A Century of Crisis and Conflict in the International System

Michael Brecher

A Century of Crisis and Conflict in the International System

Theory and Evidence: Intellectual Odyssey III

Michael Brecher
McGill University
Montreal, QC, Canada

ISBN 978-3-319-86090-9   ISBN 978-3-319-57156-0 (eBook)
DOI 10.1007/978-3-319-57156-0

© The Editor(s) (if applicable) and The Author(s) 2018
Softcover reprint of the hardcover 1st edition 2017
This work is subject to copyright. All rights are solely and exclusively licensed by the Publisher, whether the whole or part of the material is concerned, specifically the rights of translation, reprinting, reuse of illustrations, recitation, broadcasting, reproduction on microfilms or in any other physical way, and transmission or information storage and retrieval, electronic adaptation, computer software, or by similar or dissimilar methodology now known or hereafter developed.
The use of general descriptive names, registered names, trademarks, service marks, etc. in this publication does not imply, even in the absence of a specific statement, that such names are exempt from the relevant protective laws and regulations and therefore free for general use.
The publisher, the authors and the editors are safe to assume that the advice and information in this book are believed to be true and accurate at the date of publication. Neither the publisher nor the authors or the editors give a warranty, express or implied, with respect to the material contained herein or for any errors or omissions that may have been made. The publisher remains neutral with regard to jurisdictional claims in published maps and institutional affiliations.

Cover Image: © INTERFOTO/Alamy Stock Photo
Cover Design: Samantha Johnson

Printed on acid-free paper

This Palgrave Macmillan imprint is published by Springer Nature
The registered company is Springer International Publishing AG
The registered company address is: Gewerbestrasse 11, 6330 Cham, Switzerland

BOOKS BY MICHAEL BRECHER

THE STRUGGLE FOR KASHMIR (1953)
NEHRU: A Political Biography (1959)
THE NEW STATES OF ASIA (1963)
SUCCESSION IN INDIA: A Study in Decision-Making (1966)
INDIA AND WORLD POLITICS: Krishna Menon's View of the World (1968)
POLITICAL LEADERSHIP IN INDIA: An Analysis of Elite Attitudes (1969)
THE FOREIGN POLICY SYSTEM OF ISRAEL: Setting, Images, Process (1972)
ISRAEL, THE KOREAN WAR AND CHINA (1974)
DECISIONS IN ISRAEL'S FOREIGN POLICY (1975)
STUDIES IN CRISIS BEHAVIOR (ed.) (1979)
DECISIONS IN CRISIS: Israel 1967 and 1973 (with Benjamin Geist) (1980)
CRISIS AND CHANGE IN WORLD POLITICS (with Patrick James) (1986)
CRISES IN THE TWENTIETH CENTURY: Vol. I, Handbook of International Crises (with Jonathan Wilkenfeld) (1988)
CRISES IN THE TWENTIETH CENTURY: Vol. II, Handbook of Foreign Policy Crises (with Jonathan Wilkenfeld) (1988)
CRISIS, CONFLICT AND INSTABILITY (Vol. III of CRISES IN THE TWENTIETH CENTURY) (with Jonathan Wilkenfeld) (1989)

CRISES IN WORLD POLITICS (1993)
A STUDY OF CRISIS (with Jonathan Wilkenfeld) (1997)
A STUDY OF CRISIS [CD Rom edition] (with Jonathan Wilkenfeld) (2000)
MILLENNIAL REFLECTIONS ON INTERNATIONAL STUDIES (ed. with Frank P. Harvey) (2002)
REALISM AND INSTITUTIONALISM IN INTERNATIONAL STUDIES (ed. with Frank P. Harvey) (2002)
CONFLICT, SECURITY, FOREIGN POLICY, AND INTERNATIONAL POLITICAL ECONOMY (ed. with Frank Harvey) (2002)
EVALUATING METHODOLOGY IN INTERNATIONAL STUDIES (ed. with Frank P. Harvey) (2002)
CRITICAL PERSPECTIVES IN INTERNATIONAL STUDIES (ed. with Frank P. Harvey) (2002)
INTERNATIONAL POLITICAL EARTHQUAKES (2008)
THE WORLD OF PROTRACTED CONFLICTS (2016)
POLITICAL LEADERSHIP AND CHARISMA: Intellectual Odyssey I (2016)
DYNAMICS OF THE ARAB/ISRAEL CONFLICT: Intellectual Odyssey II (2017)

Contents

1 Multiple Paths to Knowledge — 1

2 Theory I: Core Concepts and Systems — 23

3 Theory II: Unified Model of Crisis (UMC) & ICB FrameWork — 53

4 General Findings: Foreign Policy Crises — 83

5 Theory III: Interstate Conflicts — 131

6 Select Case Study Findings On Interstate Conflicts: Africa & Americas — 147

7 Select Case Study Findings On Interstate Conflicts: Asia — 179

8 Select Case Study Findings on Interstate Conflicts: Europe and the Middle East — 211

9 Select Case Study Findings on Interstate Conflicts: Inter-Region — 261

10 What Have We Learned About Interstate Conflicts?	315
11 Critique of International Studies	327
Appendix: Reviews of Michael Brecher's Books	343
References	377
Names Index	403
Index	411

List of Figures

Fig. 2.1	Stability and Equilibrium	31
Fig. 3.1	Unified Model of Interstate Crisis	58
Fig. 5.1	Conflict Resolution Model	133

LIST OF TABLES

Table 2.1	System Attributes: Links	33
Table 2.2	Systemic Crisis and System Properties: Berlin Blockade 1948–1949	37
Table 2.3	Systemic Crisis and System Properties: India/Pakistan 1965–1966	40
Table 2.4	Unit- and System-Level Crisis Components	45
Table 2.5	Static and Dynamic Concepts of Crisis	46
Table 4.1	Case Studies: Hypothesis Testing—Time Pressure, Stress, and Behavior	111
Table 4.2	Case Studies: Hypothesis Testing—Summary of Findings	115

CHAPTER 1

Multiple Paths to Knowledge

INTERNATIONAL CRISIS BEHAVIOR (ICB) PROJECT: OVERVIEW

Origins

The past 4 decades have been a period of intense research concentration on *international crises*, that is, international political earthquakes, and *interstate conflicts*. From the outset it was apparent that the ICB project would become an ambitious, demanding, and rewarding exploration, in depth and breadth, of a large segment of the IR field: it encompassed the study of interstate military-security crises and protracted conflicts on a scale that, as the project unfolded, seemed awesome: *time*—the twentieth century since the end of World War I, November 1918, into the first 15 years of the twenty-first century (ICB dataset, Version 12); *geographic scope*—all states in the global system during that near-century; and *content*—from the *eruption* of crises, their *escalation*, *de-escalation* through attempts at successful *crisis management*, to the *outcome* and *consequences* of all international and foreign policy crises for all states. That project is now 42 years old but is still flourishing, measured by the number of scholars and students engaged in ICB research and the flow of publications, books, and articles. The origins of this project were closely linked to earlier periods and topics of my research. After more than two decades on a select number of crises and conflicts in two volatile regions—from the India/Pakistan conflict over Kashmir (1947) to the Arab/Israel October-Yom Kippur crisis-war (1973–1974)—the time seemed ripe to launch an inquiry into crises, conflicts, and wars in the world at large over an extended period of time. The result was my initiation of the ICB project in 1975.

Its aims were ambitious. One was to generate *comprehensive datasets* on *foreign policy* and *international crises* in the twentieth century, for none existed at the time, unlike the closely related phenomenon of war. The other was *to frame* and *test a unified model of international crisis and crisis behavior*. Both proved to be demanding tasks on a vast scale.

The few persons consulted, in 1974–1975, before taking the plunge, were skeptical, particularly of the ambitious scope of the project, which, they cautioned, could take decades; it did, with the end not yet in sight. Perhaps they were right; they certainly proved to be correct about the time frame. Their views were considered, with great care; but in the end, declined, and the saga began. (The evolution of this project, its publications, and major findings thus far, will be presented later in this book.)

Colleagues, Coders and Advisers

Since 1977, *Jonathan Wilkenfeld* has been my closest ICB colleague during what has become a very long-term research phase. Jonathan and I differ in many respects: educational background (McGill-Yale and Maryland-Indiana); research skills and methodological dispositions (*qualitative, case study* and *quantitative, aggregate data analysis*); an age difference, 17 years; physical distance—we lived on two continents and in three countries, Canada/Israel and the U.S. during virtually the entire history of the ICB Project, and most of it was before the coming of e-mail, and temperament. We learned a great deal from each other, with mutual respect. This cooperative endeavor facilitated a *multi-method study* of *crises* and *conflicts* in *world politics*. Our close collaboration—and our friendship—continues undiminished and unimpaired after 40 years!

In the early 1980s, we were joined by *Patrick James*, a very talented former Ph. D student of Jon Wilkenfeld, who has made major contributions to the concepts, models, and methods of the ICB project and has become a high-profile, accomplished IR scholar, serving as President of the International Studies Association (ISA) and Peace Science Society in 2018-2019.

The ICB project also benefited from a vibrant and stimulating group of colleagues and graduate students in three universities in three states—McGill, University of Maryland, and the Hebrew University of Jerusalem. It also had the good fortune of attracting many eager and committed research assistants in the seemingly endless task of creating reliable datasets of international crises, foreign policy crises, and protracted conflicts: for the initial, longest research period, 1929–1979—it took more than a decade, 1975–1987—*Hemda Ben Yehuda, Gerald Bichunski, Diana Brecher, Ofra Einav, Robert Einav, Alex Forma, Etel Goldmann/Solingen, Sharon Greenblatt, Rutie Moser, Hanan Naveh, Arie Ofri, Lily Polliak, Mordechai Raz, Michel Reichman, André Rosenthal, Joel Schleicher, Bruce Slawitsky,* and *Sarah Vertzberger* (in Jerusalem); and *Mark Boyer, Doreen Duffy, Steve Hill, Patrick James, Cindy Kite, Maureen Latimer, Eileen Long* (in Maryland); for the period, 1980–1985, *Joel Schleicher* (in Jerusalem), *Brigid Starkey* and *Alice Schott* (in Maryland); for the periods, 1918–1928 and 1985–1994, *Tod Hoffman, Eric Laferriere, Michelle Lebrun, Mark Peranson,* and *Michael Vasko* (at McGill); and *Ronit Lupu, Iris Margulies, Meirav Mishali, Noam Shultz,* and *Sarah Vertzberger* (in Jerusalem), and, from 1995–2015, *Kyle Beardsley, David M. Quinn,* and *Pelin Erlap* (at Maryland).

Many scholars gave generously of their time and knowledge as regional specialists, with many benefits to the ICB project: *Douglas Anglin, Naomi Hazan,* and *Saadia Touval* (on Africa); *Alexander de Barros, Thomas Bruneau, Nelson Kasfir, Jorge Dominguez,* and *Edy Kaufman* (on the Americas); *Ehud Harari, Ellis Joffe, Paul Kattenburg, Guy Pauker, Leo Rose, Martin Rudner, Yaakov Vertzberger,* and *George T.C. Yu* (on Asia); *Luigi Bonanate, Karen Dawisha, Galia Golan, Kjell Goldmann, Amnon Sella,* and *Robert Vogel* (on Europe); and *Richard H. Dekmejian, Alan Dowty, Benjamin Geist, Jacob Landau,* and *Yaakov Shimoni* (on the Middle East).

Rationale and Methods

Like other scholars immersed in IR research, the senior ICB scholars have a longstanding policy interest, that is, a wish and hope that our findings on crisis, conflict, and war, especially on how decision-makers behave under (often escalating) stress, might make a contribution in the quest for a more tranquil world, through advice on conflict resolution and even on war prevention. We had no illusions that the contribution would be decisive. But we did—and do—place a high value on trying to 'bridge the gap' between academe and the decision-makers' world.

The ICB approach to the systematic study of crisis, conflict, and war derived from a deep commitment to *pluralism* in the quest for knowledge, that is, to *complementary*, not *competing methodologies*: this commitment to pluralism is not confined to the issue of *qualitative vs. quantitative methods*. It includes recognition of the merit of both *deductive* and *inductive* approaches to *theory-building*. And it extends to a focus on both *large N* and *small N datasets*: ICB has produced—and utilized—both types in its multifaceted inquiry.

ICB began with a *single-state foreign policy crisis decision-making model* and a set of research questions. This model and the questions were designed to direct case studies of decision-making using a common framework and therefore to facilitate generalizations about behavior under the stress of crisis. A series of in-depth studies of individual interstate crises was launched—and nine volumes have been published since 1979; these volumes are set out below.

Within 2 years (1977) and with Jonathan Wilkenfeld's invaluable input, ICB moved to a second, parallel track, namely, *studies in breadth* of a large number of crises to complement the *in-depth case studies*. Each of these paths posed different questions. One dataset was appropriate to the *system or interactor (macro) level of analysis*, the other to the *unit or actor (micro) level of analysis*. One cluster of questions was designed to generate comparable data on the *four phases* of an international crisis—*onset, escalation,* de-*escalation,* and *impact*. The data were used to test hypotheses on the conditions most likely to lead to the *eruption* of a crisis, its *escalation* to peak hostility, often with violence at the eruption and/or escalation stage(s), the 'winding down' process leading to *termination*, and its *consequences*. The second cluster focused on the *behavior of decision-makers* at different levels of stress in the *pre-crisis, crisis, end-crisis*, and *post-crisis periods* of a state's *foreign policy crisis*.

During the past 42 years, we pursued both paths simultaneously, viewing them as complementary, not competitive sources of *findings on international and foreign policy crises* and on *interstate protracted conflicts*. Path I, 29 qualitative case studies, ranges from *Ethiopia's decisions* in the *1935–1936 Ethiopia/Italy crisis and war* and the *U.K. decisions* in the *Munich Crisis of 1938* to *Iraq and U.S. decisions* in the *Gulf Crisis and War of 1990–1991* and the *North Korea (DPRK)* and *U.S. decisions* during *several crises in the North Korean Nuclear protracted conflict since 1993 ('vertical' research)*. Path II has taken the form of *quantitative aggregate data analysis of 476 international crises and 1052 foreign policy crises since the end of World War I ('horizontal' research).*

Objectives
ICB research on international crises before, during, and after the Cold War focused on *five objectives*. *One* was *to develop the concept of international crisis as an international political earthquake* and to present a *comparison of such earthquakes since the end of World War I:* along many attributes such as *trigger, triggering entity, duration, number of decisions, decision-makers, their attitudinal prism,* and *values;* and along many dimensions such as *geography-region, time, system structure, conflict setting, bloc alignment, peace–war setting, violence, military power, economic development,* and *political regime.*

A *second,* closely related *aim* was *to create and apply concepts, indicators, indexes, and scales designed to measure the severity (intensity)* and *impact (consequences) of international crises* viewed as *international political* earthquakes. These are based on the premise that such precise measurement is scientifically possible.

A *third goal* was to bring closure to the persistent debate on which *international structure* is the *most*—and the *least*—*stable,* that is, the least—and the most—disruptive of the global international system—*bipolarity, multipolarity, bipolycentrism,* and *unipolarity [or unipolycentrism].* The rationale for this debate and research question is that international stability is—or should be—a high value for all states and nations/peoples in an epoch characterized by *weapons of mass destruction (WMDs),* the *persistence of anarchy* despite the proliferation of international and transnational regimes, the *increase of ethnic and civil wars,* and the growing preoccupation with *worldwide terrorism.* All these sources of turmoil enhance the *normative value* of stability. Thus illuminating the *polarity–stability nexus* has important long-term implications for foreign policy and national security decision-makers and the attentive publics of all states.

A *fourth objective* has been to extend and deepen our *knowledge* of *coping/crisis management* by in-depth case studies, focusing on how decision-makers coped with the peak stress crisis period during diverse political earthquakes (crises) in each *structural era* of the past near-century: *multipolarity* (mid-November 1918 [end of World War I]–early September 1945 [end of WWII]), *bipolarity* (early September 1945–end 1962 [termination of the Cuban Missile crisis]), *bipolycentrism* (beginning 1963–end 1989 [end of the Cold War]), and *unipolycentrism* (beginning 1990–ongoing).

The *final aim* has been to provide a novel *test of the validity of neo-Realism*. The discovery of no or minor differences in the *patterns of crisis* and *crisis behavior* during the four structural eras would indicate strong support for the neo-Realist contention that structure shapes world politics, as well as the foreign policy-security behavior of states, its principal actors. However, the presence of substantive differences in the patterns of crisis and crisis behavior during the four structural eras since the end of WW I would seriously undermine the claim of neo-Realism to be the optimal paradigm for world politics throughout history and in the decades ahead. Taken together, the general objective of the ICB inquiry since 1975 has been to enrich and deepen our knowledge of *international crisis* and *interstate conflict* in the twentieth century and beyond.

Formative Publications (1977–1980)

The late 1970s was also a period of several ICB-related publications which became guides to the Project's research program, especially its theoretical framework and its in-depth case studies: two Brecher journal articles, "Toward a Theory of International Crisis Behavior," in the International Studies Quarterly (1977) and "State Behavior in International Crisis: A Model," in the Journal of Conflict Resolution (1979). The following year, the first ICB in-depth case study volume was published, Brecher with Geist, <u>Decisions in Crisis: Israel, 1967 and 1973</u>. This book, as noted, served as the conceptual and methodological model for the seven other ICB case study volumes (analyzing 15 crises) that were published from 1980 to 1994, as well as for the 14 unpublished graduate student case studies of foreign policy crises.

Case Studies—Qualitative Analysis

All ICB case studies applied the *foreign policy crisis model*, initially presented as journal articles in 1977 and 1979, as noted above. The ICB case study volumes are as follows:

  *Brecher with Benjamin Geist, <u>Decisions in Crisis: Israel 1967 and 1973</u> (1980).
  Dawisha, Adeed I., <u>Syria and the Lebanese Crisis</u> (1980).

*Shlaim, Avi, _The United States and the Berlin Blockade, 1948–1949_ (1983).
*Dawisha, Karen, _The Kremlin and the Prague Spring_ (1984).
*Dowty, Alan, _Middle East Crisis: U.S. Decision-Making in 1958, 1970, and 1973_ (1984).
*Jukes, Geoffrey, _Hitler's Stalingrad Decisions_ (1985).
*Hoffmann, Stephen: _India and the China Crisis_ (1990), and Anglin, Douglas G., _Zambian Crisis Behavior: Confronting Rhodesia's Unilateral Declaration of Independence, 1965–1966_ (1994).

[*These six books were published from 1980 to 1990 by the University of California Press in a series, Studies in Crisis Behavior, edited by Brecher.]

The case study volumes and the unpublished crisis studies generated comparable findings which provided a valuable database for testing hypotheses on state behavior in crises. The published ICB books and other in-depth case studies analyzed 15 foreign policy crises of individual states. Fourteen other crises have been researched by my graduate students. These 29 crises served as the empirical basis for Part B ("Qualitative Analysis") in Brecher, International Political Earthquakes (2008); the findings from that inquiry are presented later in this book.

Datasets and Aggregate Analysis

A dozen years, 1975–1987, were devoted to data gathering (coding) and analysis of crises and conflicts from 1929 to 1979, the initial time frame of the ICB Project: it was a collective research enterprise whose success owed much to the devoted coding of our research assistants, under the direction of Brecher and Wilkenfeld. Given the complexity of the Project, it took 2 years to complete the process of publication. In 1988, the first two volumes of a three-volume work, _Crises in the Twentieth Century_, were published as _Handbook of International Crises_ (Brecher and Wilkenfeld) and _Handbook of Foreign Policy Crises_ (Wilkenfeld and Brecher). The next year, the third volume containing analytic papers on this dataset appeared as _Crisis, Conflict and Instability_ (Brecher and Wilkenfeld).

Almost a decade later (1997), a substantially revised and significantly enlarged aggregate dataset and analysis segment of the project appeared, _A Study of Crisis_ (Brecher and Wilkenfeld). It presented the updated dataset at both the system-level and actor-level of analysis and an array of findings on crisis, conflict, and war from late 1918 to the end of 1994. [Important findings from that book are presented later in this book.]

Millennial Reflections on Crisis and Conflict

In 1999–2000, as President of the International Studies Association, I confronted the task of conceiving and organizing the theme panels for the annual conference. In meeting this challenge I had the invaluable collaboration of my talented Program Chair for ISA 2000, Frank Harvey, a McGill Ph. D (1993) and, at the time, Professor of Political Science at Dalhousie University and Director of its Center for Foreign Policy Studies. The imminent millennial change seemed an auspicious time to reflect on the state of International Studies (IS).

To accomplish this task, a large number of prominent contributors to IS were invited to prepare papers for the envisaged eight clusters of panels on the main theme of the conference in 2000—**Millennial Reflections on International Studies**. The panelists represented all branches of International Studies and included scholars from many universities in Australia, Canada, Europe, Israel, the United Kingdom, and the United States.

Advocates and Critics

The first cluster comprised six papers by proponents, critics, and a revisionist of **Realism**, the dominant paradigm in International Relations during the state-centric Westphalia era, 1648–1990:

John J. Mearsheimer(University of Chicago).
Joseph M. Grieco (Duke University and Catholic University of Milan).
John A. Vasquez (Vanderbilt University, later, University of Illinois).
Kalevi J. Holsti (University of British Columbia).
Manus I. Midlarsky (Rutgers University).
Patrick James (University of Missouri, later, University of Southern California).

The second cluster of reflections on IR paradigms comprised four papers on **Institutionalism**:

David A. Lake(University of California, San Diego).
Robert O. Keohane (Duke University, later, Princeton University).

Joseph S, Nye Jr. (Harvard University).
Oran Young (Dartmouth College).

A diverse group of **Alternative and Critical** perspectives on International Studies was represented in the third cluster:

Steve Smith (University of Wales, later, Essex University) [**Overview**]
Robert W. Cox (York University, Toronto) [**Critical Theory**]
Michael Cox (Editor, *Review of International Studies*, later, University of Wales) [**Radical Theory**]
Ernst B. Haas (University of California, Berkeley) and *Peter M. Haas* (University of Massachusetts at Amherst) [**Constructivism**]
Yosef Lapid (New Mexico State University) [**Post-Modernism**]
R.B.J. Walker (Keele University, later, University of Victoria) [**Post-Modernism**]
James N. Rosenau (George Washington University) [**System Change**]

There were six papers on **Feminist and Gender** perspectives on International Studies:

L.H.M. Ling (Institute of Social Studies, The Hague).
V. Spike Peterson (University of Arizona).
Jan Jindy Pettman (Australian National University).
Christine Sylvester (Institute of Social Studies, The Hague).
J. Ann Tickner (University of Southern California).
Marysia Zalewski (Queen's University of Belfast).

Reflections on **Methodology** in International Studies comprised nine papers:

Four were on **Formal Modeling**:
Michael Nicholson (Sussex University).
Harvey Starr (University of South Carolina).
Bruce Bueno de Mesquita (Hoover Institution/Stanford and New York University).
Steven J. Brams (New York University).

Three papers focused on **Quantitative Methods**:
Dina A. Zinnes (University of Illinois).
James Lee Ray (Vanderbilt University).

Russell J. Leng (Middlebury College).

Two papers discussed **Qualitative (Case Study) Methods**:
Jack S. Levy (Rutgers University).
Zeev Maoz (Tel Aviv University, later, University of California, Davis).

The cluster of millennial reflections on **Foreign Policy Analysis** comprised papers by four authors:

Yaacov Y. I. Vertzberger (Hebrew University of Jerusalem).
Stephen G. Walker (Arizona State University).
Ole R. Holsti (Duke University).
Jonathan Wilkenfeld (University of Maryland).

There were five papers on **International Security, Peace, and War**:
Edward A. Kolodziej (University of Illinois).
Davis B. Bobrow (University of Pittsburgh).
J. David Singer (University of Michigan).
Linda B. Miller (Wellesley College).

Three papers focused on **International Political Economy**:
Helen Milner (Columbia University, later, Princeton University).
Robert T. Kudrle (University of Minnesota).
Lisa L. Martin (Harvard University).

(The participants are listed above in the sequence with which their papers appeared in Brecher and Harvey (Eds.), <u>Millennial Reflections on International Studies</u>, 2002.)

Although some esteemed colleagues were unable to accept the invitation, the group of 44 participants was a veritable 'blue ribbon commission' of the International Studies field; it included 13 former presidents of the International Studies Association (ISA).

Rationale

The essence of the Millennial Reflections Project is evident in the Introductory Statement by the editors of the volume that contained all the Reflections papers.

"When one of the editors was introduced to International Relations (IR)/World Politics at Yale in 1946 the field comprised international politics, international law and organization, international economics, international (diplomatic) history, and a regional specialization. The hegemonic paradigm was Realism, as expressed in the work of E.H. Carr, W.T.R. Fox, Hans J. Morgenthau, Nicholas Spykman, Arnold Wolfers and others. The unquestioned focus of attention was interstate war and peace."

"By the time the other editor was initiated into International Relations at McGill in the mid-late 1980s the pre-eminent paradigm was neo-Realism. However, there were several competing claimants to the 'true path': institutional theory, cognitive psychology, and postmodernism; and by the time he received his doctoral degree, other competitors had emerged, notably, critical theory, constructivism, and feminism."

"The consequence, at the dawn of the new millennium, was a vigorous, still-inconclusive debate about the optimal path to knowledge about International Studies (IS), most clearly expressed in competing views: that it is a discipline—International Relations {IR} or World Politics—like economics, political science, sociology, anthropology, history; or that it is a multidisciplinary field of study, the 'big tent' conception held by the premier academic organization, the International Studies Association (ISA). It was in this context that the Millennial Reflections Project was conceived."

The origin and rationale of the conference idea may be found in the central theme of my presidential address to the ISA conference in Washington in February 1999: "International Studies in the Twentieth Century and Beyond: Flawed Dichotomies, Synthesis, Cumulation" (International Studies Quarterly, 1999). Whether a discipline or a multidisciplinary 'big tent' *mélange*, International Studies has developed over the last half-century with diverse philosophical underpinnings, frameworks of analysis, methodologies, and foci of attention. This diversity is evident in the papers that were presented at the panels at the Los Angeles conference and revised for this state-of-the-art collection of essays at the dawn of the new millennium.

Diversity in International Studies

In an attempt to capture the range, diversity, and complexity of International Studies, we decided to organize the 44 'think-piece' essays into eight clusters. The mainstream paradigms of **Realism** and **Institutionalism** constitute the first two concentrations. The others were

Critical perspectives (including **Critical Theory, Post-Modernism, Constructivism,** and **Feminism** and **Gender** perspectives); **Methodology** (including quantitative, formal modeling, and qualitative [case studies]); **Foreign Policy** analysis; **International Security, Peace, and War**; and **International Political Economy.**

The *raison d'etre* of the Millennial Reflections Project was set out in the Theme Statement of the conference, titled "Reflection, Integration, and Cumulation: International Studies, Past and Future." First, new debates, perspectives the number and size of subfields and sections have grown steadily since the founding of the International Studies Association in 1959. This diversity, while enriching, has made increasingly difficult the crucial task of identifying intra-subfield, let alone inter-subfield, consensus about important theoretical and empirical insights. Aside from focusing on a cluster of shared research questions related, for example, to globalization, gender and international relations, critical theory, political economy, international institutions, global development, democracy and peace, foreign and security policy, and so on, there are still few clear signs of cumulation.

If, we declared, the maturity of an academic discipline is based not only on its capacity to expand but also on its capacity to select, the lack of agreement *within* these research communities is particularly disquieting. Realists, for instance, cannot fully agree on their paradigm's core assumptions, central postulates, or the lessons learned from empirical research. Similarly, Feminist epistemologies encompass an array of research programs and findings that are not easily grouped into a common set of beliefs, theories, or conclusions. If those who share common interests and perspectives have difficulty agreeing on what they have accomplished to date or do not concern themselves with the question of what has been achieved so far, how can they establish clear targets to facilitate creative dialogue across these diverse perspectives and subfields?

With this in mind, the objective was to challenge proponents of specific paradigms, theories, approaches, and substantive issue-areas to confront their own limitations by engaging in self-critical reflection within epistemologies and perspectives. The objective was to stimulate debates about successes and failures but to do so by avoiding the tendency to define accomplishments with reference to the failures and weaknesses of other perspectives.

It is important to note that our call to assess the 'state of the art' in International Studies was not meant as a reaffirmation of the standard proposition that a rigorous process of theoretical cumulation is both possible and necessary. Not all perspectives and subfields of IS are directed to cumulation in this sense. Some participants found the use of such words as synthesis and *progress* suspect, declaring in their original papers that they could not address, or were not prepared to address, these social science-type questions. We nevertheless encouraged these individuals to define what they considered to be fair measures of success and failure in regard to their subfield, and we asked them to assess the extent to which core objectives (whatever they may be) have or have not been met, and why.

Our intention was not to tie individuals to a particular set of methodological tenets, standards, assumptions, or constraints. We simply wanted to encourage self-reflective discussion and debate about significant achievements and failures. Even where critiques of mainstream theory and methodology are part of a subfield's *raison d'etre*, the lack of consensus is still apparent and relevant.

As a community of scholars, we are rarely challenged to address the larger question of *success* and *progress* (however one chooses to define these terms), perhaps because there is so little agreement on the methods and standards we should use to identify and integrate important observations, arguments, and findings.

To prevent intellectual diversity descending into intellectual anarchy, we set out 'guidelines' for the contributors in the form of six theme questions or tasks. The panelists were requested to address one or more of these themes in their essays.

1. Engage in self-critical, state-of-the-art reflection on accomplishments and failures, especially since the creation of the ISA more than 40 years ago.
2. Assess where we stand on unresolved debates and why we have failed to resolve them.
3. Evaluate the intra-subfield standards we should use to assess the significance of theoretical insights.
4. Explore ways to achieve fruitful synthesis of approaches, both in terms of core research questions and appropriate methodologies.
5. Address the broader question of progress in international studies.
6. Select an agenda of topics and research questions that should guide your subfield during the coming decades.

The result was an array of thought-provoking 'think pieces' that indicate shortcomings as well as achievements and specify the unfinished business of IS as a scholarly field in the next decade or more, with wide-ranging policy implications in the shared quest for world order.

Assessment of the Field

The essence of each paper in the eight clusters was summarized in the introductory chapter of the Brecher-Harvey edited book. At the end of the volume, the editors presented findings on the six theme questions about International Studies: paradigms, methodologies, and the three broad substantive research areas namely foreign policy analysis; international security, peace, and war; and international political economy. They concluded with five general observations about **progress**, more accurately the **lack of progress**, in International Studies.

"First, new debates, perspectives, theories, and approaches are proliferating much faster than old debates are being resolved—indeed, few if any of the 'old' debates have ever been resolved. To the extent that consensus exists at all, it usually emerges in the context of narrowly-defined research programs encompassing small communities of scholars who focus on less significant issues."

"Second, if we haven't yet achieved closure on key theoretical and methodological debates, we never will; a symposium in 1972 arrived at the same conclusion."

"Third, for those who remain convinced that constructive dialogue and consensus is still possible, our most discouraging observation is that there are no solutions."

"Fourth, self-critical reflection does not come easily to most scholars.

Finally, in response to the advice of one of the elders in the field, James Rosenau, 'we need to acknowledge our own limitations and alert those we train to the necessity of breaking with past assumptions and finding new ways of understanding and probing the enormous challenges....,' we declared that these assertions beg crucial questions. What precisely do we tell our graduate students to keep or discard. What is the 'real world' and how should it be studied? The debate continues." (681–684)

<u>*Millennial Reflections on International Studies*</u> (2002) [Eds. Brecher and Frank P. Harvey]

Intellectual Odyssey: Phases, Themes, Concepts

Phases

The first of my three long-term research Phases (1950–1969) focused on the **politics, international relations, and modern history** of **South Asia, mostly India**.

The second Phase (1960–1980) concentrated on articulated **perceptions of the Arab/Israel Conflict by political leaders, officials and intellectuals** from Egypt and Israel, and their **behavior** in a complex protracted conflict.

The third, on-going Phase, which began in 1975, has been devoted to the quest for theory, aggregate data, and case studies of **international crises** and **protracted conflicts**.

The three phases, as noted early in this book, were linked intellectually but the areas of study and the duration of each phase were not neatly pre-arranged. They emerged in response to changing stimuli and varying concerns over time about *sources of turmoil* in the global system. This conception of research phases provided a framework for an assessment of (a) **political leaders**, notably those who profoundly shaped the political evolution of newly independent states in two regions, South Asia and the Middle East, specifically, India and Israel, since their Independence; (b) the **Arab/Israel Conflict**; and (c) the **theory and practice of inter-state crises** and **protracted conflicts** in the near-century since the end of World War I.

Themes

Political Leadership and Charisma (Odyssey I)
This theme explored a selection of the literature on *political leadership* and some notable *political leaders* in Canada, the U.K., India, and Israel from 1944 to 1978: Trudeau (Canada); Attlee and Mountbatten (the U.K.); Nehru and Krishna Menon, along with many less visible but highly influential Indian politicians in those years, including Lal Bahadur Shastri and Morarji Desai, two other prime ministers in the post-Nehru era (India); and Ben-Gurion, Sharett, Eshkol, and Meir, the first four prime ministers of Israel, along with the prominent second-generation figures, Allon, Dayan, Eban, and Peres. This theme and the findings

were the focus of attention in the first of three books that, together, traversed my intellectual odyssey since 1950: **Political Leadership and Charisma: Nehru, Ben Gurion, and Other Twentieth-Century Political Leaders** (2016).

Arab/Israel Conflict (Odyssey II)

The second theme centered on *perceptions* of a complex unresolved conflict by eight prominent political leaders of Israel during the first three decades of independence (1948–1977) and by Egyptian officials and intellectuals during the decade of Sadat's presidency in the 1970s, before his epochal visit to Jerusalem in 1977 and the Egypt–Israel peace agreement in 1979. There were also explorations of crucial decisions by Israel, with profound consequences: *to make Jerusalem the capital of Israel* in December 1949; *to accept German reparations in 1952*; *to launch a pre-emptive strike against Egypt* in October 1956 and *against Egypt and Syria in June 1967*; *not to launch an interceptive war in October 1973, and the Egypt–Israel peace process, 1977–1979, culminating in a formal peace agreement in 1979.* The findings from many years of research on this in-depth conflict were presented in my **Dynamics of the Arab/Israel Conflict** (2017).

Interstate Crises and Conflicts (Odyssey III)

This theme focuses on *international and foreign policy crises*—their *onset phase/pre-crisis period, escalation phase/crisis period, de-escalation phase/end-crisis period, and impact phase/post-crisis period*, for all independent states in the global system since the end of World War I, along with 33 *interstate protracted conflicts*—by states, major powers and international institutions, from late 1918 to 2017. This phase includes the major findings from in-depth case studies of *decisions, decision-makers, and the decision process by principal adversaries in 29 foreign policy crises and 11 protracted conflicts* from all polarity structures, geographic regions, types of political régime, levels of power, and levels of economic development.'

Concepts

The quest for theory, insights, and findings on the three main themes was guided by ten concepts in the field of **International Relations–World Politics–International Studies (IR–WP–IS)**.

Concept 1 Subordinate State System, an intermediate level of analysis between the **dominant subsystem** (interactions among the major powers of the global system) and a **state**. A subordinate system requires six conditions:

1. Its *scope* is delimited, with primary emphasis on a *geographic region*.
2. It comprises *at least three state actors*,
3. Together, they are objectively acknowledged by other state actors and international organizations as constituting a *distinctive community, region, or segment of the global system.*
4. The *members* of the subsystem *identify themselves* as such.
5. The *level of power* among subsystem members is *relatively inferior to that of states in the dominant system*, using a sliding scale of power in both.
6. *Changes in the dominant system have greater effects on the subordinate system than the reverse.*

This concept of a subordinate state system grew out of extensive research on South Asian international relations, in particular, the India–Pakistan conflict since the late 1940s (Brecher 1963).

[Three scholars presented somewhat different definitions of a subordinate system and a focus on three other regions: Binder (1958 Middle East), Modelski (1961 South East Asia), and Hodgkin (1961 West Africa)].

Concept 2: Foreign Policy System This concept, which took the form of a *pre-theory of foreign policy*, was developed in the mid-late 1960s and was first published as "A Framework for Research on Foreign Policy Behavior," in the Journal of Conflict Resolution, 1969, and was elaborated in my book The Foreign Policy System of Israel (1972).

The research design was based on a simple proposition: the *concept of system is no less valid in foreign policy analysis than in the study of domestic politics.* Like all systems of action, a foreign policy system comprises an *environment* or setting, a group of *actors*, *structures* through which they initiate *decisions* and respond to challenges, and *processes* which sustain or alter the flow of demands and products of the system as a whole.

Underlying this research design is the view that the *operational environment*, reality, affects the results or *outcomes of decisions* directly but influences the *choice among policy options*, that is, the *decisions* themselves, only as they are filtered through the *images* [*perceptions*] of decision-makers. Thus, the *link* between *perceptions* and *decisions* is the *master key to a valuable framework of foreign policy analysis*.

This relationship of the two environments—*operational* and *psychological*—also provides a technique for measuring 'success' in foreign policy decisions. To the extent that decision-makers perceive the operational environment accurately, their foreign policy acts may be said to be rooted in *reality* and are thus more likely to be 'successful.' To the extent that their images are inaccurate, policy choices will be 'unsuccessful'; that is, there will be a gap between elite-defined objectives and policy outcomes.

The *boundaries* of a foreign policy system are vertical, that is, they *encompass all inputs and outputs that affect decisions*, whose content and scope lie essentially in the realm of International Relations, World Politics. As such, the boundaries fluctuate from one *issue* to another. It is necessary, therefore, to explore the content and interrelations of these key variables—*environment, actors, structures, decisions, processes* and *issues*—all placed within a framework of demands on policy or *inputs*, and products of policy or *outputs*.

A foreign policy system may thus be likened to a flow into and out of a network of structures or institutions that perform certain functions and thereby produce decisions. These, in turn, feed back into the system as inputs in a continuous flow of demands on policy, the policy process, and the products of policy. All foreign policy systems, then, comprise a set of components which can be classified into three general categories, *inputs, process,* and *outputs*, a concept of the political system pioneered by David Easton in a <u>World Politics</u> article (1957). All data regarding foreign policy can be classified into one of these categories.

Concept 3: International System Two questions about *international system* were posed in 1980 by a prominent IR scholar, Dina Zinnes: (1) 'how do we know one when we see one' and (2) 'what distinguishes one from another'? A new definition of international system, that provides answers to these questions, was presented in a 1984 joint paper with an ICB associate, Brecher and Hemda Ben-Yehuda.

An *international system* is a set of [state] actors who are situated in a configuration of power (*structure*), are involved in regular patterns of interaction (*process*), are separated from other units by *boundaries* set by a given *issue,* and are constrained in their behavior from within (*context*) and from outside the system (*environment*).

The essential properties of an international system are *structure, process, equilibrium,* and *stability.*

Structure refers to how the actors in a system stand in relation to each other. Its basic variables are the number of actors and the distribution of power among them, from unipolar through bipolar to multipower or polycentric.

Process designates the interaction patterns among the actors of a system. A link between structure and process is postulated: every structure has a corresponding interaction process, and a structure creates and maintains regular interaction.

Issue is another distinctive property of a system, which serves to demarcate its boundaries. This concept may be defined as a specific shared focus of interest for two or more actors. There are *war–peace* issues, *economic and developmental* issues, *political, cultural, status,* and *technological* issues within broader categories of issue-areas.

Every system has *Boundaries* which differentiate two kinds of effects on the behavior of actors—*contextual*, those arising *from within* a system, and *environmental*, those *from outside*. *Context* and *Environment* incorporate all geographic, political, military, technological, societal, and cultural elements that affect the structure and process of a system, from within and from outside the system, respectively.

The definition of international system presented above enables us *to identify* a system. Other concepts are needed *to distinguish* among *systems.* These are *Stability* and *Equilibrium,* system attributes. The concept of *Change* is the key to the distinction between stability and equilibrium, as well as to the organic link between them. Change may be defined as a shift from, or an alteration of, an existing *pattern of interaction* between two or more actors in the direction of greater conflict or cooperation. Change may also occur in the *structure* of a system, namely, an increase or decrease in the number of actors and/or a shift in the distribution of power among them.

Stability may be defined as change within explicit bounds. *Instability* designates change beyond a normal fluctuation range. These concepts may be operationalized in terms of the *quantity (number) of change(s)* in the structure of a system, its process or both, ranging from no changes to many changes. This continuum denotes degrees of stability. The absence of change indicates pure stability, its presence, and some degree of instability. Instability in the international system can be illustrated by *change in the volume of such phenomena as wars or crises* involving essential actors.

Equilibrium may be defined as the steady state of a system, denoting change below the threshold of reversibility. Disequilibrium designates change beyond the threshold of reversibility. This meaning is broader than the notion of balance of power, a widely used synonym for equilibrium in the world politics literature. Incremental change indicates a state of equilibrium, which has no effect on the system as a whole. Step-level (irreversible) change indicates disequilibrium, which inevitably leads to system transformation, that is, a change in essential actors and/or the distribution of power among them. The new system, with properties which significantly differ from those of its predecessor, denotes a new equilibrium, that is, changes within it which are reversible.

Every system has explicit or implicit *rules of the game*. Many international systems permit resort to violence as an instrument of crisis and conflict management. This is evident in the inherent right of individual and collective self-defense, enshrined in international institutions of the twentieth-century multipower system (League of Nations), as well as the bipolar, bipolycentric, and unipolycentric systems (United Nations).

In sum, a revised definition of international system comprises six components: *actors, structure, process, boundaries, context,* and *environment*. Furthermore, the two basic system attributes, *stability* and *equilibrium*, were redefined and the links between them specified, completing the dual task of identifying and differentiating systems.

Concepts 4 and 5 *International Crisis* (presented in my articles in International Studies Quarterly 1977, The Journal of Conflict Resolution 1979, and many other publications during the past three decades, culminating in my book, International Political Earthquakes [2008]), occurs at two levels of analysis.

An *international* (*macro-level*) crisis is conceived as an international political earthquake. It denotes (1) a change in type and/or an increase in intensity of disruptive interactions between two or more states, with a heightened probability of war/military hostilities that, in turn, (2) destabilizes their relationship and challenges the structure of an international system. A *foreign policy* (*micro-level*) *crisis* derives from three interrelated *perceptions* by a state's decision-makers of (1) a threat to one or more basic values, (2) finite time for response, and of (3) heightened probability of military hostilities before the challenge is overcome. The two levels of analysis are distinct but interrelated.

Concept 6: Unified Model of Crisis(UMC) is an analytical device to explain *interstate crisis* as a whole. It builds upon the logic of a model of *international crisis* and a model of *foreign policy crisis* and integrates them into an integrated model of *interstate crisis*. It also attempts to incorporate the models of the *onset, escalation*, and *de-escalation phases*, and a model of *impact*, into a systemic, unified model. This synthesis is the prototype of a theory of interstate crisis.

Concepts 7 and 8 *Crisis Severity* and *Crisis Impact* refer to *different types of change in different time frames.*

Severity is a composite of *situational attributes during* an international crisis (international political earthquake). The term refers to the *volume of disruptive change* between/among crisis actors *from onset to termination* of an international crisis, that is, an international political earthquake, and denotes the extent of *instability*. Severity measures the *intensity of disruptive change* during the course of the earthquake. It is a composite of scores for *six indicators* of *Severity* of an international crisis, each on a *four-point* scale: *number of crisis actors, gravity of values threatened, violence, major power involvement, geostrategic salience*, and *duration*.

Impact is a composite of *effects* of an international crisis (political earthquake) on an international system and/or subsystem(s), as well as on the relationship between/among principal adversaries, *after* the end of a crisis. It refers, in system terms, to the extent of *structural change* or *irreversibility* and thus denotes the presence or absence of *equilibrium*. To capture the multiple effects, *impact* is measured by *four indicators* of change, each, like the indicators of severity, on a *four-point* scale: *change in actors, power relations, alliance configuration*, and *norms* or *rules of behavior*.

In sum, Severity refers to the extent of disruptive interaction while an international political earthquake (international crisis) is in motion (instability). *Impact refers to structural change after an earthquake (crisis) has ended (disequilibrium)*.

Concept 9: Protracted Conflict —the initial formulation (Brecher 1993) and elaborations of this concept (as noted, to Brecher 2016 L) were cited in the introduction to the analysis of 13 twentieth-century protracted conflicts earlier in this book. The less-than-crystallized intellectual origins of this concept date to my early research phases, specifically, to the protracted conflicts between the Arab states and Israel, and between India and Pakistan over Kashmir, which I first encountered in 1948–1951 and 1950–1952, respectively; both conflicts remain unresolved almost seven decades later.

Concept 10 *Polycentrism* was initially formulated and applied in Brecher and Wilkenfeld, Crises in the Twentieth Century: Handbook on International Crises (Vol. I), 1988. Its conceptual kin—*Bipolycentrism* and *Unipolycentrism*—were developed and applied in Brecher, International Political Earthquakes (2008).

CHAPTER 2

Theory I: Core Concepts and Systems

CORE CONCEPTS

International Crisis and Protracted Conflict

An international crisis, later identified as an international political earthquake, begins with a disruptive act or event, a *breakpoint (trigger)*, that creates a foreign policy crisis for one or more states; for example, the crossing of the Thag La Ridge in India's North East Frontier Agency (NEFA) by People's Republic of China (PRC) forces on September 8, 1962, setting in motion the *China/India Border Crisis-War*; and the dispatch of Egypt's 4th Armored Division into the Sinai Peninsula on May 17, 1967, along with its overflight of Israel's nuclear center at Dimona in the Negev desert the same day, leading to the *June-Six-Day War*.

An international crisis ends with an act or event that denotes a qualitative reduction in conflict activity. In the cases noted above, crisis termination was marked by the unilateral declaration of a ceasefire by China on December 1, 1962, and the end of the Six-Day War on June 11, 1967, respectively.

A *militarized interstate dispute* [*MID*], the *Correlates of War* [*COW*] project counterpart of the ICB concept of international crisis, has been defined as "a set of interactions between or among states involving threats to use military force, displays of military force, or actual uses of military force."

The majority of post-WW I twentieth and early twenty-first century international crises, 58%, occurred within the context of an on-going interstate protracted conflict; however, the overall frequency of crises revealed a substantial decline—from 273 international crises, with a total of 619 crisis actors during the half-century, 1929–1979, to 84 crises, with a total of 209 crisis actors during the quarter century that followed, 1990–2015.

International crisis and *protracted conflict* are closely related but not synonymous. The focus of *crisis* is usually a single issue or a specific episode—a territorial dispute, an economic boycott, a threat to a political regime, an act of violence, etc. By contrast, *protracted conflict* has been defined as "hostile interactions which extend over long periods of time with sporadic outbreaks of open warfare fluctuating in frequency and intensity.... The stakes are very high.... They [protracted conflicts] linger on in time.... [They] are not specific events ..., they are processes" (Azar et al. 1978).

Protracted conflicts are lengthy, at least 10 years, many of them several decades, centuries, or more. All fluctuate in intensity. Many move from war to partial accommodation and back to violence (e.g., *India/Pakistan* since 1947). Other conflicts have been characterized by continuous war but of varying severity (Vietnam 1964–1975). All arouse intense animosities with spillover effects on a broad spectrum of issues. And conflict termination, where it occurs, is often complex.

Even when an international crisis is very long it can be distinguished from a protracted conflict, as with the (first) India/Pakistan crisis-war over Kashmir in 1947–1948, one of 12 international crises, including four wars, during the India/Pakistan protracted conflict over many issues, tangible and intangible, since the end of British rule over the subcontinent in 1947. So too with the (first) Arab/Israel crisis-war in 1948–1949, one of 30 international crises during their largely unresolved protracted conflict, including nine wars [to be summarized later in this book].

Using a modified version of the Azar et al. definition—deleting violence as a *necessary* condition because it did not accord with reality—ICB uncovered 33 protracted conflicts since the end of World War I: for example, at the global level, the *East/West* conflict and, at the regional level, *Ethiopia/Somalia* (Africa), *Ecuador/Peru* (Americas), *China/Japan* (Asia), *France/Germany* (Europe), and *Iraq/Iran* (Middle East), among others.

An overall majority of international crises during the near-century, late 1918–late 2017, 58%, occurred within an interstate protracted conflict, with a notable decline over time—from 59% of 1918–1994 crises to 52% of crises from 1995 to 2015. The other international crises occurred outside that setting; that is, they emerged in an environment without the prior condition of *prolonged dispute* over one or more issues and without the *spillover effects of cumulative crises between the same adversaries*.

Operationally, for a dispute between states to qualify as a *protracted conflict* (conflict), there must be three or more international crises between the same pair or cluster of adversaries over one or more recurring issues during a period of at least 10 years (The concept, protracted conflict, is similar to that of *"enduring rivalry"* (ER), with three conditions: at least five militarized interstate disputes (MIDs) between the same adversaries, each lasting at least 1 month; 25 years from the first to the last dispute within the rivalry, and a gap of no more than 10 years between two of these disputes). This definition of an interstate protracted conflict provided the conceptual basis for the classification of international crises, and for the research questions that guided the analysis of international crises and protracted conflicts.

Are there differences in the configuration of crises that occur within and outside protracted conflicts, and, if so, what are they? Specifically, how does the attribute of protracted conflict affect the crisis attributes and dimensions from onset to termination? Crises that erupted within conflicts were more likely than others to have been triggered by violence, to generate the perception of grave threat, and to entail the use of violence in crisis management. Despite these indicators of crisis *severity*, the international system has often been unable to deal with these crises effectively, either through its international organizations or through the attempts at crisis resolution by major powers.

The notion that international crises within protracted conflicts are more likely than others to be triggered by violence derives from a conflict's distinctive characteristics. First, prolonged hostility between the same adversaries creates mutual mistrust and expectation of violent behavior. Second, the likely presence of several issues within an on-going interstate conflict, a characteristic of many but not all protracted conflicts, strengthens this anticipation. Third, resort to violence in the past relationship between adversarial states reinforces the belief that violence will recur. And finally, the importance of the values at stake creates a disposition to initiate violence against an adversary.

Conceptually and empirically, crisis is also closely linked to *war*. Most international crises erupt in a non-war setting. Some do not escalate to war (notable e.g., *Berlin Blockade*, 1948–1949, *Cuban Missile Crisis*, 1962). Other crises begin in a non-war setting and escalate to war later (*Entry into World War II*, 1939). And still others occur during a war, such as defeat in a major battle, *Stalingrad*, in 1942–1943, for Germany, or the dropping of atomic bombs on *Hiroshima and Nagasaki*, in 1945, for Japan. These *intra-war crises* (IWCs) profoundly affected the decisions of German and Japanese leaders during World War II.

All types of international crisis manifest its necessary conditions, namely, more intense, or a basic change in, *disruptive interactions* and a perceived likely outbreak of *military hostilities* (or, for an intra-war crisis, a perceived adverse *change in the military balance*), which undermine the relationship between the adversaries and pose a challenge to system stability. Moreover, the effects of the IWCs cited here were more significant than most non-IWCs for state behavior and the evolution of world politics. *In sum*, a crisis can erupt, persist, and end with or without violence, let alone war. Perceptions of value threats and stress do not require war. Nor do they vanish with war. Rather, the occurrence of war at any point in the evolution of a crisis intensifies disruptive interaction, along with perceived harm and stress.

Since war does not, per se, eliminate or replace crisis, IWCs were integrated into the overall set of international crises from late 1918 to the end of 2015 in the ICB Dataset. At the same time, IWCs have one distinctive attribute, a war setting. Of the 476 international crises that then comprised the ICB Dataset, 86 cases (18%) were IWCs.

The most elaborate presentation of the dataset in an ICB publication, *A Study of Crisis* (Brecher and Wilkenfeld 1997, 2000), provided an analysis of international crises from the perspective of seven significant contextual attributes of the international system and its member-states: *polarity* and *geography*, as fundamental structural characteristics in which international crises unfold; *ethnicity* and *regime type* (democracy/non-democracy) as constraints and influences on decision-making in crisis; the *conflict setting* (protracted conflict/non-protracted conflict), and *extent of violence* as criteria by which the international community judges the potential danger a crisis poses for the system as a whole; and *third-party intervention* as a potential response by the system and its actors. Each of these contextual attributes was examined with data on international political earthquakes spanning the entire twentieth century since the end of World War I and the first 15 years of the twenty-first century. Each of the seven sections concluded with a summary of key findings pertaining to the more than 50 hypotheses examined in *A Study of Crisis*, along with the significance of these empirical findings for the international system as it approached the beginning of the twenty-first century.

Severity and Impact

In the midst of preparation of the large-scale report on ICB empirical and analytical findings, A Study of Crisis, a 'first cut' analysis of two crucial ICB concepts, by Brecher and Patrick James, was published in *Crisis and Change in World Politics* (1986). Its central contribution was to point the way: it was the first published version of the concepts, Crisis *Severity* and Crisis *Impact*, which were elaborated and refined in later Brecher publications, 1993 and 2008 (to be presented below).

SYSTEM AND CRISIS

This chapter attempts to overcome a major obstacle to a creative *system* orientation in international relations—a dearth of knowledge about *system-level change*. To accomplish this goal, two tasks are necessary. First, building upon earlier contributions, a new definition of international system is offered and its essential properties—*structure, process, equilibrium, stability*—are presented and discussed. The second requirement is to create a new approach to *crisis* and to forge links between its *unit* and *system* levels. This, in turn, will facilitate the analysis of crises as catalysts to system change, that is, serving as international earthquakes.

International System

In an early critique, Zinnes (1980) argued persuasively that a satisfactory definition of international system must address two basic questions: (1) 'how do we know one when we see one' and (2) 'what distinguishes one from another'? The first can be met by a definition which builds upon earlier writings but restores the balance between *structure* and *process* within an integrated set of system components.[1]

An international system is a set of actors who are situated in a configuration of power (*structure*), are involved in regular patterns of interaction (*process*), are separated from other units by *boundaries* set by a given *issue*, and are constrained in their behavior from within (*context*) and from outside the system (*environment*).[2]

Structure refers to how the actors in a system stand in relation to each other. Its *basic variables* are the *number of actors* and the *distribution of power* among them, from *unipolar* through *bipolar* to *multi-power* or *polycentric*. *Process* designates the *interaction patterns* among the actors of a system. *The basic interaction variables* are *type*, identified along a conflict/cooperation dimension, and *intensity*, indicated by the volume of interaction during a given period of time.[3] A link between structure and process is postulated: every structure has a corresponding interaction process, and a structure creates and maintains regular interaction.

International systems (and crises) *do not require* the physical proximity of actors, though this trait is frequently present. Another distinctive property of a system, which serves to demarcate its boundaries, is *issue*. This concept may be defined as a specific shared focus of interest for two or more state actors. There are *war–peace issues*. K.J. Holsti (1972: 452–455) noted several issues at the base of 77 international conflicts and crises from 1919 to 1965: territory; composition of a government; rights or privileges to bases; national honor; unlimited aggrandizement or imperialism; liberation, and unification. There are *economic* and *developmental* issues. Keohane and Nye (1977, part II) analyzed fishing, commercial navigation, offshore drilling, and military uses in the issue-area of ocean space and resources, as well as exchange rates, reserve assets, international capital movements, and adjustment, liquidity, and confidence in a regime within the international monetary issue-area. There are also *political, cultural, status,* and *technological* issues within broader categories of issue-areas (Potter 1980).

The inclusion of *subsystems* within this definition enables us to resolve a paradox in the globally oriented concept of international system and thereby to address the other system properties, namely, *boundaries, context,* and *environment*. The paradox is simple yet fundamental. Every system has boundaries which demarcate members from other units. However, the *global* international system excludes a priori the possibility of non-member units and, therefore, of boundaries. It has the additional shortcoming of negating the existence of an environment as a phenomenon distinct from the system itself. That in turn makes impossible a distinction between two kinds of effects on the behavior of actors— *contextual*, those arising from within a system, and *environmental*, those from outside. As Young (1968a: 23) observed, a global system can be characterized only by its context since "there is nothing outside the system which can be labeled environment." The concept of environment, he continued, is useful when dealing with subsystems, for these "may be affected by various factors (including other organized entities) located outside its boundaries in spatial terms."

There are several usages of the concept of *boundaries* in international politics. They may be conceived in vertical terms, that is, boundaries in time (Rosecrance 1963, Chap. 11; Haas 1974); as horizontal, that is, in spatial terms (Singer 1971: 12–13); or diagonal, that is, time and space boundaries together (Rosenau 1972: 149). The notion of boundaries presented here is derived from the generic definition of international system above. As such, they make possible the spatial distinction between context and environment. *Context* and *environment* incorporate all geographic, political, military, technological, societal, and cultural elements which affect the structure and process of a system, from within and from outside the system, respectively.

These two concepts can be combined along two dimensions: *extent of similarity* and *degree of integration*. Four types of effects can be specified:

1. *Similar-Integrative*—homogeneity in religion and culture facilitates negotiation and compromise among actors in a system;
2. *Similar-Disintegrative*—the presence of ethnic minorities of similar origin in contiguous states increases turmoil and the tendency to hostile behavior;
3. *Dissimilar-Integrative*—economic and technological heterogeneity among actors leads to increasing interdependence, specialization, and mutual cooperation;
4. *Dissimilar-Disintegrative*—political regimes with different ideologies induce competition for leadership and spheres of influence.

The definition of international system presented above enables us to identify a system. Other concepts are needed to distinguish among systems. These are *stability* and *equilibrium*, system attributes which have been dealt with extensively in the mainstream of international relations literature. In general, more emphasis has been given to stability. Moreover, its relationship to equilibrium has not been fully developed.[4] The argument proposed here is the necessity of restoring equilibrium to a coequal status with stability among the attributes of an international system, as a precondition to developing the concept of system-level crisis.[5]

Closely related tasks are definitions of stability and equilibrium and a specification of relationships between them so as to permit us to distinguish among international systems.

The concept of change is the key to the distinction between stability and equilibrium, as well as to the organic link between them. *Change* may be defined as a shift from, or an alteration of, an existing pattern of interaction between two or more actors in the direction of greater conflict or cooperation. It is indicated by acts or events which exceed the bounds of normal fluctuations or a 'normal relations range' (Azar 1972; Azar et al. 1977: 196–197, 207). Following Ashby (1952: 87), four types of change may be distinguished: *full function*—no finite interval of constancy; *part function*—finite intervals of change and finite intervals of constancy; *step function*—finite intervals of constancy separated by instantaneous jumps; and *null function*—no change over the whole period of observation. Change may also occur in the structure of a system, namely, an increase or decrease in the number of actors and/or a shift in the distribution of power among them.

Stability may be defined as change within explicit bounds. *Instability* designates change beyond a normal fluctuation range. These concepts may be operationalized in terms of the quantity (number) of change(s) in the structure of a system, its process or both, ranging from no changes to many changes. This continuum denotes degrees of stability. The absence of change indicates pure stability, its presence, and some degree of instability. Any system can thus be designated as stable or unstable. Instability in the international system can be illustrated by change in the volume of interaction inherent in such phenomena as wars or crises involving essential actors. The presence of one of these processes may also induce structural change and thereby accentuate system instability.

Equilibrium may be defined as the steady state of a system, denoting change below the threshold of reversibility. *Disequilibrium* designates change beyond the threshold of reversibility. This meaning is broader than the notion of balance of power, a widely used synonym for equilibrium in the world politics literature. These concepts may be operationalized in terms of the quality (significance) of change in structure, process or both, ranging from total reversibility to total irreversibility. This continuum denotes degrees of equilibrium. Incremental change indicates a state of equilibrium which has no effect on the system as a whole. Step-level (irreversible) change indicates disequilibrium, which inevitably leads to system transformation, that is, a change in essential actors and/or

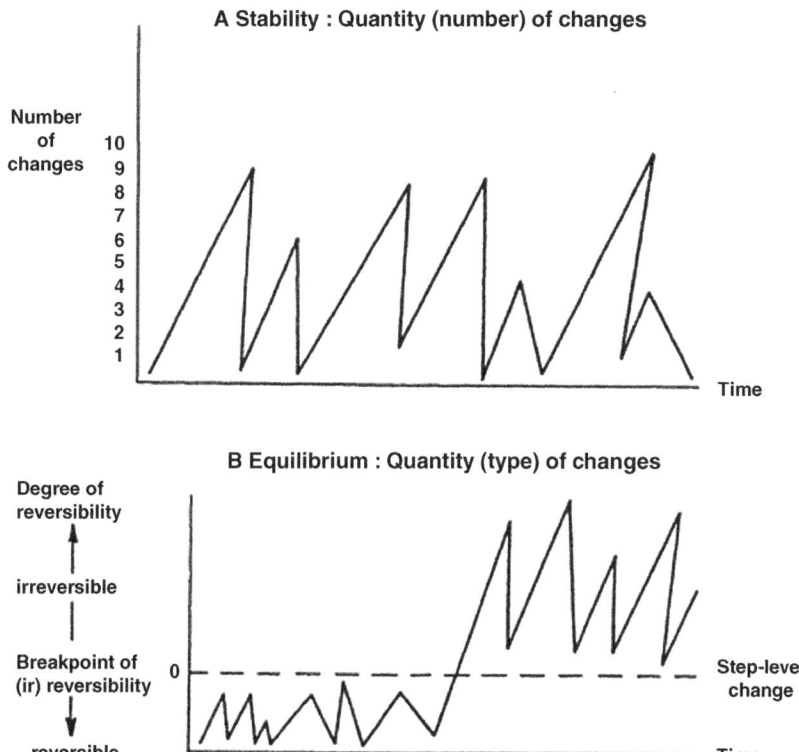

Fig. 2.1 Stability and Equilibrium

the distribution of power among them. The new system, with properties which significantly differ from those of its predecessor, denotes a new equilibrium, that is, changes within it which are reversible. These system attributes are presented in Fig. 2.1.

Every system has explicit or implicit rules of the game. Many international systems permit resort to violence as an instrument of crisis management, its legitimacy deriving from the legal sovereignty of international actors. This is evident in the inherent right of individual and collective self-defense, enshrined in the international institutions of the twentieth-century multi-power system (League of Nations) and bipolar system, and in the late twentieth and early twenty-first century unipolycentric and renewed multipolar systems (United Nations). Violence which exceeds the bounds of a normal fluctuation range, even when legitimized by the 'rules of the game,' constitutes, in our terms, instability, but not disequilibrium, unless this violence challenges the structure of the system.

Acute disruptions in an existing structure or process or both may, or may not, lead to disequilibrium. This potential linkage was illuminated by Keohane (1981): "a 'distortion' [i.e., instability] *per se*—an increase in temperature in an air-conditioned room, the rise of a single powerful state in a balance of power system, or a sharp increase in price because of a sudden upsurge in demand—does not suggest that a system is in disequilibrium: rather, it tests that hypothesis by allowing us to see whether adjustments take place. Does the air-conditioning bring the temperature back to the normal level, do coalitions form to counter the power of the rising state, do new sources of supply appear in response to price increases? ... Disequilibrium of a system ... appears only when the 'forces tending to restore the balance' (Arrow's phrase in a discussion of equilibrium) fail to operate. Air-conditioning that heats a room to 100 °F.; 'bandwagoning' that leads to hegemony by a single power; prices that rise sharply and continuously without bringing forth new supply—these are indications of disequilibrium."

There are additional linkages. Four states of a system, along with illustrations and systemic outcomes, are presented in Table 2.1.

In sum, approaches to international systems have been assessed. A revised definition has been proposed based upon six system components: *actors, structure, process, boundaries, context,* and *environment.* Furthermore, the two basic system attributes, *stability* and *equilibrium*, have been redefined and the links between them specified. Thus, the dual task of identifying and differentiating systems has now been completed. The next section will focus on the concept of *systemic crisis* both within a given system and as a catalyst to system transformation.

Systemic Crisis

Definitions of systemic crisis, based upon concepts related to international systems, can be classified into two groups: process and combined interaction structure.

Process definitions view systemic crisis as a turning point at which there occurs an unusually intense period of conflictual interactions. According to McClelland (1968: 160–161), "a crisis is, in some way, a 'change of state' in the flow of international political actions ..."

Table 2.1 System Attributes: Links

	Equilibrium		Disequilibrium
Stability	No change or few *reversible* changes in either structure or process and thus no effect on the system as a whole	A	Few, *irreversible* changes in either structure or process which lead to system transformation
	Ideologically based coalition groups in bipolar system and flexible alignment patterns in balance of power system preserve existing structure	B	Exit of major actor from bloc leading to loosening of bloc system and basic change in system polarity
	System unchanged	C	System transformed: new equilibrium
Instability	Many but *reversible* changes in structure, process or both which do not lead to system transformation	A	Many *irreversible* changes in structure, process or both which lead to system transformation
	Limited wars in a multipolar or bipolar system	B	World war—likely to lead to destruction of existing structure, in either multipolar or bipolar system
	System unchanged: equilibrium maintained, stability restored	C	System transformed: new equilibrium, new stability

Code A State of the system, *B* Illustration, *C* System outcome

Elsewhere (1972: 6–7) crisis "interaction is likely to affect the stability or equilibrium of the system …" Similarly, for Azar (1972: 184), "Interaction above the … upper critical threshold… for more than a very short time implies that a crisis situation has set in." These definitions emphasize stages of conflictual behavior among states, different types of activity, the direction and speed of behavioral change, and shifts that indicate changes in the interaction processes.

Well-operationalized concepts exist (Azar et al. 1972). And scales facilitate the ranking of various behavioral groups (Azar et al. 1977; Corson 1970; McClelland 1968; Tanter 1966). The shortcomings are analytical. The logic for designating the beginning and end of a crisis was not precisely indicated. Changes in process were not related to structure. There was no attempt to uncover causes and effects of systemic crisis. The result is a group of studies more valuable for their empirical findings than for understanding the phenomenon of systemic crisis (e.g., Burgess and Lawton 1972; Eckhardt and Azar 1978; McClelland 1968, 1972; Peterson 1975; Tanter 1974; Wilkenfeld 1972).

Combined *structural-interaction* definitions view a systemic crisis as a situation characterized by basic change in processes which might affect structural variables of a system. Thus Young (1968c: 15) identified "a crisis in international politics [as] a process of interaction occurring at higher levels of perceived intensity than the ordinary flow of events and characterized by ... significant implications for the stability of some system or subsystem ..." Integrating structure into a process definition serves as a good analytical starting point by specifying the essential conditions and effects of crisis situations. There is, however, little operationalization of the crucial concept of structure. The result is highly abstract theoretical writings.

There was another group, comprising Kaplan, Pruitt, Waltz, and others, for whom systems were characterized by normal periods of equilibrium and stability with occasional shifts to disequilibrium and instability. Although such situations are not explicitly termed systemic crises, these transitions are clearly related to the concept of crisis. Except for Kaplan, however, emphasis was placed on the traits of a specific system, not on changes from one system to another.

A problem common to systemic crisis definitions was the mixture of unit- and system-level concepts. For Young (1968c: 10, 14), "crisis concerns the probabilities that violence of major proportions will break out," a point which "explicitly refers to subjective perceptions about the prospects of violence rather than to a more objective measure of the probability of violence." Another striking illustration was Wiener and Kahn's (1962) 12 generic dimensions of crisis. Among them are system-level indicators such as a turning point in a sequence of events, a new configuration of international politics as a crisis outcome, and changes in relations among actors. There were also unit-level indicators: a perceived threat to actor goals; a sense of urgency, stress, and anxiety among decision-makers; increased time pressure; and so forth.

In sum, there were several shortcomings in system-level definitions of crisis:

1. they did not integrate all the key concepts—change in interaction, type of structure, degree of disequilibrium, and instability;
2. they focused clearly on interaction processes but did little to explain their sources and diverse effects on a system; and

3. they mixed system concepts with unit-level components such as perception, stress, and values.

Moreover, there was little attempt to link definitions at the two levels of crisis (McCormick 1978; Tanter 1978).

In an effort to overcome these weaknesses, a new definition of international systemic crisis is presented, based upon the system properties discussed in the first section of this chapter. *A systemic crisis may be defined as a situational change characterized by two necessary and sufficient conditions:*

1. *an increase in the intensity of disruptive interactions among system actors and*
2. *incipient change within the structure of an international system, more precisely, in one or more structural attributes—power distribution, actors/regimes, rules, and alliance configuration.*

This definition refers to crises in the *military-security issue-area* only. Conditions (1) and (2) denote a higher than average increase in intensity of conflictual interactions and strain to the structure. By average, we mean normal fluctuations as discussed earlier, that is, not beyond the bounds of the 'steady state' of the system. Systemic crisis encompasses change. System change need not occur by leaps and jumps, that is, crises; it may result from cumulative events. However, such change is the product of something other than a crisis.

The definition presented here specifies *change in process and structure*. It is also linked to *stability and equilibrium*, for these conditions indicate a shift in the state of a system from stability-equilibrium to instability-equilibrium or stability-disequilibrium or instability-disequilibrium, as illustrated in Table 2.1. In schematic terms: *few distortions in process or few challenges to a structure denote low instability, whereas many changes indicate high instability; minor distortions (reversible) in process or minor challenges to a structure denote equilibrium, while major changes (irreversible) indicate disequilibrium. Instability, defined as change beyond a normal fluctuation range but within bounds,* is present in all systemic crises; *disequilibrium, that is, irreversible change,* is not.

Berlin Blockade Crisis 1948–1949

The two crisis conditions and the linkages among system properties can be illustrated by the Berlin Blockade Crisis of 1948–1949. Tension between the Western powers and the Soviet Union centered on the issue of occupied Germany. The 1945 Potsdam Agreement had divided Germany into four zones of occupation, by France, the UK, the USA, and the USSR, but had provided that they were to be treated as one economic unit under the Allied Control Council. On June 7, 1948, the three Western powers published the recommendations of the March 1948 London Conference (to which the Soviet Union had not been invited), calling for a merger of their zones in Germany. This conflictual-type act broke an existing, though fragile, East–West consensus on Germany and set in motion several changes in rapid succession. The Soviet Union responded on June 24 by blocking all Western transportation by land into and out of Berlin. President Truman countered on June 26 with an order to step up the US airlift into Berlin, which had begun 2 months earlier, and continued with plans for the rehabilitation of Germany as part of Western Europe. Talks between the crisis actors began on August 2, 1948. An informal consensus on the future of Germany was reached by the four powers on March 21, 1949. An agreement was signed on 12 May formalizing the partition of Germany into two quasi-independent states, the Federal Republic of Germany [FRG, West Germany] and the German Democratic Republic [GDR, East Germany]. These events indicated an accommodation by the system, the May 12, 1949 event marking the end of the Berlin Blockade Crisis.

In systemic crises, changes vary in quality, as well as in quantity: they are reversible in some cases, irreversible in others. Thus a sharp increase in conflictual interactions between the Western powers and the USSR clearly indicated system instability between June 7, 1948 and May 12, 1949. The Berlin crisis also affected the East–West equilibrium. Distortions were step-level in nature; that is, neither the interaction pattern nor the structure of the dominant system in world politics at the time was the same before and after the crisis. The agreement of May 12, 1949 illustrates this point. It left Germany divided, creating the foundation of two new international actors, the Federal Republic of Germany (FRG, West Germany) and the German Democratic Republic (GDR, East Germany), and tightened the polarization between the superpowers. Furthermore, the interaction pattern between the Western powers and the Soviet Union after the agreement on Berlin came into effect differed

Table 2.2 Systemic Crisis and System Properties: Berlin Blockade 1948–1949

	Dominant system components		Dominant system attributes	
Crisis phase	Interaction	Structure	Stability	Equilibrium
1. Pre–June 7, 1948	Interaction among the powers ruling Germany within a normal relations range	Embryonic bipolarity	Stable	Equilibrium
2. June 7, 1948– March 21, 1949	Rapid increase in (irreversible) conflictual interaction between the USSR and the Western powers	Grave challenge to the existing structure	Unstable	Disequilibrium
3. March 21–May 12, 1949	Decline in conflictual interaction and a system accommodation	Tight bipolarity	Stable	(New) equilibrium

substantially from that during the occupation of Germany by the four powers. The system during the Berlin Blockade crisis was in a state of high instability leading to disequilibrium. As such, it helped to catalyze the transformation of the transitional international system of embryonic bipolarity (1945–1948) to tight bipolarity.

The threshold events between phases of the Berlin Blockade Crisis, as well as the overall links between crisis conditions and the system attributes of equilibrium and stability, are summarized in Table 2.2.

India/Pakistan Crisis Over Kashmir 1965–1966

A similar analysis will now be undertaken for an international crisis at the subsystem level, the India/Pakistan struggle over Kutch and Kashmir in 1965–1966. A South Asian regional system had emerged in 1947 with the transfer of power from the United Kingdom to India and Pakistan. For almost a quarter of a century, until the sundering of Pakistan in the crisis leading to the creation of Bangladesh in 1971, India and Pakistan were the relatively equal major powers in the South Asian system, with several small or very small powers on the geographic periphery of the sub-continent, Ceylon (Sri Lanka) from 1948, Afghanistan from 1949, Nepal since 1950, and Bangladesh.

The normal pattern of interaction between India and Pakistan was characterized by mistrust and verbal hostility, with periodic disruptions of an intensity sufficient to mark international crises, as that over the post-partition *territorial issues* of Junagadh, Kashmir, and Hyderabad (1947–1949) and the Punjab war scare (1951). There were also long-standing conflicts over diverse issues like *refugee compensation and repatriation*, and the *division of river water in the Indus Valley*. Among them was the princely state of Kutch. Its ruler had acceded to the Indian Union in 1947, but Pakistan claimed that the northern section of the Rann of Kutch was part of its Sind province. Incidents occurred in 1956, but Indian control over the disputed territory was quickly restored.

The India–Pakistan systemic crisis over Kutch and Kashmir began in April 1965 and ended in January 1966. The initial breakpoint occurred on April 8, when India launched an attack on the disputed Kutch border. Pakistan responded with a counter-attack the same day. Much higher-than-normal hostile interaction continued until the end of June 1965. Pakistani forces initially repelled local Indian troops. In response, on April 26, India placed its armed forces on alert, thereby escalating the crisis. A British call for a ceasefire and negotiations was accepted in principle on 11 May, but hostilities continued until June 30 when both parties agreed to all the terms of a UK-mediated package—mutual withdrawal of forces, direct negotiations, and arbitration if these failed to settle the dispute. *High instability characterized the subsystem* during those months, but its basic *equilibrium remained un*changed. Third-party intervention led to partial accommodation of the South Asian subsystem.

A second phase of this systemic crisis began in August 1965 and lasted until January 1966. The breakpoint occurred on August 5 when Pakistan-supported guerrillas infiltrated into the Indian-held part of the former princely State, Jammu and Kashmir, in an attempt to spark a large-scale uprising against India's rule. The overall distribution of power between India and Pakistan was at stake, making the challenge to the structure of the regional system much greater than in the April–June phase over the Rann of Kutch. India responded on August 25 by sending several thousand troops across the 1949 Kashmir ceasefire line, capturing most areas through which the infiltrators came. The crisis escalated further on September 1, when Pakistan sent an armored column across the ceasefire line in southern Kashmir threatening the vital road linking the Kashmir capital, Srinagar, with the plains of India. This led to a further escalation, India's invasion of West Pakistan on September 5.

The sharp increase in the volume of disruptive interaction indicated *greater system instability*. This was accentuated by China's denunciation of India's 'aggression' against Pakistan and its 'provocation' on the Sikkim–Tibet border. Moreover, Peking (later, Beijing) issued an ultimatum to Delhi to dismantle all border military fortifications and to stop all alleged intrusions into Tibet. While rejecting China's demands on the 17th, India hinted at a willingness to make minor concessions. The next day Chinese troop movements were reported to be within 500 m of Indian border positions. However, on September 21, China withdrew its ultimatum, announcing that India had complied with Peking's demands. This moderate decrease in conflictual interaction denoted further partial accommodation at the systemic level; change had not risen above the threshold of irreversibility.

The threat of direct Chinese military involvement in a South Asian crisis generated mediation efforts by the superpowers through the Security Council. A ceasefire resolution in mid-September, which also provided for a UN observer group in Kashmir, was accepted by India and Pakistan. This did not, however, indicate an exit point in the system-level crisis, for both armies continued to occupy each other's territory, a situation which was soon followed by violations of their ceasefire agreement. Another pacific strand of third-party intervention began on September 17 when Soviet Prime Minister Kosygin offered to convene a conference in Tashkent between President Ayub Khan of Pakistan and Indian Prime Minister Shastri. The conference was held between January 4 and 10, 1966. It ended with a declaration affirming the intentions of both parties to restore diplomatic and economic relations following the withdrawal of their troops from all occupied territory, as well as the repatriation of prisoners of war. Thus, January 10, 1966 marked the end of the crisis and a successful accommodation by the South Asian system. The challenge to its structure had been overcome, the pre-crisis equilibrium had been restored, and instability had reverted to its long-term norm of passive distrust.

As with the Berlin Blockade Crisis of 1948–1949, the *links between crisis conditions and the system attributes of equilibrium and stability* in the 1965–1966 India–Pakistan crisis are presented schematically in Table 2.3.

Table 2.3 Systemic Crisis and System Properties: India/Pakistan 1965–1966

Subsystem components		Subsystem attributes		
Crisis phase	Interaction	Structure	Stability	Equilibrium
1. April 8–June 30, 1965 (Kutch)	Increase in (reversible) conflictual interaction between India and Pakistan	Bipolarity	Unstable	Equilibrium
2. July 1–August 4, 1965	Decline in conflictual interaction and a partial system accommodation	Bipolarity	Stable	Equilibrium
3. August 5–September 16, 1965 (Kashmir)	Rapid increase in (irreversible) conflictual interaction between India and Pakistan	Grave challenge to the existing structure	Unstable	Disequilibrium
4. September 17, 1965–January 10, 1966	Marked decline in conflictual interaction and effective system accommodation	Bipolarity	Stable	Stable (restored) equilibrium

Severity and Impact

At the outset of this chapter, two questions were raised regarding international systems: how do we know one when we see one; and what distinguishes one from another? The same questions can be posed about international crises. We have already indicated how to recognize a crisis. It remains to explain how to distinguish one crisis from another. For this exercise, two additional concepts, severity and impact (importance), must be introduced.

Severity is a composite indicator of crisis attributes from the beginning to the end of an international crisis. It refers to the *volume* of conflictual interactions among the crisis actors and thus denotes the extent of system *instability* during a crisis.

Impact (*Importance*) is a composite indicator of crisis attributes *after* the conclusion of an international crisis. It refers to the *quality of structural change* or irreversibility and, as such, indicates the effects of a crisis on the *equilibrium* of a system.

Severity can be operationalized by six indicators. One is the *number of crisis actors*: the larger the number, the more disruptive will be hostile interactions, the greater the likelihood of superpower or major power involvement, and the more difficult the system's accommodation, all pointing to greater severity. Another indicator is the *geostrategic salience* of the location of an international crisis in terms of its natural resources and distance from major power centers. An underlying assumption is that the broader the geostrategic salience, the more severe will be the crisis. Salience ranges from a single regional subsystem (e.g., Afghanistan–Pakistan crisis over Pathanistan, 1955) to the global system (Cuban missiles, 1962). A third indicator is the extent of *heterogeneity* among crisis adversaries, measured by the number of attribute differences in terms of military capability, political regime, economic development, and culture (maximal heterogeneity—*Mayaguez*, 1975, between Cambodia and the United States). Here, too, the operative assumption is that the greater the heterogeneity among adversaries, the more severe the crisis.

A fourth indicator of *Severity* is the *extent of superpower involvement* in an international crisis, ranging from situations in which both the USA and the USSR are crisis actors to a crisis in which neither was involved in any form. In general, the greater the involvement by superpowers, the greater the challenge to the structure of a system and, therefore, the more severe the international crisis. A fifth indicator of severity is *issues*. Crises may focus on one or more issues within one or more *issue-areas—military-security, political-diplomatic, economic-development,* and *cultural-status.* The first issue-area creates the most severity. Moreover, the larger the number of issues, the more severe th*e crisis is likely to be.* Finally, severity is indicated by the *extent of violence* in a crisis, ranging from full-scale war, through serious clashes short of war, to minor clashes, to no violence.[6]

The *impact* (*importance*) of an international crisis can be operationalized by four *indicators.* One is *actor change* as a consequence of a crisis. This ranges from the creation or elimination of one or more actors (e.g., *Bangladesh,* 1971; *South Vietnam,* 1975), through a change in regime type (e.g., *Czechoslovakia,* 1948, democracy to communism), to a change in regime orientation (e.g., *Guatemala,* 1954, pro-Soviet to pro-USA), to no change in actors or their regimes. Another indicator is the extent of *alliance change* flowing from an international crisis, the most important being the formation or termination of an alliance (*China Civil War,* 1948–1949, and the PRC-USSR alliance, 1950), followed by the entry or exit of one or more actors into or from a formal or informal alliance (Greece–Turkey–*Truman Doctrine*, 1946–1947), an increase or decrease in cohesiveness in an existing alliance (*Prague Spring*, 1968) to no change in alliances.

Power change is a third indicator of crisis importance, extending from the entry or exit of an actor into or from the ranks of the most powerful states in a system (Japan's *atomic bomb* crisis, 1945), through a change in rank among the most powerful members of a system, to a change in relative power, but not in power rank, among the adversaries, to no change. Finally, the importance of a crisis is indicated by the extent of *change in rules of the game*. There may be new rules, codified or tacit (*Prague Spring*, 1968 and the *Brezhnev Doctrine*), an increase or decrease in actor consensus about existing rules, or no change in rules.[7]

Two international crises—one at the dominant system level (*Berlin Blockade*, 1948–1949), the other at the subsystem level (*Kashmir*, 1965–1966)—were examined in terms of several core concepts, *system, stability, equilibrium,* and *crisis*. These same cases will now be evaluated in terms of *severity* and *importance*.

The *Berlin Blockade* crisis of 1948–1949 was the first major *direct* confrontation between the two superpowers, though both had been adversaries in the 1945–1946 *Iran Hegemony* crisis. There were four *crisis actors* in the first Berlin crisis, the USA, USSR, UK, and France. Its *geostrategic salience*, as with all Berlin crises after 1945, was high, for it impinged on the balance of power in the dominant East–West system, as well as on the distribution of influence in the East Europe and West Europe subsystems. Among the adversaries, near-maximal *heterogeneity* is evident between France (or the UK) and the Soviet Union: while the former had a democratic political regime, the USSR had a civil authoritarian system of government; they were major military powers, it was a superpower; and cultural differences between Paris (or London) and Moscow were fundamental. As for *superpower involvement*, the Berlin case was at the apex of severity for, as noted, both the USA and the USSR were intensely hostile crisis actors. There were several *issues* at stake, including territory, hegemony, security, and status. Only with respect to the *violence* indicator did the Berlin case rank low: there was none. Taken together, however, its composite overall severity places the Berlin Blockade among the most severe international crises since the end of the Second World War.

The *impact (importance)* of this crisis was no less grave. The 1948–1949 Berlin case marks the first great divide in East–West relations. One of its structural consequences was the crystallization of basic changes then in motion, leading to the *formation of two new German states*, the FRG and GDR, on the ashes of the old. Another was the *change from embryonic bipolarity* in the post-World War II dominant system *to tight bipolarity*. As for alliance configuration, the Berlin Blockade hastened the *formalization of NATO* (1949) and moved the Communist states of East Europe *towards the Warsaw Pact* (1955). The Berlin Blockade outcome did not result in a change in the composition of the most powerful states in the dominant system or in their relative rank, but the USSR failed to achieve its objective, while the western powers did so. Berlin was more consequential, however, in *changing the rules of the game*: the blockade and direct confrontation indicated the end of the Potsdam phase in East–West relations; overt conflictual interaction became the norm thereafter. Thus the overall importance of the 1948–1949 Berlin crisis, like its severity, was very high.

In the *South Asian crisis* of 1965–1966 there were, as noted, *three crisis actors*, India, Pakistan and, for a very brief period, the PRC, along with three highly involved actors, the USA, USSR, and UK; their involvement, however, was confined to the political realm. *Geostrategic salience* was at the bare minimum, for the location of the crisis over Kutch and Kashmir had no relevance to any subsystem other than South Asia, let alone the dominant international system. There was limited *heterogeneity* between the principal adversaries, namely, in political regimes (India's western-type democracy versus Pakistan's military rule) and in culture (Hinduism versus Islam). There was *no superpower confrontation*, direct or indirect, only political involvement. Both *military and political issues* were at stake—territory and hegemony. As for *violence*, there was a *full-scale war* between India and Pakistan in September 1965. Taken together, the overall severity of the 1965–1966 India–Pakistan crisis was low.

In terms of *impact*, this crisis ranks very low. There was *no meaningful change in power distribution*, neither in the narrow sense of the crisis outcome, which was a political compromise, nor in the rank of the two major South Asian powers, India and Pakistan. Unlike their subsequent crisis over Bangladesh (1971), there was *no change in actors* nor in the type or orientation of their regimes. Only the existing *alliance pattern changed*, with Pakistan moving from an unqualified pro-western posture, formalized through its membership in SEATO and CENTO, to a more even-handed attitude toward the superpowers and an improvement in its relations with the USSR following the Tashkent Agreement. There was *no change in the rules of the game* within the South Asian subsystem:

both in war and diplomacy, the crisis actors adhered to established rules of behavior. The *impact* of the 1965–1966 international crisis, that is, its overall importance, was *minimal.*

Thus far this analysis has focused exclusively on the systems level. The next section will address the *level-of-analysis* problem with respect to crisis, that is, the crucial dimension of system change.

Unit–System Linkages

In all branches of knowledge there are several levels of analysis, each with distinct concepts, research questions, and methodologies. Every level is capable of illuminating a segment of knowledge within a discipline but no more. To provide insights into a part of any whole is admirable. However, the ultimate challenge is to link the findings at all levels into an aggregate of the whole and its parts in order to comprehend as much as possible of the total universe of knowledge in any field.[8]

This perspective derives from a conviction that the competitive focus on a single level of analysis is counter-productive. To examine the two levels—unit and system—would enable us to move beyond the position of blind men attempting to grasp the elephant. In the words of Robert North (1967: 394): "As research scholars and would-be theorists in international relations we might all derive at least three useful lessons from the old fable about the blind men and the elephant. The first is that the elephant [crisis] presumably existed; the second is that each of the groping investigators [at the unit and system levels], despite sensory and conceptual limitations, had his fingers on a part of reality; and the third is that if they had quieted the uproar and begun making comparisons, the blind men might—all of them—have moved considerably closer to the truth." It is in this spirit that we now approach the task of linking the unit (micro) and system (macro) levels of crisis analysis.

Since the early 1960s, there has been a large body of research on state behavior in international crisis, the counterpart to studies of conflictual interactions among adversary states (Hopple and Rossa 1981; Holsti 1980; Tanter 1978). They differ in definitions, conceptual frameworks, and techniques of analysis, as they must. This chapter emphasizes points of convergence while maintaining a clear-cut distinction between the two levels and their diverse effects.

A unit-level, *foreign policy crisis* derives from perceptions, whereas a *systemic crisis* is objective. Stated differently, the focus of the former is

Table 2.4 Unit- and System-Level Crisis Components

Component	Definition level	
	Unit-level (perception)	System-level (reality)
Threat	Threat to basic values	Challenge to system structure
Violence	Increase in war likelihood	Increase in disruptive interaction

image and action by a state's decision-maker(s), while that of the latter is reality and interaction. There is no one-to-one relationship between unit and systemic crises: the former occurs for a single state; the latter is predicated upon the existence of distortion in the pattern of interaction between–among two or more adversaries in an interstate system.

A definition of systemic crisis has been presented early in this book. From the perspective of a single state, a foreign policy crisis is a situation with three necessary and sufficient conditions, deriving from a change in its external or internal environment. All three are *perceptions* held by the highest-level decision-makers of:

a *threat to basic values*, along with the awareness of *finite time for response* to the external value threat, and a *high probability of involvement in military hostilities*[9]

At the unit level, there are *crisis actors*, that is, states whose decision-makers perceive the conditions of crisis. There are parallel concepts at the system level, as presented in Table 2.4.

For the threat component, the counterparts are basic values of decision-makers and structure of the system. Basic values, such as *existence*, *influence* in the global and/or regional systems, *territorial integrity*, *economic welfare*, and others are the elements which guide goals, decisions, and actions of states. Similarly, at the system level, *structure* provides the setting for continuity in interaction processes. Threat at the unit level indicates (subjective) perceptions by decision-makers. Challenge at the system level means an (objective) possibility of change in the structure. A challenge to the system structure may or may not materialize, just as a threat to basic values and an increase in war likelihood may or may not be realized.

In the 1948–1949 Berlin Crisis, the *threat to Soviet and USA influence in Germany* and, more generally, *to the international system* generated a sharp increase in conflictual interaction. This distortion, the counterpart of an increase in perceived likelihood of military hostilities, posed a challenge to the existing structure of the system, namely, to the number of actors (two or more Germanys) and the tighter polarization around the superpowers as a result of the crisis.

An international crisis may thus be addressed in macro-level and micro-level terms. While the former deals with a system as a whole, the latter focuses on each state crisis actor. There are situational changes in which only one state perceives a crisis for itself, that is, actions by one (or more) state(s) which trigger perceptions of threat, time pressure, and war likelihood for a single actor (e.g., the massing of Indian demonstrators on India's border with Goa in 1955, creating a crisis for Portugal). In other instances, two or more states experience a crisis over the same issue, as with the Western Powers and the USSR over Berlin in 1948–1949, 1958–1959, and 1961.

The link between unit- and system-level concepts of interstate crisis may be illustrated by two different cases: when a crisis for all state actors is identical in time; and when their crises overlap but are not identical in time. Establishing this link requires the clarification of *static* and *dynamic* concepts at both levels. The former is *trigger/termination* at the unit level and *breakpoint/exit-point* at the system level. The latter is *escalation/de-escalation* and *distortion/accommodation*, respectively. These concepts are presented in Table 2.5.

At the *unit level*, a *trigger*, a *static act*, is defined as the *catalyst* to a *foreign policy crisis*. In the 1948–1949 Berlin Blockade crisis, the trigger to the Soviet Union's foreign policy crisis was, as noted, the publication by the Western Powers on June 7, 1948 of the recommendations of their March 1948 London Conference. The *trigger* for the United States, Britain, and

Table 2.5 Static and Dynamic Concepts of Crisis

Nature of concept	Crisis level	
	Unit	System
Static	Trigger/termination	Breakpoint/exit-point
Dynamic	Escalation/de-escalation	Distortion/accommodation

France was the *Soviet decision on June 24 to block all Western transportation, by land and sea, into and out of Berlin*. In terms of a *dynamic* process, a *trigger denotes* an *escalation* in perceived threat, time pressure, and the likelihood of military hostilities.

The *termination* of a crisis at the *unit level*, that is, a *foreign policy crisis* is the point in time when decision-makers' perceptions of threat, time pressure, and war likelihood decline to the level existing prior to the crisis trigger. In the Berlin Blockade case, the termination date for each of the four powers was May 12, 1949, when an agreement regarding West and East Germany as separate entities was signed. Thus the triggers did not coincide but the termination dates for the various actors did. In *dynamic process* terms, *termination for crisis actors* marks the *final de-escalation in perceived threat, time pressure, and war likelihood during a crisis*.

At the *system level*, parallel notions exist—*breakpoint* and *exit-point* as counterparts of *trigger* and *termination*. A *breakpoint* is a disturbance to the system created by the entry of an actor into a crisis. A systemic crisis erupts with an initial breakpoint event, such as the Western powers' challenge to Moscow on June 7, 1948 regarding the integration of their zones of occupation in Germany. In dynamic terms, this change denoted distortion in the pattern of East–West interaction. Similarly, an exit-point refers to a significant reduction in conflictual activity, such as the formal agreement among the four powers on May 12, 1949 about the future of Germany and the lifting of the Soviet Union blockade. This change indicated *accommodation*, that is, a shift to a less intense level of hostile interaction than that during the systemic crisis.

The *duration* of a system-level crisis is measured from the *first breakpoint* to the *last exit-point* which, in unit-level terms, means from the *trigger for the first crisis actor* to the *termination by the last crisis actor*. For the initial breakpoint to occur, there must be two or more adversarial state actors in higher-than-normal conflictual interaction. They may both or all be crisis actors simultaneously; a rare occurrence for this requires triggers the same day, as in the 1965–1966 India–Pakistan crisis over Kutch–Kashmir. More often, they comprise one crisis actor and one adversary who triggers the crisis; the latter may later become a crisis actor, as with Belgium and the Congo in the 1960 Congo Crisis,[10] or it may not. A variant is one initial crisis actor and one adversary, with the latter joined by another in the process of becoming crisis actors, as with the USA and the USSR-cum-Cuba in the 1962 Missile Crisis.[11] Another variation is one crisis actor at the outset with several adversaries who later become crisis actors simultaneously, as with the USSR and the USA–UK–France in the 1948–1949 Berlin Crisis. As for the winding down of a system-level crisis, the majority of cases reveal a simultaneous termination for all crisis actors and, therefore, simultaneous accommodation by the system, as in the Berlin and India–Pakistan cases noted above.

Distortion may be gradual or rapid; so too with *accommodation*. In general, system-level interstate crises are characterized by multiple breakpoints, that is, *gradual distortion* and, by contrast, few exit-points, that is, rapid accommodation. The reason is that the onset of a systemic crisis is usually a process in which crisis actors cumulatively challenge one another. The result is that breakpoints tend to differ in time and, therefore, distortion is gradual. Accommodation, however, usually requires agreement, either formal or tacit. Thus exit-points tend to coincide in time. However, as long as any crisis actor has not terminated its foreign policy crisis, accommodation has not yet been completed: termination of the unit-level crisis for the last participant and the end of the system-level crisis are identical in time.

Breakpoints and *exit-points* also indicate the *entry* and *departure of actors* in a system-level crisis. Each breakpoint denotes an increase in conflictual interaction relative to the pre-crisis phase, whereas exit-points signal accommodation at the system level. *Linking unit upward to system*, the effects of trigger/termination on breakpoints/exit-points are immediate and direct; that is, a *trigger* at the unit level *always denotes a breakpoint at the system level* and *thus a further distortion in systemic interaction*. In the Berlin Blockade case, both June 7 and June 24, 1948, which were triggers at the unit level for the Soviet Union and the three Western powers, respectively, were also immediate breakpoints in the system-level crisis. However, *when systemic crisis is linked downward to actors*, the effects of exit-points on de-escalation are immediate and direct for some but may be delayed and indirect for others. Stated differently, *not all system-level changes affect all units at once and equally in a readily identifiable way*. The Berlin Blockade Crisis provides an example of direct and immediate effects: the last system level exit-point, on May 12, 1949, denotes final de-escalation for the four powers simultaneously. In general, systemic crises have more significant effects than unit-level crises because they pose a dual danger, namely, to the structure of the system and to its actors, whereas unit-level crises affect actors only.

In sum, a *system-level crisis requires behavioral change on the part of at least two adversarial actors leading to more intense conflictual interaction*.

Although a crisis is catalyzed by behavioral actions, these actions, the trigger to a unit-level crisis, can always be traced to their perceptual origin. Here lies *the organic link between the two levels of crisis*.

The concepts and definitions elaborated above have several possible uses in IR, IS, and WP research. Empirical data on system-level crises can be collected, classified, compared, and measured. Types of systemic crises can be described and can then serve as indicators of crisis anticipation. Sources of system-level crisis can be uncovered and rank-ordered. Factors such as decision-making process, type of regime, power distribution in the dominant system or subsystem, and other state-oriented or system-derived attributes can be examined in order to explain diversity in the emergence, type, and outcome of system-level crises. Finally, *conceptual clarity on system and crisis* paves the way for the analysis of crises as *international earthquakes, that is, as catalysts to system change*.

Notes

1. The major attempts to integrate system concepts into international relations theory focused on the great powers in world politics. Moreover, they meant by international system either the global system or, more often, the dominant system, a synonym for Singer and Small's (1972: 381) "Central Sub System," that is, "the most powerful, industrialized, and diplomatically active members of the interstate system, generally coinciding with the 'European state system'." Kaplan (1957: 4, 9) referred to a "system of action" as a set of five interrelated variables whose relationship is characterized by behavioral regularities—essential rules, transformation rules, actor, capability and information variables—but he did not explicitly define an international system. For Hoffmann (1961: 207), the concept of international system is blurred by its all-inclusive nature; it incorporates the structure of the world, the nature of the forces which operate across or within the major units, capabilities, pattern of power, and political culture of the units. Rosecrance (1963: 5, 6) acknowledged the importance of international systems and treated historical systems at length but distinguished among them mainly by "significant changes in diplomatic style." Aron (1966: 94, 95) appears to restrict the term, international system, to an 'ensemble' of political units capable of being implicated in a generalized war. E. Haas (1964: 62–63) noted the need for "definitional clarity, verbal and operational," among key system properties—inputs, outputs, units, environment, attributes, structures and functions—but the links were not developed. McClelland (1966: 20) distinguished between boundaries and environment but

confined the meaning of system to interaction. Young (1968a: 6) specified four essential components of a system: actors, structure, process and contextual limitations, but his distinction between *structure* and *process* is blurred. Keohane and Nye (1977: 20–21) clarified this distinction by identifying the former with "the distribution of capabilities among similar units" and the latter with "bargaining behavior within a power structure." Waltz (1979: 40), too, asserted the need for a clear-cut demarcation of structure and interaction but, like McClelland with process, he overemphasized structure.

2. Conceptually, an international system ranges across a broad spectrum, from the global system through the dominant system to subsystems. There are two strands in the subsystems literature: geography and issue. On the first see Binder (1958), Modelski (1961), Brecher (1963), Hoffmann (1963), Russett (1967), Zartman (1967), Bowman (1968), Kaiser (1968), Cantori and Spiegel (1970), M. Haas (1970), Dominguez (1971). Among the most careful in using a geographic criterion is M. Haas (1974: 336–356), whose empirical analysis of 21 subsystems combined geographic and issue criteria, providing a rare link to the second strand in the subsystems literature. On issue subsystems see Hanrieder (1965), Russett (1967), Zimmerman (1972), K.J. Holsti (1972), M. Haas (1974), Dean and Vasquez (1976), Keohane and Nye (1977), and Lampert (1980), who was the most direct in asserting the primacy of issue over geography as the basic component of subsystems. For an overview of the international subsystems literature see Thompson (1973). A later variation on the systems theme is the literature on international regimes (e.g., Krasner 1982). A regime, in the largest sense, may be termed an issue subsystem and, in narrower terms, the rules of the game within such a system.

3. In the literature on systems—though not on international systems—process is also used to denote growth and decay, concepts which are closely linked to system transformation. The latter, though not the central focus of this chapter, will be discussed in relation to stability and equilibrium.

4. Kaplan (1957: 21, 35–36) designated his "six distinct international systems" as "six states of equilibrium of an ultrastable international system"; that is, equilibrium is synonymous with system. Equilibrium is the normal state of a system; and his concern was with "the expectations for stability of each of the systems." The concept of "ultrastable system" was developed by Ashby (1952: 100–122). The first wave of analysts in the on-going debate over the relationship between systemic polarity and systemic stability (Waltz 1964; Deutsch and Singer 1964; Rosecrance 1966; Young 1968b) virtually omitted discussion of the concept of equilibrium. Hoffmann (1961: 208) distinguished between two types of system,

'stable' and 'revolutionary,' but he made no reference to equilibrium. Aron (1966: 100–101) barely mentioned stability and instability; and while he had an extensive discussion on equilibrium, it was treated as a policy, not a concept. For Rosecrance (1963: 220–221), "a system aiming at stability" comprises four elements: "a source of disturbance or disruption (an input)"; a regulator; a list of environmental constraints; and outcomes. While emphasizing interactions in his analysis of nine historical systems from 1740 to 1960, he made only a passing reference to equilibrium. Young (1968a: 42) was precise in defining stability both statically and dynamically: "In static terms, stability refers to the continuance of the essential variables of an international system (i.e., actors, structures, processes, and context) within the bounds of recognizability over time. In dynamic terms, on the other hand, stability can be thought of as the tendency of a system to move in the direction of equilibrium following disturbances." What is missing is the content of equilibrium. Waltz (1979: 161–162), too, was clear on stability, to which he related structure (1967: 229, fn. 18): "By 'structure' I mean the pattern according to which power is distributed; by 'stability,' the perpetuation of that structure without the occurrence of grossly destructive violence." Thus a change in structure means system transformation and a new stability. Just as Kaplan equated system with equilibrium, so Waltz equated system with stability. Several international relations scholars did focus on equilibrium. In this they share the emphasis of general systems theorists and economists who identify stability and instability as "states of equilibrium" (Arrow 1968: 384, 387). Richardson's conception of stability "referred simply to any set of conditions under which the system would return to its equilibrium state ..." (Deutsch and Singer 1964: 391). Liska (1957: 13) relied "mainly on the ideas of progressive, stable, and unstable equilibrium." Pruitt (1969: 20, 23–24, 36–37) addressed the relationship of these concepts rigorously: "Instability is defined as the *likelihood of sudden (basic) change* and stability is defined as the opposite of instability." Moreover, "Stable relations are usually characterized by oscillations around an equilibrium point..." However, Pruitt was less clear on the meaning of change and equilibrium. On stability see also Gilpin (1981: 50–105).

5. Michael Haas' treatise on international conflict (1974), for example, has a 23-page appendix on "Definitions of Concepts," in which equilibrium is conspicuously absent. By contrast, Gilpin (1981: 156–185) devotes considerable attention to this core concept.
6. The rationale for these indicators of Severity, the scales for each, and their relative weight in the overall severity of systemic crises are elaborated in Brecher and Wilkenfeld (1988: 119–141).

7. The rationale for the indicators of the Importance-Impact of international crises, along with the crisis impact model, and the hypotheses and findings on Impact are presented in Brecher (1993: 290–298, 318–334).
8. Among the pioneers of systems theory in the social sciences, Boulding (1956: 202, 201) introduced the idea of system rungs or levels. McClelland (1955: 34; 1958) was perhaps the first to specify levels in the study of world politics. Deutsch (1974: 152–156) set out a 10-level political system, including four levels in international politics. The 'level-of-analysis problem' was first given explicit formulation by Singer (1961, also 1971). See also Andriole (1978).
9. A crisis defined here refers to the war-peace issue-area. However, breakpoints may occur in any foreign policy issue, and the study of international political, economic, and status crises might yield no less valuable findings. For these types, an appropriate change is necessary in the second condition specified above.
10. The crisis trigger for Belgium, on July 5, 1960, was a mutiny among soldiers of the *Congolese Force Publique*, which rapidly turned into a general movement against Belgian and other European residents. Belgium responded on the 8th by announcing its intention to send military reinforcements to the Congo. A crisis was triggered for the Congo two days later when Belgian troops went into action.
11. The Missile crisis for the United States was triggered on October 16, 1962 when photographic evidence of the presence of Soviet missiles in Cuba was presented to President Kennedy. The US major response, on 22 October, was a decision to blockade all offensive military equipment on *route* to Cuba. This, in turn, triggered crises for the Soviet Union and Cuba.
12. Brecher and Ben-Yehuda, "System and Crisis in International Politics" (1984).

CHAPTER 3

Theory II: Unified Model of Crisis (UMC) & ICB FrameWork

UNIFIED MODEL OF CRISIS

The *Unified Model of Crisis*, which is designed to create a general theory of *Interstate Crisis*, is based upon an integration of six partial models, for: (1) the crisis *onset* phase/*pre-crisis* period, (2) the crisis *escalation* phase/*crisis* period, (3) the *de-escalation* phase/*end-crisis* period, and (4) the *impact* phase/*post-crisis* period, the four phases of an **international crisis** and the four periods of a state's **foreign policy crisis**. The UMC also builds upon two partial models of *crisis*—at the *international* (macro) and *state* (micro) levels of analysis.

In essence, these two partial general models are necessary but insufficient for a comprehensive analysis of crises in world politics. *International crises* encompass much more than the behavior of a single state in a *foreign policy crisis* and more than the crisis interactions among adversarial states in international crises. Thus, it was found necessary to integrate the four phase-period models and the two international and state level models into a **Unified Model of Crisis**, in order to capture the insights provided by each model and level of analysis and to explain accurately and fully the complex phenomenon of **Interstate Crises**.

Conceptual Guidelines: Overview

A **system** approach to knowledge in the social sciences (Bunge 1994), of which the Unified Model of Crisis is the ultimate expression in

International Relations–World Politics, is based upon the following six conceptual guidelines.

1. The concepts, *international* and *foreign policy crisis*, denote dynamic processes over time with separate *phases* such as *onset, escalation, de-escalation,* and *impact*, and their analytical counterpart at the level of a foreign policy crisis for a state such as *pre-crisis, crisis, end-crisis,* and *post-crisis periods.*
2. The distinguishing trait of each *phase—incipient distortion, peak distortion, accommodation,* and *non-crisis* interaction, and of each *period* namely *low, high, declining,* and *non-crisis stress*—can be explained by different sets of *enabling variables: system, interactor, actor,* and *situation* attributes, acting through *decision-makers' perceptions* of *value threat, time pressure,* and *war likelihood* (these concepts and their interrelationship will be clarified in a diagram of the Unified Model below).
3. The *two levels* of crisis, *international* and *state*, are analytically distinct but generate interrelated processes, each helping to explain the other, and both levels constitute integral parts of a larger unified whole, *interstate crisis* (Unified Model).
4. The four phase-period models and the two-level models capture parts of a multi-layered reality.
5. An explanation of cause–effect relationships in an Interstate Crisis requires the analysis of *perceptions* and *behavior* by the participating states (*crisis actors*), for crises occur and evolve as a result of choices by their decision-makers.
6. A synthesis of the two levels of analysis, *international* and *state* into a *unified model,* will achieve a comprehensive explanation of interstate crisis.

I turn now to one of the two major conceptual and theoretical innovations of the **Unified Model**, incorporating the *four phases* and *four periods* of a *crisis,* the *two levels of analysis,* the *crucial variables,* and the *perceptions* that shape *decision-makers' behavior* in foreign policy crises. (The concepts of **Severity** and **Impact**, along with the **Severity–Impact Model**, are discussed at length in Brecher, International Political Earthquakes (2008), Chaps. 6 and 7).

What is the meaning of the *Unified Model of Crisis?* In essence, it is a conceptual device to explain interstate *crisis* as a whole. To achieve that aim it builds upon the logic of a model of *foreign policy crisis* [state level of analysis] and of a model of *international crisis* [interactor level of analysis] and integrates them into a model of **Interstate Crisis** [system level of analysis] (**UMC**). Moreover, it incorporates the four *phase* and four *period* partial models—for *onset, escalation, de-escalation,* and *impact,* the four phases of an *international crisis,* and the four periods of a *foreign policy crisis* such as *pre-crisis, crisis, end-crisis,* and *post-crisis*— into the *Unified Model*. Third, the empirical data to test this integrated model of Crisis are drawn from the findings acquired in the testing of hypotheses derived from the four phase models, based upon two strands of evidence: aggregate, quantitative data on 97 years of international crises (late 1918–end 2015) and qualitative data from 29 case studies of state behavior in foreign policy crises.

The concepts, international crisis and foreign policy crisis, denote dynamic processes over time. The key traits of each *phase* (of an *international crisis*) and each *period* (of a *foreign policy crisis*), namely, *distortion* and *stress*, respectively, are explained by clusters of *enabling variables— system, inter-actor, actor,* and *situational*—operating through decision-makers' perceptions of *value threat, time pressure,* and *probability of war* (military hostilities). The *two levels of analysis* are distinct but interrelated. The models of international crisis and foreign policy crisis capture segments of a complex reality. Moreover, cause–effect relationships at the international level require the prior analysis of perceptions and behavior by the crisis actors (state level). The task of integrating the two levels of analysis is demanding. However, a synthesis is the essential precondition for a valid theory of interstate crisis.

Onset Phase–Pre-crisis Period: Hypotheses on Onset; Crisis Onset Model

How does an interstate crisis begin? It erupts first as a *foreign policy* crisis for a state through one of three kinds of trigger: a *hostile act*, a *disruptive event*, or an *environmental change*. The catalyst may be *internal* or *external*. It may be a *verbal threat*, for example, state A may issue a threat to expel B's citizens if B persists with propaganda against A's leaders. State A may commit a *hostile political act*, such as severing diplomatic relations with B. It may impose an *economic embargo* on B's exports. It may take *non-violent military* action, such as mobilization of reserves, maneuvers, or a show of force. It may also resort to *indirect violence*, attacking B's client.

An interstate crisis may also be set in motion by one of several types of *external change*: the development of a new weapon or weapon system or, more generally, an innovation in military technology that affects the balance of power between adversaries; change in the configuration of the global system or the salient regional subsystem, etc. An *internal verbal or physical challenge* to B's regime may occur with the support of A's leaders. It may take the form of a *coup d'état*, assassination, act of terror or sabotage, demonstration, strike, mutiny, or revolt. It may be the fall of a government or the proclamation of a new regime or a new state.

One example of a catalyst or *trigger* to a foreign policy crisis for a state will suffice: an air battle between Syrian *MIGs* and Israeli *Mirages* on September 13, 1973 triggered Israel's and Syria's foreign policy pre-crises, which escalated to an international crisis (and war), the October-Yom Kippur Crisis-War of 1973–1974 *(direct violent act)*.

There is, in short, an array of *triggers* to a *foreign policy crisis*. However, in order for state B to experience a foreign policy crisis, the catalyst/trigger, whether it is an act, event, or environmental change, must be perceived by B's decision-makers as a source of higher-than-normal value threat. That perception, in turn, generates modest stress, indicating the beginning of B's *pre-crisis* period. However, the change is not yet and may not develop into a full-fledged *international crisis*.

Stated in terms of the **Unified Model of Crisis**—see the graphic representation of this model below—the *outbreak of a foreign policy crisis* for a state *is a defining condition of an international crisis*. It is necessary but not sufficient; that is, the *pre-crisis period for a state* is a *prerequisite to, but not synonymous with,* the *onset phase* of an *international crisis*.

Whether or not B's pre-crisis period will set an *international crisis* in motion depends upon its perception and response. If it ignores A's trigger as posing a marginal or transitory threat—and does nothing—B's incipient foreign policy crisis will be aborted and an international crisis will not ensue. There are many such 'failed' international crises in world politics since the end of World War I. More often than not, B's decision-makers will perceive a trigger from A as seriously threatening one or more basic values and will respond in accordance with the dictates of a universally shared *security dilemma* by states that arise from the underlying anarchy of the interstate system; all states must be aware of the need to prepare to engage in self-help in an environment of system anarchy.

B's preliminary response may be a verbal, political, economic, non-violent military act, or a violent act (the same categories as triggering acts) or it may take the form of a multiple response, including or excluding violence. Whatever B's response, other than 'do nothing' or compliance with A's hostile behavior, it will generate a reciprocal perception of threat by A's decision-makers and with it A's pre-crisis period. If A responds, then *more-than-normal hostile interaction between A and B* would follow. That, in turn, would transform a pre-crisis period for both A and B into the *onset phase* of an international crisis characterized by incipient distortion; that is, at that point in the A–B relationship an *international crisis* erupts.

While this process traces the incipient link between the two levels of analysis, state level and international level, at the beginning of an interstate crisis, what explains the change from non-crisis to pre-crisis period for the adversaries and then to the onset phase of an international crisis? An unambiguous, theoretically valid causal formula is not possible because interstate crises are pervasive in time and space, affecting virtually all members of the global system. What is possible is to specify the cluster of *enabling variables*, that is, the *system, inter-actor,* and *actor attributes* whose presence makes the *outbreak* of an interstate crisis most likely. The more of these conditions that are present, the more likely is the jump *from non-crisis to incipient foreign policy crisis for one or more adversarial states and the onset of an international crisis.*

Crisis Onset Model

These conditions were derived from the **crisis onset model**: it postulates that *a foreign policy crisis* and later an *international crisis are most likely to be catalyzed when*

> the dispute between A and B occurs *within* a *polycentric structure*;
> it erupts *within* a *subsystem of world politics*;
> it occurs in a setting of *protracted conflict*;
> there is *no or marginal power discrepancy between the adversaries*;
> their *political regimes* are *non-democratic or mixed*; and
> the adversaries are *geographically contiguous* (Fig. 3.1).

Two other puzzles about 'crisis take-off' merit attention in the context of the Unified Model. First, what *enabling variables* explain the *most likely set of conditions for crisis initiation by a state*? Second, if A's action triggers B's pre-crisis period and generates low stress for B's

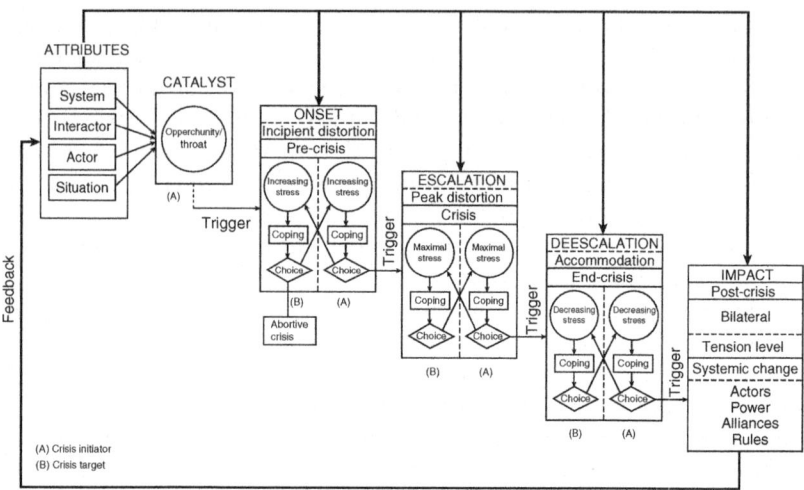

Fig. 3.1 Unified Model of Interstate Crisis

decision-makers, what does the **UMC** indicate as the *most likely pattern of coping* in that initial period of an interstate crisis?

The task of explaining foreign policy crisis initiation, too, takes the form of specifying the *most likely conditions* in which a state will trigger a *military-security crisis* for another member of the global system. According to **Proposition 2**, the most likely conditions are when a state

is a *young* or *newly independent entity*;
is *militarily stronger* than its adversary;
has a *non-democratic regime*;
confronts *internal political, social, and/or economic instability*;
is *geographically contiguous to its adversary*; and
has a *large territory*.

Given the prevalence of low stress between–among the decision-makers of adversaries in the onset phase, their behavior (*coping*) during their pre-crisis period is likely to take the form of a preliminary probe of each other's intention, capability, and resolve. Bargaining is not likely to be of the coercive diplomacy type; for the *heightened probability of military hostilities* and *time pressure*, the two other defining conditions of a foreign policy crisis are not yet or are only dimly perceived by the adversaries; and the *value threat*, the third defining condition, is still modest in the *onset* phase. In short, the adversaries are likely to consider one or more *pacific techniques of crisis management*, notably *negotiation* or *mediation*.

For the same reasons—low, though higher than normal, value threat, unawareness of time constraint, and the perception of war as unlikely—*decision-making* in the pre-crisis period of the adversaries will differ little from its non-crisis norm. Decision-makers will not exhibit a more intense *search for information* about the disputed issue(s) or the adversary's intention, capability, and behavior. The *processing of information* will remain essentially the function of bureaucrats. And their 'gatekeeper' role on the type and amount of information to flow upwards to senior decision-makers will, as in non-crisis situations, have a profound effect on the latter's [mis]perceptions and behavior in the pre-crisis period.

Consultation, too, is likely to follow the non-crisis norm. Senior decision-makers will become slightly more active because a new or enhanced threat is perceived, requiring some attention and response by those authorized to decide and act for a state. They will meet more frequently and seek more advice from military and civilian advisors but without a display of pressure for rapid choice.

They may be open-minded about *alternative ways of responding* to the perceived threat, though not averse to reliance on standard operating procedures (SOPs) to cope with the challenge. And the *decisional forum* is likely to remain a non-crisis unit, whether Cabinet, National Security Council, Politburo, Revolutionary Command Council, Standing Committee, or other institutional variants. In general, the *decision process* will be unhurried and largely free from dysfunctional stress.

The many (29) ICB case studies of decision-making in foreign policy crises alluded to earlier provide strong but not total support for the expected *coping pattern* in the pre-crisis period. There was *no change in information processing* in an overwhelming majority of the cases, and where change occurred it was confined to a modest increase in information flow. Decision-makers did not perceive a *need for more information* and did not resort to *extraordinary channels of communication*. As for *consultation*, exceptions to the Unified Model's anticipated continuation of non-crisis behavior were the USSR's consultation with leaders of other Warsaw Pact states in the 1968 *Prague Spring* pre-crisis period, and the formation of an ad hoc group, the "Malvinas Team," by Argentina's Foreign Ministry in its 1982 *Falklands/Malvinas* pre-crisis period.

Similarly, there were exceptions to an anticipated continuation of the non-crisis norm for *decisional forums* in the pre-crisis period—in several foreign policy crises. Change from the non-crisis norm is evident in: the UK's 'Inner Cabinet' in the *Munich Crisis* (1938); Israel's 'Kitchen Cabinet' in the *October-Yom Kippur Crisis-War* (1973–1974); and Syria's 'decision-making Committee' in the *Lebanon Civil War I* crisis (1975). Finally, some *alternatives* were considered in several cases during the pre-crisis period, for example, Hungary in the *Hungarian Uprising* (1956) and India in the *India/China Border Crisis* (1959–1962), but the search for options in these cases was minimal. *In sum, coping with pre-crisis* did not differ markedly from the non-crisis norm. The fundamental reason was a perceived modest value threat and the perceived remoteness of military hostilities or time pressure for choice.

In the Unified Model, the *duration* of the onset phase is postulated as flexible. This phase will continue as long as the initial value threat for all crisis actors remains unchanged and decision-makers' perceptions are free from heightened expectations of war or acute time pressure, and at the international level, as long as disruptive interaction among the crisis adversaries is modest. Thus, the duration of onset may be very brief, less than a day, or *very long, many months, even longer.*

The *number of decisions*, too, is expected to vary greatly, from one to many. This will depend upon: the *duration of the onset phase*, the *number of crisis actors* at that stage, the *geographic distance* between the adversaries, the *gravity of values* at risk, and the extent of salience to major powers. Whatever the individual linkage, there is likely to be fewer decisions during the onset/pre-crisis period than in the escalation phase/crisis period.

The key *concepts* that illuminate the pre-crisis period of a state's foreign policy crisis are *trigger, stress, coping,* and *choice. Coping* by both A and B, in fact by as many adversaries as there are in an international crisis, will correspond to a *non-crisis norm*, that is, to *established routines* of *information processing, consultation* with bureaucratic subordinates, *limited* if any *search for alternatives, assessment of options* in the *institutionalized decisional forum* and, more often than not, a *decision* that follows *standard operating procedures.*

This mutual process of perception, coping, and choice at the state level in the pre-crisis period will generate *modest distortion* at the *interactor level*, in the *onset phase*. There may be only one action–reaction exchange; there may be many.

How and when does the initial *phase change* occur, that is, from *onset to escalation?* The Unified Model of Crisis identifies the catalyst to phase change. As evident in the figure of the UMC above, the key is a *new constellation* of system and/or inter-actor and/or actor attributes, strengthened by some traits of the crisis itself that generate for at least one of the adversaries a perception of *more acute value threat*, along with an *awareness of time pressure* and a *higher than normal expectation of involvement in military hostilities* before the disruptive challenge is overcome. With that fundamental *perceptual change*, that is, a deepening of the anticipation of harm, the onset phase will move to *more intense action and reaction* that heralds the coming of the *escalation* phase. The actors will experience a *corresponding change from pre-crisis to crisis period behavior*. The termination dates for phase and period are often, but need not be, identical. And when phase/period change in an interstate crisis occurs, the *coping* pattern *undergoes basic change* as well.

Escalation Phase—Crisis Period

Escalation refers to a dynamic process in the evolution of an interstate crisis: it denotes a shift from one equilibrium state to another. At the interstate level, the indicators of escalation are an increase in the intensity and/or a change in the type of disruptive interaction between/among adversaries, including a heightened probability of military hostilities. At the state level, the indicators are a perception by decision-makers of more acute value threat, awareness (or, if it existed in the pre-crisis period, greater awareness) of time constraint on choice, and unlike pre-crisis, an image of substantial increase in the perceived probability of war.

How does escalation begin? As specified in the *Figure of the Unified Model of Crisis* above, the process from pre-crisis period to onset phase is replicated. State A may commit a hostile act against B or vice versa. It may be verbal, political, economic, non-violent military, or violent. Or the catalyst may be a disruptive event or environmental change. The target may comply, that is, yield to the adversary's demand, in which case the crisis will terminate abruptly in victory/defeat, the counterpart to 'abortion' in the onset phase. More likely, the target will perceive the new trigger as a step-level change in hostility and respond accordingly. The combination of A's new trigger and B's response, or vice versa, completes the initial jump from onset phase/pre-crisis period to escalation phase/crisis period.

Some interstate crises gestate slowly; that is, they undergo a lengthy onset phase in which the adversaries do not threaten or employ violence or engage in coercive diplomacy. This pattern operates when lesser values are at stake and especially when time, though salient, is not crucial to the outcome. Other crises escalate quickly, with a short onset phase and the early threat or use of violence. This pattern tends to correlate with high values at risk such as existence, influence, or territory. Where minor values are at stake, time pressure will be absent or minimal, and war will be perceived as unlikely, thus making escalation remote and therefore imposing no/few demands on the adversaries to abandon pre-crisis behavior. Where basic values are perceived to be under threat, a premium is placed on violence and the time for choice and action will be restricted. *In sum*, the duration of the onset phase will be a function of the gravity of values threatened and, to a lesser extent, the awareness of time constraints on choice.

Hypotheses on Escalation

Sooner or later, events or acts or both will generate for at least one state actor perceptions of more acute value threat, a heightened probability of war, and time pressure, inducing more disruptive interaction and thereby a jump to the escalation phase. The shift from onset to escalation is an integral part of the crisis process except in those cases that abort or fail to materialize. The key question in this context is *under what conditions is escalation most likely to occur?* These conditions are as follows:

> crisis occurrence *within a polycentric structure*,
> *outside the dominant system*, and
> *in a protracted conflict setting*:
> *geographic proximity between the adversaries*,
> *more than two adversaries in the onset phase*, and
> *several cross-cutting issues* in dispute.

Although not theoretically necessary, the step-level jump from onset to escalation phase and from pre-crisis to crisis period is most likely to be catalyzed by a threat of violence or its actual use. Even if the trigger is a verbal, political or economic act it will contain an implied threat of violence. By contrast, the catalyst to crisis onset will most likely involve non-violent acts, non-violent events, or non-military environmental changes.

Under what conditions is the trigger to the escalation phase/crisis period most likely to be some form of violence? And *why should this be so?* The enabling variables for *violent escalation* of an international crisis are as follows:

All of the conditions for a jump from onset to escalation phase specified above, along with
military or other types of authoritarian regime between the crisis adversaries,
power discrepancy between the crisis adversaries, and
military aid by patrons to clients engaged in the crisis.

As for escalation of an international crisis from no/low to severe violence, all the above conditions are relevant. The two additional enabling conditions are as follows:

the *trigger to escalation* takes the form of a *violent act* and
the *target* responds with *equal severity or stronger violent acts.*

Why should violence be expected in the trigger to crisis escalation? Stated formally, escalation signifies a *step-level jump* in the pattern of hostility, a qualitative increase in the intensity or a change in type of disruptive interaction. For that to occur the trigger must be a much more powerful inducement to change—in disruptive interaction between adversaries, in decision-makers' perceptions of threat, time pressure, and war likelihood, and in crisis management. The most powerful catalyst to crisis escalation is violence, actual, threatened, or implied.

The process of *step-level change* from pre-crisis to crisis period for the crisis actors and from onset to escalation phase of the international crisis was analyzed in 29 case studies. One illustration of this process will suffice. The dispatch of a British naval task force to the South Atlantic on April 5, 1982 indicated to Argentina's decision-makers a heightened probability of war with the U.K. in the near future, a visible escalation of its foreign policy crisis and the international crisis over the *Falklands/ Malvinas (non-violent military* act).

There are many differences between onset and escalation phases and between pre-crisis and crisis periods. One is the extent of *disruptive interaction*: it is more intense in the escalation phase. The other is the *depth and scope of perceived hostility by decision-makers*: low value threat in the pre-crisis period; more acute value threat reinforced by time pressure and heightened probability of war, in the crisis period. This perception, in essence a more basic anticipation of harm, points up a third difference: it generates *higher stress than in the pre-crisis period*. And that in turn has a profound effect on the behavior of decision-makers in the two periods.

Still another difference relates to the *number of decisions* in an interstate crisis. The *Unified Model of Crisis* postulates that the *number of important decisions* by the adversaries is likely to be *higher in the crisis period*. The reason is a combination of higher stakes, emergent time salience, and greater expectation of war in the crisis period. Pre-crisis, as noted, is generally confined to low value threat and low stress. The demands on decision-makers are proportionate to the threat-stress level. They perceive little need to make hard choices, that is, core decisions about an incipient crisis. The threat perceived in the pre-crisis period is not such as to induce an abnormal pattern of choice. Time does not impose constraints. And the perceived remoteness of military hostilities leads to an avoidance of decisions whose consequences cannot be anticipated. The tendency therefore is to make few if any strategic or even tactical decisions in the pre-crisis period and onset phase lest violent options to cope with escalation of a crisis be foreclosed.

Once a more hostile act, stressful event or disquieting environmental change triggers the threefold perception of higher threat of harm that marks the beginning of a crisis period, and the target state responds, escalation is set in motion. This phase too may be brief or lengthy. It too may be characterized by one albeit more intense action–reaction exchange or many interactions. It may be non-violent or violent, more likely the latter for reasons noted earlier. Major Powers may or may not become involved in support of a client or ally; they are more likely to do so than in the onset phase of an interstate crisis. This also applies to international organizations.

According to the Unified Model, decision-makers will adopt more elaborate crisis management techniques during the crisis period of a foreign policy crisis. They will engage in a *more intense search for information* and *process it quickly at the highest level of decision-maker(s)*. They will *broaden the scope of consultation*, to draw upon the expertise of specialists in violence and possibly include competing elites in order to enhance national unity. They may create an ad hoc *decisional forum* in order to expedite and enhance the efficiency of the decision-making process. And they will embark upon a *more careful search for, and consideration of, alternatives* to manage the crisis. Time becomes more salient. Military hostilities will be viewed as increasingly probable. Stress will be high. Choice is more likely to be novel, to deal with a more serious threat.

Escalation also relates to *coping* with the challenge of a more intense crisis. In some respects, adversaries will follow the pre-crisis pattern. They will seek to uncover each other's intention, capability and resolve, that is, to assess their 'critical risk.' But the emphasis of the search will shift: to the adversary's disposition to use violence or diplomacy (or both) to achieve its objectives, to relative military capability, and to the likelihood that the adversary will stand fast on its demands, rather than compromise or yield. More important, *this search* and all other aspects of crisis management *during the crisis period* will be *much more intense* because of the higher stress generated by the threefold perception of harm—of more acute value threat, increased time pressure, and heightened war likelihood. Crisis actors will also negotiate, directly or indirectly, and will seek support from one or more major powers, other states and international organizations. Moreover, because the stakes are higher and the risks greater than in the pre-crisis period, actors are more likely to adopt a strategy of coercive diplomacy as the basis for crisis bargaining.

Bargaining will take the form of *verbal and physical acts.* If violence has not yet occurred, actors may mobilize reserves and/or place their armed forces on alert. They may hold visible maneuvers. They may threaten to use violence, if necessary. They may activate commitments of allies and friends to provide assistance in situations of crisis or war. And they may seek legitimacy from international organizations and law for demands that are based upon *raison d'état* and superior power.

If violence erupts in the escalation phase, either as the trigger or in the course of bargaining, coercive diplomacy will give way to the strategy of force, designed to achieve victory at minimal cost—in casualties, weapons, morale, national unity, status in the international system, and the perceptions held by friends, enemies, and neutrals. The use of violence as a crisis management technique is much more likely in the crisis period/escalation phase than in pre-crisis/onset, for reasons cited earlier. Whatever its scope and severity, violence will intensify disruptive interaction and generate higher stress for the target and, assuming reciprocal violence, for the initiator as well. In general, coping with escalation in a context of violence is more stressful than coping with pre-crisis or with a non-violent crisis period.

Higher stress, the **UMC** contends, *will also affect information processing*. Bureaucrats will play a lesser role and senior decision-makers will become more directly involved in their crisis period than in pre-crisis. Many of the laborious and time-consuming intermediary layers will be eliminated, with more information being elevated rapidly to the top of the decision-making pyramid. The result is that senior decision-makers' perceptions under high stress will be formed largely from their direct access to information relevant to a crisis. Sources of information will be broadened. And higher stress will create a tendency to rely on extraordinary and improvised channels.

Consultation, too, will undergo *substantial change* in the crisis period–escalation phase. The cost of miscalculation and decisional errors will be higher. Military hostilities are more likely. And if they have occurred, more intense violence is expected. That too accentuates stress. Under these conditions, decision-makers are likely to broaden the consultative network and seek the views of persons outside the core decision-making group, especially when existence or some other core value is at stake, so as to maximize national unity at the peak of a crisis. For these reasons too, decision-makers will consult more frequently among themselves, deriving reassurance and confidence from more face-to-face contact. They will also rely on ad hoc forms of consultation.

The *search for, and consideration of, alternatives* too will not be impervious to the higher stress of the crisis period. Because one or more basic values are perceived to be under threat, *decision-makers will enlarge the scope of their search for viable options*. Moreover, *alternatives will be assessed with greater care*. However, because of perceived time constraints on choice, decision-makers will be *more concerned with the immediate than the long-term future*.

According to the Unified Model of Crisis, *change* will also occur in the *decisional forum* of crisis actors during their high-stress crisis period. The institutional unit for choice in non-crisis and pre-crisis periods will tend to give way to an ad hoc or combined ad hoc-institutional body, usually small and homogeneous in composition and devoted to the political leader to whom this group provides advice about the most cost-effective path to crisis management. At the same time the members of the selected decisional unit will exhibit a greater felt need for decisive leadership. Once a decision is reached the greater will be the likelihood of a consensus.

For the crisis period, too, the *29 foreign policy crises* examined provide *substantial evidence in support of the Unified Model's postulates*. There was *a felt need for more information* in almost all cases. The crisis actors also intensified and diversified their search. The *pattern of consultation too was broader in almost all cases*. Ad hoc *decisional forums flourished in the crisis period* of most of the 29 crises. The *evidence on alternatives* provides even stronger support for expected behavior in the crisis period: *options were sought and thoroughly assessed in the large majority of these crises*.

What produces the next phase-change in an interstate crisis? According to the Unified Model, as long as action–reaction behavior by the adversaries sustains the existing high level of mistrust, hostility, disruptive interaction, and stress, or as long as cost–benefit assessments by the main protagonists remain unchanged, the escalation phase will persist. However, sooner or later, *an act or event will indicate a willingness by a crisis actor to accommodate an adversary by reducing maximal demands or offering concessions. Mutual mistrust will diminish. Signals of openness to compromise may appear*. One or more of these developments portends another *phase change, from escalation to de-escalation*. This is preceded at the actor level by a shift *from the crisis period to the end-crisis period*, with a winding down of overt hostility.

De-escalation Phase–End-Crisis Period

The concept, *de-escalation*, like escalation, has several meanings. First, it refers to the winding down of an interstate crisis, *a process of accommodation by the adversaries*. As such, it is *characterized by* a *decline in the perceptions of threat, time, and war likelihood towards their non-crisis norms* and in *the intensity of disruptive interaction*. In this sense, de-escalation denotes phase-change and period-change, that is, at both macro- and micro-levels of analysis, conceptually, like the change from onset to escalation and from pre-crisis to crisis.

At the *actor level*, de-escalation has an additional meaning: it denotes *a shift to a strategy of crisis behavior designed to achieve the goal of accommodation between the conflicting parties*. This strategy is precisely the obverse of a strategy of force that aims at an imposed victory/defeat outcome, compared to a voluntarily arrived-at mutual compromise. An accommodative strategy, thus, is associated with a decrease in tension and perceived harm which in turn leads to less disruptive interaction and distortion in the relationship between adversaries.

How does de-escalation begin? Several scenarios are possible and are evident in twentieth-century and early twenty-first century interstate crises. This phase *may begin when one actor achieves a decisive military victory* and imposes the conditions of crisis termination. In such a case, de-escalation may take a few days to run its course. However, *it may last weeks or months* until a *ceasefire, armistice,* or *peace agreement* is framed and implemented.

At the other extreme of the transition from escalation to de-escalation is a *mutual signaling of a wish to terminate a crisis*. This may occur in the context of a costly war of attrition in which victory is unattainable by either adversary. It may emanate from a calculus by the decision-makers of both [or all] crisis adversaries that, in game-theoretic terms, a *strategy of cooperation* will generate a *more positive payoff* than a *strategy of defection*. Such a calculus may occur before military hostilities have erupted or during a war, with a *coincidence of perceptions* that continuing the war will increase one's losses, whereas accommodation (cooperation) will increase one's gains.

If the adversaries arrive at this assessment more or less simultaneously, phase-change from escalation to de-escalation would occur abruptly and is likely to be of brief duration. If there is a time lag in the adversaries' shift from a strategy of defection to one of cooperation, de-escalation may still begin—as long as the mutual perception of the relative military balance has convinced both that military victory is either impossible or too costly relative to the anticipated gains. That awareness need not be and rarely is simultaneous. One of the conflicting parties may make a bid for termination. The adversary may find the terms unacceptable or suboptimal, in which case a bargaining process will ensue. Its intensity and duration will depend upon the parties' assumptions of the military balance before or during a war.

All of these scenarios exhibit *the crucial indicator of phase-change from escalation to de-escalation: at least one crisis actor must perceive a decline in value threat and/or time pressure and/or war likelihood*. That perceptual shift marks the beginning of a 'crisis downswing' toward the pre-crisis level of perceived harm and eventually to the non-crisis norm.

Stated in terms of the Unified Model of Crisis, *phase-change is a function of period-change*. And *period-change, from crisis to end-crisis, begins with a decline in one or more of the perceptions of threat, time, and war likelihood and their derivative, high stress*. When an actor-level crisis begins to diminish, stress declines with consequences for coping. And this in turn leads to less disruptive interaction, marking the beginning of the phase-change from escalation to de-escalation.

One illustration of the shift to the de-escalation phase will suffice. The winding down of India's prolonged and grave border crisis-war with China began on November 21, 1962, when the latter announced an immediate ceasefire and a unilateral withdrawal of forces starting December 1 to a point 20 km behind "the line of actual control" (*verbal* act).

How long does the de-escalation phase last? Several variables will determine its *duration*. One is the *number of crisis actors*. All other things being equal, *the fewer the crisis adversaries the less complex will be the accommodation process*. Value trade-offs involving mutual concessions will be easier for the conflicting parties to identify and to measure and therefore to accept as a fair compromise. Any increment beyond a two-actor crisis game adds to the complexity of the accommodation process: the *dynamics of negotiation*; the *ability of each party to assess multiple combinations of gains and losses*; the *communication of bids and counter-bids*; the *greater likelihood of misperception*; mistrust of one or more adversaries' intention regarding crisis accommodation; and the *framing of a package to satisfy minimal demands and achieve mutual satisfaction*. This analysis applies to an *interstate crisis in which the adversaries' relative equality of power dictates a compromise outcome*. However, if crisis escalation includes war and a decisive victory/defeat outcome, the duration of de-escalation is likely to be short, only long enough for the victor to frame surrender terms for the vanquished.

The duration of de-escalation will also be influenced by the *extent of major-power activity*. *The less involved the major powers are in an interstate crisis, the longer will be the process of accommodation by the adversaries*. If major powers are active militarily in support of a client, they can exert pressure in favor of a compromise outcome to a crisis; and this they will prefer so as to minimize the risk of major power confrontation and the consequent threat to stability and equilibrium in the global system. Low-level activity, verbal, political, or economic, will reduce the major powers' leverage with clients or non-client adversaries in the accommodation process.

Several other factors will affect the duration of the de-escalation phase. One is the *geo-strategic salience* of an interstate crisis. The more remote it is from the vital interests of the major powers the less likely it is that they will intervene and therefore the less influence they will exert on crisis termination. This absence, in turn, will tend to make de-escalation longer. In such a case, its evolution will depend largely on internal dynamics between the lesser powers that are the principal crisis adversaries.

The *type of crisis management techniques* will also affect the duration of de-escalation. If a crisis escalates to war, accommodation will be more difficult, unless one party achieves decisive military victory and can impose the terms of war termination. Moreover, the *fewer the issues* the shorter will be the de-escalation phase, because the quest for mutual compromise will be easier to achieve. Similarly, *the less basic the perceived values at stake* the less difficult will be the framing of terms that will be mutually acceptable to the conflicting parties.

Hypotheses on De-escalation

Under what conditions is an international crisis *most likely to wind down and terminate in an agreement?* This is most likely to occur when

a crisis unfolds in a *non-protracted conflict setting*;
the adversaries are *relatively equal in military power*;
there are *few adversarial actors*;
the *major powers are less active* in the crisis;
the *international organization* is *highly involved* in *quest of a peaceful settlement*; and
the adversaries rely on *non-violent crisis management techniques.*

Earlier in this analysis, several differences between the *onset phase/pre-crisis period* and the *escalation phase/crisis period* were noted. A similar comparison can be made between the escalation phase/crisis period and the de-escalation phase/end-crisis period. The volume of disruptive interaction is expected to decline in the latter, as will the intensity of perceived harm on the part of one or more crisis actors. As a result, the decision-makers' stress level will decline. And behavior will be correspondingly affected. Finally, the number of decisions in the end-crisis period too is expected to decline, relative to the peak stress crisis period.

The *29 case studies exhibited these changes as* an *interstate crisis de-escalated.* Disruptive interaction continued but at a distinctly lower level of intensity. This occurred because the crisis actors perceived a lower value threat and with it less stress from time pressure and/or expectation of war or an adverse change in the military balance. In all of these cases, whatever the trigger and duration, there was a decline in both perceived harm and disruptive interaction. That in turn led to less stress for decision-makers. Whether as a result of a ceasefire or more formal termination of hostilities, or a military victory or even defeat or a faded outcome, the world looked less menacing to decision-makers than in the crisis period. Stated in terms of the *Unified Model* and *the definition of crisis, high stress,* derived from a composite perception of harm, *diminished in the end-crisis period.* The number of decisions in this period too is expected to decline for all of these reasons.

All of the themes relating to the preceding crisis phases and periods apply to the de-escalation phase/end-crisis period as well, with appropriate changes because of declining perceptions of harm and stress. Generally, *interaction* between the crisis adversaries will be *less intense and hostile*—because there is a perception of less threat, less time pressure, and a decreasing probability of war.

Coping mechanisms too will undergo change. The *quest for information* about the adversary's intent and capability will be *less intense* than in the crisis period and will give way to a focus on accommodation and crisis termination; and *information processing is likely to revert to the pre-crisis norm,* with bureaucrats once more playing a crucial role. Moreover, the adversaries will seek support from the international organization and major powers, where possible. Adversaries will also continue to engage in *bargaining,* but *more* via *verbal and political than physical acts.*

Consultation beyond the core decision-making group is *expected to contract.* The *decisional forum* too is *likely to revert to its institutional, pre-crisis norm*—since the need to elicit support from a broad section of the political public, to share the burden of difficult decisions, has diminished. The *search for,* as well as *consideration of, alternatives will involve much less decision time* because the stakes will be perceived as less important. *Stress* too *will decline.* And *choice* is likely to be of the *standard operating procedure,* routine type.

Impact Phase–Post-Crisis Period

Thus far, the *Unified Model of Crisis* has offered an explanation for eruption (onset/pre-crisis), crystallization (escalation/crisis), and the winding down process (de-escalation/end-crisis), leading to crisis termination. However, the end of an interstate crisis does not mark the end of its role in the on-going flow of world politics. Crises have multiple effects—on the actors, on their relations, and on one or more international systems.

The UMC tries to capture this post-crisis dimension by the concept of *impact*.

Although it is treated schematically as another domain/phase of crisis, in the figure on the UMC above, impact differs from the other three phases in several respects. Its *time frame* is *arbitrary, 20 years after crisis termination*. It has *no coping dimension*. It is less precise than onset, escalation, and de-escalation, and their counterpart actor-level periods, pre-crisis, crisis, and end-crisis; that is, *empirical traces* of the post-crisis impact are *more difficult to discover* than the evidence of a crisis proper, that is, the three earlier phases and periods. There is also *less* of a *consensus on its duration and scope*. Nonetheless, while recognizing these constraints, the Unified Model of Crisis contends that the boundaries and content of the impact phase can be designated and its effects measured, though with somewhat less confidence than the measurement of its conceptual counterpart during the crisis proper, namely, *severity*.

The concept of impact is a device to capture the *consequences* of an interstate crisis. At the *bilateral* level, the task is to discover how a crisis affects *subsequent relations between-among the principal adversaries*. Its legacy is defined in terms of more or less distrust, hostility, and tension. And the tangible indicator is the *occurrence or non-occurrence* of one or more military-security crises between the adversaries in the 20 years following crisis termination.

What determines this aspect of impact? According to the Unified Model, the crucial explanatory variables are *outcome*, both *content* and *form*, and the *intensity* of a crisis. The UMC postulates that, all other things being equal, a clear zero-sum victory/defeat outcome is much more likely to have a negative impact than a blurred, ambiguous outcome, in which none of the adversaries achieved all of its goals during their interstate crisis or when the *status quo ante* remained unchanged. Either of these outcomes, *compromise or stalemate, will reduce the likelihood of more hostile relations* after a crisis has ended.

The UMC also contends that the *form of outcome* too has spillover effects on *post-crisis relations between the adversaries*. Thus *a crisis that ends through agreement*—*a* ceasefire, truce, or armistice in case of violence, or a formal document setting down the procedure for dispute settlement, or even an exchange of letters of peaceful intent—is *much more likely to leave a positive residue on relations between the adversaries than termination through a unilateral act*, such as decisive military invasion or even humiliating unilateral withdrawal or by covertly inspired regime change in the adversary.

Like overall *intensity*—the *severity* of a crisis during its occurrence—the overall *impact* of a crisis is the product of a set of situational attributes. Its indicators are *types of change* generated by a crisis during a 20-year period after termination.

One is the extent of change in the distribution of power [*power change*]. This ranges, in the ascending order, along a four-point scale, from *no change* [point 1], if the outcome is *compromise or stalemate*, to *change in relative power between the adversaries* [point 2], to a *shift in ranking within the power hierarchy* [point 3], to the *inclusion of a new state in, or the exclusion of a pre-existing member from, the apex of the power pyramid* [point 4].

Another indicator of impact is *actor change*. As with power, there may be *no change* [point 1]. However, a crisis may affect the political regime of one or more adversaries, either their *foreign policy orientation* [point 2] or, more basically, the *regime type*, for example, a crisis-induced shift from authoritarianism to democracy or the reverse [point 3]. In rare cases a crisis may lead to the *creation, elimination,* or *restoration of a state* [point 4], as with Bangladesh as a result of the 1971 India/Pakistan crisis-war.

Alliances too may undergo *change* as a consequence of an interstate crisis. To capture this aspect of impact another four-point scale was constructed, ascending from *no change* [point 1], through an *increase or decrease in cohesiveness within a pre-existing alliance* [point 2], to the *entry or exit of an actor into or from an alliance* [point 3], to the *formation or elimination of an alliance* [point 4], as with the transformation of the alliance configuration as a result of the *Entry into World War II Crisis* of 1939 and the six-year upheaval that followed. Finally, and most difficult to measure, interstate crises may generate *changes in rules of the game*, formally or informally.

How to measure the impact of an interstate crisis was a crucial *methodological* problem? So too was a *theoretical task*, namely, to generate deductively the conditions of most likely impact on inter-actor relations and the system(s) of which they are members. To this end, the UMC postulated expectations about change at both levels of analysis, indicated the underlying logic, and framed these assumptions in a form that could be tested.

Hypotheses on Impact

Suffice it to note the postulate relating to *systemic consequences* of an *interstate* crisis: the *higher the severity* of an international crisis, the *greater will be its impact*, high severity being expressed by

many crisis actors,
high major power activity in an interstate crisis,
high geo-strategic salience,
several issues in dispute, and
intense violence.

The broadest possible scope of crisis impact is system transformation: the systemic legacy of an international crisis is most likely to be transforming when

All of the conditions specified above operate, and when
the *catalyst* to crisis escalation is *extreme*;
violence is the *primary crisis management technique*;
the crisis is of *lengthy duration*; and
the *outcome is other than formal agreement*.

The *impact* of an interstate crisis merits attention on several grounds. Conceptually, it is an integral part of the phenomenon of Crisis viewed holistically: without this *post-crisis* dimension the analysis of Crisis would be incomplete. Moreover, the impact phase provides an indispensable dynamic link between a specific, time-and-space-bound disruption, an interstate crisis, and global politics writ large. Without *impact*, the dynamism of the Unified Model of Crisis is confined to the perception-decision-behavior-interaction flow from phase to phase and period to period, *within* an interstate crisis per se. Impact traces the feedback from an interstate crisis to the system, inter-actor and actor attributes of the larger environment from which a crisis originated. As such it links crisis to the array of events, acts and changes that together constitute the flow of world politics.

Interstate crisis is but one of many sources of global instability and disequilibrium. Nevertheless its capacity for disruption is enormous, as evident in some of the transforming crises of the twentieth century: the *1914 Crisis*, which revolutionized the structure of world politics, destroying and creating empires and states as a result of the military upheaval, World War I, that followed; the *1939 Entry into World War II Crisis*, which exceeded its predecessor in the scope of change—the replacement of multipolarity by bipolarity, with two superpowers, global decolonization amidst the decimation of empires, etc.; and the *Cuban Missiles Crisis* which, in the post-Cold War perspective, stabilized superpower relations in an era of rapid, potentially destructive technological change. For all of these reasons, impact is no less crucial than the other three phases of an interstate crisis—onset, escalation, and de-escalation. Finally, in policy terms, the ability to trace the post-crisis impact, especially of high severity crises, can enhance the way in which political leaders and foreign policy decision-makers, sensitized to potential multiple consequences, will respond to future incipient crises among the ever-growing number of autonomous members of the global system. Such is the rationale for the inclusion of the *impact phase/post-crisis period* in the Unified Model of Crisis.

This model purports not only to *describe* and but also *represent reality*. Rather, like all models, it is an analytical device designed *to explain reality*, in this case the phenomenon of interstate crisis. What functions, then, are performed by the *Unified Model of Crisis*? In the largest sense, the UMC *guided and shaped a systematic inquiry* into the meaning of interstate crises in the twentieth and early twenty-first centuries. It provided the intellectual *rationale for* the *phase-period models*. It generated the *logic for the inferences derived from these models*. As such, it made possible the *testing of theoretical expectations with the abundant evidence of interstate crises* from the end of 1918 until the end of 2015, facilitating the crucial confrontation between theory and reality. In so doing the Unified Model has laid claim to being the core of a *scientific research program* on crisis, conflict, and war (ICB), for it aims to discover which logically derived propositions about crises and state behavior are falsified and which are supported, though *formal, definitive* confirmation of the findings remains elusive. Brecher, <u>**Crises in World Politics: Theory and Reality**</u> (1993)

CHANGES IN ICB STRUCTURE

Recent Additions to Crisis-Conflict Project

Soon after the publication of the three-volume <u>*Crises in the Twentieth Century*</u> (1988–1989), awareness of the scope of unanswered questions and unexplored dimensions of the vast world of interstate crises and conflicts led the ICB team, notably Brecher and Wilkenfeld, to persist in the quest for knowledge about vast and complex phenomena in world politics. During the decade that followed we were also encouraged by newly discovered sources and valuable suggestions by colleagues and devoted research assistants. The result was many changes in the structure, framework, analysis, and content of ICB inquiry, which enlarged and enriched our knowledge of this challenge to humanity's survival. Our findings were presented in the longest and most comprehensive book in this project, *A Study of Crisis* (1997, 2000) [Brecher and Wilkenfeld], the culmination of two decades of research on crisis, conflict, and war.

First, the *time span* was extended: whereas our 1988–1989 books covered the period 1929–1979, this volume began with cases in late 1918, just after the end of World War I, and continued to the end of 1994. [Since then, the scope of ICB data has expanded to the end of 2015]

The *number of cases* increased by more than 50%, from 278 to 476 international crises and from 627 to 1052 foreign policy crises for individual states. Moreover, some cases were merged and others split, in light of newly discovered evidence.

There were changes too in the *dataset*. *New variables* were constructed to tap hitherto neglected dimensions (e.g., ethnicity, mediation). And many of the key variables (e.g., value threat, form of outcome) were checked and recoded as part of an on-going attempt to achieve maximal accuracy, clarity, rigor, and salience in the overall objectives of the inquiry.

Another basic change relates to the *framework of analysis*. While the earlier ICB version (1988) examined crises at both the international (system) and state (actor) levels, A Study of Crisis (1997, 2000) applied the *Unified Model of Crisis*, as set out in Crises in World Politics: Theory and Reality (Brecher 1993) and summarized above. Thus, Part I of A Study of Crisis presented an integrated framework for the two levels of analysis. Part II specified the combined methodology—quantitative (aggregate data) and qualitative (comparative case study). And Part III offered comparable summaries of all the crises, interweaving the flow of events from a system perspective to the behavior of the principal actors, along with the roles of the involved major power(s) and international organization(s).

Noteworthy, too, was the *enlarged conceptual and substantive scope* of the 1997/2000 book. While *crisis* remained the primary focus, much greater attention was given to *interstate protracted conflicts*. This change was evident in the presentation of the cases in a format designed to make a large body of knowledge more user-friendly and more relevant. All crises were classified into two types instead of being presented in a simple chronological sequence: those that formed part of a protracted conflict—60% of the international crises—and those that were unrelated to a conflict. The former was grouped into 33 protracted conflicts, some that have ended (e.g., France/Germany, East/West conflicts), others that are still unresolved (e.g., Arab/Israel, India/Pakistan conflicts). A brief background commentary on a conflict was followed by a summary of each crisis within that conflict, in chronological sequence, providing a broader conflict perspective for the unfolding of related crises between the same adversaries. The other 40% of the international crises were grouped by region (Africa, Americas, Asia, Europe, Middle East, and Inter-Region) and were presented chronologically. A multiple cross-reference system in Part III of the 1997/2000 book and the Master Table, which contained information about the key dimensions of each of the then-researched 412 international crises, were designed to ease the reader's task.

This book also attempted to break *fresh ground in the analysis of crisis, conflict and war* (Part IV). The innovation took the form of an intensive inquiry into seven enduring topics/themes in World Politics: *polarity, geography, ethnicity, democracy, protracted conflict, violence, and third-party intervention*—their roles and effects on the configuration of crises and conflicts. Most of these distinct analytical 'cuts' were guided by models from which hypotheses were derived and tested against the voluminous evidence generated by the *International Crisis Behavior* (ICB) Project. The objectives of these analyses were twofold: *theory construction*, through a systematic and rigorous search for patterns of turmoil in most of the twentieth and the first 15 years of the twenty-first century and an indirect *contribution to world order*, through the generation of knowledge to be communicated to policymakers and the attentive public about this pervasive phenomenon in the global system.

From early in the *Crisis-Conflict* project, Jonathan Wilkenfeld and I were convinced that no single *path to knowledge* is flawless or even adequate. Competing claims to the 'correct' *method* struck us as arrogant and counter-productive. We recognized that *deductive logic* is capable of generating models and hypotheses to guide systematic inquiry. We were also convinced that generalizations can be derived from *inductive research*, both from *comparative case studies* and from *aggregate data analysis* through large *N* studies. In short, we tried to demonstrate the merit and validity of *multiple paths to knowledge* (a concept expounded in Brecher (1989)).

Overview of Findings

The approach of a new millennium coincided with the emergence of a fundamental change in the structure of the international system, the outlines of which were just beginning to crystallize when we were writing <u>A Study of Crisis</u>. With the end of the Cold War and the demise of the Soviet Union (1989–1990), the United States emerged as the dominant power in the international system, that is, the sole *superpower*, though other autonomous *centers of decision* persisted, notably China, France, Germany, Russia, and the UK. Does the fact that the international system managed the transition from *bipolycentrism* [*bipolar* in terms of power configuration, *multi-power* in terms of decisional autonomy by existing states] (1963–1989), to *unipolycentrism* [*unipolar*, that is, power pre-eminence of a single state since 1990, along with many autonomous centers of decision], without an international catastrophe similar to the one that accompanied the end of multipolarity in 1945, signal maturing of the international system and its actors and institutions? It was too early to render a verdict in 1994.

What is unmistakable in 2017—and was already evident in the late 1990s—is a basic change in the predominant *location* of international crises, namely, a shift from Europe to Africa, Asia and the Middle East beginning, gradually, after the end of World War II. Structurally, this change has been accompanied by a decline in international crises– international political earthquakes at the dominant system level and an increase within geographically and power subordinate subsystems. Moreover, neighboring crisis actors were more likely to experience and employ violence in their crises. Not surprisingly, major powers, with the widest geographic reach, were the most likely to be involved in crises far from their borders. Global reach will likely continue to be an important factor in the rest of the twenty-first century, in light of fundamental technological changes, which also affect the capability of states to wage war far from their borders.

Ethnicity, too, emerged as a major international force, as evident in many high-visibility crises in the post-Cold War era. We asked: is ethnicity's current high profile likely to pass once the international system and its member-states make the accommodations necessary to recognize its roots and cope with its demands? Our data point to a relatively steady frequency of crises with an ethnic dimension throughout the twenty-first century, but some of their unique characteristics bear watching. Ethnicity-related crises, particularly if they occur within protracted conflicts, are particularly susceptible to escalating violence, undoubtedly attributable to the high level of perpetual hostility existing among the adversaries. These crises are also characterized by very high levels of threat perception, particularly when territorial issues are involved. And crises with an ethnic dimension are characterized by a high rate of dissatisfaction with the terms of the agreements that are often associated with their termination; that is, they are poised for subsequent and serious eruptions. Here too the evidence on the central role of ethnicity was inconclusive in 1994, the end of the time frame for *A Study of Crisis*. It was evident, however, that international organizations have generally been more involved and more effective than the major powers as intermediaries in ethnicity crises.

Just as the International Relations empirical literature has found a strong general link between *democracy* and *peace*, so too our research confirmed this link among states involved in international crises: the higher the proportion of democracies among the adversarial actors in an international crisis, the less likely it is that violence will be employed in crisis management; and when employed, the less likely it is that such violence will escalate to a high level. Left unanswered in the euphoria over the emergence of new democracies in virtually every corner of the globe are two questions. Will an international system dominated by a plurality of democracies exhibit the same peaceful tendencies that were associated with democracies when they were relatively few in number? Secondly, will democracies in process, that is, transitional democracies, be likely to play the same 'peace' role vis-à-vis a democratic adversary that has been discovered in the behavior of mature democracies toward democratic adversaries in situations of disputes?

Much has been learned about the *role of violence* in international crises. A *bipolycentrism* structure—two power centers, along with more than two centers of autonomous decisions (1963–1989)—was particularly susceptible to violence in both triggers and crisis management. Regions differed in terms of the extent and severity of violence. At the same time, regardless of region, contiguity was a strong predictor of violence among crisis adversaries. As noted, ethnicity, too, was a strong predictor of violence during interstate crises. Democracy among crisis adversaries dampened the tendency toward the use of violence in crisis management. Moreover, the more protracted a conflict in which a crisis was embedded, the more likely it was for the crisis trigger to be violent and for actors to have employed violence in crisis management. Finally, decision-maker *stress*, *societal unrest*, and *power discrepancy* among principal adversaries all contribute to the likelihood that violence in crises will escalate.

What has been the role of *international organizations* and *major powers* in crisis management? While the UN Security Council has consistently accounted for roughly two-thirds of international organization activity, the role of the General Assembly declined during *bipolycentrism*, while that of the Secretary-General was enhanced. The post-Cold War *unipolycentric* system—one power center and several or many autonomous decision centers—provided some preliminary evidence of a reinvigorated role for the Security Council, but not always accompanied by effectiveness.

Major powers during *multipolarity*—several power centers and several decision centers—were far more likely to become involved in international crises than the two superpowers during *bipolarity* and *bipolycentrism*. Indeed, a close examination of the superpowers as actors and intermediaries in international crises reveals the great care with which they interacted in the global arena: the USA and the USSR were almost never highly involved or crisis actors simultaneously in the same crisis as principal adversaries.

Overall, *A Study of Crisis* created an analytical framework within which foreign policy crises, international crises, and protracted conflicts can be examined from a comparative perspective. Although we presented a panorama of international crises in the twentieth century, we did not provide answers to all questions about crises. One goal, throughout the decades of research, has been to facilitate learning by foreign policy decision-makers as they attempt to avoid repeating the mistakes of the past. For the scholarly community, the objective has been to strengthen the accumulation of knowledge in the domain of crisis and conflict, and particularly with regard to the seven key themes, noted earlier in this chapter, that served as a focus of analysis in this book.

[The 1997 edition of *A Study of Crisis* consisted of more than 1000 pages. In 2000, the original print version was transformed into a

300-page soft-cover book: all of Part III in the original Work, the summaries of every international crisis from November 1918 to the end of 1994, appeared in an innovative CD-ROM format, one of the earliest International Relations books to be presented in this form.]

Aggregate data analysis, that is, *in-breadth, horizontal analysis*, and *Case-studies*, that is, *in-depth, vertical analysis*, have been the two pillars of the ICB Project. However, important dimensions have been added to its research program since the publication of A Study of Crisis. A new data subset on *mediation* in international crises has been created by Jonathan Wilkenfeld, with extensive analysis of the findings. The phenomenon of '*near-crisis*' among states, an important segment of the Conflict domain that has been neglected until now, has been conceived and a dataset created by Patrick James. Another topic that has been the focus of wide-ranging ICB research has been the role of '*non-state actors*,' including *ethnic groups*, in international crises: this addition, developed by Brecher and Ben-Yehuda, was stimulated by basic changes in the structure and actors of the international system since the turn of the millennium.

When this inquiry into the *Crisis-Conflict* domain of world politics began, in 1975, the state was still the pre-eminent actor in the global system. Since then, the state-centric model of world politics, which held sway since the Treaty of Westphalia ended the European Thirty Years War in 1648, has been increasingly challenged by some scholars as no longer an accurate representation of global reality. A plethora of *non-state actors* has acquired high visibility—*transnational, international, nongovernmental, intergovernmental*, and *sub-national*. And *nationalism*, often in the guise of ethnicity, has re-emerged as a powerful force in the domain of crisis, conflict and war. We took note of this important development, both in updating the ICB Dataset, e.g., the specification of non-state actors as triggering entities, and in our analyses. This has been accomplished by applying the *concepts* and *methods* developed for the analysis of *interstate* crises to *domestic/internal* crises, focusing on ethnic minorities and other non-state actors, the *intrastate* level of analysis, that is, *domestic (internal)* crises. *In sum*, the ICB Project has spawned and developed several additional branches to its two core segments, quantitative and qualitative analysis of crises at the macro (interstate) level and the micro (state) level of analysis.

At the same time, interstate turmoil continued unabated in the post-Cold War years: from 1990 to 1994, there were 21 international crises—many of which escalated to war, and from the beginning of 1995 to the end of 2004, another 33 crises among states erupted. The most violent were *Gulf Crisis-War I* in 1990–1991 and the interstate *cum* intrastate conflict that wreaked havoc in former *Yugoslavia* from 1991 to 1995. Both were followed by further violent upheavals, including the NATO-Serbia crisis-war over *Kosovo* in 1998–1999, *Gulf Crisis-War II*, which raged in Iraq in 2003, along with the war in *Afghanistan* since 2002.

Other post-Cold War, high-profile crises within unresolved interstate protracted conflicts, most without violence, contained a potential for grave crises that undermined regional and global stability. Notable were the *India/Pakistan Nuclear* crises of 1990 and 1998 (along with their mini-war over *Kargil* in northern Kashmir, in 1999), and the cluster of crises over the *North Korea Nuclear Weapons program* since 1993–1994, along with a cluster of crises between Iran and the *P5+1* major powers (France, the PRC, the UK, the USA, the USSR + Germany), supported by the UN, from 2005 until agreement was reached between the six major powers and Iran in 2014. And in 1995–early 1996, there were 8 more international crises, of which one, between the People's Republic of China (PRC) and Taiwan in 1995, indicated that their protracted conflict continues to pose a threat to stability in Northeast and Southeast Asia, with potential fallout far beyond those regions.

In terms of the *structure* of the *international system*: despite the disavowal of the state-centric IR paradigm by many academics, dozens of nationalities/ethnic groups continue to seek self-determination, more precisely, the right to create an independent state, with all of the rights to statehood that the global system confers on its members. Thus, while the state is no longer the virtually exclusive actor in terms of crisis, conflict, and war, it remains the *most important actor in both the military-security and political-diplomatic* issue-areas of world politics.

CHAPTER 4

General Findings: Foreign Policy Crises

What have we learned about the **Crisis-Conflict** domain of world politics—in particular, about the closely related but distinct phenomena, **international** and **foreign policy crisis** and **interstate protracted conflict**? The ICB Project uncovered abundant evidence relating to its *five objectives*, which were noted earlier in this book:

1. to illuminate foreign policy crises and international crises (international political earthquakes) since the end of World War I, along seven *attributes* and 10 *dimensions*;
2. to create and apply concepts, indicators, indexes, and scales to facilitate the *measurement* of *severity* and *impact* of crises as international political earthquakes;
3. to discover which is the *most and least stable* of *four structures* of the global system during the past century—*bipolarity, multipolarity, bipolycentrism,* and *unipolycentrism*;
4. to enhance our knowledge and understanding of *crisis management* via qualitative case studies of how foreign policy-national security decision-makers coped with high or rising stress during the past near-century; and
5. to present a *novel test of the validity of Neo-Realism* as the optimal paradigm for the field of World Politics among the many competing claimants.

The most important finding, for both intellectual insights and foreign policy choices by decision-makers of states attempting to cope with interstate crises, is that the evidence from 29 crises, below, many very important and highly stressful for decision-makers, seriously challenges two long-established beliefs about *state behavior during interstate crises-international political earthquakes:*

first, that ***high stress seriously undermines the quality of foreign policy-national security decision-making—it does not***; and
second, that ***the great diversity of crises and crisis actors leads to great diversity*** in ***crisis management*** **behavior**—***it does not***.

Both of these conventional views are fundamentally flawed, as will be evident in the *qualitative case-study* findings presented below. So too were the related perceptions and foreign policies that derived from these two beliefs.

DATASET: 29 FOREIGN POLICY CRISES

The qualitative, case study findings in this book are derived from 29 in-depth studies of *foreign policy crises* for states which occurred within 23 *international crises* from 1935–1936 to 2002–2003: they are listed here in chronological sequence, along with the *international crisis* of which they are an integral part, and the *international system structure* and *region* in which they occurred:

Ethiopia, Ethiopian [Abyssinian] War 1935–1936, (multipolarity, Africa);
Italy, Ethiopian [Abyssinian] War 1935–1936, (multipolarity, Africa);
U.K., Munich Crisis 1938 (multipolarity, Europe);
Netherlands, Fall of Western Europe 1939–1940 (multipolarity, Europe);
USA, Berlin Blockade 1948–1949, (bipolarity, Europe);
USSR, Berlin Blockade 1948–1949, (bipolarity, Europe);
Italy, Trieste II 1953 (bipolarity, Europe);
Guatemala, Guatemala 1953–1954 (bipolarity, Americas);
Hungary, Hungarian Uprising 1956 (bipolarity, Europe);

USA, Iraq-Lebanon Upheaval 1958 (bipolarity, Middle East);
USA, Berlin Wall 1961 (bipolarity, Europe);
India, China/India Border War 1962 (bipolarity, Asia);
USA, Dominican Intervention 1965 (bipolycentrism, Americas);
Zambia, Rhodesia's Unilateral Declaration of Independence (UDI) 1965–1966 (bipolycentrism, Africa);
Israel, June-Six-Day War 1967 (bipolycentrism, Middle East);
USSR, Prague Spring 1968 (bipolycentrism, Europe);
USA, Black September/Syria-Jordan Confrontation 1970 (bipolycentrism, Middle East);
India, Bangladesh War 1971, (bipolycentrism, Asia);
Pakistan, Bangladesh War 1971, (bipolycentrism, Asia);
Israel, October-Yom Kippur War 1973 (bipolycentrism, Middle East);
USA, Nuclear Alert 1973 (bipolycentrism, Middle East);
Syria, Lebanon Civil War 1975–1976 (bipolycentrism, Middle East);
Argentina, Falklands-Malvinas 1982 (bipolycentrism, Americas);
Iraq, Gulf War I 1990–1991, (unipolycentrism, Middle East);
USA, Gulf War I 1990–1991, (unipolycentrism, Middle East)
Yugoslavia (FRY), Kosovo 1999 (unipolycentrism, Europe);
NATO, Kosovo 1999 (unipolycentrism, Europe);
Iraq, Iraq Régime Change/Gulf War II 2002–2003 (unipolycentrism, Middle East);
USA, Iraq Régime Change/Gulf War II 2002–2003 (unipolycentrism, Middle East).

The findings from these 29 foreign policy crises served as the database for the following *qualitative analysis of state behavior during* the *high-stress crisis period of international political earthquakes from 1935–1936 to 2002–2003.*

CONTEXT DIMENSIONS

An array of dimensions is represented in this cluster of cases:

Geography—Africa, Americas, Asia, Europe, Middle East, Inter-Region;
Time—eight of the nine decades of the post-WW I era;
System Structure—multipolarity, bipolarity, bipolycentrism, unipolycentrism;

Conflict Setting—protracted conflict, non-conflict;
Bloc Alignment—inter-bloc, intra-bloc, non-bloc;
Peace–War Setting—non-war, pre-war, war; (intra-war crises [IWCs] are excluded);
Intensity of Violence—no violence, minor clashes, serious clashes, war;
Power Level—major powers, middle powers, minor powers, mixed major/minor power, mixed middle/minor power;
Economic Level—developed, developing, developed–developing;
Political Regime—civil authoritarian, military, democracy, democracy-civil authoritarian, democracy-military.

The findings below will focus mainly on key *attributes* of crisis actors, framed in the form of research questions:

What was the catalyst or *trigger* to the onset of a state's foreign policy crisis?
Who was the *triggering entity*?
How long did a crisis last, that is, what was its *duration*?
How many *decisions* did the crisis actor make in the peak stress crisis period?
Who were the *decision-makers*?
What was their psychological framework for defining the situation, that is, their *attitudinal prism*?
What was the most *basic value(s)* that they *perceived to be at risk*?
Can any *patterns* be discerned?
First, I turn to the contentious issue of the preferred **method** for analyzing these findings.

METHODOLOGY IN CASE STUDIES: AN UNRESOLVED DEBATE

The question of *case-selection criteria* and the larger topic of *methodology in qualitative research* has been the object of continuing debate in political science, especially in the past 25 years. King, Keohane, and Verba [KKV] crystallized the *criticism of single or few case studies as a valid basis for generalization and theory construction*, in their <u>Designing Social Inquiry: Scientific Inference in Qualitative Research</u> (1994, Chap. 4). Several scholars responded with criticism of the King, Keohane, and Verba volume: their articles are reprinted in Brady and Collier, <u>Rethinking Social Inquiry: Diverse Tools, Shared Standards</u> (2004).

For the purpose of evaluating the qualitative case-study findings below, the relevant issue is whether the case selection for this study of international political earthquakes meets the optimal criteria for qualitative research. The King, Keohane, and Verba volume provides several instances of defective qualitative research design.

1. *More explanations (inferences) than cases.* KKV argue that the number of observations (cases) must be larger than the number of explanations. They criticize Alexander George's method of 'structured focused comparison' because it might lead to more explanations than observations. The large number of observations in this study of international political earthquakes (29), with a much smaller number of possible explanatory variables (10), clearly overcomes this problem.
2. *Multicollinearity*—any situation where it is possible to predict one explanatory variable from one or more of the remaining explanatory variables, that is, perfect correlation between two explanatory variables. A set of 29 cases demonstrate that no such perfect correlation exists between any 2 of the 10 explanatory variables.
3. *A sufficient number of observations*—KKV emphasize the need to enlarge the number of observations, that is, cases (N) as much as possible. It is doubtful that any other project in International Relations/World Politics is based on a larger number of *in-depth* cases (29).
4. *Limiting the number of explanatory variables*—'not to explain a lot with a lot.' As long as the number of explanatory variables is significantly lower than the number of observations, which is the case in this project (10 and 29), this criterion is met.
5. *Randomness and intentional selection*—KKV contend that, in a relatively small N of existing observations (cases) for qualitative study, random selection can cause serious problems, notably a risk of missing crucial cases. Further, they argue that an intentional selection after some knowledge of the cases has been acquired, to avoid selection bias, is a better method of selection. This is the selection method exercised in this project.
6. *Avoiding selection bias*—KKV emphasize that it is important to avoid a selection of a cluster of cases that confirm the favorite hypothesis, although other cases might disprove it. The large N of observations—for a qualitative study (29) and the variation in

a much smaller number of explanatory variables (10)—overcome this problem.
7. *Selection bias on the dependent variable*. This too does not pose a problem in this project: coping with high stresscrisis management behavior might vary between the observations and the number of cases.

Moreover, the qualitative segment of this inquiry into international crises during the past near-century (late 1918–end 2015 meets the KKV rules for intentional selection of observations).

Rule 1 *selecting observations on the explanatory variables—to ensure variation in the values of the explanatory variables*; this requirement is met.
Rule 2 *selecting a range of values of the dependent variable—to avoid selection of cases with no variation on the value of the dependent variable*; this requirement, too, is met.

In sum, the research design and case selection in this inquiry meet the criteria of King–Keohane–Verba for optimal qualitative research in political science. The *problem of indeterminate research design is not present in this project*. The *intentional selection of a large number of cases,* the *smaller number of explanatory variables, and variation in* both the *explanatory and dependent variables* meet all the requirements specified by KKV for a superior qualitative research design.

Two relevant chapters in the Brady and Collier volume discuss the issues of case selection and selection bias. Both Rogowski and Collier et al. argue in favor of selecting cases with extreme values on the dependent variable: these abnormal cases, they contend, can refute a theory or refine a theory, and account for the difference between selection bias across cases and within one case. This opposition to the King–Keohane–Verba premises is relevant only when choosing a single case study or a very small N of cases, but it is not relevant to qualitative research in this inquiry, with its substantively larger N Dataset, 29 cases.

Critics of the King–Keohane–Verba approach to qualitative research, in Brady and Collier, Preface, Chaps. 1 and 13, have alleged serious flaws. First, the KKV volume "does not adequately address the basic weaknesses within the mainstream quantitative approach it advocates." Further, its "treatment of concepts, operationalization and measurement" are "seriously incomplete." Third, the "claims that it provides a general framework for 'specific inference in qualitative research'" is rejected. More generally, contributors to the Brady–Collier critique deplore the "failure to recognize the distinctive strengths of qualitative methods" and their tendency to "inappropriately view qualitative analysis almost exclusively through the optic of mainstream quantitative methods."

A more forceful criticism of the King–Keohane–Verba approach to qualitative case studies was expressed by George and Bennett (2004: Chap. 1, especially pp. 10–16, and Chap. 8).

...we find it necessary to qualify DSI's [Designing Social Inquiry's] argument that there is one 'logic of inference'.... If...the logic of inference refers to specific methodological injunctions on such issues as the [negative] value of single-case studies, the procedures for choosing which cases to study, the role of process-tracing, and the relative importance of causal effects...and causal mechanisms as bases for inference and explanation... then we disagree with the overall argument.

We also critique DSI for emphasizing almost exclusively the epistemic goal of hypothesis testing...the 'logic of confirmation,' neglecting other aspects of theory development such as the formation of new hypotheses or the choice of new questions to study.

Another concern is that DSI pays little attention to problems of causal complexity, particularly equifinality and multiple interaction effects.

On the methodological level, we take issue with DSI's arguments on case selection criteria, the value of single-case studies and 'no variance' research designs, the costs and benefits of increasing the number of cases studied, and the role of process-tracing.... DSI's arguments on all these methodological issues may be appropriate to statistical methods, but in our view they are ill-suited or even counterproductive in case study approach. (10–15)

It will be clear, from the following analysis of 29 international political earthquakes, many of them among the high-profile, significant interstate crises in the past near-century, where I stand in this contentious, and at times acrimonious, methodological debate.

General Findings on Attributes of Foreign Policy Crises

Trigger

Eight of the nine types of *trigger [catalyst]* to crisis onset are represented in the group of 29 foreign policy crises since the 1930s that were selected for in-depth research. The largest cluster of triggers was *verbal acts* (8 cases), e.g., *Ethiopia (Ethiopian [Abyssinian] War 1935–1936)*. This was followed by *political* and *non-violent military acts* (5 crises each), e.g., *Zambia (Rhodesia's Unilateral Declaration of Independence [UDI] 1965–1966)*, and *Argentina (Falklands-Malvinas 1982)*, respectively; 3 cases of *indirect violent acts*, e.g., *Syria (Lebanon Civil War 1975–1976)*; 3 cases of *economic acts*; 2 cases of *external change;* and 1 case in each of two other trigger categories, *other non-violent act,* and *internal physical or verbal challenge to régime.* The most striking finding on crisis triggers is thus *pervasive diversity.*

Triggering Entity

The evidence also reveals a very broad range of triggering entities: 12 *states* (China, Egypt, Germany, India, Iraq, Italy, Jordan, Rhodesia, the U.K., the USA, the USSR, and Yugoslavia); *multi-state, non-state actor, international organization*—League of Nations and United Nations— and *military alliance*—NATO, as triggering entities. Most of these catalyzed one crisis each, but several were multiple triggering entities: multi-state, 4 cases, e.g., the USA, the U.K., and France triggered a foreign policy crisis for the USSR (*Berlin Blockade 1948–1949*); non-state actors, 4 crises, e.g., for the USA (*Dominican Intervention 1965*); for Iraq and the USSR, 3 crises each, e.g., the former catalyzed a crisis for the USA (*Gulf War I 1990–1991*), the latter, a crisis for the USA (*Berlin Wall 1961*); and 3 states catalyzed two crises each, e.g., *Germany* triggered a foreign policy crisis for the U.K. (*Munich 1938*), *Yugoslavia* triggered a crisis for Italy (*Trieste II 1953*), and the USA, for Iraq (*Gulf War II 2002*). *In sum,* like *triggers,* the *triggering entities in the 29 foreign policy crises exhibit great diversity.*

Duration

Duration, in this project, is calculated from the beginning of the peak stress crisis period to the end of the entire foreign policy crisis for a state. There was only *one short case* (1–14 days) among the 29 foreign policy crises that were explored in depth—the USA in the *1973 Nuclear Alert* crisis (1 day). Three cases were of *medium* duration (15–30 days), e.g., the U.K. (*Munich*), 19 days. The *long* (31–182 days) and *very long* categories (more than 182 days) are more numerous: the former, 17 cases, e.g., India (*China–India Border 1962*), 138 days; and the latter, 8 cases, e.g., Ethiopia (*Ethiopian [Abyssinian] War*), 331 days. On this crisis attribute, too, *diversity* is conspicuous.

Several traits of duration are noteworthy. First, the *range* of foreign policy crises is *vast*, from 1 day (the *US Nuclear Alert*) to 331 days (*Ethiopia—Ethiopian [Abyssinian] War*). Second, the *overwhelming majority* of the 29 foreign policy crises were *long or very long*, 59% and 28%, respectively. Parenthetically, this is similar to the distribution of all crises in the ICB Dataset, long (43%) and very long (29%). Third, there is *great variation among the crises of individual states*: USA (8 crises)—1–322 days; the USSR (2 crises)—114–320 days; Iraq (2 crises)—135–210 days; Italy (2 crises)—57–118 days, etc. Fourth, there is *no discernible pattern* in the *duration* of these 29 crises—by region, system structure, conflict setting, power level, economic level, political régime type, or any other crisis dimension. *In sum*, the most conspicuous trait of duration in this cluster of foreign policy crisis case studies, too, is *diversity*.

Decisions

The *number* of *strategic or tactical*, that is, important *decisions* in the high-stress crisis period ranges from 1 (the USA in its 1973 *Nuclear Alert* crisis, during the *October-Yom Kippur War*), to *13* (the *USSR*, in the *1968 Prague Spring* crisis). There were *12* cases at the high end of the number of important decisions, including *Guatemala* in the 1953–1954 *Guatemala* crisis, and the *USA* in the 1965 *Dominican Intervention* crisis, 11 decisions each; *Israel*, 10 decisions, in the 1973 *October-Yom Kippur* crisis-war; the *U.K.*, 9, in the 1938 *Munich* crisis;

5 cases with 8 decisions in the high stress crisis period, e.g., *Zambia, Rhodesia's UDI* crisis *1965–1966*; and 3 cases with 7 decisions, e.g., *Italy, Trieste II*. There were also crises with 2, 3, 4, 5, and 6 decisions. *In sum,* the *number* of *important decisions,* too, reveals great *diversity.*

Decision-Makers

The number of key decision-makers was small in most of the 29 in-depth cases: 1 pre-eminent decision-maker in 10 crises, e.g., *Mussolini* (Italy) and *Emperor Haile Selassie* (Ethiopia), *Ethiopian [Abyssinian] War, Stalin* (USSR), *Berlin Blockade*; 2 principal decision-makers in 4 crises, e.g., *Nehru* and Defense Minister *Krishna Menon* (India), *China-India Border War*; 3 decision-makers in 2 crises, e.g., the USA, *Berlin Blockade (President Truman, Secretary of State Marshall* and *General Clay,* Military Governor of the US zone in Germany and Commander of US forces in Europe, 1945–1949); 4 decision-makers in 5 crises, e.g., Pakistan, *Bangladesh War* 1971 *(President-General Yahya Khan, Generals Pirzada* and *Hamid,* and *Z.A. Bhutto,* a political leader of West Pakistan, later prime minister of the truncated Pakistan). There were 2 cases with 5 decision-makers; 1 case with 6 key decision-makers; 2 crises with 8; 1 with 9; 1 case with 16 decision-makers—the leaders of all 16 members of NATO, in the *Kosovo crisis-war* 1998–1999; and 1 crisis with 21 decision-makers—Israel's seven party/faction National Unity Government, the *June 1967 crisis-war*. Moreover, most of the crisis actors (states) in the 29 case studies moved to a larger decision-making group at some point in their crisis, and diversity is conspicuous in this context. *In sum,* the *enlarged decisional forums* point to **diversity** in this crisis actor attribute as well.

Attitudinal Prism

Diversity is also pronounced in the attitudinal prism of crisis decision-makers, that is, the lens through which their perceptions were filtered, which, in turn, shaped their behavior; for examples,

> The *U.K., Munich 1938*—peace was the highest value, appeasement was preferable to war, and Hitler was trustworthy;

Guatemala, Guatemala 1953–1954—"Yankee imperialism" would not tolerate a socialist régime in the Americas, and US military strength was vastly superior;
Hungary, Hungarian Uprising 1956—an internal upheaval was threatening the Communist régime in Hungary, and Moscow's opposition to basic reform was certain;
Israel, October-Yom Kippur War 1973—the flawed "Conception" held by Israel's political and military elites: Egypt would not launch a war against Israel without sufficient air power to dislocate Israel's airfields, a capability which Egypt lacked; Syria would not initiate war without the active involvement of Egypt; *ergo*, the frontline Arab states lacked a military option.
In sum, there were almost as many attitudinal prisms as the number of crises!

Values

All but 2 of the 8 types of threatened values uncovered in ICB research are represented in the 29 cases:

Influence [14 cases], e.g., the *USA* (*Nuclear Alert* crisis, during the October-Yom Kippur Crisis-War), the *USSR* (*Prague Spring*), *Syria* (*Lebanon Civil War*), and *Iraq* (*Gulf War I*);
Territory [5 cases], e.g., *Italy* (*Trieste II*);
Political [3 cases], e.g., *Iraq* (*Gulf War II*);
Existence [3 cases], *Ethiopia* (*Ethiopian [Abyssinian] War*), the *Netherlands* (*Fall of Western Europe 1939–1940*), and *Israel* (*June-Six-Day War*);
Economic [2 cases], e.g., *Zambia* (*Rhodesia's-UDI* crisis); and
Other [2 cases], *U.K.* (*Munich*), and *NATO* (*Kosovo*).

As evident, *threat to influence* was the *primary threatened value* in *almost half of the in-depth cases (14 of 29)*, including most of the US crises. The second most frequent value was a *threat to territory*, 5 cases—2 in Asia, 2 in Europe, 1 in the Americas. And the core value, *existence*, was present in slightly more than 10% of the 29 cases, 1 in Africa, 1 in Europe, and 1 in the Middle East. *In sum, diversity is pronounced* among the *values perceived to be at risk*, as with all the other actor attributes discussed above.

Findings on Coping—Crisis Management

In general, decision-makers of states confronted with national security crises employ one, some or all of four *coping mechanisms* to deal with escalating stress in the crisis period of a foreign policy crisis. They *seek and process information*—about their principal adversary's intentions and capabilities, the attitudes of potential allies and patrons, and the adversary's allies and patrons. They *consult* their military and bureaucratic specialists, opposition political leaders, allies, patrons, and international organizations. They create an ad hoc, or employ an existing, *decisional forum*. And they *search for, and consider, alternatives* prior to making decisions.

What does the evidence from the 29 in-depth case studies reveal about **coping/crisis management**?

Information Processing

The decision-maker(s) in *almost all* (27 of 29) cases felt the need for, and sought, information about the crisis that they confronted: decision-makers in almost all of the foreign policy-national security crises manifested a *felt need*—and *engaged* in *a quest—for more information* about: the gravity of the perceived threat, that is, the *intent, capability* and *resolve* of their *adversary*; the *time available for response*; the *probability of war*; the *extent and reliability of support*—military, political, diplomatic and/or economic—that could be expected *from allies, a patron or patrons,* and/or *international organizations,* the *options* available to cope with the threat, and the *most likely outcome* of the crisis.

At the same time, *information processing* varied; that is, it did not unfold in an identical way, robot-like, by the decision-maker(s) of the target states. Some were more, others less, actively engaged in the search for information than others. Some were more trustful, others less trustful, of the sources and content of information. Some were more, others less, successful in processing often contradictory information. However, the *evidence* of a *near-universally shared attitude to information*—a *felt need and quest for more*—and the *processing,* as well as the *rapid transfer, of information to the most senior decision-makers—is compelling*. In this respect, the multiple diversities among crisis attributes and crisis dimensions were irrelevant, for they were subsumed in the *commonality of the challenge faced by decision-makers,* all of whom experienced escalating stress with the escalation of threat, time pressure, and the higher likelihood of military hostilities.

Consultation

Consultation by decision-makers during the peak stress crisis period of most foreign policy crises was *broader* and *more intense* than in the *pre-crisis period*; that is, its scope and depth correlated with the intensity of the crisis and the stress generated in the *pre-crisis period* (low stress) and *crisis period* (high stress). There were several notable exceptions: *Ethiopia* and *Italy* in the 1935–1936 *Ethiopian [Abyssinian] crisis-war*, the *USSR* in the *Berlin Blockade* and the *Prague Spring* crises, *Iraq* in *Gulf War I* and *Gulf War II* (*Iraq Regime Change*), and *Yugoslavia* in the *Kosovo* crisis. The explanation is simple: in all of these cases, an *authoritarian regime was in power*. In most of them, *one person was pre-eminent* in terms of decisional influence and authority—Emperor Haile Selassie in Ethiopia, Mussolini in Italy, Stalin in the USSR (in 1948), Saddam Hussein in Iraq (both Gulf War cases), and Milosevic in Yugoslavia, the FRY. The USSR continued to be authoritarian in 1968, but it was the Communist party leadership, not an individual, that held power. In all other cases, the escalation of stress led to a broadening and deepening of the consultation process.

Decisional Forum

The findings on decisional forums during the peak stress crisis period of the 29 foreign policy crises are mixed:

15 of the 29 cases exhibit *no change* from the low-stress pre-crisis period—*Ethiopia* (1935–1936), *Italy* (1935–1936 and 1953), the *USSR* (1948–49 and 1968), the *USA* (1961, 1973, 1990–1991 and 2002–2003), *India* (1971), *Pakistan* (1971, *Argentina* (1982), *Yugoslavia* (1998–1999), and *Iraq* (1990–1991, 2002–2003); 9 of the 15 were authoritarian regimes of various types—monarchical, Fascist, Communist, military, and Ba'athist; the other 6 were democratic; 9 cases witnessed an *enlarged decisional forum*—the *U.K.* (1938), the *Netherlands* (1940), *India* (1962), the *USA* (1965), *Zambia* (1966), *Israel* (1967 and 1973–1974), *Syria* (1975–1976), and *NATO* (1998–1999); 7 of the 9 were democratic; and

5 cases experienced a *smaller decisional forum*—the *USA* (1948–1949, 1958, and 1970), *Guatemala* (1954), and *Hungary* (1956); 4 of

the 5 were democratic (one of them with prominent communist influence), and 1 was communist.

SEARCH FOR, AND CONSIDERATION OF, ALTERNATIVES

Because of the centrality of this coping mechanism for crisis decision-making, writ large, the *search for,* and *consideration of, alternatives* in all 29 selected foreign policy crises will be reported below.

Multipolarity

Ethiopia (1935–1936) The emperor was open to—and pursued—several options during the *Ethiopia–Italy crisis-war*. One, actively implemented by Ethiopia's ruler, Haile Selassie, was *to appeal to the League of Nations and the European powers, especially Britain, for needed diplomatic and great power support in its existence crisis.* A second option, which the Emperor was cautious about initiating because of the uncertain loyalty of Ethiopia's autonomous *rases* (kings), was *to mobilize Ethiopia's human and material resources to confront the anticipated Italian military assault.* A third option, which he also pursued, on the advice of "La Trinité," his three foreign advisers, was *concessions to Italy*. Although his preferred option was the *status quo ante, war* was the least attractive alternative. Thus he did not exclude *direct negotiations* with Italy but faced unacceptable demands, in essence, total surrender. In the hope of avoiding a full-scale Italian invasion, *Haile Selassie accepted*—but *Mussolini rejected*—*a British-French concessions plan*, drafted without consulting Ethiopia, that would have given part of the vast *Ogaden Desert and far-reaching economic privileges to Italy,* drastically reducing Ethiopia's sovereignty.

Italy (1935–1936) Mussolini did not seriously consider any alternative to *invasion*—he was bent on conquering Ethiopia. His only worry was that the United Kingdom might decide to impose economic sanctions. He gambled, correctly, that Britain would not intervene militarily, which would have been devastating for Italy. He even *rejected* the very favorable British-French *Hoare–Laval Plan* of December 9, 1935, in the midst of war, calling on Ethiopia to cede to Italy three areas bordering Italy's East Africa colonies, Eritrea, and Italian Somaliland, and to grant Italy exclusive economic rights in large parts of southern Ethiopia. *In sum,* while rejecting, a priori, all alternatives to invasion, he sought the *optimal diplomatic tactics* to avoid a confrontation with Britain and France.

United Kingdom (1938) Many options were considered, and several were adopted, by the United Kingdom during the rising stress phase of its *Munich* crisis period: *cooperation with Germany*, implemented by Prime Minister Chamberlain at his three summit meetings with Hitler in Germany (at Berchtesgaden, Godesberg, and Munich); *cooperation with France*, expressed in their Joint Proposals of September 18, 1938, signaling Britain's intention *to stand by France* and *support Czechoslovakia*, if invaded by Germany; *mobilization of the British navy*; the use of *Mussolini as a mediator*; and ultimately, the *sacrifice of Czechoslovakia (appeasement)*.

Netherlands (1939-1940) Many options were adopted and implemented (some in its pre-crisis period) : *proclaiming a state of war status* in March 1939; *mobilization* in August; a *declaration of neutrality* in September; a *diplomatic offensive* in London, Paris, and Brussels to reinforce its claim to neutrality, beginning in November 1939; and *intensified low-level military consultations with France and the United Kingdom*, starting in January 1940. During the higher stress crisis period, the Netherlands proclaimed a *state of siege*, including the cancelation of all leaves in Holland's army, in April 1940, and set in motion *active military steps*, notably the blowing up of bridges, in response to the German invasion on May 10.

Bipolarity

United States (1948-1949) *Several high-risk alternatives were considered during the United States' Berlin Blockade crisis period: planned withdrawal from West Berlin*, rejected as unworthy; the *dispatch of a train with American troops aboard, across East Germany to West Berlin*, implemented; the *use of nuclear weapons*, a *contingency directive by President Truman*, not implemented; and the *airlift*. The primary US concern was the maintenance of the flow of essential supplies to West Berlin, a short-term goal. The strategic chosen US option, *to stay in Berlin at all costs*—the airlift was a means to achieve that goal—was not the result of a formal rational choice calculus; rather, it was improvised and intuitive, namely, derived from President Truman's belief that yielding on West Berlin would have been tantamount to accepting Soviet hegemony in Europe.

USSR (1948–1949) Four options were identified during the Soviet Union's *Berlin Blockade* crisis period, all high risk: *to take over West Berlin with conventional Soviet military forces; to organize mass action in Berlin against the Western powers, which Moscow would then support militarily; to interfere with the airlift;* and, fourth, *to negotiate with the United States and seek a peaceful agreement that would provide the Soviet Union with a face-saver.* The first option was not seriously considered; the second and third were considered and rejected because of the perceived high risk of war with the USA. For Stalin, the optimal way to cope with the Berlin crisis was to make sure that the United States knew the Soviet Union did not intend to escalate the crisis to war—because the "correlation of forces" at the time was perceived then as unfavorable to the USSR. Thus the only perceived feasible alternative, the one Moscow chose, was to negotiate a face-saving agreement with the USA, while the blockade was still in force.

Italy (1953) Several options were considered by Italy during its *Trieste* crisis period, all tactical, designed to achieve the strategic goal, namely, Italy's sovereignty over at least Trieste's Zone A. One was the *transfer of administrative authority to Italy in Zone A in incremental steps,* along with the *mutual Italy–Yugoslavia withdrawal of troops from Trieste* and an *exchange of guarantees with Yugoslavia.* Another was *an attempt to work out a definitive solution at a conference* and, if inconclusive, the *implementation of the October 8 decision calling for partition of Trieste between Italy and Yugoslavia.* A third option was *to hold a preparatory meeting to search for a solution.* Yugoslavia was amenable to three substantive solutions—a *plebiscite in the entire territory of Trieste, partition along ethnic lines,* and *partition along the zonal border,* as provided by the October 8 decision.

Guatemala (1953–1954) Five options were considered by Guatemala's Left-wing government at different stages of its peak stress crisis period: **first**, *to reduce Guatemala's isolation in Latin America,* via a *flurry of friendly diplomatic initiatives*; **second**, *to improve relations with a hostile United States,* aimed at ending American support for the Castillo Armas-led rebel movement; **third**, *to enlist UN Security Council support*—after the outbreak of violence; **fourth**, *to enhance Guatemala's military capability* by purchasing arms from abroad and *an* (abortive) *attempt to form a militia*; and, finally, *to reduce the highly visible communist role in the*

Arbenz government, the core issue for its adversaries, the United States and Honduras. All but the last option were adopted and implemented.

Hungary (1956) Two polar alternatives were seriously considered by Hungary's leaders during its crisis period—*to crush all demands for liberal reforms by force and repression* or to pursue a middle path and *to offer concessions without yielding on the party's monopoly of power*. The options of *introducing a multiparty political system or withdrawal from the Warsaw Pact or proclaiming neutrality* were favored by some but were beyond the pale for party leader Gérö in the early stage of the crisis period. Even Nagy, his much more popular and relatively liberal successor, did not favor, though he did consider, *inviting Western military intervention* or *offering military resistance to the Soviet invasion* and he did *proclaim Hungary's neutrality* on November 1.

United States (1958) There was a *wide search for strategic and tactical military options* but not for basic political alternatives to the *use of force* during the United States' crisis period in the *Iraq-Lebanon Upheaval*. A *summit meeting* was frowned upon, as were *diplomatic initiatives* in Lebanon. The US response was characterized by tactical rationality, leading to a *rejection of all proposals for military intervention in Iraq* or to *stimulate a broader Middle East conflict involving Israel and/or Turkey as US proxies*.

United States (1961) The search for, and evaluation of, alternatives by the United States was extensive in its *Berlin Wall* crisis period—by the Berlin Task Force, created following the Kennedy-Khrushchev Vienna summit in early June, in a study by former Secretary of State Acheson, and by Kennedy himself. The polar alternatives were *deterrence that relied on US military power or deterrence via negotiations with the Soviet Union*. After the construction of the Wall on August 13, the options considered by the USA ranged from *passive acceptance of the new status quo in Germany* to *re-imposition of the status quo ante by political and economic retaliation*. Other options were available but were not seriously considered: *tearing down the barbed wire barriers, imposing an economic embargo on East Germany, and sending more US troops to West Berlin*. The ultimate choice was *to send a protest note to Moscow, without taking any tangible action*.

India (1962) During the pre-war phase of the *India–China* Crisis, India's behavior was shaped by a rigid *attitudinal prism*, namely, that fundamental hostility by China created the border dispute, the need for firm Indian counterforce to China's infiltration into Indian territory, and the low likelihood of major war; this set of perceptions was not conducive to a search for strategic alternatives. With the coming of war, India's *options*, hitherto considered inconceivable, were rapidly assessed and chosen under maximal stress—an *appeal for US air cover over India's cities in the east* and *an implied willingness to enter a military alliance with the long unfriendly superpower*, which would have meant abandonment of the hallowed foundation of India's foreign policy since independence, non-alignment.

Bipolycentrism

United States (1965) The outbreak of civil war in the Dominican Republic on April 24 and the US perception of American lives and property in grave danger created very little time to consider alternatives—and only one was considered. On April 28, the United States chose what President Johnson regarded as the only option, *military intervention* ("we had no choice"). That day, 400 American troops were sent to the Dominican Republic; within 3 weeks, this force grew to 22,000. All foreign citizens were evacuated. Thereafter, the United States opted for *diplomacy—bilateral, inter-American, and UN negotiations*—to achieve the "Act of Dominican Reconciliation," which ended the civil war and the *Dominican Republic* Crisis on August 31, 1965.

Zambia (1965–1966) Despite its predominant perception of constraints on the search for, and consideration of, alternatives, Zambia sought and assessed many options during its *Rhodesia Unilateral Declaration of Independence Crisis*: *development of alternative outlets to the sea*, a long-term option for a landlocked state; *demands for UK military retaliation against Rhodesia*—pursued insistently but without success; and the option of a *"Quick Kill" strategy against Rhodesia*, recommended by British Prime Minister Harold Wilson and accepted by Zambia's President Kaunda, which ended the crisis.

Israel (1967) Many more options were sought, considered, accepted, and implemented during Israel's June-*Six-Day War* peak stress crisis period, from May 17 to June 6, than during its pre-crisis period: *mobilization of reserves, partial and then large-scale*; *diplomacy*—an active search for support from the three Western powers, notably the USA; *delay*, in making a decision, to provide Israel's armed forces time to prepare for war; *deception*—acts designed to persuade Egypt that Israel would not fire the first shot; and the *initiation of interceptive (pre-emptive) war*. The high-risk military option, late in the war, *to advance on Syria's capital, Damascus*, was considered but rejected; and joint USA-USSR pressure on Israel to ceasefire was accepted on June 11.

USSR (1968) A wide range of options was considered during the Soviet Union's *Prague Spring* crisis period: *direct political pressure* on the communist reformers in Prague; *economic incentives and sanctions*; the *permanent stationing of Soviet bloc (Warsaw Pact) forces in Czechoslovakia*; the *use of these forces to restore pro-Soviet communist orthodoxy in Prague*; the *use of European communist leaders to persuade the Czechoslovak reformers to relent*; and *military invasion*, the chosen option of last resort.

United States (1970) Many options were considered by the United States during the crisis period of *Black September/Syria-Jordan Confrontation*, mostly military and strategic: *pressure on Moscow to force Syria to withdraw its troops from Jordan*—accepted and implemented; *preparation of a credible military option* if King Hussein's regime were overthrown—accepted; *direct US military intervention* to save King Hussein—rejected; *"going public"*—rejected because it would make it more difficult for Syria to retreat; a direct or indirect *approach to Syria and/or the USSR and/or the UN Security Council*—rejected because uncertain outcomes exceeded any perceived gain; and using the *threat of Israeli intervention*, by air and, if necessary, by ground forces, as a US proxy—accepted and decisive in forcing Syria's withdrawal from Jordan and terminating the crisis.

India (1971) Until early July, still its pre-crisis period in the *Bangladesh* Crisis, India pursued a *political-diplomatic* option, dispatching diplomats in May–June to persuade Western powers to press Pakistan to seek a mutually acceptable political solution to the crisis in East Pakistan. When that failed, India adopted the *military* option, in principle. Prime Minister Gandhi prepared the ground by visiting Western states—Austria, Belgium, France, the United Kingdom, West Germany, and the United States—from October 16 to November 13—to convey India's determination *to intervene if Pakistan did not change its policy.* India's military intervention was decisive in terminating Pakistan's control over East Bengal–East Pakistan. However, the prime minister and her civil servant advisers rejected a proposed *high-risk supplementary military option—to "liberate" the Pakistani-controlled part of Kashmir* on the western India/Pakistan front—urged on India's Cabinet Political Affairs Committee on December 4 by the defense and finance ministers, soon after the full-scale war began.

Pakistan (1971) The military leaders of Pakistan considered and tried, briefly, a *political* option in the pre-crisis period of its *Bangladesh* Crisis, namely, *to split East Pakistan's* dominant political party, the *Awami League, by offering greater autonomy to an alternative leadership.* They responded to East Pakistan's declaration of independence on March 26 with massive force. The *military option* remained the sole option pursued by Pakistan until the end of the war with India and the loss of East Pakistan. It was also unsuccessful in active *attempts to secure military support from* its long-time patron, the *United States,* and its ally, *China.*

Israel (1973) The *October 1973* pre-war crisis period, unlike the 1967 pre-war crisis period, lasted only one day. Thus its search for, and consideration of, alternatives were overwhelmingly related to military-strategic issues. The first, high-risk, problem of choice occurred only hours before the war—*to launch a pre-emptive air strike against Egypt or to take the first blow.* Prime Minister Meir's "Kitchen Cabinet" opted for the latter, for political reasons—concern about the need to ensure US weapons support, if necessary. During the war, there were several problems of choice between options: *to accept or to reject a ceasefire in place, on October 12*—accepted, *pro forma*; *to cross the Suez Canal two days later or to wait*—it opted to cross; *to accept or reject the first and second ceasefire*—accepted, so as not to alienate the United States; *to relax or not to relax its vise-like encirclement of, and allow the passage of food to, the Egyptian Third Army*—accepted for the same reason; and *to continue or halt the advance on Damascus*—halted because of expected high Israeli casualties.

United States (1973) Its *Nuclear Alert* crisis lasted one day. There was no time to search for, or consider, alternatives, except to respond or not to respond to the Soviet threat of military intervention in the

October-Yom Kippur War. The only option considered and adopted by the USA was *to warn the USSR of its high-risk threat by a demonstrative US non-violent military act*; it placed all US Strategic Air Forces on DEFCON 3, the highest state of alert, a clear message to Moscow that the United States would respond to Soviet military intervention on the Middle East battlefield. The US crisis ended abruptly, and the October-Yom Kippur War, soon after.

Syria (1975–1976): President Assad perceived clear alternatives before several crucial decision points during Syria's *Lebanon Civil War* crisis period. The first was *to intervene or not to intervene*; he opted to intervene indirectly by sending the Syria-controlled Palestine Liberation Army's [PLA's] Yarmouk Brigade to prevent the near-certain collapse of the Lebanese-Muslim-Palestinian alliance. The second issue was *to intervene or not to intervene directly with Syrian troops*: the former option was chosen after assurances, especially from Israel, of non-opposition. And, third, Syria considered whether *to threaten or not to threaten an attack against PLO forces in Mount Lebanon*, the Christian Lebanese heartland, unless they withdrew within 5 days; the former option was chosen.

Argentina (1982) Several options were considered by Argentina's military *junta* during its *Falklands-Malvinas* crisis period, despite its commitment to "liberating" the UK-controlled islands. One was *mutual withdrawal of Argentine and UK forces from the disputed territory and acceptance of the right of self-determination by the islanders, without a precondition of Argentine sovereignty*; this option was accepted and then reneged. Another option was a USA-sponsored *mutual withdrawal of forces and an UN-supervised transition to Argentine sovereignty by the end of 1982*—accepted by Argentina, but rejected by the United Kingdom. A third option was a *ceasefire, mutual withdrawal, and later talks on the future of the islands*—rejected by Argentina, mainly because of the British sinking of the Argentine naval ship, the General Belgrano, with heavy casualties.

Unipolycentrism

United States (1990–1991) Substantive *options* were considered at several crucial decision points in the United States' *Gulf War I* crisis period. Following a meeting of the senior US decision-makers, the "Principals," on October 30, 1990, a *strategic decision* was made *to set in motion a process leading to war against Iraq*, at the behest of President Bush, National Security Advisor Scowcroft, Defense Secretary Cheney, and Vice-President Quayle. The first follow-up tactical issue was *whether or not to prepare for a land campaign*; the same decision-makers ensured a positive decision. With the rapid advance of USA-led Coalition forces on the battlefield, two other crucial problems of choice demanded attention. First, *should US forces enter Baghdad and overthrow the Saddam Hussein regime?* This option was rejected on the grounds that it would destabilize Iraq and the entire oil-rich Gulf region. Soon after, a related issue arose—*when should the war be terminated?* It was erroneously believed by American political and military leaders that all Iraq Republican Guard divisions had already been destroyed. Because of an acute fear of regional instability, the option of immediate war termination was chosen. Although options were carefully considered on many war–peace and regime change issues, the decision-making process was not thorough or systematic. In short, US decision-makers seriously considered and chose only *one strategic option in 1990–1991, to expel Iraq from Kuwait by force.*

Iraq (1990–1991) Saddam Hussein had *three options* in the pre-*Gulf War I* crisis period, while trying to cope with the impending UN deadline for Iraq's *withdrawal from Kuwait*—January 15, 1991. One was *withdrawal from Kuwait, total and unconditional,* as demanded by the USA-led Coalition, *or partial,* and in either case, *immediate or phased.* Another option was *to do nothing,* calculating that Bush I and the UN Coalition were bluffing. The third alternative was *to wage war,* either defensive war or a strike against Saudi oil fields or Israel or both. Hints and rumors of a Saddam Hussein withdrawal continued until the UN deadline, but he made no move in that direction; nor did he initiate war. Rather he chose to do nothing. During the war, he had to consider alternatives in other high-risk choice situations*: to accept or reject the (friendly) Soviet plan* in late February 1991 to wind down the crisis—he opted in favor and, most important, *to accept or reject the USA-led UN Coalition terms for surrender* a few days later—he chose to accept those terms as less costly for Iraq than other possible outcomes.

Yugoslavia (1998–1999) The Federal Republic of Yugoslavia (FRY) pursued a *limited cooperation with NATO* strategy in its *Kosovo* pre-crisis period. Once NATO's "Operation Allied Force" was launched, the

FRY chose the option of *standing firm*, although with conspicuous military restraint—it avoided attacking NATO troops and ships and avoided alienating Russia, its sole, but not entirely reliable, patron. Those two negative choices were considered the most effective for Yugoslavia, especially because of its awareness of its own military constraints and its (flawed) assumptions about NATO's fragile unity and cohesion.

NATO (1998–1999) No *strategic alternatives* to *sustained bombing* were seriously considered by NATO during its *Kosovo* crisis period because of Miloševic's intransigence. The first of two noteworthy *tactical options* was a *phased air campaign*, with pauses allowing *negotiations*, an idea supported by Italy, Greece, and Germany. It was rejected as likely to be ineffective, given the failure of previous negotiations with Miloševic, backed by the threat of force. The *ground troops* option gained more and more support toward the end of NATO's crisis period. At a meeting of foreign ministers in Bonn on May 27, 1999, the British government announced that it was ready to commit 50,000 troops if a decision on that option was made. President Clinton responded that he was ready to send ground troops but did not believe it was necessary; it proved not to be.

Iraq (2002–2003) Throughout its *Gulf War II pre-crisis period* (from Bush II's "Axis of Evil" speech on January 29, 2002 to his speech to the UN General Assembly on September 12, 2002), Iraq had two options— *to stall for time* and hope that Washington was bluffing or *to cooperate by complying in full with UN inspections*; it declared in September that it would readmit inspectors. There was also an Iraq option of *striking American targets in the Persian Gulf and Kuwait before they attacked*, but it is not known how seriously this was considered. While the substance of discussions in Baghdad is unknown, its actions indicate that it was not serious about *compliance* and instead hoped that *either the Americans were not serious or military action could be blocked at the UN*, as Saddam Hussein was reportedly assured by French and Russian diplomats. Thus, the preeminent option, and the one chosen by Iraq, was *do nothing*.

United States (2002–2003) Probably from 9/11 onward, certainly after January 29, 2002, Bush II never seems to have seriously contemplated a *strategic alternative* to *regime change* in Iraq during the interstate crisis that led to *Gulf War II*. Thus the consideration of options focused on how, not whether, to topple Saddam Hussein and his Ba'athist regime. The available US *tactical options* included *sponsoring a coup in Iraq*, a *unilateral or UN-sanctioned, USA-led invasion*, and *applying pressure via the UN over Iraq's assumed weapons of mass destruction (WMD) programs*. Another crucial US tactical choice point was *whether or not to seek another UN resolution explicitly authorizing war*. Strenuous attempts to do so convinced Bush II that another such resolution was not attainable and that he would have to proceed with his "coalition of the willing." His choice was to invade Iraq, without UN authorization, to achieve regime change with a coalition including forces from many states, notably the UK and France, and two Arab states, Egypt and Syria.

What does the evidence on a *search for*, and *consideration of*, alternatives in foreign policy crises from 1935 to 2003 reveal? Did national security–foreign policy decision-makers seriously consider *one, few, or many options* while coping with more stressful perceived threat, time pressure, and the higher likelihood of war, in the crisis period than in the pre-crisis period, that is, while confronting challenges under *maximal stress*? Moreover, did they consider options *more frequently* in the crisis period than in pre-crisis?

One option was considered in 7 interstate crises: by *Italy, invasion* of Ethiopia; by the *United States, military intervention* in the Dominican Republic; by *Pakistan, resort to force* against the East Pakistan secession, Bangladesh; by the *United States*, which chose to *place its strategic air forces on nuclear alert*; by the *United States*, which opted to *expel Iraq from Kuwait by force*; by *Yugoslavia*, the choice of *military restraint*, that is, non-use of force against NATO's 'Operation Allied Force' in the crisis-war over Kosovo's *independence*; and by the United States, the sole option of achieving *regime change in Iraq, by force*.

Two options (2 cases): *India*, first in time, selected a *diplomatic* option, an attempt to persuade Western major and minor powers to press Pakistan to seek a political solution with the dominant Awami League in East Pakistan; when that failed, India chose a *military* option—direct Indian military intervention; *NATO*, too, first chose the option of *diplomatic persuasion* and then the *use of force* to expel Yugoslavia (the FRY) from Kosovo.

Several options (20 cases) Multiple options, as noted above, ranged from three to seven: *three options* (5 cases, e.g., *Ethiopia, Ethiopian [Abyssinian] War*); *four options* (4 cases, e.g., the *USSR, Berlin Blockade crisis*); *five options* (4 cases, e.g., *Guatemala*, Guatemala crisis); *six options* (5 cases, e.g., the United Kingdom, Munich crisis); and *seven* options (2 cases, e.g., Hungary, Hungarian Uprising).

In sum, there was a *substantial search for, and consideration of, options in 20 of the 29 foreign policy crises (70%), often very extensive* and *very thorough*, before strategic and tactical decisions were taken. *In two other crises, polar alternatives were seriously debated by the decision-makers.* Among the seven cases in which only one strategic option was considered, four can be termed idiosyncratic: two were *opportunity crises, triggered by a leader's glory complex (Mussolini* re Ethiopia, 1935–1936*)* and an *ideologically driven foreign policy agenda (*the *Bush II administration re regime change* in *Iraq, 2002); and two were urgent immediate responses to a perceived "no choice" threat to unprotected citizens and property (US President Johnson and his advisers re Dominican Intervention in 1965) and a perceived no-time-to-respond direct challenge to the regional and global balance of power by one superpower to another (*the *United States re its 1973 Nuclear Alert).* Two of the remaining *three cases* in this group exhibited a *perceived fundamental threat* of *territorial disintegration (Pakistan's military junta re Bangladesh* in 1971 and Serbia's President *Milošević* re the *Kosovo secession* in 1998–1999*),* and a *superpower's perception of basic threat to its deterrence credibility and vital economic interests (*the *United States in Gulf War I, 1990–1991).* And even *in these cases, 24% of the cases explored in depth, tactical options, often many, were considered and frequently adopted* by the decision-makers.

Two other findings from the case studies are noteworthy. *First, coping in the crisis period was more efficient in the vast majority of cases under high stress than in the low-stress pre-crisis period. Second, decision-makers in democratic regimes coped with stress better than those in authoritarian regimes.*

COPING WITH FOREIGN POLICY CRISES: NEW EVIDENCE CONFRONTS CONVENTIONAL WISDOM

Thus far, this chapter has presented an array of findings, notably on the four coping mechanisms that, together, illuminate decision-making in the peak stress crisis period—*information processing, consultation, structure, and size* of the *decisional forum, and the search for, and consideration of, alternatives*. As such, these findings shed light on the general question, *how do states cope with high stress?*

Two related questions also merit careful attention. First, *is there a pattern of common response to the stress experienced by decision-makers in crises, or is diversity the norm?* Second, *is the conventional wisdom that high stress has a severe injurious effect on decision-making an accurate portrait of the stress-behavior linkage in foreign policy crises?* The following discussion on *conventional wisdom* versus *new evidence* will attempt to answer these crucial questions.

Earlier in this book attention was focused on 10 **dimensions** of crisis (*geography, time, system structure, conflict setting, bloc alignment, peace-war setting, intensity of violence, power level, economic level, and political regime*), and in this chapter on seven **attributes** of crises and their actors (*trigger, triggering entity, duration, decisions, decision-makers, their attitudinal prism*, and *threatened values*). The *central finding* of that empirical analysis was *pervasive diversity on all of the dimensions and all of the attributes of international political earthquakes-international crises*.

Did this conspicuous and documented diversity generate a diverse—or common—response among crisis actors to the challenge posed by crisis escalation? Did decision-makers cope well or badly under high stress? These are important questions, with far-reaching policy implications, as well as social-scientific research interest. An earlier inquiry (Brecher 1993) uncovered findings that challenged conventional wisdom on these questions. Twenty-five years later, I did an elaborate re-testing of 19 hypotheses on the behavior of decision-makers in almost twice as many foreign policy crises, 29–16.

Hypotheses 7, 14, 15, 17, and 18 focus on the effects of *Time*. All other hypotheses focus on the impact of *Stress* and are framed in terms of, "the higher the crisis-induced stress…"

Cognitive Dimension

Hypothesis (H.)1 The higher the crisis-induced stress, the more concerned the decision-makers will be with the immediate rather than the long-run future.

H.2 The higher the crisis-induced stress, *the greater the felt need, and consequent quest, for information*.

H.3 The higher the crisis-induced stress, *the more closed (conceptually rigid) to new information the decision-maker(s) become.*

H.4 The higher the crisis-induced stress, *the more the decision-maker(s) will supplement information by relying on past experience as a guide to choice.*

H.5 The higher the crisis-induced stress, *the more active the information search is likely to become but also more random and unproductive.*

H.6 The higher the crisis-induced stress, *the more information about a crisis tends to be elevated to the top of the decisional pyramid.*

Decisional Dimension

Consultation/Communication
H.7 The longer the crisis decision time, *the greater the consultation with persons outside the core decisional unit.*

H.8 The higher the crisis-induced stress, *the greater the reliance on extraordinary channels of communication.*

H.9 The higher the crisis-induced stress, *the higher the rate of communication with international actors.*

Decisional Forum
H.10 The higher the crisis-induced stress, *the smaller the decision group tends to become, that is, the greater the tendency to centralized decision-making.*

H.11 The higher the crisis-induced stress, *the greater the tendency for decisions to be reached by* ad hoc *groups.*

H.12 The higher the crisis-induced stress, *the greater the tendency to "group-think," that is, to conformity with group norms.*

H.13 The higher the crisis-induced stress, *the greater the felt need for face-to-face proximity among decision-makers.*

H.14 The longer the crisis decision time, the greater the felt need for effective leadership within the decisional unit.

H.15 The longer the crisis decision time, the greater the decision-makers' consensus on the ultimate decision.

Alternatives
H.16 The higher the crisis-induced stress, the less careful the evaluation of alternatives.

H.17 The shorter the crisis decision time, the greater the tendency to premature closure.

H.18 The shorter the crisis decision time, the more likely are decisions to be made with inadequate assessment of consequences, that is, with less sensitivity to negative feedback.

General

H.19 High stress is dysfunctional; that is, cognitive and, therefore, decisional performance will be greatly influenced by psychological biases and will deteriorate markedly.

The findings on the *extent of support* and *non-support*, and *mixed support*, for each hypothesis relating to the cognitive and decisional aspects of coping are provided in numerical form in Table 4.1.

The findings are most instructive. As in the earlier analysis (Brecher 1993), but with a much larger set of cases (29), 9 of the 19 hypotheses, selected from a very large number framed by other researchers, reveal strong support and 1 moderate support, and 4 are strongly disconfirmed, as postulated by this writer, that is, **14 of the 19 hypotheses.**

- Two of the six *cognitive* hypotheses, *a felt need for information* (H.2) and *reliance on past experience* (H.4), are very strongly supported (27–30 and 21–32, respectively). So too with Hypothesis 6, the *rapid transfer of information to the top of the decision-making pyramid* (25–31), and the first part of Hypothesis 5, the *search for information will be more active* (20–23).[4]
- The three hypotheses on *consultation and communication* (H.7, H.8, and H.9), too, are strongly supported (19–26, 20–27, and 26–32, respectively).

4 GENERAL FINDINGS: FOREIGN POLICY CRISES   111

Table 4.1 Case Studies: Hypothesis Testing—Time Pressure, Stress, and Behavior

The Higher-The Crisis-Induced Stress...	Ethiopia (Ethiopian War)	Italy (Ethiopian War)	United Kingdom (Munich)	Netherlands (German Invasion)	United States (Berlin Blockade)	USSR (Berlin Blockade)	Italy (Trieste II)	Guatemala (Guatemala)	Hungary (Hungarian Uprising)	United States (Iraq-Lebanon)
Information										
H.1	S	NS	M	NT	NS	S	NT	NS	S	M
H.2	S	S	S	S	S	S	S	S	S	S
H.3	NS	M	NS	M	S	NS	NT	MD	NS	S
H.4	M	S	MD	S	S	S	NT	S	S	S
H.5	S/NS	S/NS	S/NS	S/MD	NS	S/M	S/NS	MD	S	S
H.6	S/NS	S	S	MD	S	S	M	S	S	S
Consultation										
H.7	S	NS	NS	S	S	NS	NT	S	S	NS
H.8	S	NS	NS	S	S	NS	NS	NS	S	S
H.9	S	S	S	NS	S	S	NS	S	S	S
Decisional Forum										
H.10	S	S	S	NS	S	S	NS	S	S	S
H.11	NS	NS	NS	S	S	NS	NS	N	NS	S
H.12	NS	NS	S	S	NS	NS	NS	NS	S	NT
H.13	MD	S	S	MD	S	NS	NS	MD	S	S
H.14	NS	S	S	MD	S	S	NS	S	S	S
H.15	NR	S	S	NS	NS	MD	NS	NS	NS	NS
Alternatives										
H.16	NS	M	NS	S	NS	MD	NS	NS	NS	NS
H.17	NS	NS	NS	NS	NS	NS	NS	NS	M	NS
H.18	NS	M	S	S	NS	NS	NT	NS	S	NS
H.19	NS	NS	NS	NR	NS	M	NS	S	S	NS

(continued)

112   M. BRECHER

Table 4.1 (continued)

The Higher-The Crisis-Induced Stress...	United States (Berlin Wall)	India (China-India Border)	United States (Dominican Intervention)	Zambia (Rhodesia UDI)	Israel (June-Six Day War)	USSR (Prague Spring)	United States (Black September)	India (Bangladesh War)	Pakistan (Bangladesh War)	Israel (October-Yom Kippur War)
Information										
H.1	NS	S	NT	S	S	NS	S	NS	S	S
H.2	S	S	S	S	S	S	S	S	M	S
H.3	NS	S	NT	NS	M	S	S	NS	S	N
H.4	NT	NT	S	S	S	S	S	S	S	S
H.5	NS	MD	S	S/NS	S/NS	S	S	S/NS	S	S
H.6	NT	S	S[a]	S	S	S	S	S	S	S
Consultation										
H.7	NT	S	S[a]	S	S	NS	S	ND	NS	S
H.8	NT	S	S	S	S	S	S	NS	S	S
H.9	S	S	S[a]	S	S	M	S	S	S	S
Decisional Forum										
H.10	S	NS	NS	NS	NS	NS	NS	S	S	NS
H.11	S	NS	S	NS	NS	S	NS	S	NS	NS
H.12	NT	S	S	MD	S	MD	NT	M	S	S
H.13	S	S	S	MD	S	S	S	MD	NS	S
H.14	NT	S	NS	MD	S	MD	S	S	NS	S
H.15	NT	S	NS	MD	S	S	S	S	S	S
Alternatives										
H.16	NS	S	S	NS	NS	NS	NS	M	S	NS
H.17	NS	NS	S	NS	NS	NS	NS	NS	S	NS
H.18	NS	MD	NS	MD	NS	NS	NS	NS	S	NS
H.19	NT	NS	S[a]	NS	NS	NS	NS	S	S	NS

(continued)

Table 4.1 (continued)

The Higher-The Crisis-Induced Stress…	United States (Nuclear Alert)	Syria (Lebanon Civil War)	Argentina (Falkland-Malvinas)	United States (Gulf War I)	Iraq (Gulf War I)	Yugoslavia (Kosovo)	NATO (Kosovo)	Iraq (Gulf War II)	United States (Gulf War II)
Information									
H.1	S	NS	S	NS	NS	S	S	MD	NS
H.2	S	S	S	S	NS	S	S	S	S
H.3	S	NS	NT	NS	S	S	NS	MD	S
H.4	S	S	NT	S	S	NS	NS	MD	S
H.5	S	S	NT	S/NS	MD	MD	M	S	NS
H.6	S	S	S	S	S	S	S	MD	S
Consultation									
H.7	S	S	S	S	NS	S	S	MD	S
H.8	S	S	S	NS	MD	NS	S	S	NS
H.9	S	S	S	S	S	S	S	S	S
Decisional Forum									
H.10	S	NS	NS	S	S	S	S	MD	NS
H.11	S	NS	NS	S	NS	NS	S	S	S
H.12	NT	NT	S	NS	NS	S	S	MD	NS
H.13	S	S	NT	S	MD	S	S	MD	NS
H.14	S	NS	NT	S	S	S	S	MD	S
H.15	S	MD	NT	S	NS	S	S	MD	S

(continued)

Table 4.1 (continued)

The Higher- The Crisis- Induced Stress...	United States (Nuclear Alert)	Syria (Lebanon Civil War)	Argentina (Falkland- Malvinas)	United States (Gulf War I)	Iraq (Gulf War I)	Yugoslavia (Kosovo)	NATO (Kosovo)	Iraq (Gulf War II)	United States (Gulf War II)
Alternatives
H.16	NS	NS	NT	NS	S	S	M	MD	S
H.17	NS	NS	S	NS	S	NS	NS	MD	NR
H.18	S	NT	S	NS	S	NS	NS	MD	NR
H.19	NS	NS	S	NS	MD	NS	NS	MD	NS

Source The sources of hypotheses generated by others are as follows: H.2 Paige 1968, 292; H.4 Paige 1968, 295; Milburn 1972, 274; Holsti and George 1975, 281; H.5 March and Simon 1958, 116; H.6 Paige 1972, 47; H.7 Paige 1972, 52; H.8 Holsti 1972, 75; H.9 Hermann 1972, 202–204; H.10 Lentner 1972, 130; H.11 Paige 1968, 281; H.14 Paige 1972, 52; H.19 Holsti and George 1975, 278

Note S supported; *NS* not supported; *S/NS* supported/not supported; *M* mixed findings; *MD* missing data; *NT* not tested; *NR* not relevant

[a] Partly supported
[b] Present throughout the crisis

- So too are two of the six hypotheses on the *decisional forum*, Hypotheses 13 and 14 (17–24 and 18–25, respectively), with moderate support for Hypothesis 15 (14–18).
- The three hypotheses on the *consideration of alternatives* (H.16, H.17, and H.18) are rejected, as I argued elsewhere (Brecher 1993), one of them decisively, and two hypotheses, substantively (7–16, 4–22, and 7–15).
- Most important, the conventional wisdom that *high stress* is *dysfunctional in decision-making* (H.19) is clearly *Not Supported* (5–18), as I discovered in Brecher 1993 (Table 4.2).

Some illustrations of the findings on behavior by states experiencing high stress in a foreign policy crisis highlight their significance.

Table 4.2 Case Studies: Hypothesis Testing—Summary of Findings

S	NS	M	MD	NT	NR	Overall Results
H.1	13	10	2	1	3	1	Neither support nor rejection 13–10
H.2	27	10	1	1	3	1	Strong support 27–0
H.3	10	2	4	2	3	1	Neither support nor rejection 10–10
H.4	21	3	1	2	1	1	Strong support 21–2
H.5a)	20	11	1	4	1		Strong support 20–3
5b)	10	1	2	5	2		Neither support nor rejection 10–11
H.6	25	6	1	2	1		Strong support 25–1
H.7	19	7	1	2	5		Quite strong support 19–6
H.8	20	2	1	1	1		Quite strong support 20–7
H.9	26	12	1	1	2		Strong support 26–2
H.10	16	16	3	3	2		Neither support nor rejection 16–12
H.11	12	9	1	7	1		Neither support nor rejection 12–16
H.12	11	4	1	4	2		Neither support nor rejection 11–9
H.13	17	5	1	4	1		Strong support 17–4
H.14	18	8		2			Strong support 18–5
H.15	14	16		1			Moderate support 14–8
H.16	7	22		3			Rejection 7–16
H.17	4	15		2			Strong rejection 4–22
H.18	7	18					Rejection 7–15
H.19	5						Strong rejection 5–18

Source The sources of hypotheses generated by others are as follows: H.2 Paige 1968, 292; H.4 Paige 1968, 295; Milburn 1972, 274; Holsti and George 1975, 281; H.5 March and Simon 1958, 116; H.6 Paige 1972, 47; H.7 Paige 1972, 52; H.8 Holsti 1972, 75; H.9 Hermann 1972, 202–4; H.10 Lentner 1972, 130; H.11 Paige 1968, 281; H.14 Paige 1972, 52; H.19 Holsti and George 1975, 278

Note S supported; NS not supported; M mixed findings; MD missing data; NT not tested; NR not relevant

The higher the crisis-induced stress, the greater the felt need, and consequent quest, for **information**. *In order to enhance the quality of* **USSR** *decision-making, rather than yielding to premature closure* during the *Prague Spring crisis* in 1968, a steady flow of delegations to and from Moscow funneled a large body of fresh information to the Soviet decision-makers, on the basis of which options were framed and evaluated and choices made. With slight variations, this was the **common information pattern** in **27** of the **29 crises** during the period of highest stress.

The postulate that **consultation** would be *broader and more intense as stress increased*: the **UK** inner cabinet of four consulted the full cabinet, French leaders, and members of the British Commonwealth at the height of the Munich Crisis before making the fateful U.K. decisions concerning Czechoslovakia in 1938; Prime Minister Meir's "Kitchen Cabinet" of four consulted the full **Israel** cabinet of 18 and many others in Israel's 1973 *October-Yom Kippur crisis period*. And President Assad broadened the **Syrian** consultative circle from four to 43 for some crucial decisions relating to its intervention in the *Lebanon civil war* (1975–1976).

There were, as noted, several exceptions: **Italy** in the *Ethiopian [Abyssinian] War* (1935–1936); the **USSR** in the *Berlin Blockade* crisis (1948–1949); the **United States** in the 1958 *Iraq-Lebanon Upheaval*; the **USSR** in the 1968 *Prague Spring* crisis; **Pakistan** in the 1971 *Bangladesh* crisis-war; and **Iraq** in *Gulf War I* (1990–1991). All of these exceptions, other than the United States, were authoritarian regimes, civil or military, and in four cases the regime was dominated by one leader—Mussolini (Italy), Stalin (USSR) Yahya Khan (Pakistan), and Saddam Hussein (Iraq).

A similar *pattern of enlargement* is evident in **decisional forums** during the high-stress crisis period. While President Truman remained the final US decision-maker, ad hoc groups and the National Security Council were used to make many **US** decisions in coping with the 1948–1949 *Berlin Blockade* crisis. In the 1953 *Trieste* crisis, **Italy's** decision-making became more decentralized, with more reliance on Foreign Ministry officials. In **India**, the *emergency committee of the cabinet* emerged as the principal decisional forum at the height of the 1962 China/India border crisis-war. Five of the six exceptions to the broadening of consultations noted earlier apply to the decisional forum as well.

The predominant trait of the crisis period was *extensive search for, and careful evaluation of,* **alternatives**. The **United States**, as noted, considered a *planned withdrawal from Berlin, an armed convoy,* and *the use of nuclear weapons*, apart from the *airlift*, at the height of the Berlin Blockade crisis. The **Soviet Union**, too, exhausted an array of options before resorting to military intervention to crush the Prague Spring: *political pressure, economic incentives, third-party intermediaries,* and *stationing troops near the Czechoslovak capital*. However, there were exceptions in the search for, and consideration of, alternatives, as noted earlier, notably the states that considered only one alternative in their crisis decision process. A very similar pattern of behavior emerges from an aggregate data analysis of the *impact of regime type and issues in 1052 foreign policy crises since the end of World War I*. There is robust evidence that "as issues became… more intense, the behavior of crisis actors as witnessed in the choices of primary crisis management technique became more similar regardless of the type of regime" (Trumbore and Boyer 1999).

In sum, the *evidence* in the 29 foreign policy crises selected for this inquiry *is compelling* on the *first of the two crucial questions posed earlier about coping with high or higher crisis-induced stress:* there was a **widely shared response** *to more severe perceived threat, more time pressure, and perceived higher probability of military hostilities in* the **crisis period of the two central domains of crisis management—the quest for information and the search for, and consideration of, alternatives—despite the wide-ranging diversity in crisis dimensions and crisis attributes..**

This finding may seem counter-intuitive to many, for it has long been regarded as a consensual truth among scholars that racial, cultural, historical, political, ideological, and socio-economic differences must result in different behavior, including state behavior in foreign policy crises. This linkage is undoubtedly correct in some spheres of human activity—but not all.

Despite the cogent and, in some respects, persuasive criticism of Realism from competing interpretations of what moves foreign policy decision-makers and entities to act the way they do, it remains **beyond doubt** that, **throughout history**, from the city-states of Greece and their counterparts in the Chinese, Indian, and Middle East systems of antiquity, to the principalities of Renaissance Italy and early modern Europe, the polyglot empires of the seventeenth to the twentieth centuries, and the new nation-states of the nineteenth and twentieth centuries, *autonomous political entities sought power*, that is, sought to attain enlarged relative power, or to undermine an existing balance of power with rivals, *notwithstanding their racial, cultural, historical, political regime, and/or other differences.*

The discovery of a widely shared **pattern of coping with high stress in foreign policy crises** falls into this category. Stress is a universal phenomenon experienced by all humans under certain conditions. So, too, coping with stress is a universal challenge. Decision-makers of all states need to make choices in situations of complexity and incomplete information. They all attempt to maximize gains and minimize losses, though different cultures may define gains and losses differently. They all seek to enhance "national interests," though the content of those national interests may vary. The evidence uncovered here demonstrates that these **universal** elements in world politics are more significant than **diversity** among state members of the global system.

What is the **explanation** for **the triumph of widely shared elements in coping with crises by states over diversity in the dimensions and attributes of interstate crises?** The answer, it is contended here, lies in the **concept of commonality**. Stress is a shared challenge, an indicator of impending harm and danger. States and political leaders have common traits that outweigh their diversity, especially the need to survive and to minimize harm from external foes. And most foreign policy–national security decision-makers, in coping with crisis-generated stress, act as humans do in all comparable situations of perceived impending harm. In essence, **the commonality of statehood, stress, and human response to expected harm overrides variations among states and their national security decision-makers, and generates a widely shared pattern of coping with foreign policy crises.**..

I turn now to the second specific question posed early in this chapter: **is the impact of high or rising stress on the behavior of foreign policy-national security decision-makers, in interstate crises, negative, neutral, or positive?**

The **quest** for, and **accumulation** of, **knowledge** on the **stress-performance linkage** of states in foreign policy crises has not been free from controversy. Most visible has been the continuing verbal "war" between political psychologists and rational choice theorists. The former assert the innate limitations on rationality, acknowledging, at most, "bounded rationality." The latter assume a capacity for unqualified rational calculus by decision-makers. The difference between the contending views is highlighted by the **inverted U-shaped curve** that relates stress to performance.

Political psychologists, drawing upon the findings of research on **individual** Psychology, claim that, during foreign policy crises, *as in all crises confronting humans*, high or rising stress leads to diminished performance by decision-makers. In contrast, advocates of rational choice claim that stress level correlates with the importance of the task at hand: attentiveness will increase under high stress and enhance performance. Thus the stress-performance link will be at or near the top of the inverted U-shaped curve during the peak phase of stress for decision-makers, that is, the crisis period of a state's foreign policy crisis.

Conventional wisdom among IR scholars on this controversy has been formalized in the last of the 19 hypotheses that were tested above. *High stress is dysfunctional; that is, cognitive and, therefore, decisional performance will be greatly influenced by psychological biases and will deteriorate markedly.* This issue has far-reaching practical implications. Are decision-makers able to read correctly the signs of impending crisis and potential escalation to war? Can they calculate the costs and benefits of alternative courses of action, free from the effects of stress—or other cognitive constraints? Can they search for and process information or search for and consider options unhindered by high stress? Are they able to brake the thrust to violence and the adverse consequences of a spiral effect that can lead the adversaries into the unknown arena of war in an era of proliferating weapons of mass destruction? *In short, can they cope effectively with higher, often much higher-than-normal, value threat, time pressure, and heightened probability of war so as to achieve their goals without horrendous costs to their adversaries, themselves, their neighbors, far-off lands and peoples, and the global commons, that is, the fragile environment for all?*

The classic International Relations scholarly statement on the adverse effects of high and/or escalating stress was Ole Holsti's summation almost 40 years ago.

> A vast body of theory and evidence [from individual psychology] suggests that intense and protracted crises tend to erode rather than enhance... cognitive abilities.

Among the more probable casualties of crises and the accompanying high stress are the very abilities that distinguish men from other species: to establish logical links between present actions and future goals; to search effectively for relevant policy options; to create appropriate responses to unexpected events; to communicate complex ideas; to deal effectively with abstractions; to perceive not only blacks and whites, but also to distinguish them from the many subtle shades of grey that fall in between; to distinguish valid analogies from false ones, and sense from nonsense; and, perhaps, most important of all, to enter into the frame of reference of others.

Holsti concluded "Low-to-moderate stress may facilitate better performance, but high stress degrades it". (1979: 405, 410)

This is a formidable catalog of the assumed high costs of high stress in foreign policy crises and a dismal portrait of human cognitive and decisional abilities. If it is accurate, the ability of decision-makers to manage crises effectively is—and will continue to be—disturbingly deficient. What, then, is **the record in the 29 diverse foreign policy crises** explored in this book?

There was *support for the postulate that high stress will be dysfunctional in three cases*—the behavior of **Hungary** *decision-makers in 1956 (Hungarian Uprising)*, of **Pakistan** *in 1971 (Bangladesh Crisis-War)*, and **Argentina** *in 1982 (Falkland/Malvinas crisis-war)*. In *six other cases, the results are not entirely clear*:

The **Netherlands** *in 1939–1940*, when reliable warnings of a German invasion were disbelieved almost until it occurred, on May 10, 1940, though *not because of high stress but rather the reverse*, leading to a coding of Not Relevant (NR) for Hypothesis 19 in that case;

The **USSR** *in 1948*, when Stalin left Moscow for a 10-week "vacation" in September 1948 during the Berlin Blockade crisis, *not because of high stress, for he coped very well in his determination to avoid* war with what he perceived, correctly, to be a more powerful United States in 1948–1949, leading to a coding of Mixed (M) for that case;

India's Nehru, *at the height of the 1962 China–India crisis-war*, when, perhaps under the impact of high stress, he sought US air cover against a feared Chinese bombardment of Indian cities in eastern India—*though,* *in perspective, this qualifies as a rational response to correctly perceived high threat, rather than as an irrational response to high stress*, leading to a coding of Not Supported (NS) in that case;

Iraq's Saddam Hussein's *behavior in Gulf Wars I and II*, when he misjudged the likely/unlikely USA resort to war, though *there is no evidence that his judgment was the result of high stress*, leading to a coding of Missing Data (MD) in both cases; and

Serbia's Mi*lošević's misjudgment of NATO's likely/unlikely resort to war in 1999*; but, as with Saddam Hussein, there is *no evidence that this was a result of high stress*, thus a coding of Missing Data (MD).

In the other 20 crises, high stress did not impair overall performance.

The evidence that has been cited here regarding the stress-performance link in foreign policy crises (Hypothesis 19) is reinforced by independent concluding assessments of authors of ICB in-depth case studies.

- **United States**, in the 1948–1949 *Berlin Blockade* crisis: "it is reasonably clear from the actual historical record... that stress can have positive effects which outweigh the negative effects on the performance of selected cognitive and decision-making tasks.... On the whole, the American policy-makers stood up to stress well and coped fairly effectively and even creatively with the acute dilemmas posed by the Soviet ground blockade... [It] was in essence a rational and calculated process of decision-making" (Shlaim 1983: 422).
- **Italy**, in the 1953 *Trieste II* crisis: "crisis actually enlarged the perceived range of alternatives and led to a relatively more thorough and imaginative search, as well as to a timely re-evaluation of choice in light of new information... It was precisely during the period of higher stress (October–November 1953)... that Italian decision-makers operated at their best.... Rising stress did not lead to group think... There were no clear instances of premature closure... The increase in stress... cannot be said to have disrupted performance in any significant way" (Croci 1991: 330, 439–440).
- **Zambia**, in *Rhodesia's 1965–1966 UDI* crisis: "the evidence does suggest that crisis-induced stress accounted for some impairment in

the cognitive abilities of decision makers in Zambia. Nevertheless, the degree of deterioration was nothing like as catastrophic as implied in Ole Holsti's catalog... On the contrary, the level of cognitive performance... was commendably high" (Anglin 1994: 326–327).
- **Syria,** in the 1975–1976 *Lebanon Civil War* crisis: three of the four Syria decisions in the crisis period were "rational choice decisions... the outcome of lengthy and exhaustive meetings in which all the high-level political interests participated" (Dawisha 1980: 182).

In light of these findings, based on in-depth studies of many crises, from different cultures, regions, system structures, power and economic levels, political regimes, and other dimensions of crisis, **this crucial hypothesis would seem to be seriously flawed**. Holsti and George (1975) sensed that their finding of dysfunctional behavior by international crisis decision-makers under high stress, *based solely upon the US experience*, might not have universal experience and might have "more limited applicability for other nations." That surmise is correct. More significantly, their finding on the stress-performance linkage is not supported by the experience of many developed states as well, including the **United Kingdom** in the 1938 *Munich* crisis, **Italy** over *Trieste* (1953), the **USSR** in the *Prague Spring* crisis (1968), and *6 of the 8 US cases in the group of 29* (it was supported in only one US case, *Dominican Intervention* (1965), and it was not tested for US behavior in the *Berlin Wall* crisis). Overall, **this pivotal hypothesis was supported in 5 cases, not supported in 19.**

What more do these findings reveal on **coping with high or escalating international crisis-induced stress**? First, there is now powerful evidence in support of the following **behavior by decision-makers** from diverse cultural and geographic settings, with variations in power, economic development, size, etc.

- **Cognitive dimension**: decision-makers feel a *greater need for information and enlarge their quest* accordingly, and they supplement such information with a growing reliance on personal past experience as a guide to choice among options.
- **Information processing**: their *search for information becomes more active*, and, as a crisis escalates, information moves swiftly to the senior decision-makers, severely weakening the role of bureaucrats in the decisional process.

- **Consultation**: the *scope of consultation grows, not declines*, under the impact of increasing stress in most foreign policy crises. Decision-makers seek extraordinary channels to communicate bids to adversaries in the negotiation process during an escalating crisis, and they communicate more with allies, adversaries, and other international actors.
- **Decisional forum**: decision-makers feel a *greater need for face-to-face proximity* as stress grows, and, as crisis escalates, they feel a greater need for effective leadership from the principal decision-maker(s).
- More important for an understanding of coping with international crisis-induced high or escalating stress is a cluster of *negative* findings about **Alternatives:**
- Increasing time pressure leads to a *less careful evaluation of options—it does not*;
Decision-making suffers from *premature closure*, before all alternatives are carefully assessed and ranked—*it does not*;
Decisions are reached with an *inadequate assessment of consequences—they are not*, and the most compelling negative finding:
High stress is dysfunctional for cognitive performance and, therefore, the decisional process as well—*it is not*.

All of these findings are qualitatively robust. They point inexorably to the existence of discernible patterns in the behavior of decision-makers during foreign policy and international crises relating to security. In fact, there is an inner logic to the process in which crises erupt, escalate, wind down, and terminate.

To conclude on the core questions posed at the beginning of this chapter, with the **two central findings** from the 29 in-depth case studies of foreign policy crises:

1. In contrast with the findings from *individual psychology*, **high stress does not have a negative effect on the quality of decision-making in foreign policy crises; in fact, the impact is the reverse.**
2. There was a **common pattern of coping with international crisis-generated high or rising stress, across regions, time, system structures, power levels, economic levels, types of regime, and other dimensions.**

The reason is that stress is a shared challenge, an indicator of impending harm and danger. States have common traits that outweigh their diversity, especially the need to survive and to minimize harm from external foes. Foreign policy-national security decision-makers, in coping with crisis-generated stress, act as humans do in comparable situations of perceived impending harm. In essence, the *commonality of statehood, stress, and human response to expected harm overrides variations among specific states and generates a widely shared pattern of coping in a foreign policy crisis.*

These findings *compel a fundamental rethinking about how states cope with foreign policy crises, that is, about crisis management* in world politics.

TEST OF NEO-REALISM: EVIDENCE FROM 29 CRISES

The earliest formulation of the Realist paradigm for International Relations can be traced to the internecine strife of the Greek city-state and Indian princely state systems of antiquity (by *Thucydides* and *Kautilya*, respectively). It was enriched by several classical Western philosophers, notably *Machiavelli, Hobbes,* and *Rousseau*. Classical Realism continued to be pre-eminent in the first half of the twentieth century, through the writings of *Niebuhr* 1932, *Carr* 1939, 1946, *Wolfers* 1940, *Spykman* 1942, *Morgenthau* 1946, 1948, *Wight* 1946, and others. Several alternative paradigms have emerged since the 1970s, all challenging Realism on theoretical and empirical grounds, notably neo-institutionalism, critical theory, constructivism, and feminism.

The most recent important variant of Realism, neo-(structural) Realism (*Waltz* 1979, *Gilpin* 1981, and *Mearsheimer* 2001), identified a causal relationship between the structure of the international system and the unfolding of world politics, including the behavior of its member-states. This fundamental postulate of neo-Realism was examined in my International Political Earthquakes, 2008, Chap. 12, through a rigorous test of its core thesis. This test focused on the *behavior of crisis actors*, that is, states whose decision-makers identify a foreign policy crisis for their state and confront the value threat, time pressure, and higher-than-normal expectation of war that accompany such a political earthquake. The *logical underpinning of the test* was that a discovery of *substantive differences in the patterns of crisis behavior during the four structural eras—multipolarity* (late 1918–September 1945), *bipolarity* (late September 1945–end 1962), *bipolycentrism* (1963–1989), and *unipolycentrism* (1990 continuing) *would indicate strong support for the neo-Realist view that structure shapes world politics, as well as the foreign policy–security behavior of states*, its principal actors. However, should an inquiry into the structure–behavior link find *either no or minor differences in the patterns of crisis behavior during the four structural eras, it would seriously undermine the claim of neo-Realism to theoretical primacy*. What does the evidence reveal?

Evidence from 29 Cases

First, as noted above, the most prominent trait of *crisis dimensions*—geography, time, power level, economic development, and political régime, among others—and of *crisis attributes*—trigger, triggering entity, attitudinal prism and values, etc.,—is *diversity*. Moreover, diversity encompasses both the entire period of this inquiry, from late 1918 to 2017, as well as the four structures of the international system since the end of World War I: *there are no distinct patterns of crisis dimensions and crisis attributes among the four structures; rather, diversity is evident* within *multipolarity, bipolarity, bipolycentrism,* and *unipolycentrism*.

The more significant test of the neo-Realist thesis is the evidence on how crisis actors (states) coped with higher perceived threat, time pressure, and likelihood of war, that is, crisis behavior. The *evidence* on this test is *incontrovertible:* for *all four coping mechanisms* and processes, noted in the above discussion, there was **support for 10 hypotheses and, as postulated, disconfirmation of 4 hypotheses, that is, 14 of 19 hypotheses** generated by **other studies of crisis behavior.**

The extent of support for most hypotheses on many aspects of behavior ranges from *strong to very strong*, in a group of 29 crisis actors in all four system structures. Some of these hypotheses are:

Information
 The higher the crisis-induced stress,
 The *greater the felt need, and quest, for information, 27–0*;
 The *greater the reliance on past experience, 21–2;*
 The *more active the search for information, 20–3;*
 The more *information will be transmitted to senior decision-makers, 25–1.*

Consultation:
  The longer the crisis decision time,
  The greater the consultation outside the core decisional unit, 19–6;
  The greater the reliance on extraordinary channels of communication, 19–8;
  The higher the rate of communication with international actors, 26–2;

Decisional Forum:
  The higher the crisis-induced stress,
  The greater the felt need for face-to-face proximity among decision-makers, 17–4;
  The greater the felt need for effective leadership within the decisional unit, 18–5;

Alternatives:
  The higher the crisis-induced stress, the less careful the evaluation of alternatives, rejected by 16–7, as I argued;
  The shorter the crisis decision time, the greater the tendency to premature closure, rejected by 22–4, as I argued;
  The shorter the crisis decision time, the more likely decisions will be made with inadequate assessment of consequences, rejected by 15–7, as I argued;

Stress:
  High stress is dysfunctional, cognitive and decisional performance will deteriorate markedly, rejected by 19–5, as I argued.

  In sum, 13 of the 19 tested hypotheses by other scholars are clearly supported (or clearly rejected, as I argued), some strongly, others very strongly.

Even more significant, in the context of the *neo-Realist theory that structure determines external state behavior, as well as world politics, more generally, there is no discernible pattern of structural differentiation in these findings:* that is, *all four system structures in the near-century (late 1918-end of 2017 are amply represented in the majority, often decisive, support for, or postulated rejection of, these 13 hypotheses.* Moreover, the *absence of any clear structural differentiation is also evident in the cases that do not support the hypotheses.* Suffice it to illustrate the *multi-structure distribution of the 29 cases for the 19 hypotheses* by noting the system structure identity of non-support cases for 4 hypotheses with a large majority support.

Hypothesis 7 *the longer the crisis decision time, the greater the consultation outside the core decisional unit*—Supported, 19 cases, Not Supported, 6 cases; (there was missing data for 2 cases, and 2 cases were not tested). The non-support cases comprise the following:

Italy (Ethiopian [Abyssinian] War 1935–1936) multipolarity, hereafter *M*;
USSR (Berlin Blockade 1948–1949) bipolarity, hereafter *B*;
USA (Iraq-Lebanon Upheaval 1958) B;
USSR (Prague Spring 1968) bipolycentrism, hereafter *Bipol*;
Pakistan (Bangladesh War 1971) Bipol;
Iraq (Gulf War I 1990–1991) unipolycentrism, hereafter *U*.
In sum, the six non-supporting cases occurred in all four system structures.

Hypothesis 8 *the longer the crisis decision time, the greater the reliance on extraordinary channels of communication*—Supported, 19 cases, Not Supported, 8 cases; (there was missing data for 1 case, and 1 case was not tested). The non-support cases comprise the following:

Italy (Ethiopian [Abyssinian] War 1935–1936) M;
USSR (Berlin Blockade 1948–1949) B,
Italy (Trieste II 1953) B,
Guatemala (Guatemala 1953–1954) B,
India (Bangladesh War 1971) Bipol,
USA (Gulf War I 1990–1991) U,
Yugoslavia (Kosovo 1998–1999) U, and
USA (Gulf War II 2002–2003) U.
In sum, the eight non-supporting cases occurred in all four system structures.

Hypothesis 14 *the longer the crisis decision time, the greater the felt need for effective leadership within the decisional unit*—Supported, 18 cases, Not Supported, five cases; (there was missing data for 4 cases, and two cases were not tested). The non-support cases comprise the following:

Ethiopia *(Ethiopian [Abyssinian] War 1935–1936) M*;
Italy *(Trieste II 1953) B*;
USA *(Dominican Intervention 1965) Bipol*,
Pakistan *(Bangladesh War 1971) Bipol*, and
Syria *(Lebanon Civil War 1975–1976) Bipol*.
In sum, the five non-supporting cases occurred in three system structures.

Hypothesis 19 *High stress is dysfunctional; that is, cognitive and, therefore, decisional performance...will deteriorate markedly*—Supported, five cases, Not Supported, 19 cases; (there were missing data for 2 cases, 1 case had mixed findings, 1 case was not tested, and 1 case was not relevant). The support cases comprise the following:

Guatemala (Guatemala 1953–1954) B,
Hungary (Hungarian Uprising 1956) B,
USA (Dominican Intervention 1965) Bipol,
Pakistan (Bangladesh War 1971) Bipol, and
Argentina (Falkland/Malvinas 1982) Bipol.
In sum, the five supporting cases occurred in two system structures.

The *central finding* from this analysis is clear. The *Realist theory* that system structure determines state behavior in world politics *does not accord with reality, certainly not the reality of foreign policy crisis behavior by states*. The fact that the foreign policy crisis behavior of states from all system structures exhibits non-support for many hypotheses indicates that *crisis behavior is the outcome of several, probably multiple, pressures, and inducements*, of which the *structure of the international system is, at most, one source*, and not necessarily the most influential cause of crisis behavior.

In sum, the most important finding from in-depth research on the stress-behavior relationship is that two long-held beliefs about *state behavior during international crises are fundamentally flawed:*

first, that **high stress seriously undermines the quality of foreign policy-national security decision-making** and

second, that *the great diversity of crises and crisis actors leads to great diversity* in behavior, *not to a shared pattern in crisis management.*
Both of these conventional views, derived from the evidence on one state, the USA, are seriously undermined by the multiple qualitative case study findings above.
(Brecher, *International Political Earthquakes* (2008))

CHAPTER 5

Theory III: Interstate Conflicts

The ICB concept, *Protracted Conflict*, was introduced 25 years ago, in Brecher, *Crises in World Politics: Theory and Reality* (1993, 5, 7–8, 59, 71–73, 145–146, 543–545), building on a pioneering definition by Azar (1978). [The conflict concept was further developed in Brecher and Wilkenfeld, *A Study of Crisis* (1997, 5–6, 34–35, 65–66, 659–660, 788–792. 820–834, 837–838), and in Brecher, *International Political Earthquakes* (2008, 6–7, 13–18, 28–35, 40–41, 264–267). It was treated most extensively in Brecher, *The World of Protracted Conflicts* (2016 L, *passim*)]. In terms of *geographic scope*, conflict is one of five levels of the concept, CONFLICT, in descending order: *global system conflict, regional sub-system conflict, interstate protracted conflict, non-state ethnic, religious, racial, tribal group conflict, and domestic-internal conflict*. As indicated most recently, "there are three necessary conditions of a protracted conflict: at least three interstate crises between the same principal conflict adversaries; *perceptions* by their decision-makers of a higher-than-normal threat to one or more *basic values, finite time* for response, and the higher-than-normal *likelihood of involvement in military hostilities* before the value threat is overcome; and minimal *duration* of *ten years*" (Brecher 2016 L. 7). "All protracted conflicts are lengthy, some of them several decades or more. All have fluctuated in intensity: many have moved from war to partial accommodation and back to violence (e.g., *India and Pakistan since 1947*); others have been characterized by continuous war, but of varying severity (e.g., Vietnam War 1946–1975). All have aroused intense animosities, with spillover to a broad spectrum of issues. And conflict termination has yet to occur in many of them" (Brecher and Wilkenfeld 1997, 5) Fig. 5.1.

CONFLICT RESOLUTION MODEL

Among the 33 protracted conflicts that have been active during most or part of the past century [late 1918–2017], 20 have been resolved, while 13 persist, as noted above. Why did some end and others persist well into the twenty-first century? More generally, can one identify, a priori, the conditions most likely to lead to conflict *resolution*, the conceptual counterpart to the conditions most likely to generate *onset* and *persistence* of an interstate conflict? Other related dimensions of these conflicts demand attention, notably which *Condition(s)* or cluster of Conditions can be identified as the most significant *Basic Cause(s)* of conflict Termination? Formally, the answer is to be found in a Model designed to explain the most likely conditions for resolution of interstate conflicts, of which 60% since the end of World War I have been characterized by *violence* that ranges from *minor clashes* to *serious clashes* to full-scale *war*.

BASIC CAUSES OF CONFLICT RESOLUTION

This model postulates that there are *six basic causes* of *Conflict Resolution*. One is a collective feeling of **Exhaustion** by a substantial proportion of the population of at least one of the conflict principal adversaries. Another is a qualitative change in the **Balance of Capability**, human and material, between-among the principal adversaries. A third Basic Cause is **Domestic Pressure(s)** on the principal adversaries in favor of conflict termination. A fourth is **External Pressure(s)** on the principal adversaries to pursue the objective of conflict resolution in good faith. A fifth Basic Cause is a discernible **Reduction in Discordant Objectives** of the principal adversaries. And a sixth is a qualitative **Decline in Conflict-Sustaining Acts** *by the principal adversaries.* All of these Conditions (Basic Causes) constitute the *Independent Variables* of the **Conflict Resolution Model**.

An additional cause—most likely Condition—of conflict resolution, acting as an *Intervening Variable* in the *Conflict Resolution Model*, is a **Perceptual Calculus** by the decision-maker(s) of the principal

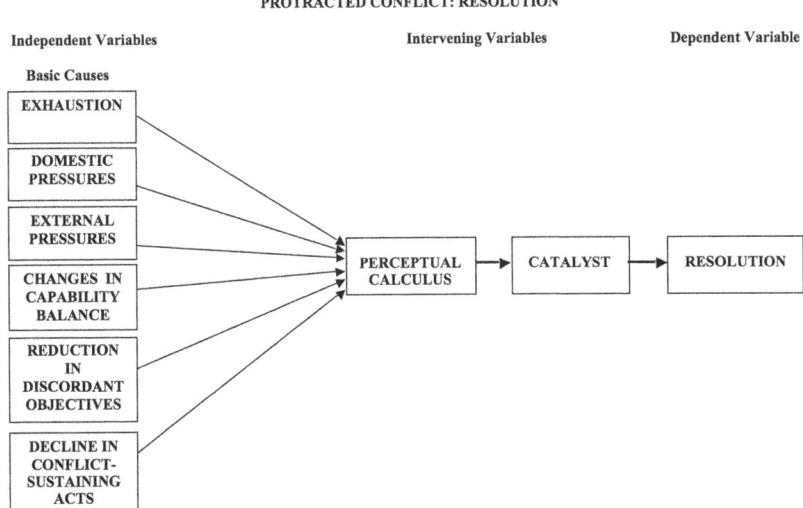

Fig. 5.1 Conflict Resolution Model

adversaries of some, most or all of these Conditions: intolerable *exhaustion*; an unfavorable *capability balance* at the time conflict resolution is being assessed, along with negative future prospects of that balance; awareness of strong *domestic* and *external pressures* in favor of conflict termination; of substantive *reduction in discordant objectives* by the adversaries; and of a substantive *decline in their Conflict-Sustaining Acts*.

Each of these *Causes* is a *sufficient condition* for conflict resolution. None is a *necessary condition*. The model also postulates that the *likelihood of conflict resolution increases with an increase in the number of favorable conditions present at the time* the *conflict termination option is evaluated by decision-makers* of the conflict's principal adversaries. When *many* of these *causal conditions are present, termination of an interstate protracted conflict is highly likely*, and *when all favorable conditions are present*, conflict *resolution is virtually certain to occur*. The *causal links between likely Conditions and likelihood of conflict resolution* are presented in Fig. 5.1. The rationale of this causal chain is presented in the following discussion.

Exhaustion

Two types of exhaustion may be experienced by the population of protracted conflict actors, *physical* and *psychological*. The former derives from *intolerable high casualties* and/or *insufferable material destruction* caused by enemy bombing or shelling, or by weapons of mass destruction, in long duration wars or massive single occurrences of violence. Physical exhaustion may also result from *deprivation*—shortage of edible food and potable water, damage to living quarters and schools, and/or the cumulative effects of long-term, high unemployment, notably the drastic reduction in income. The second type, psychological exhaustion, may result from a conflict of uncertain duration, with no assurance of relief in a lengthy conflict, accentuated by frequent or persistent outbursts of violence between the principal adversaries. Exhaustion may derive from either *source* or from both. It may be experienced by the mass public of one or more conflict adversaries or by their political and military elites and/or attentive publics, or by their entire population. Exhaustion may penetrate only one or both, possibly multiple, adversaries in an interstate protracted conflict.

A *quantitative measurement* of the *effect of collective exhaustion* is elusive. However, a *qualitative assessment* of the *cause–effect linkage between exhaustion and the likelihood of protracted conflict resolution* is logically plausible: the *higher the casualties*, the *greater the material damage*, and/or the *longer the period of collective and individual pain* experienced by the population of principal adversaries during an interstate protracted conflict, the more likely will conflict termination occur. Moreover, when *both types of exhaustion, physical* and *psychological*, are operating to generate collective fatigue in one adversary, the impact of exhaustion on the likelihood of conflict resolution will be *great*. *It will be greater* when *both the mass public and elites of one principal adversary* are affected by exhaustion, and *greatest* when *all principal adversaries* are experiencing acute exhaustion. In the broadest formulation of this cause–effect linkage, the *likelihood of interstate protracted conflict resolution will be great when all types and sources of exhaustion are experienced by all principal adversaries, simultaneously*. These propositions will be tested by the evidence from selective interstate conflicts that have been active during the past century.

CAPABILITY BALANCE

In quest of a priori explanatory power regarding the conditions most likely to lead to resolution of an interstate protracted conflict, a second basic cause is the *Balance of Capability* between-among the principal conflict adversaries. In performing the role of an independent [causal] variable, *Capability* comprises several dimensions. One is effective or ineffective *political leadership* by a state's decision-maker(s), that is, the ability or inability of leaders to mobilize strong support from their elites and attentive and mass publics for their choice of one or more policy options that can cope successfully with the challenge(s) and/or threat(s) posed by a competing principal adversary or adversaries during a protracted conflict. Political leaders, who are *endowed with strong support* by their elites and attentive and mass publics, and who perceive that their state will be unlikely to achieve core goals by prolonging a protracted conflict—because of a *high level* of collective *exhaustion* among its population, higher than that of its principal adversary, and/or because of a *qualitative decline* in their state's *material capability*, relative to that of its adversary—would be able, nonetheless, to initiate or participate in a process of accommodation with their principal adversary(ies) designed to attain mutually acceptable resolution. Conversely, a *weak political leadership*, which recognizes or perceives a deeper *exhaustion* among its population than that of its principal adversary, and an adverse *balance of capability* with that adversary, with little or no prospect of reversing these basic conditions within their conflict, will be more likely to accept conflict resolution, even with imposed major concessions to the adversary. In essence, the presence of *effective or ineffective, strong or weak political leadership* in one or both (all) of the principal adversaries is *an important component of the causal variable, Balance of Capability*, in explaining if, when—and what type of—conflict resolution is most likely to occur. This proposition, too, will be tested against the evidence on conflict resolution to be presented in the following chapter.

The same reasoning applies to the *military* component of the *Capability* variable. This refers to the ability–inability of political and military leaders to mobilize a state's human and material resources, notably the *size, level of preparedness,* and *commitment* of its *armed forces,* and the *volume* and *quality* of its *military technology* and *weapon systems,* that would be able to achieve basic objectives and defend core interests if violence erupts in the relationship with one or more principal adversaries. The military dimension of Capability also includes the *alliance potential* of state actors during a protracted conflict; that is, the presence or absence of a reliable ally (allies) and/or national security patron(s), for one or both (or all) principal adversaries, would also be incorporated into an assessment of the *Capability Balance* in a specific interstate conflict.

This reasoning also applies to the *economic* dimension of *Capability*, which combines *material* and *human* aspects: the availability of, or reliable access to, ample *natural resources*, and a *developed economic structure*, or lack thereof; the presence or absence of a well-trained *labor force* capable of utilizing the technology of a twentieth and twenty-first century industrial and agricultural economy; with or without a skilled *economic leadership* able to manage a state's economy effectively, to sustain its material capability, and thereby contribute to a state's security in both peace and war phases of an interstate conflict. Here too the conflict resolution model postulates that successful leadership in the economic domain will be more likely to achieve a favorable resolution of its external conflict than an ineffective display of economic management.

For all three components of a state's *Capability—political, military, and economic*—there are two relevant aspects for an analysis of the most likely conditions of conflict resolution. One is the presence of *relative equality or inequality between the principal adversaries in a specific protracted conflict, not the absolute level* of sophistication in the human and material elements of Capability in one conflict, that is, *symmetric or asymmetric* conditions within a specific conflict, not its Balance of Capability compared with the Capability Balance in other protracted conflicts. For example, the relevant comparison in exploring the conditions that made conflict resolution likely in the *Chad/Libya* conflict (1971–1994) was the Balance of Capability *between the two principal adversaries in that protracted conflict*, Chad and Libya, in 1994, not the overall level of Capability—political, military and economic—in the *Chad/Libya* conflict, compared with the overall level of Capability in the *USA/USSR* conflict or the *India/Pakistan* conflict.

The second relevant aspect of Capability as a causal variable that can lead to, or delay, or influence the type and content of, conflict resolution is the presence or absence of *deterioration in the Capability Balance* between the principal adversaries *during* a specific conflict. States that are adversaries in an interstate protracted conflict, like other political, military, and economic organizations, experience change, including deterioration in the quality and effectiveness of their political, military, and/or economic leaders, and/or the volume, technological quality and productivity of their civilian and military economies. When one conflict principal adversary experiences a *qualitative relative decline* in one or more dimensions of *Capability*, the *resolution* of its protracted conflict, whether or not accompanied by violence, will most likely occur in the form of a *victory-defeat outcome*. By contrast, the *absence of a qualitative decline in Capability*, including *leadership of any principal adversary* and *its material productivity*, will most likely lead to *conflict persistence* or a *shared-benefit conflict termination* for the adversaries; that is, if conflict resolution occurs in a condition of stable leadership in all the principal adversaries and relative equality in their material component of Capability, the *basic cause(s)* of conflict resolution will be *one or more* of the other independent (causal) variables specified in the conflict resolution model, namely, collective *exhaustion, domestic,* and/or *external pressures on the adversaries* to seek a peaceful resolution of their protracted conflict, or a *reduction in discordant objectives*, or a *decline in conflict-sustaining acts* by the principal adversaries.

Domestic Pressures

In all states, persons and/or institutions that are authorized to frame and conduct policy toward all other members of the global system are the object of pressures emanating from their domestic political system, among many other sources. The *volume, form, intensity,* and *impact* of domestic pressures will vary greatly, from the *minimal number* of *transparent* acts of pressure, of *low intensity*, and *modest impact*, in states with authoritarian regimes, both Left (e.g., USSR) and Right (e.g., Nazi Germany), to a *large, continuing flow* of mostly unconcealed *transparent* acts from a *multitude* of interest groups, many of *high intensity*, with *considerable impact* on decision-makers, in states with democratic regimes (e.g., UK and USA). In no state among the 110 states that played a role as a principal adversary in one or more interstate protracted conflicts during the time frame of this inquiry (late 1918–2017), were decision-makers on issues relating to an interstate protracted conflict immune from domestic system pressures.

The *forms* of *domestic pressure* range from *oral* and *written communications* by respected individuals and organizations, and governmental leaders and institutions [polite pressure], to public, often angry and violent, demonstrations by dissenting individuals, groups and institutions, designed to thwart a decision or act on a divisive issue by persons or governmental bodies [drastic pressure], or designed to prevent or at least undermine the legitimacy of an act by the demonstrators as a violation of some national or international norm. Some dramatic acts of domestic pressure exerted a profound influence on policy and decisions relating to, and generating, the behavior of a principal adversary during an interstate protracted conflict: a notable example was the effect of cumulative anti-Vietnam War demonstrations in the United States, in the mid-late 1960s, on the Johnson Administration's fundamental shift in policy in 1968, replacing the goal of total military victory over North Vietnam to a serious attempt to negotiate a compromise peace.

A thorough discussion of *domestic system pressures* is beyond the scope of this presentation of the Conflict Resolution Model. Further examples of the effect of these pressures were cited in case studies, testing this model with the evidence from a selection of conflicts that were active during the near-century, late 1918–2016 (Brecher 2016 L). Suffice it for this conceptual exploration of the conditions most likely to lead to resolution of interstate protracted conflicts to note that pressures emanating from a principal adversary's domestic political system tend to be *spasmodic* and *highly visible* only in conflicts in which at least one of the principal adversaries epitomizes a democratic political system, and even within this context, only when the mass public within states attached to this political system becomes aroused and angry over a highly controversial specific decision or policy by their political leaders that stimulates an act of 'drastic pressure.' Thus the influence of *Domestic Pressures* as a causal variable in the conflict resolution model is much less evident and less significant than the role of *Collective Exhaustion* and the *Balance of Capability* in contributing to a 'state of mind' among principal conflict adversaries that, at certain points during a protracted conflict, take an initiative to pursue conflict resolution or to accept such a proposal, emanating from the hostile adversary, a well-wishing patron, ally, or empathetic intermediary, as a welcome outcome. [The proposition that Collective Exhaustion and a favorable Balance of Capability will be more significant than Domestic Pressures in a decision process whether or not to initiate, or to welcome, a proposal to pursue the path of conflict resolution, will also be tested against the evidence of conflicts that have been active since the end of World War I.]

EXTERNAL PRESSURES

Principal adversaries in interstate protracted conflicts, like all states, are members of the global system and, most of them, one or more regional and sub-regional systems. These interactions—economic, political, military, cultural, and other—provide both opportunities and settings for influencing the behavior of one or more conflict adversaries, through an array of *forms of external pressures*. They may be *active or passive*, or both. They may be communicated *verbally* or by *tangible acts, supportive or hostile*. They may be directed to government institutions and/or officials, *or* to one or more economic, political, cultural, religious, or social *groups within a neighboring state or a more distant member of a sub-system* in which the initiator of pressure and its target state(s) share membership. Pressure may or may not be effective in influencing policy choices and actions by the target(s), that is, one or more principal conflict adversaries.

Pressures on conflict adversaries exist in all interstate systems, as an integral part of the relations among their members. However, the *volume* and *scope* of external pressures on conflict adversaries in the twentieth and early twenty-first centuries have been more extensive than in earlier historical eras because of the technological and communications transformations from antiquity and early modern epochs to the contemporary global system. To the traditional *means of communication* among states—visits by officials from State A to their counterpart in a target state and written documents laboriously transported, sometimes for days or longer—have been added an *array of techniques*, via telephone, telegram and fax, instant internet communication, and for non-governmental sources of pressure, daily, weekly, monthly newspapers, social networks, blogs, videos and photographs of public demonstrations, in favor of, or hostile to, proposed legislation or acts by a conflict adversary.

In the inter-World War era, and especially since the end of WWII, the *multiple sources of external pressures on conflict adversaries have been, and continue to be, vast, a myriad of institutions and societal groups, and states that generate and transmit, often instantly, pressure on conflict adversaries*, including (often unequivocal) demands for conciliatory acts designed to facilitate conflict resolution. Notable, among a formidable list of *international institutions* at the global system level which have attempted to exert pressure on protracted conflict adversaries, are the League of Nations Council and Assembly (1920–1939, formally, to 1946); the United Nations (since 1946), with an array of institutions—the Security

Council, General Assembly, and a myriad of specialized agencies—the International Monetary Fund (IMF), World Bank (IBRD), International Atomic Energy Agency (IAEA), and economic commissions for all regions; military organizations, e.g., NATO; multi-purpose regional organizations, e.g., the European Union (EU), cultural, and educational organizations, e.g., UNESCO; and judicial bodies, the International Court of Justice (ICJ). Many states, too, have exerted pressure on conflict adversaries, especially two inter-World War major powers, France and the UK, and the major powers during most of the period since the end of WWII, the USA, USSR, UK, France, and China. Such pressure has not always been successful, but conflict adversaries have often been unable to resist these external attempts by international organizations, more powerful states and the media in those states, to achieve resolution of conflicts by less powerful states. Because of the unequal distribution of power within the global and regional systems, it is hypothesized that, among external sources of pressure for conflict resolution, major powers that attempt to influence conflict adversaries to pursue conflict resolution will be more successful than pressure emanating from international organizations or non-state interest groups.

Reduction in Discordant Objectives

In the **Conflict Resolution Model**, the *continued presence* of one or more of the four major Discordant Objectives of adversarial states—over *Territory, Power, Ideology,* and/or *Material* (Economic) Benefit—would be a serious obstacle to Conflict Resolution; that is, the continuance of disputes over any of these discordant issue-areas and issues, and even more an increase in the scope and intensity of disagreements among conflict adversaries makes the task of conflict resolution more difficult and more distant, for both adversaries and third-party mediators. Conversely, the reduction of discordant objectives by the principal adversaries is a likely condition of Conflict Resolution: the reason for this crucial causal role of the *reduction in discordant objectives* among states for the attainment of interstate conflict resolution is the *centrality* of these four issues and issue-areas.

Among these discordant issues, the preoccupation with Territory, in its multiple manifestations, looms very large in the behavior of virtually all states in the post-World War I global system, as in all known past interstate systems. The overall reason is that Territory is the indispensable pre-condition of statehood. There are several strands of interstate discordance, including active disputes over territory. One is that the acquisition of territory is necessary for the attainment of integrity by a state. Another is the substantive and symbolic value attached to regaining ownership and control over 'lost territory': when both, more so, all, principal adversaries identify the same territory as 'lost,' the impact of that discordance is intensified to the point that the reduction of that discordance is essential, though not necessarily sufficient for conflict resolution by states. Moreover, the possession of territory is the foundation of a state's quest for national security. Territory is also vital because it is necessary for access to raw materials, many of which are essential for economic development. Thus, the acquisition of territory, including additional territory, is justified by states on several grounds, including historical links, the quest to regain 'lost' territory, shared ethnicity with the population of disputed territory, and the needs of national security. Not all disputes and claims over territory generate violence, though it often accompanies such discord.

Interstate competition for more *power* to achieve a state's goals, including the struggle for influence on the *behavior* of other states, also generates discordant objectives, contributing further obstacles to conflict resolution. Specifically, the attempt to change an existing balance of power with a rival state serves as an obstacle to conflict reduction or resolution. Moreover, the quest for more power by a state, whether by its own efforts to enlarge its military capability, both its armed forces and its weapon systems, is often rationalized as necessary to cope with grave threats by rivals, including threats to existence of both statehood and populations. As with discord over territory, the reduction of power rivalries, especially attempts to change an existing power balance between states, is an important requisite for conflict resolution.

The same pattern of dispute, tension, conflict, and often, violence is evident in situations of discordant objectives between adversaries arising from competing *Ideologies*, notably among Communism, Democracy, Fascism, Islamism, Nationalisms, etc. Discord driven by competing ideas on optimal economic and political systems may be important sources of discordant objectives on their own, or they reinforce discords on objectives driven by rivalries over territory, power, or material benefits. They may be modest sources of discord, but they are unlikely to be irrelevant. As such, the reduction of interstate discord over *territory* or the *distribution of power among states* is a vital task in the pursuit of paths to conflict resolution.

This observation applies to discordant objectives over *Material Benefits* as well. Discordance may occur on the terms for direct material benefits, notably financial aid by affluent to needy states and foreign investment in developing economies, access to valuable natural resources in developing economies, or for long-term benefits related to economic development—technological and organizational, including access to vital interstate waterways. Although economic disputes are less prone to violence, it is not unknown in conflicts which include competition over material issues.

In sum, the significance of reduced discordant objectives among states for the resolution of interstate conflicts derives from the reality that, notwithstanding the impressive growth in the institutions, rules and norms designed to regulate the relations among states in the twentieth and early twenty-first centuries, states retain a decisive degree of autonomy in their behavior, especially in the military-security issue-area of international relations, where interstate protracted conflicts are located.

Reduction in Conflict-Sustaining Acts (CSAs)

Hostile acts by principal adversaries in a protracted conflict have been grouped into four types, namely *political hostility, violence, economic discrimination,* and *verbal hostility-propaganda*. They all share the same attribute of hostility to the rival adversary(ies). Moreover, as with *discordant objectives, conflict-sustaining acts* (CSAs) are part of the *causal chain* in the Resolution Model. The continuance of conflict-sustaining acts, whether political, violent, economic, or verbal, are all *hostile* acts, directed at the adversary(ies), that implement hostile decisions, thereby helping to *sustain* their conflict. In sharp contrast, a *reduction* in conflict-sustaining acts by a conflict actor toward its adversary would be perceived by 'the other' as a positive signal, thereby contributing to a process of accommodation between adversaries, which is likely to enhance the likelihood of *conflict resolution*.

To recall the role of CSAs in the **Resolution Model** causal chain, six Basic Causes were specified as the **Independent** or **Causal Variables**. The content of these Basic Causes is filtered through a **Perceptual Calculus** by decision-makers of the principal adversaries, one of two **Intervening Variables** in this Model. That Calculus proceeds to the **Catalyst**, the second intervening variable, which takes the crucial form of a *qualitative reduction* in the volume and intensity of the four types of Conflict-Sustaining Acts specified above. Performing the function of a trigger mechanism, that decline in CSAs is expected to increase significantly the process of accommodation by the principal adversaries that will more likely culminate in **Conflict Resolution**.

Perceptual Calculus

Policy toward a conflict adversary and decisions on a core issue of potentially great significance for both (all) of the principal adversaries—to sustain, even to intensify, their conflict, or to welcome an opportunity for conflict termination, even actively to encourage a process designed to culminate in conflict resolution—will also be influenced by the **Perceptual Calculus** of decision-makers, an *intervening variable* in the Conflict Resolution Model.

What do they *perceive* to be the *optimal conditions* for a decision to initiate, or to respond affirmatively to, an adversary's proposal of a termination of their conflict? One is a dual image of *exhaustion*—its *intolerability for their own population* and/or, closely related, *greater exhaustion among its people than for the populace* of their principal adversary. Another condition is *a calculus of an unfavorable balance of political, military, and economic capability*, relative to that of its adversary(ies), especially in the military domain. A third is *awareness of domestic pressures for conflict resolution*, supported by elites in their society, as well as their attentive public and mass public opinion. A fourth condition is unmistakeable *evidence of external pressures for termination*, emanating from a patron, ally, major power, international organization, and/or the media, or from several of these sources. There is also a realization by decision-makers of a substantive reduction in discordant objectives with its principal adversary(ies) as their conflict unfolded. Finally, there is a recognition of a decline in conflict-sustaining acts by its principal adversary(ies), leading to doubt about the wisdom of perpetuating a conflict with primarily negative consequences—persisting casualties, continuing material damage, and likely symbolic costs relating to its status in the global system and relevant international sub-systems.

In addition to changes in core conditions that generated conflict onset and persistence, a principal adversary's decision whether or not to pursue the goal of conflict resolution will be influenced by a formal or informal *Cost–Benefit* analysis. Decision-makers will assess their and their adversary's *security, material, and status costs of pursuing conflict resolution as a high priority goal*, and they will seek to weigh the *maximal and minimal benefits* to be derived from a decision to initiate or to respond favorably to an offer of conflict termination by their principal adversary(ies). If their *Perceptual Calculus* of core conditions and their cost–benefit analysis generate a negative outcome *vis-à-vis* their principal adversary, that is, costs exceeding estimated benefits and an unfavorable balance of capability, decision-makers are likely to accept conflict resolution as an unavoidable, less burdensome outcome of a protracted conflict, even if the *calculated cost* is significantly larger than any possible benefit of conflict termination.

Did these changes in the six Basic Conditions and the Perceptual Calculus, postulated by the Resolution Model as conducive to conflict resolution, exist in all or many or few or any of the 20 post-WWI resolved conflicts, and were these conditions absent in all or many or few or none of the 13 conflicts that persist in the second decade of the twenty-first century? Stated in terms of the *Model on Resolution* presented above, is a pattern of postulated favorable conditions for conflict resolution discernible during two-thirds of the interstate conflicts that were active during the near-century since the end of WWI and have been resolved?

Catalyst

The *Catalyst* in the **Resolution Model** is the conceptual counterpart of *Precipitating Cause* in a model designed to explain the *Onset* of Protracted Conflict, discussed elsewhere (Brecher 2016 L, Chap. 4). Both are closely related to *Basic Causes* but are analytically distinct. In both models, concepts are characterized by three differences.

One is *duration*. *Basic Causes* of Resolution, as of *Onset*, refer to *long-term, underlying* determinants of the *termination* (and *beginning*) of interstate protracted conflicts. *Catalyst*, like *Precipitating Cause* of *Onset*, is a *short-term* concept that identifies the mechanism leading to termination (resolution) of a conflict; however, though the latter is a finite-specific causal event, a Catalyst may comprise several related events that crystallize in Resolution.

A second difference is their *conceptual role* in the models of Resolution and Onset. *Basic Causes* are the *independent variables* in both models, the conditions that are most likely to lead to the termination (and outbreak) of a protracted conflict. As evident in Figure 5.1, above, those fundamental causes are different, but their role in explaining why a conflict ends is decisive in understanding the phenomenon of protracted conflict and the processes that culminate in resolution. The Catalyst (and Precipitating Cause, in the Onset model) serves as an *intervening variable*, in the causal flow from Basic Cause to crystallization as Conflict Resolution, the *dependent variable* in the Resolution Model.

The third difference between these concepts, *Basic Causes* and *Catalyst* (or Precipitating Cause), relates to *time sequence*. *The former precedes the latter*. In the protracted conflict *causal chain*, Basic Causes are the indispensable Step 1: without them a protracted conflict cannot occur. The *Catalyst*, like the *Precipitating Cause*, is an intermediate Step 2 that transforms the causal process to Step 3, *Resolution* or Persistence at the end of the causal chain. Thus, both Basic Causes and Catalyst-Precipitating Cause are integral parts of the resolution (and persistence) models.

The evidence on *crisis management* within, and *conflict resolution* of, protracted conflicts, to be presented in the following chapter, will focus on the *causal conditions*, along with the *perceptual calculus*, likely to lead to decisions to respond favorably to a proposal for conflict resolution. It will also address the important question of generalizability: is a cost–benefit calculus by conflict adversaries *generalizable* or ad hoc and unique, varying with decision-makers' diverse assessments of optimal conditions, costs, benefits, and opportunities for shared outcomes? Moreover, the evidence will present the findings on alternative paths to conflict resolution; that is, if the goal of conflict resolution was to be pursued, was it sought, and the benefits pursued, by *direct negotiation* with the principal adversary(ies) or by *indirect negotiations* via a third party? If a *third party* was preferred, what type was sought by the principal adversaries: a state friendly to both (all) principal adversaries; a high-profile person trusted by both (all) principal adversaries; an appointee by an international organization, global or regional; one person or a small-n committee? What role and powers were granted to a mediator? Finally, the evidence will enable the testing of the following nine hypotheses, implied at the beginning of this chapter and derived from the **Resolution Model**.

Hypotheses on Conflict Resolution

H.1 Resolution of an Interstate Protracted Conflict is *likely to occur* when one or more of the following Conditions characterize at least one of the principal adversaries: *Collective Exhaustion, Unfavorable Balance of Capability, Domestic Pressures, External Pressures, Reduction in Discordant Objectives, Decline in Conflict-Sustaining Acts,* and an *unfavorable Perceptual Calculus of these Basic Causes of Resolution*.

H.2 The *larger the number* of Basic Causes, that is, Conditions favorable to Conflict Resolution, that are present, the *more likely* is an interstate protracted conflict to be resolved.

H.3 The *most likely single Basic Cause* of (condition favorable to) interstate conflict resolution is *Collective Exhaustion* by at least one principal adversary.

H.4 The *most likely cluster of Basic Causes* of conflict resolution is one in which *Collective Exhaustion is the primary cause*.

H.5 The *higher the casualties*, the *greater the material damage* and *the longer the period of collective pain* experienced by one or more principal adversaries during a conflict, the *more likely* will conflict resolution occur.

H.6 The *likelihood of protracted conflict resolution* will be *greatest* when *all **types** of exhaustion (physical and psychological)* and *all **sources** of exhaustion (high casualties, widespread material damage, lengthy period of collective pain)* are experienced by *all principal adversaries*.

H.7 Political leaders endowed with strong support by their elites and attentive and mass publics are able to initiate or participate in a process of accommodation with their principal adversary, designed to attain mutually acceptable conflict termination, whereas a weak political leadership, which recognizes an adverse balance of capability with its principal adversary, is likely to accept conflict termination with major concessions imposed by the adversary.

H.8 A principal adversary, whose leadership possesses an ability to mobilize effectively its human and material resources in the military domain, will be more likely to pursue and achieve a favorable conflict resolution outcome than an ineffective political-military leadership.

H.9 Collective Exhaustion and an unfavorable Balance of Capability will be more significant than Domestic or External Pressures in a decision whether or not to initiate, or to welcome, a proposal to pursue the path of conflict resolution.
(Brecher, *The World of Protracted Conflicts*, 2016 L, Chapter 12).

CHAPTER 6

Select Case Study Findings On Interstate Conflicts: Africa & Americas

The most salient findings on **Historical Roots**; **Conflict Behavior** such as *Decisions, Decision-Maker(s), Decision Process*; **Conflict-Sustaining Acts** such as *Violence, Political Hostility, Propaganda, Economic Discrimination*; and **Crisis Management** and **Conflict Resolution**, from an illustrative group of thirteen protracted interstate conflicts in six regional clusters—*Africa, Americas, Asia, Europe*, Middle East, and *Inter-Region*—will be presented over the course of the next four chapters (6–9). Case studies include the following:

Africa	*Chad/Libya, Ethiopia/Somalia, Western Sahara*
Americas	*Costa Rica/Nicaragua*
Asia	*Afghanistan/Pakistan, China/Vietnam*
Europe	*Finland/Russia-USSR, Poland/Russia-USSR*
Middle East	*Iran/Iraq*
Inter-Region	*Georgia/Russia-USSR, Inter-Korea North Vietnam/USA, Taiwan Strait*

This chapter focuses on African and American cases

Africa

Chad/Libya Conflict (Resolved)

Behavior

Decisions
Many of the major decisions and implementing acts by the two principal adversaries in this 23-year African sub-system, interstate conflict (1971–1994) were inter-linked in a direct cause–effect relationship, mostly Chad's reaction to Libya's hostile initiatives. Thus, their decisions will be presented together, noting the linkage wherever relevant.

The *onset* of this conflict, in 1971, was triggered by Libya's first *strategic* decision—*to support an attempted coup by the pro-Libya Front Liberation Nationale de Tchad (FROLINAT) to overthrow Chad President Tombalbaye*. The decision (precise date unknown) was made by a group of young Libyan military officers, headed by *Col. Muammar Gadhafi*, sometime after they had seized power in Libya in 1969, overthrowing *King Idris*, and was implemented on August 27, 1971. The attempted coup and Libya's concealed intervention failed to achieve Libya's objective—bringing the friendly FROLINAT to power in Chad, with expected benefits to Libya, namely, virtually unlimited access to the reputed valuable material resources such as uranium, oil, iron, etc., in the northern part of Chad, the *Aouzou Strip*, long a disputed territory, to which Libya aspired and laid claim.

Libya's first major decision triggered a foreign policy crisis for Chad and its first responsive decision—*to sever diplomatic relations with Libya*. That act, in turn, generated a responsive decision by Libya, which took the form of *recognizing FROLINAT as Chad's legitimate government*, on September 17, 1971. External pressure by France on both of the principal adversaries led to an initially shared conciliatory decision by Chad and Libya: they resumed diplomatic relations in mid-April 1972.

The next episode of serious hostility between these Africa neighbors occurred 6 years later, when FROLINAT forces, supported by Libya, advanced to within 100 miles of Chad's capital, N'Djamena. France, long the pre-eminent colonial power in the Saharan region, responded to an urgent decision by Chad's President *Malloum to request immediate French military aid*, dispatched 1700 troops in an airlift from near-by

French bases in other former French colonies and created a defense perimeter around Chad's capital. In this Libya-generated crisis, Libya decided *to intervene directly, with indirect benefit to FROLINAT*: it *invaded parts of northern and central Chad with 800 troops*. Confronted by French military pressure, both FROLINAT and Libyan forces withdrew, and the Chad state survived once more.

In a variation of Libya's 1971 decision to recognize FROLINAT as Chad's legitimate government, Gadhafi and the FROLINAT leader, *Goukouni Oueddei*, announced a plan in January 1981 *to merge Chad and Libya*. This was greeted with strong public opposition by many African states and, especially, France, which increased its military presence in Chad. Once more, Libya responded with an announced decision *to withdraw its large military contingent in Chad, estimated at 7000–12,000 troops*. However, only a few were withdrawn, leading to a schism between Libya and FROLINAT. Eventually, Libya's forces were withdrawn by agreement in late 1981.

During the 5 years that followed, several political and military developments in Chad set in motion profound changes in the behavior of the two principal adversaries. One was a split in the Goukouni–Gadhafi alliance, largely due to the former's discontent with Gadhafi's initial refusal to withdraw Libya's forces from Chad in early 1981. This led to a split within the FROLINAT–Goukouni-led forces and FAP; clashes between Goukouni's splinter from PAP and the forces of another Libya ally in Chad; and cooperation between Goukouni's post-PAP forces and those of the Chad government. Together, this enlarged, merged Chad government army succeeded, for the first time, in mounting a counter-offensive north of the long-established informal line between Libya's and Chad's influence, the 16th Parallel. France's forces, long established in Chad, provided valuable forms of military aid, notably an air defense system, bombing Libyan airstrips in Chad, and a flow of weapons for Chad's forces. The Chad counter-offensive was surprisingly successful, culminating in the first Chad military invasion of Libya. The capital of the disputed *Aouzou Strip*, the town of Aouzou, was captured, along with a Libyan airbase within Libya proper.

This successful Chad military offensive, late in their interstate-intrastate conflict, led to attempted mediation of the Chad/Libya conflict. When that failed, the two adversaries made a shared decision in 1990—*to seek a judicial ruling on their conflicting claims to the long-disputed Aouzou Strip*: the shared decision was implemented by the submission of their dispute to the International Court of Justice for a binding ruling. The ICJ ruled in 1994 in favor of Chad almost unanimously: the vote was 16-1. Libya accepted the Court's decision and withdrew all of its forces from the Aouzou Strip within a few months, a rare example of protracted conflict termination generated by an international judicial ruling.

Chad and Libya: Decision-Makers

Throughout this post-World War II Africa conflict, the dominant decision-maker for Libya was the charismatic Muammar Gadhafi: he retained that role for the entire period of his authoritarian rule (1969–2011). For Chad, too, there was one commanding figure in decision-making on issues related to this conflict—but only for the period in office as President of Chad. Notable among them were *Francois Tombalbaye*, the first Chad president, who was assassinated in 1975, *Felix Malloum*, and *Hissené Habré*. There were other influential Chad leaders, notably *Goukouni Oueddei*, commander of the PAP forces in Chad, long an ally of Gadhafi, until 1981, but he did not have direct power in the making of Chad's decisions. Moreover, none of the presidents of Chad possessed the power exercised by Gadhafi as dominant decision-maker for Libya in all major issues relating to its conflict with Chad.

Chad and Libya: Decision Process

Although hard evidence is lacking on the making of Libya's decisions, it is likely that, for the major decisions in the early years of this conflict, members of the military junta that assumed power in 1969 were involved; this was before Gadhafi eliminated all rivals to his power in the junta. By the mid-1970s, he had succeeded in establishing undisputed control over every aspect of Libya's public policy, in which the on-going conflict with Chad ranked high for Gadhafi, as it would have for any leader—and did for *King Idris*, his predecessor as Libya's ruler (1951–1969).

While little is known about the Chad decision process, beyond the primacy of its presidents during their tenure, the lack of a commanding figure and the existence of multiple Chad ethnic communities suggests that, on some issues, notably the disputed Aouzou Strip, Chad's presidents consulted with leaders of some of these communities for possible benefits enhancing their power or costs of ignoring all but those sharing power and its benefits in highly restricted political elites. Notable among Chad's communities were the *Sara*, the most populous and influential ethnic group in Chad, and the *Tebu*, the most populous ethnic group in the pivotal disputed region within this conflict, the Aouzou Strip.

Conflict-Sustaining Acts

Among the four conflict-sustaining techniques (CST) and acts that contribute to the persistence of interstate conflicts, *political hostility* and *violence* were of relatively equal frequency and impact in this conflict, political hostility in *Phase I (1971–1978)* and violence in *Phase II (1978–1987)*. Both *verbal hostility* and *economic discrimination* were inconsequential, the former more so.

Political Hostility: It was manifested in the behavior of both principal adversaries, primarily by Libya, in three distinct forms—attempted Libyan coups in Chad, financial and military backing by Libya for Chad rebel groups, and the severance of diplomatic relations. The first, highly visible, hostile political act, the catalyst to *Chad/Libya I*, the first of eight interstate crises in their protracted conflict, was Libya's active support for a (failed) coup against Chad President Tombalbaye on August 27, 1971, by the most prominent Chad rebel group, FROLINAT which, throughout this interstate–intrastate conflict, served as Gadhafi's instrument for penetration of Chad's political system and society. As noted, Chad responded by breaking diplomatic relations with Libya, and Libya retaliated by recognizing the FROLINAT as the legitimate government of Chad. Relations between Chad and Libya were restored in April 1972, as a result of material incentives to both adversaries by France, the pre-eminent power in Saharan and much of North Africa during the last half of the nineteenth and the pre-World War II part of the twentieth century. Libya occupied the disputed mineral-rich border area of Chad, the Aouzou Strip, in April 1972. Chad ceded the territory to Libya in November 1972, and Libya again occupied the Aouzou Strip in 1973 (retaining control until Chad's brief successful invasion of Libya in September 1987—see below). Chad's President Tombalbaye was overthrown in a coup by Malloum in April 1975. He, in turn, was the target of another Gadhafi failed assassination attempt, in 1976.

Violence: There were renewed FROLINAT attacks on Chad's government in 1977. And in January 1978 Libya provided active support for a FROLINAT attack on the crucial administrative center of northern Chad, Faya-Largeau, one of several such attacks by Libya's proxy in Chad. This triggered the *Chad/Libya II* crisis and set the tone and pattern of continuous hostile military attacks, mostly by Libya, during six subsequent Chad/Libya crises from 1979 to 1987. During that period, there were three major occurrences of violence. The first was an invasion of northern Chad by 2500 Libyan troops in June 1979, directed at the strategic center, Faya-Largeau. Chad responded with a counter-offensive which, with the military aid of France, notably bombers and reconnaissance planes, the first use of aircraft in this conflict, compelled Libya to withdraw its forces (*Chad/Libya IV*). The second violent episode occurred in June 1983, the onset of *Chad/Libya VI*, when Libya-supported forces of the Goukouni-led Chad faction occupied Faya-Largeau on June 24. Military aid to the *Habré* regime in Chad from France, Zaire, and the USA led to the recapture of the prized city in northern Chad on July 30. Libya attacked the contested city the next day, and France countered by sending troops from the neighboring Central African Republic. France and Libya terminated this violent episode by agreeing to withdraw their forces from Chad. The final phase of violence began in December 1986, when Libyan forces attacked Chad troops in northern Chad who, surprisingly, recaptured Libya-occupied cities north of the 16th Parallel, the de facto boundary between Chad and Libya agreed-to by France and Libya in 1984. The violence persisted for 6 months, with the Aouzou Strip captured by Chad troops in August 1987 and then recaptured by Libya the same month. In early September, for the first time, Chad troops invaded Libya and occupied a major air base. A ceasefire, initiated by the Organization of African Unity (OAU), terminated the third and last intense episode of violence and *Chad/Libya VIII* on September 11, 1987. Their conflict was resolved on May 30, 1994 when Libya formally transferred the Aouzou Strip to Chad, in accordance with an ICJ near-unanimous ruling 4 months earlier, on February 3, 1994, supporting Chad's claim to the disputed territory. (The eight interstate crises in the Chad/Libya conflict, like all crises discussed in this book, are summarized in the ICB Data Viewer).

Ethiopia/Somalia Conflict (Dormant)

Behavior

Somalia: Decisions and Decision-Makers
Viewed in terms of *decisional behavior* by Somalia, one of the two principal adversaries in this unresolved Horn of Africa conflict, there were four

phases: *Phase I* Independence (1960–1969); Phase II Regime Change, War, and Instability (1969–1991); Phase III Collapse (1991–2004), and Phase IV Islamist War. (In the last two phases, as will be evident below, this unresolved conflict was dormant because Somalia descended into chaos, disintegration, and civil strife.)

There was one *strategic* decision by Somalia in *Phase I*, the pre-condition for any relations between Somalia and Ethiopia: after a 10-year UN trusteeship by the UK and Italy over former British and Italian Somaliland (1950–1960), the two Trust Territories held elections, and 5 days after independence they decided *to form the United Republic of Somalia*. Among several *tactical decisions* soon after the creation of a new state, the founders decided *to send* an *unequivocal irredentist message to Ethiopia (and Kenya)*, the most directly affected neighbors of Somalia, by issuing a five-star national flag, identifying five territories in the Horn of Africa that Somalia asserted, in 1960 and since then, rightfully belonged to Somalia by virtue of the Somali ethnicity of its pastoral population. The largest of these Somalia-claimed territories was the *Ogaden*, a vast desert frequented mainly by Somali pastoralists, which had been recognized as an integral part of Ethiopia, in an 1897 treaty between Ethiopia and the UK, the then-leading Great Power in Africa and the world. From the onset of the *Ethiopia/Somalia* conflict, this disputed territory has been the core discordant issue of their still-unresolved conflict.

The Ogaden, one of the five stars in Somalia's flag, was never remote from the concern and aspiration of Somalia's political and military elites, but it was not a source of officially directed hostile activity toward Ethiopia by either of Somalia's presidents during the first phase of this conflict, *Aden Abdullah Osman Daar* (1960–1967) or *Abdi Rashid Ali Shermarke*, who was elected president in 1967 but was overthrown in a 1969 coup. However, hostile activity was not wanting: the most visible manifestation of Somalia's persistent claim was the visible role among Somalis in the disputed Ogaden territory by a state-supported interest group, the Western Somali Liberation Front (WSLF).

Somalia's state behavior toward Ethiopia changed only after a *coup d'état* brought *Muhammad Siad Barré* to power in 1969, but the change did not occur immediately. In *Phase II* of Somalia's behavior during this interstate conflict, the authoritarian regime headed by Barré made the second Somalia *strategic* decision, in 1977—*to issue a formal declaration of war against Ethiopia* and *to invade the Ogaden region*.

It was ill-advised: in 1978, Somali forces were expelled from the disputed territory, and within a few years, domestic opposition to Barré's rule became evident. A third Somalia *strategic* decision in this phase, part of the political fall-out of its severe defeat in the war with Ethiopia, was *to sever its longstanding alignment with the USSR, expelling Soviet advisers, and seeking support from the United States.* Another consequence of that military defeat was a fourth Somalia *strategic* decision, by an increasingly weaker Barré-led regime—*to sign a formal peace treaty with Ethiopia in 1988.*

Ironically, the mutual obligation undertaken by the principal adversaries in that treaty, to respect their existing borders, became a catalyst for escalating political instability in Somalia. The provision calling for Somalia's cooperation with Ethiopia to eliminate rebellious factions in the Ogaden, notably the Somali National Movement (SNM) and the Ogaden National Liberation Front (ONLF), further undermined the Barré-led regime.

Its descent into state collapse, *Phase III*, began in 1991, with Barré's ouster after two decades at the helm of Somalia's functioning government. Civil strife was rampant for 13 years, highlighted by territorial fragmentation within Somalia—the 1991 Declaration of Somaliland Independence from Somalia and the 1998 Declaration of Puntland Independence, leading, in turn, to a territorial dispute between them over northern regions of Somalia. As a consequence of Somalia's deterioration into the status of a 'failed state,' the Somalia/Ethiopia conflict became dormant during Phase III: there were no strategic decisions, while Somali factions were immersed in a struggle over the succession to the defunct Barré regime. Attempts to restore a semblance of unity to the Somali state characterized *Phase IV* of Somalia's woes (2004–2015); however, since 1991 the Ethiopia/Somalia conflict was dormant.

Somalia: Decision Process
Throughout the three decades (1960–1991) and two phases (1960–1969, 1969–1991), in which Somalia was an active principal adversary in this conflict, its *decision process* was dominated by inter-clan relations. Presidents of Somalia were, first and foremost, clan leaders, dependent upon support by the members of their clan, and engaged in inter-clan relations, designed to maximize support from within one's clan, to weaken competing clans, and to attain and sustain political power by constructing alliances or effective coalitions with friendly clans.

Overall, such an *inter-clan political system* functioned like inter-party systems in Western democracies. During the two decades in which Siad Barré was Somalia's authoritarian political leader, he retained power by an adept skill in mobilizing intra-clan support and loose alignments with one or more other clans, with ties of kinship and/or shared interests and political goals. During that long *Phase II* (1969–1991), notwithstanding his serious error in waging war against a more powerful Ethiopia in 1977–1978, his clan-based political regime was a viable, generally effective principal adversary against a more powerful foe.

Ethiopia: Decisions
The pattern of Ethiopia's behavior in this conflict was similar to that of the other principal adversary. As in Somalia, there were two phases. The first phase (1960–1974) was dominated by Ethiopia's twentieth-century long-time ruler, *Haile Selassie*, who was restored to his throne by the UK in 1941, after it defeated Italy in an early World War II East Africa military campaign. Ethiopia's *Phase II* began with the overthrow of Haile Selassie in 1974 by a military coup and lasted until 1991: as in Somalia, it too was dominated by an authoritarian ruler for 14 years (1977–1991), *Mengistu Haile Mariam*, the counterpart of Siad Barré in Somalia: Mengistu was head of the Military Junta, known as the 'Derg,' the Coordinating Committee of Ethiopia's regular army, police, and territorial army.

As the stronger regional power, in occupation of the Ogaden with the UK's sanction since 1897 and long before, Ethiopia's policy throughout this conflict was *defensive*, aimed at maintaining the status quo; it was the counterpart of Somalia's *revisionist* policy toward the disputed territory. Thus the two major decisions by Ethiopia in its *Phase I* (Haile Selassie) were only indirectly relevant to the Ogaden. In 1962, it enlarged the image and reality of its primacy in the Horn of Africa by annexing the neighboring territory of Eritrea. Two years later, Ethiopia formed an alliance with Kenya, whose North West District was explicitly identified as one of the five stars in Somalia's flag, that is, an irredentist territory rightfully belonging to Somalia because of its Somali ethnic majority.

Phase II for Ethiopia began with another decision and act indirectly relevant to the protracted conflict with Somalia: having triumphed in its 1974 coup, the *Derg* re-affirmed the federalist character of Ethiopia, including the annexed territory of Eritrea. Three years later, Ethiopia made the most important *strategic* decision in this phase—*to engage in full-scale defensive warfare against Somalia's invasion of the Ogaden*. The result was a decisive Ethiopia military victory in 1978, leading to the expulsion of all Somalia forces from the disputed territory.

In perspective, that decision and act marked the de facto end of the Ethiopia/Somalia conflict. However, it took another decade for that outcome to be sealed in the decision of Ethiopia (and Somalia) *to sign a peace treaty that formalized the pre-war existing border*. Although Somalia's five-star flag, including the explicit identification of the Ogaden as 'lost' territory remained unchanged, the 1988 treaty constituted *Somalia's recognition of Ethiopia's sovereignty over the entire disputed territory* by imposing an obligation on the two signatories, essentially, Somalia, as noted, to cooperate in eradicating insurgent pro-Somalia forces from the Ogaden Desert. Even before the signing of the 1988 border treaty, Ethiopia had reinforced its primacy in the Horn of Africa and Somalia's relative weakness by renewing, in 1984, its 1964 alliance with Kenya, the location of another irredentist star in Somalia's national flag.

Ethiopia: Decision-Makers and Decision Process

The similarity in the behavioral structure of the two principal adversaries in this interstate conflict extends to their *decision-making process*. In Somalia, it was characterized by a highly authoritarian structure, led by General *Siad Barré*, from 1969–1991. In Ethiopia, the decision process was also highly authoritarian, both in Phase I, with the Emperor as the *dominant decision-maker* from 1960 (and long before) to 1974, and in Phase II, with General Mengistu as the *dominant decision-maker* from 1974 to 1991. Both Barré and Mengistu also espoused a Left-Socialist ideology though it was never clear whether this was an ideological commitment or a tactical choice to ensure the very substantial military assistance provided by the USSR for most of their tenure in power. The authoritarian leaders in both adversarial states also operated under structural and personal constraints: in Somalia, *inter-clan relations and pressures* limited Barré's freedom of choice, and in Ethiopia, Haile Selassie often experienced *dissent, even opposition, from lesser kings in Ethiopia's regions*, while Mengistu operated within the constraints of a military junta. *In sum*, there were many similarities in the decision process of the two principal adversaries in this Horn of Africa interstate conflict.

Ethiopia/Somalia: Conflict-Sustaining Acts

<u>Violence</u>—Ethiopia was the status quo adversary throughout this conflict, with the primary goal of retaining control and sovereignty over the disputed Ogaden Desert. Somalia has been the *revisionist* adversary since this conflict's inception in 1960. However, the initiation of wars and military-security crises was almost equally divided between the adversaries. Somalia precipitated one of the *two wars* (*Ogaden II*, July 22, 1977– March 14, 1978), via its proxy, the Western Somalia Liberation Front (WSLF), which launched an attack on the Ogaden region of Ethiopia in its on-going quest to wrest control of this territory. Soviet and Cuban aid to Ethiopia led to Somalia's withdrawal from the Ogaden. In October 2006, Ethiopia invaded Somalia, defeating the Union of Islamic Courts (UIC), which had declared a holy war against (Christian) Ethiopia. Of the *three violent interstate crises*, Somalia initiated the brief *Ogaden I* crisis (February 7–March 30, 1964), with an attack on an Ethiopian frontier post. A ceasefire seven weeks later led to the withdrawal of Somali forces to the original frontier. Ethiopia triggered the other two violent crises: *Ogaden III* (June 30–August 1982), when Ethiopian troops invaded the Hiran region and threatened communication between the two parts of Somalia, and USA military and economic aid to Somalia led to an inconclusive fading of the crisis, and the *Todghere Incident* (February 12–April 1987), when Ethiopian-supported irregulars attacked half a dozen Somali villages. Ethiopia apologized to Somalia, and the violence ended with a ceasefire in early April. A year later, the two conflict adversaries agreed to demilitarize their border and to resume diplomatic relations.

<u>Political Hostility</u>—Frequent hostile political acts were initiated by both adversaries. Notable among Somalia's conflict-sustaining political acts was the *formal approval of its constitution*, which proclaimed the goal of unification of all ethnic Somali majority territory and the authorization of Somalia's provision of weapons to achieve that objective. Moreover, Somalia became a member of the Arab League, to secure aid and support for this most fundamental of its goals, generating an Ethiopian perception of 'enemies at [most of] the gates.' Ethiopia, too, contributed several high-profile conflict-sustaining political acts, all of them perceived by Somalia as gravely threatening: Ethiopia succeeded in securing formal approval of the 'inviolability of state frontiers' as a basic principle of the

Organization of African Unity (OAU), thereby pre-empting Somalia's claims to ethnic-majority territories in several neighboring states. It formed a military alliance with Kenya in 1963, another unfriendly neighbor of Somalia, which Somalia perceived as a thinly disguised hostile act by its 'common enemy' [Somalia has long claimed Kenya's North West District because of its large ethnic Somali population]. Moreover, the rulers of Ethiopia and Kenya publicly called on Somalia, at an 'East Africa Confrontation,' to renounce all of its territorial claims against Ethiopia, Kenya, Djibouti, a former French colony, and Tanzania, and to pay reparations to Ethiopia for damage caused by Somalia during their 1977–1978 Ogaden War. Finally, both Ethiopia and Somalia, as noted above, drew the two superpowers into their protracted conflict by securing from them military equipment and political support to their African proxy—the USA as patron of Ethiopia from 1953 to 1977, with the USSR playing that role for Somalia in the 1960s and most of the 1970s, including a Treaty of Friendship, followed by a reversal of both superpower Horn of Africa alignments in 1977.

Verbal Hostility (propaganda)—this type of conflict-sustaining activity was subsumed within the most relevant acts of political hostility by both adversaries, discussed above.

Economic discrimination—the paucity of economic relations between the two adversaries in this conflict meant a virtually non-existent role for this type of conflict-sustaining acts, except for Somalia's emphasis throughout the unresolved conflict on the economic deprivation of the pastoral Somali majority in the Ogaden Desert caused by Ethiopia's denial of unhindered access to land and water in the disputed territory.

Western Sahara Conflict (Unresolved)

Behavior

Morocco and Polisario-SADR: Decisions
Both of the principal adversaries in this unresolved conflict made and implemented three *strategic* decisions during their four decade-long conflict (1975). In all of these, the adversaries adopted directly conflicting positions on the contending issues; thus their decisions will be examined together.

The first *strategic* decision by Morocco, in the late 1970s, was designed *to deny the Polisario Front*, its non-state adversary in the early years of their conflict, *direct physical access to large parts of Western Sahara, including five of the six largest and most important cities in this disputed territory:* the implementation of this decision took the form of an unusual, controversial series of high-profile acts from 1980 to 1986, the building of six massive sand walls in the Western Sahara's southern provinces, surrounded by minefields and guarded by Moroccan troops. [An earlier, important *tactical* decision, *Moroccan March* (*1975–1976*), in which Spain, Morocco, Algeria, and Mauritania were crisis actors, did not involve the *Polisario*].

The *sand wall* decision and its dramatic implementing project expressed the determination of Morocco to achieve sovereignty and permanent physical control over the colonial territory that Spain had vacated in 1975, transferring two-thirds of the territory to Morocco, the rest to Mauritania which, soon after, yielded its part to Morocco. The sand wall project also reflected the basic *defensive strategy* of Morocco during Phase I of this conflict (1975–1991): the sand walls would, it was hoped, defend the population and whatever centers of economic activity existed in Western Sahara and limit the physical damage that could be created by Polisario raids. Moreover, the defensive strategy had the merit of minimizing the attention paid to the conflict over Western Sahara by international organizations, notably the UN and some of its functional agencies, and states inimical to Morocco's interests, in the Islamic and African worlds. By contrast, a 'forward' policy by Morocco, including attacks on refugee camps, where many Polisario guerrillas live, even more so, *Sahrawi* refugee camps in Algeria, would have brought the wrath of world public opinion down on Morocco; a low-profile strategy was safer.

By contrast, the *Polisario* movement (and its formal state successor, the Saharan Arab Democratic Republic [SADR]), proclaimed in February 1976, adopted an *offensive strategy,* with the aim of causing sufficient physical damage and personal insecurity among the people protected by the sand walls that Morocco would yield the disputed territory to an aspiring nationalist movement. That movement was endowed with a determined, effective leadership and widespread support among the *Sahrawi*, and it enjoyed the benefit of financial and military support from Algeria, long Morocco's rival for primacy in the *Maghreb*, Arab West Africa. Evidence of the *Polisario-SADR* offensive strategy was most clearly expressed in its initiative in precipitating all but one of the 10 crises that erupted within this conflict, most of them (6 of 9) by military raids against Morocco: *Tan Tan* 1979; *Goulimime-Tarfaya Road* 1979; *Operation Iman* 1980; *Galtat Zemmour I* 1981; *Sand Wall* 1987; and *Galtat Zemmour II* 1989. The first three crises in this conflict—*Nouakchott I* 1976, *Nouakchott II* 1977, and *French Hostages in Mauritania* 1977—were triggered by Polisario attacks against Mauritania, when it was occupying part of the former Spain colony of Western Sahara.

A second *strategic* decision by both of the principal adversaries in this conflict was their acceptance of the 1991 *UN Settlement Plan*, devised by former US Secretary of State *James Baker* (Baker Plan I). This included a ceasefire agreement between Morocco and the Polisario-SADR, still in force more than two decades later. Even more significant, in terms of a potential political solution, was a provision for a referendum the next year that would include the option of independence for Western Sahara. However, disagreement between the conflict adversaries about the criteria for voter eligibility led to continuing delays in its implementation: Morocco insisted that recently arrived Moroccan settlers in Western Sahara be allowed to vote, while Polisario-SADR refused. This persistent disagreement rendered Baker Plan I obsolete. An attempt by the Houston Plan in 1997 to restore the referendum idea also failed.

The third *strategic* decision by the principal adversaries in this conflict formalized the impasse early in the twenty-first century. In 2003, Baker Plan II proposed 4–5 years of transitional autonomy for Western Sahara—under Morocco's supervision, to be followed by a referendum on "self-determination," that is, independence. The eligible voter list was enlarged, to include persons, almost all Moroccans, who had resided in Western Sahara since the end of 1999, that is, 4 years. Despite this Plan's conspicuous pro-Morocco bias on several crucial issues—Western Sahara autonomy for several years, under its supervision, and the granting of voter rights to recent Moroccan settlers—Morocco rejected the Baker Plan II referendum proposal, indicating that independence was not an acceptable option under any conditions; the Polisario-SADR accepted the Plan. There has not been any further progress toward a political solution of this conflict, despite further negotiations by Morocco and Polisario-SADR under UN auspices, in 2007–2008, to be summarized later in this report. The impasse in this protracted conflict continues.

Morocco: Decision-Makers

There were very few key *decision-makers* in Morocco's conflict behavior, as with most states engaged in a protracted conflict. Notwithstanding its formal governmental structure, a constitutional monarchy (see below), major decisions on all issues of public policy have been the monopoly of the Sultan (King) of Morocco. The two persons who have held this position during the 43 years of the most contentious issue in Morocco's foreign policy, the conflict over Western Sahara, with far-reaching implications for Morocco's status and role in northwest Africa, have been *Hassan II*, a highly authoritarian and flamboyant ruler for almost 4 decades (1961–1999) during most of the protracted conflict with Polisario-SADR, and his son, *Mohammed VI* (since 1999), Morocco's decision-maker on the Baker II Plan (2003) and the subsequent negotiations under UN auspices. To the extent that Morocco's ruler solicits advice on important issues, the most visible role is associated with his Royal Advisory Council for Saharan Affairs: it was this body that proposed the status of autonomy for Western Sahara, rather than independence, at the negotiations with Polisario-SADR in 2007–2008—at the urging of Morocco's principal allies, France, Spain, and the USA. One or more senior political figures, notably the Prime Minister and Foreign Minister, were also probably consulted as well. However, the ultimate Morocco decision-maker on all major issues of public policy was/is the reigning monarch.

Polisario-SADR: Decision-Makers

The most important Polisario-SADR *decision-maker* for the entire period of this conflict, since 1975, except the first year, has been its Secretary-General since 1976, *Mohammed Abdul-Aziz*. There were three others who held this highest-ranking position in Polisario briefly since it was founded in 1973. It can be presumed that other decision-makers—names not known—were senior members of the highest decision-making organ of Polisario, the National Secretariat. Given the character of this nationalist organization, it is also assumed that decision-making authority-power was not concentrated in one person, as in Morocco's monarchy.

Morocco: Decision Process

Formally, Morocco is a constitutional monarchy, with a British type of political structure, notably a government headed by a Prime Minister that possesses executive power and shares legislative authority with a bicameral legislature. Since 1996, there has been an Assembly of Representatives of Morocco, with 325 members, 295 elected for 5-year terms in multi-seat constituencies, 30 from national lists of women, and an Assembly of 270

Councilors, elected by local councils and professional organizations for nine-year terms. Formally, the legislature has the authority to approve bills, including the annual budgets, and can dissolve a government by a vote of no confidence. However, built into the 1996 constitution is a set of formidable royal powers long exercised by Morocco's monarchs: to appoint the Prime Minister and members of the government; to dismiss any minister; to dissolve any government; and to suspend the constitution or rule by decree. *In sum*, authority and power are concentrated in the monarch. He can, and undoubtedly does, consult select persons in government, and it is reasonable to assume that he consults the Royal Advisory Council for Saharan Affairs on all matters related to this unresolved conflict. However, this is his choice, not an obligation. He is not bound ever to accept advice. Thus, while Morocco's decision process may, and probably does, involve inputs from political aides at the request of the monarch, the ultimate decisions are at the discretion of Morocco's Sultan-King.

Polisario: Decision Process

The decision process of Polisario-SADR would seem to be more complex than in Morocco, with authority and power more widely distributed in the Polisario-SADR context. At the apex of the decision pyramid, power is exercised by the Secretary-General and a 41-member National Secretariat, both elected by the General Popular Congress (GPC) every 4 years. The GPC, in turn, consists of delegates from the Popular Congresses of the residents of refugee camps and members of multiple organizations—for women, youth, workers, and soldiers, the last belonging to the Sahrawi People's Liberation Army (SPLA), later headed by the SADR Defense Minister, with elections at the base level. Ultimate choices in the decision-making process on important issues that may affect the survival of Polisario and, since 1976, the SADR, and the achievement of their goal of independence undoubtedly rest with the Secretariat and the Secretary-General and, probably, with the SPLA military commanders as well before the 1991 ceasefire. However, the multiple layers of political participation, from the base-level cells of the refugee camps to the Popular Congresses and refugee camp administrations, to the General Popular Congress, and the 'top tiers' of Polisario and SADR, the National Secretariat and Secretary-General would seem to have led to a much wider actual participation in the Polisario-SADR decision process than in the narrow process that characterized decision-making in Morocco.

Western Sahara Conflict: Crisis Management

In this currently dormant, 43-year-old *interstate-intra-state* Africa conflict, with three principal adversaries—Morocco, Polisario (since 1976, also known as the Saharan Arab Democratic Republic (SADR) [SAHRAWI]), and in the early years, Mauritania—*crisis management* took the form of winding down the <u>ten crises</u> between Morocco and Polisario-SADR from 1975 to 1989. The evidence on crisis management is presented here.

Moroccan March (October 16, 1975–April 14, 1976) The UN was active in attempted *multilateral* crisis management from the onset of this conflict. The Security Council, responding to Spain's appeal, passed a resolution on October 22, 1975, calling for restraint and requesting the UN Secretary-General to initiate negotiations. They were conducted on October 26–28. The Security Council met twice in November. And mediation was attempted by the Secretary-General and his Representative in March–April 1976. The Arab League [formally, League of Arab States (LAS)] sent its Secretary-General to the region, at the request of the Organization of African Union (OAU) [later, African Union (AU)]. All failed to manage the crisis because of the refusal of Morocco and Polisario to compromise. The crisis was *managed* bilaterally by two of the three principal adversaries, a Morocco-Mauritania jointly initiated succession agreement on April 14, 1976: Morocco annexed the northern two-thirds of the territory of Western Sahara, and Mauritania, the other third of the territory ruled by Spain as a colony from 1885 to 1975.

Nouakchott I (June 8, 1976): This one-day crisis was caused by a Polisario attack on Mauritania's capital. It was *managed* by a successful Mauritanian counter-attack that forced an immediate Polisario withdrawal.

Nouakchott II (July 3–late July 1977): Another Polisario attack on Mauritania's capital, on July 3, led to an airlift of 600 Moroccan troops on July 18–19 to assist Mauritania. That intervention and the completion of the reorganization of Mauritania's army by the end of July served to *manage* this crisis.

French Hostages in Mauritania (October 25–December 23, 1977): Two French engineers, working on the Mauritania railway, were abducted by

Polisario guerrillas on October 25, creating a crisis for France and Algeria. *Crisis management* was successful, via several techniques employed by crisis actors and the UN. One was a meeting of the UN General Assembly at France's request, on October 31. Another was an offer of *good offices* by the UN Secretary-General. A third was the dispatch of additional French troops to Senegal at the beginning of November. Still another was talks between French Foreign Ministry officials and Polisario leaders in Algiers from November 1 to 7. There was also a UN General Assembly resolution, adopted on November 9 calling upon UN members to respect Western Sahara's right to self-determination, an important interest for Polisario and Algeria, rejected by Morocco if the options included Western Sahara's independence. Ultimately, the crisis was *managed* by a *violent act*—the strafing of *Polisario* columns in Mauritania by French warplanes from 12–18 December, which led to the freeing of the two hostages on 23 December, ending this crisis.

Tan Tan (January 28–March 1979): A crisis for Morocco was triggered on January 28, 1979 by a Polisario attack on the Moroccan garrison town and air force base, Tan Tan. Effective *crisis management* was achieved by *reciprocal conciliatory acts* by the two principal adversaries: Morocco's Foreign Minister informed his Algeria counterpart that Morocco would not exercise its "right of pursuit" against Polisario, and Polisario forces suspended their attack, leading to a faded crisis in March.

Goulimime-Tarfaya Road (June 1–25, 1979): Another crisis for Morocco was triggered on June 1 by a large-scale Polisario military attack within Morocco proper. King Hassan's public announcement on 6 June of Morocco's intention to exercise its "right of pursuit" in future attacks on Moroccan citizens and territory catalyzed a reciprocal crisis for Algeria. Both North African states appealed to the OAU and sought UN intervention by summoning ambassadors of the five permanent Security Council members to their Foreign Ministry to publicize their future policy response to attacks on their territory. On June 15, Morocco requested an urgent meeting of the Security Council, which sought to manage the crisis by discussions at meetings from June 15 to 25, without passing a resolution. On the 25th, Morocco requested the indefinite suspension of the Security Council debate on this issue, on the grounds of a lowering of tensions, since Polisario attacks in June had ceased.

This atypical behavior by a principal crisis actor constituted *negative crisis management* in this case.

Operation Iman (March 1–mid-May 1980): Another crisis for Morocco, within the *Western Sahara* conflict, was precipitated by a major victory of Polisario forces over a column of Moroccan troops that had been dispatched to clear an area in the north of Morocco, in the direction of Western Sahara. Both adversaries sought external support. Polisario did so by submitting documents to the UN, the OAU, and the Non-Aligned Movement, charging collusion between Morocco and South Africa, the former seeking weapons to enable Morocco to take possession of Western Sahara; there was no response. Similarly, Morocco criticized Algeria and Libya for allegedly providing Polisario with North Korean weapons, with no benefit. By mid-May 1980, the clashes related to Morocco's *Operation Iman* had wound down, ending this crisis, without any attempt at crisis management by the UN or either of the two superpowers.

Galtat Zemmour I (October 13–November 9, 1981): A further crisis for Morocco was triggered by a large Polisario attack on its garrison at Galtat Zemmour on October 13, 1981, with 3000 troops, tanks and armored personnel carriers. King Hassan sought support from the presidents of France and the USA, the UN, and the OAU, accusing Algeria and Libya of providing weapons to Polisario. There were no positive attempts at external crisis management. Rather, on November 5, Soviet President Brezhnev denied that the USSR had provided SAM missiles to Polisario, and the USA dispatched a military delegation to Morocco during the crisis, conveying symbolic support for a valued ally in North Africa. Negative crisis management took the form of unilateral Morocco acts—withdrawal from Galtat Zemmour and another military base on November 7 and 9, a severe defeat in this protracted conflict.

Sand Wall (February 25–May 4, 1987): This complex crisis was set in motion by an outbreak of heavy fighting between Morocco and Polisario-SADR armed forces on February 25. In mid-April, Mauritania became a third crisis actor because the newly completed Moroccan sand wall, designed to prevent the entry of Polisario forces into a part of Western Sahara, posed a potential threat to Mauritanian territory and its economy, because of that sand wall's proximity to a vital Mauritanian railway line—a few hundred meters—that transported iron ore, a vital Mauritanian raw material, to its commercial capital, for export. The crisis became more complex when the president of Algeria, the primary rival of Morocco for influence primacy in northwest Africa, visited Mauritania and pledged support for its territorial integrity. In this crisis, too, an atypical form of *crisis management* was utilized—a summit meeting between the leaders of Algeria and Morocco at their border on 4 May 1987, arranged by King Fahd of Saudi Arabia. Although a formal agreement was not reached, the meeting reduced the tension level between the two *Maghreb* regional powers sufficiently to end the international crisis that day for all three crisis actors, Mauritania, Morocco, and Polisario.

Galtat Zemmour II (October 7–late November 1989): Notwithstanding a peace-seeking atmosphere in the *Western Sahara* conflict during the summer of 1988, following the acceptance by Morocco and Polisario-SADR of a UN-OAU peace plan on August 30, 1988 [to be elaborated below in the analysis of attempts at **conflict resolution**], the absence of progress in negotiations during the next 13 months led Polisario to break the UN-OAU-engineered truce: on October 7, 1989, it attacked Moroccan forces at Galtat Zemmour a second time. Two days later, Morocco threatened military intervention in Mauritania if Polisario attacks from that neighboring state continued. Crisis management efforts began on October 13, 1989, when the UN Secretary-General urged a resumption of meetings between King Hassan and Polisario leaders, to re-activate the UN-OAU peace plan. Moreover, on November 7, SADR, the formal quasi-state framework of Polisario, called for a dialogue with Morocco to achieve peace in Western Sahara. Nonetheless, a day later, Polisario launched another attack on Moroccan forces. However, despite further clashes on November 16, serious fighting ended in the second half of November, and the Galtat Zemmour II crisis faded. [In response to a request by the UN Secretary-General, Polisario-SADR agreed to a truce on February 21, 1990, to the end of March.]

Successful management of the last recorded military-security crisis in the *Western Sahara* conflict—before serious attempts at conflict resolution began in 1991 (see below)—was achieved largely by the persistent efforts of the UN Secretary-General. In that context, the behavior of the principal adversaries in this conflict, Morocco and Polisario-SADR, and of all other participants in the winding down of these crises did not extend to efforts at *conflict resolution*: they were confined to

6 SELECT CASE STUDY FINDINGS ON INTERSTATE CONFLICTS ... 167

the narrower realm and the more limited task of winding down specific episodes of threats of violence, threats of escalation to more intense violence, and of the challenge to terminate violence in these limited time episodes, that is, the realm of *crisis management*. In the absence of successful *conflict resolution* (see below), the formal stage of conflict termination has not begun.

Western Sahara: Failed Attempts at Conflict Resolution

The quest for resolution of the *Western Sahara* conflict—by Spain, its colonial ruler since 1885, by the principal adversaries, Morocco and Polisario-SADR, and by international organizations, the UN, the OAU—began even before the recognized *onset* of this protracted conflict in October 1975, which was the result of half a dozen inter-related developments about the uncertain future status of Western Sahara. The first was Spain's proclamation of the internal autonomy of its then-existing colony in August 1974, as the first step toward decolonization. The second was Morocco's and Mauritania's submission of their claims to sovereignty over Western Sahara to the International Court of Justice (ICJ) in early October. In September 1975, Spain announced that a referendum would be held among the residents of Western Sahara in the first half of 1976, with the options of independence or continued association with Spain. Morocco and Mauritania responded on October 1, 1975 with an agreement to partition the disputed territory between them, the former declaring its rejection of the option of independence in a referendum, as it was to do repeatedly during the next four decades. On October 15, 1975, a UN mission reported sentiment in Western Sahara favoring independence. On October 16, in a crucial decision, the ICJ ruled that, despite some historical links and legal ties between the claimants and Western Sahara, neither Morocco nor Mauritania had a valid claim to sovereignty over the disputed territory. The same day, King Hassan declared that the "links" cited by the ICJ validated Morocco's claim to sovereignty and that he would lead a march of 350,000 Moroccan civilians into Western Sahara to secure its integration into Morocco. The result was the *Moroccan March* crisis, summarized in the discussion of crisis management above, marking the onset of this protracted conflict and the failure of the first attempt at conflict resolution of this conflict.

The first, abortive attempt to resolve this conflict peacefully occurred in July 1981. The OAU had been floating the idea of direct negotiations since 1979 as the only likely successful path to conflict resolution. Algeria, the patron of Polisario from the outset, concurred, as did the UN. Polisario consistently favored an UN-supervised referendum, including the option of independence. King Hassan of Morocco, as noted, consistently rejected any reference to an independence option. In July 1981, he offered to hold a referendum. However, when Polisario accepted, conditional on the inclusion of the independence option, Morocco withdrew the offer, ending this attempt at conflict resolution.

A promising episode in the search for a mutually acceptable resolution formula occurred on August 30, 1988, when both *Morocco and Polisario-SADR accepted a UN-OAU peace plan*, which called for a ceasefire and a referendum on self-determination among the people of Western Sahara. However, there was no progress in the further negotiations, and, in early October 1989, as noted, Polisario broke the truce and launched its second attack on the Morocco base, Galtat Zemmour. UN Secretary-General Perez de Cuellar publicly urged a resumption of direct negotiations on October 13; and the Saharan Arab Democratic Republic (SADR), the political entity that represented Polisario to the world, urged a dialogue with Morocco on November 7, 1989, but Polisario ignored these urgings from the UN and its own colleagues. However, following another request by the UN Secretary-General, Polisario relented and agreed to a truce on February 21, 1990 until the end of March.

A breakthrough seemed likely with another UN-mediated ceasefire in 1991 and a rare substantive political agreement by the principal adversaries—the <u>Settlement Plan</u>, essentially the 1988 OAU plan, endorsed by Security Council Resolution 658, signed in 1991. It called for a ceasefire, which took effect on September 6, 1991, a self-determination referendum, set for 1992, an exchange of prisoners, the repatriation of refugees, and the total withdrawal of Morocco's forces from Western Sahara. However, only the ceasefire was implemented—and has been sustained ever since, with few violations. All the other provisions of the Settlement Plan floundered over one contentious issue—*who was to be included in the voter list?*

Polisario urged acceptance of the original voter list, based upon Spain's 1974 census, 74,000 Sahrawi. Morocco insisted on expansion of the list to include Sahrawi residents who fled into Morocco in the 1950s. After 2 years of deadlocked negotiations over this issue, the UN accepted Morocco's demands. The UN mission in Western Sahara, MINURSO, received 244,643 applications for Sahrawi status. From 1994 to 2000, mostly after 1998, it interviewed 198,649 applicants for the right to participate in the referendum. There were 131,036 appeals by rejected applicants, almost all from Morocco-nominated candidates. UN Secretary-General Kofi Annan, doubting that the referendum would ever be held, urged a resolution to seek an alternative. The Council accepted his advice and passed Resolution 1292 on February 29, 2000, calling for an "early, durable and agreed solution." Almost certainly, this was done at the advice of the Secretary-General's Personal Representative on the Western Sahara dispute, former US Secretary of State, James Baker III, in 1997. Polisario strongly opposed the abandonment of the Settlement Plan; Morocco was relieved because of its unqualified rejection of any plan that included the independence option.

There were two Baker plans for resolution of this protracted conflict, one in May 2001, the other in May 2003. *Baker Plan I* provided for a referendum, to be held 5 years after the beginning of the Plan's implementation. The voter list was to include all persons who had been full-time residents of Western Sahara for the preceding year. A dual system of authority was advocated by Baker for the 5-year transition period: responsibility for most *internal* affairs was to be granted to an assembly and executive elected by persons on the MINURSO list, including the 1-year residence proviso; all *external issues* and some internal affairs would be under the control of Morocco. Polisario opposed the 1-year residence criterion, viewing it as the gateway to a large number of persons from Morocco without primary allegiance to the SADR, and it was less than enthusiastic about the division of external and internal authority, and the 5-year waiting period for the referendum. Morocco seemed satisfied with Baker Plan I, which was widely perceived beyond the region, including the UN, as strongly biased in favor of Morocco. The Security Council, in its Resolution 1429, reaffirmed that any solution must "provide for the self-determination of the people of Western Sahara."

The result was a more balanced *Baker Plan II*. The time frame for the transition was made more flexible, 4–5 years. The voter list was made more rigid: it would comprise persons on the MINURSO voter list from December 30, 1999, that is, before the appeals from persons denied inclusion in the Settlement Plan-proposed voter list had been addressed; the UN High Commission for Refugees (UNHCR) repatriation list from October 31, 2000, and persons who had lived in Western Sahara since December 30, 1999. Moreover, the list of subjects granted to the

Western Saharan autonomous government was enlarged. However, the reaction of the principal adversaries was negative. Morocco rejected the inclusion of the independence option in the proposed referendum, even though it had approved Baker Plan I, which included this option. Polisario initially rejected Baker Plan II in its entirety, noting the lack of guarantees of its control over the subjects to be placed under the jurisdiction of Western Sahara's autonomous government, and the inclusion of Moroccan settlers in the referendum voting list. Later, on July 11, 2003, Spain's UN Representative announced that Polisario accepted Baker Plan II. This induced an initiative by the USA, supported by the UK and Spain, to request the UN Security Council to endorse Baker Plan II; China, France, and Russia opposed an act injurious to Morocco. The Security Council did pass a resolution, strongly supporting, but not endorsing, this Plan; and the resolution was not a prelude to UN action—for another 4 years.

The most recent attempt to resolve the Western Sahara protracted conflict occurred in 2007–2008, in response to UN pressure: Security Council Resolution 1754, passed in April 2007, called on the two principal adversaries "to enter direct negotiations without preconditions, in good faith." Morocco and Polisario held four rounds of negotiations, the *Manhasset* negotiations, in June and August 2007, and January and March 2008, over Morocco's persistent plan for regional autonomy and Polisario's persistent commitment to independence for Western Sahara. There was no compromise and no progress, then or since.

Western Sahara: Causes of Non-Resolution

Viewed in terms of the *Conflict Resolution Model* set out above, *three of the six postulated conditions* of the high likelihood of conflict resolution were evident in the *Western Sahara* conflict.

Exhaustion Neither adversary has exhibited exhaustion. Both Sultan Hassan and his son, the current ruler of Morocco, Muhammad VI, have been steadfast in their opposition to independence for Western Sahara. This rejection extended to the inclusion of independence as a legitimate option for voters in a referendum on the future status of Western Sahara—even after the large expansion of the voter list to the benefit of Morocco—except in one instance of attempted mediation, Morocco's formal acceptance of Baker Plan I (2001), which provided for this option in a proposed referendum on Sahrawi self-determination after 4 or 5 years of Western Sahara's autonomy. Moreover, that Morocco concession was nullified by Hassan's insistence on a large expansion of the voting list, far beyond the 74,000 Sahrawi identified in the 1974 Spanish census of Western Africa's population, in an attempt to ensure a majority against independence by Moroccan settlers in Western Sahara. Polisario-SADR leaders remained committed to the goal of independence for Western Sahara, though they displayed some flexibility on an expansion of the voter list for the referendum, indicating an optimism regarding a majority in favor of independence, even in a referendum with the inclusion of many Moroccan settlers in Western Sahara as voters. Furthermore, the steady growth of Polisario's military capability and its successful 'forward' policy of attacks on Moroccan military bases, and Morocco's construction of six massive sand walls in Western Sahara, in an effort to seal much of the disputed territory against invasion by Polisario guerillas, *suggest the opposite of exhaustion* by either adversary.

Changes in the Balance of Capability were conducive to conflict resolution. In the early years of this conflict, the qualitative and quantitative superiority of Morocco's armed forces and weapons was not successfully exploited by the kingdom in imposing a resolution of the conflict on Morocco's terms. Later, when the balance between Morocco's conventional forces and *Polisario's* guerrilla forces moved toward relative equality, this condition *contributed to a greater likelihood of conflict resolution* but was not sufficient to ensure termination.

Domestic Pressures There is virtually no available evidence of domestic pressures for compromise in the behavior of either principal adversary. The sole known exception was the urging by the SADR of a dialogue between its activist wing, Polisario, and Morocco, on November 7, 1989, when the fate of the OAU's 1988 conflict resolution plan hung in the balance. As noted, Polisario ignored the pressure from its political colleagues and launched a fresh attack on a Moroccan base 1 day after the pressure by the SADR.

External Pressures Among the six conditions that were postulated as likely to contribute to conflict resolution, the most visible in the *Western Sahara* conflict was foreign pressures, *one of three favorable conditions of termination.* These pressures were present in abundance since 1988: the OAU

Plan, supported by the UN in 1988–1989; frequent UN-initiated ceasefire and truce agreements, notably in 1991; an active role by two UN Secretaries-General, Perez de Cuellar and Kofi Annan, the former strongly supporting the OAU plan, the latter strongly supporting Baker Plan II; several UN Security Council resolutions calling for a fresh initiative in February 2000—urging the parties in 2000 to seek an alternative to the 1991 Settlement Plan that had reached an impasse, which led to Baker Plan I; a Security Council request for changes in the 2001 Baker Plan, leading to Baker Plan II in 2003; Security Council pressure for changes in Baker Plan II, which failed; and its 2007 resolution, calling for a renewal of direct negotiations between Morocco and Polisario, which were conducted in 2007–2008 but concluded with another impasse. There is no evidence of active external pressures on the principal adversaries in the *Western Sahara* conflict since 2008 to pursue other possible paths to definitive conflict resolution.

Reduction in Discordant Objective Both of the principal adversaries in the *Western Sahara* conflict have remained committed to their primary objective throughout this conflict—formal integration into Morocco or unqualified control over the disputed territory, for Morocco, and independence, for Polisario-SADR: there has *never been any reduction of discordance in their diametrically opposed core objective.*

Decline in Conflict-Sustaining Acts During the first 15 years of this unresolved conflict (1975–1990), there was a steady flow of conflict-sustaining acts in Western Sahara, as evident in the 10 crises between Morocco and the Polisario-SADR, most of them characterized by moderate violence. However, since 1990, this protracted conflict has been dormant, with no military-security crises between the principal adversaries. This *decline in hostile acts*, especially for an extended period, did facilitate several attempts by the adversaries to achieve conflict resolution by *third-party mediation* efforts, e.g., the two Baker Plans in 2001 and 2003, and by direct *negotiations* in 2007–2008. As such, it *supported the postulate* that a decline in conflict-sustaining acts would enhance the *likelihood* of conflict resolution. However, that goal remains elusive.

In sum, three of the six conditions postulated in the *Conflict Resolution Model* as most likely to lead to resolution of interstate protracted conflicts—*Changes* in the *Balance of Capability,* in the direction of relative equality in the military dimension of Capability,

External Pressures on the adversaries, and a *Decline in Conflict-sustaining Acts*—have been present in the *Western Sahara* conflict. However, thus far, the presence of three conditions acting as likely causes of conflict resolution, including one as highly visible and intense as foreign pressures from the late 1980s to 2008, have not been sufficient to attain that goal. Their presence, acting as Basic Causes, is *no guarantee* that conflict resolution will occur. The *enduring obstacles* to resolution of the Western Sahara conflict remain—rigidly *incompatible objectives* by the principal adversaries, especially Morocco, and the absence of collective *exhaustion* by both adversaries. Thus, this conflict remains unresolved.

In the absence of conflict resolution, there is no evidence of *Reconciliation* between the political regimes and/or societies of Morocco and Polisario-SADR.

AMERICAS

Costa Rica/Nicaragua Conflict (Resolved)

Behavior

Decisions
There were several *inter-related* major decisions by the two principal adversaries in the early and late phases of this protracted conflict. The first was an initiative by Costa Rica's military dictator, General *Federico Tinoco* (1917–1919), designed *to achieve three goals* simultaneously: *to assert Costa Rica's independence from Nicaragua*, its perennial rival in Central America, and from *the United States,* the *long-time patron of Nicaragua; to prevent an anticipated rebellion,* and *to achieve international recognition for his regime.* The decision took the form of a *pre-emptive dispatch of troops to the Nicaragua border* on 25 May 1918. However, it proved to be ill-conceived, for this provocative act aroused the active hostility of the USA, which had earlier precipitated Tinoco's overthrow and enforced exile.

Nicaragua responded with a similar provocative decision—*to recognize and support the anti-Tinoco Costa Rican rebellion against his regi*me, led by *Julio Acosta.* That Nicaragua decision was implemented by an identical act, moving troops to the Costa Rica border. The USA, as always in these tit-for-tat non-violent military exchanges, adopted a passive non-interventionist attitude that both adversaries correctly perceived as tacit support for Nicaragua's hostile act.

Three decades later, another successful military coup in Costa Rica brought General *José Figueres* and a 10-man junta to power in April 1948. Nicaragua, as always, seeking a submissive 'friendly' regime in Costa Rica, made the *strategic* decision *to seek regime change*. This was implemented in the form of a Nicaraguan invasion of Costa Rica in December 1948, with a sizeable armed force in Central America's interstate crises, 1000. Figueres responded with mobilization of all available Costa Rica manpower and the dispatch of troops to the Nicaragua border.

The bitterly disputed presidential election in Costa Rica between pro- and anti-Figueres candidates spawned a 44-day civil war, with 2000 killed, the bloodiest event in twentieth-century Central America. The victor in this civil war, Figueres and his military junta, drafted a new constitution providing for a democratically elected assembly and abolished the Military in Costa Rica, a unique condition in the Americas to the present day and virtually in the rest of the world. Soon after a peace treaty between Costa Rica and Nicaragua was mediated by the Organization of American States (OAS) in February 1949, Figueres and his junta relinquished power to the newly elected Costa Rica government, in November 1949, another unique act.

The last of the three interstate crises during this conflict (January 8–20, 1955) was a re-play of the first two crises and conflicting decisions. Nicaragua once more made a decision *to support Costa Rican rebels, with the aim of overthrowing Figueres* (He had been elected president of Costa Rica in 1953—in the first of 13 peaceful and transparent presidential elections in Costa Rica in more than half a century, until 2010). Nicaragua implemented its decision with the dispatch of troops and aerial bombings, but the OAS called on its members to provide aircraft to Costa Rica. It also succeeded in ending the crisis and mini-war and created a demilitarized zone between the two adversaries in 1955, marking the end of their protracted conflict.

Decision-Makers

The key decision-makers of Costa Rica during this interstate conflict were noted above in the discussion of decisions. They emerged during each of the crises in which Costa Rica's *strategic* and important *tactical* decisions were made and implemented: Federico Tinoco in the first major decision during the 1918 crisis, and Jose Figueres in the major decisions during the 1948 and 1955 crises.

The decision-makers of Nicaragua during this conflict can be traced to two sources. One was the Somoza family dynasty that exercised dictatorial power in Nicaragua for more than half a century (1927–1979), that is, during the second and third phases of this Central America conflict, 1948–1949 and 1955. The founder of this dynasty, *Anastasia Somoza*, commanded Nicaragua's National Guard from 1927 to 1937, and then as president from 1937 until his death in 1956. He was succeeded by his two sons from 1956 until 1979, when the family dynasty was overthrown by the Left-wing *Sandinista* Party, whose five-person *junta* ruled Nicaragua from 1979 to 1984 and whose acknowledged leader since 1981, Daniel Ortega, was elected president for 1985–1990 (and again, for 2006–2011 and 2011–2016).

Throughout their 52 years of absolute power over all decisions of any consequence in Nicaragua, including economic policy and the attempts to generate regime change in Costa Rica, the Somoza family had the unqualified backing of the United States. Moreover, the USA intervened frequently in the two adversarial states and their relations from 1909 to 1933, with occupation of one or the other by Marines from 1912 to 1933, except for 9 months in 1925. Thus senior American officials in Washington throughout this conflict, notably all who served as Secretary of State, Secretary of War, Deputy Secretary, Under-Secretary, and Assistant Secretary of State for Latin America, all the US ambassadors and consuls to Costa Rica and Nicaragua from 1918 to 1955, were decision-makers during their tenure in that period, with particular influence during the three crises between the adversaries in this conflict. (Unlike the 1965 Dominican Republic crisis, in which President *Johnson* was the active, pre-eminent US decision-maker, and several presidents who were directly involved in decisions relating to the Panama Canal, from *Theodore Roosevelt* to *Jimmy Carter*, the US president was not involved in the Costa Rica/Nicaragua conflict.)

Decision Process
The decision process in the two principal adversarial states, Costa Rica and Nicaragua, was primarily authoritarian, with decision-making power concentrated in an *individual* (Tinoco in the 1918 decision), a *junta* (led by Figueres in the 1948 decision), a *family* (Somoza throughout this conflict), and probably, an input from the Costa Rica *Assembly* in its

1955 decision. As for the decision process during this conflict in Central America, it replicated the US decision process in other conflicts in which the USA was highly involved as a conflict actor, with US diplomatic representatives in Costa Rica and Nicaragua, and at OAS meetings deliberating an issue related to their conflict—generally, diplomats and consuls in the field—acting under instructions from the US State Department.

Conflict-Sustaining Acts During the shortest of the three Americas' post-World War I interstate conflicts—*Costa Rica/Nicaragua*, 37 years (1918–1955), compared to *Ecuador/Peru*, 80 years (1918–1998), and *Honduras/Nicaragua*, 89 years (1918–2007), *political hostility* was the most frequent conflict-sustaining technique (CST), with the greatest impact. *Violence* occurred during two interstate crises between Costa Rica and Nicaragua, as did *verbal hostility*, but they were secondary in frequency and impact.

Political Hostility was evident throughout this conflict but was conspicuously intense at its onset and during its last decade. Although Costa Rica and Nicaragua were the principal adversaries, they were heavily dependent on the longstanding self-appointed hegemon of the Americas, the United States, since its proclamation of the Monroe Doctrine (1823). Thus their politically hostile relationship was intertwined with US goals, policy, and behavior in Central America since both became formally independent of Spain in 1821. At the onset of this conflict, Nicaragua was a virtual protectorate of the USA, which dominated its government and political leaders and continued this role informally long after it voluntarily ceased its direct control of Nicaragua in 1933. By contrast, Costa Rica, like the hegemon of the Americas, proudly retained its image as an 'exceptional' state and society. This incurred the hostility of the USA, which did not recognize the regime of Costa Rica's president, General Federico Tinoco, in 1917–1918. He responded with a pre-emptive military strike against Nicaragua in 1918. Tinoco was deposed in August 1919, as was his successor in 1919, because the USA refused to recognize him as Costa Rica's president. Nicaragua exhibited its political hostility to Costa Rica by supporting a rebel force that invaded Costa Rica and proclaimed a provisional government. The new regime, led by Julio Acosta, was recognized by Nicaragua, Honduras, and Guatemala.

After a lengthy period of calm between the principal adversaries (1919–1943), the conflict was renewed between Costa Rica's military-political leader, José Figueres, and Nicaragua's long-time, US-supported dictator of Nicaragua, Anastasio Somoza. When Somoza, coping with a domestic political crisis, supported a left-wing Costa Rican president in 1947, the USA intervened once more and secured Nicaragua's withdrawal of forces from Costa Rica in exchange for renewed American support for Somoza. Toward the end of this conflict, Costa Rica's President Figueros was accused by Nicaragua in 1954 of supporting a plan by Nicaragua revolutionary, Chamorro, to assassinate Somoza, reinforcing the animosity generated by acts of political hostility.

Violence was used in two of the three military-security crises during this interstate protracted conflict. An invasion of Costa Rica by 1000 Nicaraguan National Guardsmen in December 1948 led to the movement of Costa Rican troops to its border with Nicaragua and to minor clashes in January–February 1949; their second crisis was resolved by an OAS inquiry commission and a military commission to supervise activity on their border. Minor clashes in Central America also occurred in the third Costa Rica/Nicaragua crisis, from January 8 to 20, 1955: 500 Costa Rica rebels, supported by the Somoza government, crossed the frontier from Nicaragua and captured a town near Costa Rica's capital. Once more the OAS sent a fact-finding mission. The rebels were forced by Costa Rican forces to withdraw from captured Costa Rican territory, ending this crisis, with the adversaries agreeing to an OAS plan for demilitarized zones along the border. As in several other interstate conflicts, violence, during a military-security crisis, in January 1955, became the catalyst for conflict resolution, soon after termination of an interstate crisis.

Verbal hostility was employed by both of the principal Central America adversaries, especially from 1944 to 1955. It was highly personalized propaganda by the two leaders, Figueres in Costa Rica and Somoza in Nicaragua, who viewed their neighboring head of government as an enemy and strongly encouraged the overthrow of 'the other.' These frequent acts of verbal hostility contributed to the persistence of this conflict but were essentially reinforcement of a deeply rooted political hostility and rivalry between two neighbors with very different societies, incompatible outlooks, and conflicting interests since their independence after two centuries of colonial rule by Spain.

Economic discrimination was not apparent in this Central America interstate conflict.

CHAPTER 7

Select Case Study Findings on Interstate Conflicts: Asia

Afghanistan/Pakistan Conflict (Unresolved)

Historical Roots

The roots of this *unresolved* conflict in the borderland of South Asia-Central Asia can be traced to the mid-eighteenth century, to the *Durrani* era of Afghanistan's imperial expansion into northwest India, early in the period of British rule over the sub-continent. As an interstate conflict, it began with the creation of Pakistan and India on August 14–15, 1947, when the North West Frontier Province (NWFP) was allocated to Pakistan by the British Parliament's India Independence Act. An impending conflict between Afghanistan and Pakistan was already evident in July 1947, during a British Government of India-supervised referendum among the overwhelming Pushtun ethnic majority in the NWFP: the options for its electorate were integration into Pakistan or India. Conspicuously absent were two other options, urged by the Government of Afghanistan—*integration into Afghanistan*, where the Pushtuns formed the largest ethnic community, or *independence for the North West Frontier Province*, widely known by its population as *Pakhtunkhwa*. [In 2010, Pakistan formally accepted the name change, adding the preceding word, *Khyber*]. The outcome of the 1947 referendum, boycotted by the largest socio-political organization in the NWFP, the *Khudai Khidmatgars* [Servants of God]—a very close ally of the Gandhi- and Nehru-led Indian National Congress until the 1947

Partition of India—was a very large majority, of those who voted, in favor of integration into Pakistan. The referendum and its outcome were immediately rejected by Afghanistan as illegal, leading, *inter alia*, to its decisive rejection of Pakistan's initial application for membership in the United Nations, and they have never been accepted by Afghanistan as the legitimate expression of the NWFP's Pushtun population. That ethnic-territorial dispute has been the core of this interstate conflict since its onset in 1948.

Behavior

Afghanistan Decisions

The first of many *strategic* and important *tactical* decisions by Afghanistan in this unresolved, though long-dormant conflict was its repudiation of the results of a referendum conducted in mid-1947 under the terms of the UK Government's formal decision leading to the partition of India: the referendum, among the residents of the North West Frontier Province (NWFP), offered two options for their future association—legal integration into the Dominion of India or the Dominion of Pakistan, scheduled to come into existence on August 14–15 of that year. As soon as news of this impending referendum became known, Afghanistan made the *strategic* decision *to challenge its legitimacy and legality.* In March 1947, Afghanistan's decision was implemented in an official dissenting letter to the UK Government: as noted it emphasized *the overwhelming Pushtun majority of* NWFP residents and declared that *two other crucial options should therefore be included in the referendum—integration of the NWFP territory and residents into Afghanistan,* in which Pushtuns were the largest ethnic community, and *independence for the NWFP*. Both the UK and the leadership of the soon-to-be-inaugurated Dominion of Pakistan remained firm in the narrow choice of referendum options. After the results of the two-option referendum were announced—a large majority favored integration into Pakistan—Afghanistan vigorously reaffirmed its rejection of the outcome as a denial of a fundamental right of the NWFP Pushtuns to genuine self-determination.

A second *strategic* decision by Afghanistan was *to disavow, formally, its long-time acquiescence in the 1893 Durand Line Agreement* between British India and a weakened Afghan monarchy: although it had informally rejected the Durand Line as the legitimate border with Pakistan, both before and at the time of Pakistan's independence (August 15, 1947), Afghanistan's decision *no longer to recognize the Durand Line as their border was announced in July 1949*.

The unconcealed hostility of Afghanistan toward its southern neighbor was expressed frequently: an early expression of this attitude was its *tactical* decision *to vote against Pakistan's admission to the UN* on September 30, 1947, the only negative vote on this issue in the UN General Assembly. Aware of the adverse fall-out of this act led Afghanistan to withdraw its vote on October 20, 1947 and to establish diplomatic relations with Pakistan in 1948. Yet the Afghanistan commitment to reversing the outcome of the 1947 referendum in the NWFP and its integration into Pakistan, continued to rankle. Among the important *tactical* decisions that reflected this commitment was Afghanistan's *sponsorship of a Pashtunistan Government in the border city of Tirah* in 1951.

Much more significant, in terms of this South Asia-Central Asia conflict, was Afghanistan's *strategic* decision *to oppose vigorously Pakistan's 'One Unit' plan* in 1954 and 1955 *to merge all four western provinces* in this geographically divided state *into one unit, to be called West Pakistan* (East Bengal was to remain the sole province of East Pakistan). Afghanistan was enraged by what it deplored as the second phase of a conscious Pakistan denial of the NWFP Pashtuns' right to self-determination; the first phase was their imposed integration into the new state of Pakistan via the 1947 referendum that deprived the NWFP Pashtuns of their natural right to choose integration with their ethnic kin in Afghanistan or independence.

A *strategic* Afghanistan *foreign policy* decision, with roots in this conflict and belated far-reaching consequences, was *to seek aid from the USSR, when Pakistan suspended its cross-border trade on May 14, 1955*: as a land-locked state, Afghanistan was heavily dependent on Pakistan for most of its foreign trade, both imports and exports. The implementation of this decision took the form of Soviet economic and military aid that began immediately and grew considerably over time. In August 1955, Afghanistan signed a barter protocol with the USSR, assuring it of a regular supply of vital imports. In December 1955, the Soviet Union provided a $100 million development loan. The following August, Afghanistan received the first small supply of Soviet arms ($25 million). By 1960, the Soviet Union accounted for half of Afghanistan's total trade, including 90% of its oil and all of its military imports. The next year, when Pakistan once more suspended Afghanistan's cross-border trade and access to the Arabian Sea, the USSR further increased the flow of economic and military aid, which continued through the 1960s and 1970s. More than two decades after Afghanistan's initial 1955 decision, the *alignment between Afghanistan and the USSR culminated in a Treaty of Friendship* (December 5, 1978). This, in turn, provided a legal basis for the Soviet Union's disastrous military intervention-occupation of Afghanistan the next year that lasted a decade (1979–1989). For the Soviet Union, it proved to be a superpower model of very high geopolitical costs with no visible benefits that was emulated by the other superpower, the U.S., for an even longer period (2001–2014).

Afghanistan: Decision-Makers
The key *decision-makers* in Afghanistan during the most active period of its conflict with Pakistan (1947–1978) were members of the *Musahiban* royal family. Specifically, they were as follows: *Muhammad Hashim* and *Shah Mahmud*, two uncles of the young *King Zahir Shah*, who alternated as Prime Minister (1947–1953); *Muhammad Daoud Khan*, cousin of the King and Prime Minister, and his brother who served as Deputy Prime Minister and Foreign Minister (1953–1963) for King Zahir Shah (1963–1973); and Muhammad Daoud Khan, as President of Afghanistan, after a coup that overthrew the monarchy (1973–1978). Other than the first two decisions noted above, acquiescence in the results of the 1947 NWFP referendum and renunciation of the 1893 Durand Line agreement with British India, the most influential figure in shaping Afghanistan's policy toward Pakistan and key decisions for 15 years was Daoud Khan. Since 1978 this conflict has been dormant, first, when Afghanistan was under communist rule, with Soviet occupation (1979–1989), later, under the *Taliban* (1996–2001) and, since then, the U.S.-supported Afghanistan Government in the Afghanistan-*Taliban* War.

Afghanistan: Decision Process
The political structure of Afghanistan during the active period of this unresolved conflict (1947–1978) combined two systems—organized, centralized government in the relatively few urban centers and autonomy in the provinces and tribal areas. A national legislature existed with 120 members, acting as a consultative body at the discretion of the monarch, later, of the president or the prime minister. In the autonomous Tribal Areas, the basic governing unit was the *Jirga* or *Assembly*, with a higher assembly, *Loe Jirga*, that met infrequently. During the period

of Soviet occupation, an Afghan Communist structure was introduced but its institutions exercised little actual decision-making power *vis-à-vis* Pakistan. The Taliban introduced a highly authoritarian political structure during its 5 years in power (1996–2001); it was replaced by a formally democratic system, under U.S. influence. *In sum*, when the Afghanistan/Pakistan conflict was active (1947–1978), the Afghanistan decision process on major issues related to the conflict was concentrated in the small number of political leaders noted above, with informal consultation involving provincial and tribal leaders on matters of local concern, but not on matters of general national policy toward the long-time adversary, Pakistan.

Pakistan: Decisions
The other principal adversary in this interstate conflict made even more *strategic* and important *tactical* decisions. The first two major Pakistan decisions in this conflict were the obverse of Afghanistan's two earliest decisions, noted above. Both were *passive* decisions that had long-term *strategic* consequences for the adversaries and the durability of their conflict. However, they did not involve a complex decision process for Pakistan or indeed any problem of choice: there was only one perceived option for the two closely related issues. One Pakistan decision was *to welcome, with relief, the result of the NWFP referendum—a large majority in favor of integration into Pakistan, not India*. The other decision was *to acquiesce, comfortably, in the implicit confirmation of Pakistan's claim that the 1893 Afghanistan–British India Agreement on the Durand Line as their common border applied as well to the border between Afghanistan and Pakistan*, by virtue of the formal inclusion of the NWFP in the territory of the new state.

In the early 1950s, Pakistan made a major *foreign policy* decision, not *directly* related to, but with far-reaching consequences for, its conflict with Afghanistan—*to seek a close military alignment with the United States*. This decision was implemented in three high-profile national security agreements: a *Mutual Defense Assistance Act with the United States* in May 1954, which mushroomed into a half-century of valuable military aid from a superpower, greatly enhancing Pakistan's military capability in its primary national security pre-occupation, its long, acrimonious unresolved conflict with India; and *membership in two U.S.-sponsored regional alliances*, the South-East Asia Treaty Organization (SEATO) in September 1954, and the Central Treaty Organization

(CENTO), better known as the 'Baghdad Pact,' in September 1955. This military alignment with the U.S., especially the first of these three pacts, which was renewed continuously except for a brief suspension of U.S. military aid, greatly enhanced Pakistan's military capability, primarily related not only to its conflict with India but also in its conflict with a much weaker Afghanistan in all the dimensions of national power, despite the latter's (much smaller) military aid from the USSR.

Another major (domestic political) decision by Pakistan in the mid-1950s had a direct and significant *strategic* impact on the conflict with Afghanistan: it was *to merge the four provinces in the western part of Pakistan—West Punjab, Sind, Baluchistan,* and the disputed territory of the *North West Frontier Province (NWFP)—*into *'One Unit,' West Pakistan.* The plan was approved by the NWFP Assembly on November 25, 1954 and was inaugurated on October 14, 1955. As noted in the above discussion of Afghanistan's decisions, this act was perceived by Pakistan's adversary as an even more demeaning act than the 1947 two-option NWFP referendum, for it further submerged the Pushtun ethnic identity of the decisive majority of the NWFP's population in one of Pakistan's two regions. Afghanistan expressed its dismay and unalterable opposition to the 'One Unit' merger but lacked the power to undo what it perceived as the violation of a fundamental Pushtun right to self-determination by a Punjab-dominated Government of Pakistan. For Afghanistan, the 'One Unit' scheme was destined to perpetuate its conflict with Pakistan until the merger was rescinded.

On two notable occasions—there were many during this unresolved interstate conflict—Pakistan decided *to cut off transit trade from, and deny access to, its port on the Arabian Sea, to land-locked Afghanistan, once in mid-1956 and again in 1961,* the latter in retaliation against Afghanistan's closure of its border with Pakistan in 1960. Both cases had *strategic* consequences: the first, as noted above, led to Afghanistan's request for Soviet aid and the second deepened the relationship between Afghanistan and the USSR.

Another Pakistan decision, with long-term *strategic* consequences, was made in 1973 by Prime Minister *Zulfiqar Ali Bhutto,* newly appointed after a lengthy period of rule by Pakistan's politically powerful Military establishment: it was *to adopt a more aggressive policy toward Afghanistan, including support for Afghan Islamists against the regime of* Mohammad Daoud Khan, *a long-term foe of Pakistan, who had returned to power that year after a successful coup against* King Zahir Shah, *his cousin,* who had ousted Daoud in 1963 from his position as Afghanistan's leader from 1953 to 1963, as noted. Bhutto's anti-Daoud policy became entangled with—and was perceived as—a hostile policy directed at Afghanistan and Pushtuns generally. There was strong evidence supporting this perception, especially Bhutto's decisions in 1973 *to dissolve the Pushtun and Baluchi National Awami(People's) Party governments in the NWFP and Baluchistan* and in 1975 *to ban the National Awami Party*, on the grounds that they were disloyal to Pakistan. Moreover, between 1973 and 1977, when Bhutto was in power, Pakistan provided military training to an estimated 5000 young Islamist dissidents, whose goal was to overthrow the Daoud regime in favor of a pro-Islamist government in Afghanistan.

This Bhutto introduction of the 'Islamist' factor into Pakistan's relations with Afghanistan was to re-occur later in their conflict as a valued technique to secure a regime in Kabul more sympathetic to Pakistan. Soon after the USSR invasion of Afghanistan in December 1979, a decision was made by Pakistan *to oppose the Soviet occupation and the newly installed Afghan Communist regime*. This was implemented by *active military support for the Mujahuddin* [Islamist freedom fighters] *in their struggle against the Soviet occupation*, as well as *sanctuary to Afghan opponents of its proxy regime*. That support, including weapons and the opportunity to establish bases in Pakistan's tribal areas, continued throughout the Soviet occupation (1979–1989). During that decade and beyond the Taliban emerged as a steadily growing force in the struggle for control over Afghanistan, with Pakistan as a major source of economic and military aid, until '9/11' and the beginning of the U.S. war in Afghanistan. What began in the early 1970s within the Afghanistan/Pakistan conflict became a major fact in the continuing struggle over the future of Afghanistan four decades later.

Pakistan: Decision-Makers
In its first 4 years of independence (1947–1951), Pakistan's principal *decision-makers* were its 'founding father,' *Mohammed Ali Jinnah*, who served as Governor-General (1947–1948), and *Liaquat Ali Khan*, Prime Minister (1947–1951), his principal aide in the decisive last phase of the tense, bitter, and complex tripartite negotiations (British Government of India, Indian National Congress, and All-India Muslim League, 1946 and 1947) that led to the Partition of India on August 14–15, 1947 into the Dominions of the British Commonwealth, India and Pakistan.

They, particularly Jinnah, were crucial in the framing of the NWFP Referendum as a two-option choice—merger with Pakistan or India. Jinnah died in 1948, leaving Liaquat Ali as the decisive Pakistani decision-maker for Pakistan, with consultative inputs by senior members of the Muslim League leadership.

Liaquat Ali Khan was assassinated in October 1951. There were many influential decision-makers in the near-three decades after 1951, when the Afghanistan/Pakistan conflict was active. One was the person who served as Prime Minister of Pakistan. There were five prime ministers as Head of Government during that period: Liaquat Ali Khan, as noted; *Khwaja Nazimuddin* (1951–1953); *Mohammad Ali Bogra* (1953–1955); *Chaudhri Mohammad Ali* (1955–1956); and Zulfiqar Ali Bhutto (1973–1977). Other than Liaquat Ali, the only pre-eminent prime minister was Bhutto, whose decisions related to the Pakistan/Afghanistan conflict were noted above. From 1947 to 1956, Pakistan's Head of State was known as Governor-General, formally, the representative of the British monarch; Jinnah was the towering figure. Among the seven presidents from 1956 to 1988, the pre-eminent leaders were *Field Marshal Muhammad Ayub Khan* (1958–1969), *General Agha Muhammad Yahya Khan* (1969–1971), Bhutto (1973–1977), and *General Muhammad Zia-ul-Haq*, most of whose presidency (1978–1988) occurred after the conflict with Afghanistan became dormant.

Other influential decision-makers throughout those three decades were the persons occupying the position of *Army Commander-in-Chief, Pakistan Army (1947–1972)*, known as *Chief of Army Staff of Pakistan Army (COAS)* since 1972. The longest-serving and most influential military leader in decision-making on all national security issues during his tenure, including relations with Afghanistan, was *Ayub Khan* (1951–1958), who then served as President of Pakistan (1958–1969). Other prominent commanders in chief were *Yahya Khan* (1966–1971), who was also President (1969–1971) and *General Tikka Khan* (1972–1976), both of whom were crucial decision-makers in the disastrous decision process during the crisis-war over Bangladesh in 1971, and General Muhammad Zia-ul-Haq (1976–1988), who served simultaneously as president (1978–1988). Other important Pakistan decision-makers during the *Afghanistan/Pakistan* conflict, as well as on all other national security issues, were the Director of Inter-Services Intelligence (ISI), Pakistan's powerful military intelligence agency, of whom there were only three (1959–1978) during the three-decade active period of the

Afghanistan/Pakistan conflict, and the Minister of Foreign Affairs. There were only two notable decision-makers in that position: *Sir Muhammad Zafrullah Khan*, Pakistan's first, most accomplished, and long duration (1947–1954) voice to the world, and the talented, politically controversial Bhutto, who served even longer (1963–1966 and 1971–1977), as well as Prime Minister, simultaneously (1973–1977). As in most states, the institutions that they headed were active participants in the decision-making process relating to this interstate conflict (see below). However, as evident, the large majority of influential Pakistan decision-makers during the active period of this conflict, as in the more crucial conflict for Pakistan, the *India/Pakistan conflict*, were military leaders. Notable civilians were Jinnah, Liaquat Ali, Zafrullah, and Bhutto, and the first three of these four were active in the early years of Pakistan's independence and of these protracted conflicts.

Pakistan: Decision Process
The political structure of Pakistan at its creation was that of a parliamentary democracy, modeled on Westminster. The Head of State was the UK monarch, whose representative was the Governor-General of Pakistan, appointed, formally, by the king to a symbolic position lacking in political power and partiality. However, the reality of Pakistan's politics was profoundly different from its formal structure. The first Governor-General was 'the father of the nation,' undisputed leader of the Muslim League, the dominant, virtually unrivalled political party. Moreover, Jinnah was the self-conscious leader of the new nation and state, not a passive representative of the British monarch. He was also an authoritarian politician, who did not take kindly to opposition. With his passing a year after independence, the mantle of leadership passed to Liaquat Ali Khan, who lacked Jinnah's charisma. He was also more tolerant of diversity in political outlook, more comfortable with an environment in which competition among politicians and political parties was the norm. His character and personality facilitated 'the rules of the game' that characterized the British model.

Not all Pakistani politicians shared this outlook. The massive upheaval that accompanied the creation of Pakistan (and independent India)—the migration of approximately 15 million people, including the death of one million or more, combined with the widespread fear that the adversary, India, was an irreconcilable enemy that would not accept the permanent bifurcation of India, in both the west and east, and the magnitude of the tasks confronting a new nation and leadership—was not conducive to governing in accord with the niceties of a British parliamentary democracy. The result, over time, was pre-occupation with survival and an easy move to more authoritarian behavior in politics. The first of four wars with India (1947–1948), for Pakistan an irredentist war it initiated to gain control of a Muslim majority part of the sub-continent, Kashmir, occurred within 2 months of Partition and an almost unimaginable human tragedy. National insecurity was rampant, hardly an atmosphere conducive to political democracy and its accompanying decision-making environment. In perspective, the descent to authoritarian politics, with a central role for the Military, the institution that was perceived as the most reliable guardian of Pakistan's survival, in a conflict that was likely to pose frequent, often grave, threats to Pakistan, seemed inevitable, though it was not an abrupt process, from the creation of Pakistan.

As evident from the above discussion of Pakistan's decision-makers on issues relating to the *Afghanistan/Pakistan* conflict, *as on all issues of national security*, Pakistan's democratic structure generated a decision-making process that relied heavily on decision-makers primarily associated with national security, not with political parties (though the structure bred many parties). The pivotal institutions that shaped Pakistan's decision-making process for all disputed issues in interstate conflicts, with Afghanistan and India, have been the armed forces—all branches, with enormous power concentrated in the Intelligence community, the ISI. Civilian leaders of political parties have always been consulted. The skills of civil servants in the foreign ministry and occasionally other ministries are utilized. However, as the list of senior decision-makers after the early years of Pakistan's statehood indicates, the primacy of the Military in Pakistan's decision-making process dates to the beginning of the 1950s—Ayub Khan, the longest-serving Chief of the Army Staff and the longest-serving president, began his career as Pakistan's leader at the summit of military and political power in 1951 and held these positions for 18 years. Generals dominated the presidency for most of the time from 1958 to 1988. And the ISI, dominated by the Military, has been ever-present in the decision process since its known creation in 1959.

Afghanistan/Pakistan: Conflict-Sustaining Acts

Violence—compared with later outbreaks of violence in which Afghanistan was directly involved, notably the Soviet invasion of Afghanistan in 1989 and the U.S. invasion of Afghanistan in 2001, there was very little violence in the *Afghanistan/Pakistan* conflict, all of low intensity and short duration during its three interstate crises. The first of these episodes took the form of an Afghan military intrusion into Pakistan's territory on September 30, 1950 and its forced withdrawal 5 days later by Pakistani troops and aircraft, terminating their *Pushtunistan I* crisis. Another low-intensity outburst of violence occurred on March 29, 1955, 2 days after Pakistan announced its intention to incorporate its North West Frontier Province (NWFP) [known locally as *Khyber Pakhtunkhwa*], with an overwhelming Pushtun majority, into a merger of all provinces and tribal territories in the western half of the State into West Pakistan, its 'One Unit' Scheme, which triggered the second Pushtunistan crisis. Outraged Afghans caused serious damage to the Pakistan embassy in Kabul and to Pakistan consulates in Jalalabad and Kandahar. Pakistanis retaliated by attacking the Afghan consulate in Peshawar, capital of the NWFP, and Pakistan severed diplomatic and trade relations with Afghanistan. The crisis escalated with mobilization of forces by both adversaries, but no further violence erupted. The third episode of violence erupted on May 19, 1961, when 1000 Afghan troops infiltrated into Pakistan's territory, triggering the *Pushtunistan III* crisis. Two days later, Pakistan responded with air attacks on border areas. The crisis escalated on August 23 when Pakistan ordered the closure of all Afghan consulates and trade agencies in Pakistan, but there was no further violence between the two adversaries in this crisis or in their dormant but still-unresolved conflict.

Political Hostility—this type of conflict-sustaining act occurred more frequently than violence. As noted above, Afghanistan challenged the provision of the British plan for the partition of India that allocated the NWFP to Pakistan, one of the two successor states to the British *Raj* in 1947, as well as the options given the voters in a NWFP referendum on its future status—integration into Pakistan or India. Afghanistan formally demanded additional options—independence for the NWFP or merger with Afghanistan, to no avail. In 1949, the Afghan National Assembly passed a resolution nullifying all treaties signed between Afghanistan and British India, which included the designation of the Durand Line in 1893 as the formal border between Afghanistan and British India, which Afghanistan has rejected ever since the agreement was signed—it was forcibly imposed, according to Afghanistan. In July 1949, Afghanistan appointed a Pushtun notable, the Faqir of Ipi, leader of the independent state of Pakhtunistan. The next month, a youth group, the Young Afridi Party, proclaimed the formation of the Pakhtunistan Assembly in the independent state of Pakhtunistan within Pakistan's NWFP, a political act recognized by the Afghan Government. A much higher-profile act of political hostility was Afghanistan's vote against the admission of Pakistan to the UN in 1947, though it was successfully pressed by the U.S. and the UK to relent in 1948. Pakistan, too, contributed political acts that sustained and, at times, intensified this conflict: the most important was the 'One Unit' plan announced on November 22, 1954. Its formal inauguration, on October 14, 1955, including the NWFP, generated a sharp response by Afghanistan at the highest level: in November, at the end of the *Pushtunistan II* Crisis, the Afghanistan National Assembly formally reaffirmed its non-recognition of the integration of the NWFP into West Pakistan. Another conflict-sustaining act by Pakistan was the disbandment of the Awami National Party in February 1973, triggering anti-government demonstrations in the NWFP and Baluchistan, where that party had very strong support.

Verbal Hostility—at many points during the lengthy dispute over the NWFP and its Pushtun majority, especially during the three interstate crises in this conflict, both adversaries declared and reaffirmed their unshakeable views on the validity of their claim—in radio, press and, later, television statements by officials and at international conferences, whenever an opportunity arose to influence other states in favor of their case; each time they did so, the renewal of their claim served to sustain and, often, to intensify their conflict. The primary target for Afghan propaganda was the legality and, especially, the legitimacy of the 1893 Durand Line agreement, viewed by Afghanistan as a blatant imposition by a superior power and totally lacking in moral justification because it denied the right of a massive ethnic majority—Pakhtuns—to the exercise of a right to self-determination. The propaganda dimension of conflict-sustaining behavior included a battle in the late 1970s and, especially, in the 1980s between an increasingly secular, pro-Soviet Afghan regime and Pakistan's support for traditional Muslim education, including the creation of *madrassas* (Muslim religious schools) and the provision of teachers for the vast influx of refugees from Afghanistan attending these religious schools, as well as financing the activities of Muslim clerics in the tribal regions of Pakistan bordering Afghanistan: these were to provide the leadership and the bulk of the rank-and-file in the *Taliban* movement that was to play a crucial role in Afghanistan during the past two decades.

Economic Discrimination—in terms of conflict persistence, Pakistan has been—and continues to be—able to shape the economic 'rules of the game' in this conflict. Afghanistan, a land-locked state, is totally dependent on Pakistan for imports from, and exports to, virtually the rest of the world. Its access to the Arabian Sea is controlled by Pakistan, which can, almost at will, assist or retard economic growth in Afghanistan. Among the conflict-sustaining acts by Pakistan have been border closures, for example, lasting 5 months in 1955, during the *Pushtunistan II* crisis. Moreover, in the 1960s, many construction projects in Afghanistan were halted for lengthy periods because Pakistan controlled the flow of vital materials for the building and renovation of roads, factories, dams, and schools throughout Afghanistan and was prepared to exploit that structural advantage to achieve other goals; this made Afghanistan economically dependent on Pakistan. Other states, notably the USSR, especially interested in access to the Arabian Sea and the Indian Ocean, and Iran, seeking to enlarge its influence in the Middle East and Central Asia, provided alternative sources of economic aid—trade with the USSR, possible access to the Arabian Sea via a rail connection to the Iran border and the Persian Gulf. Overall, however, Pakistan possessed and frequently utilized geo-economic advantages, thereby contributing to conflict persistence.

Afghanistan/Pakistan Conflict: Crisis Management and Attempts at Conflict Resolution

As in many interstate conflicts, crisis management within the Afghanistan/Pakistan conflict, via *bilateral negotiations* and *third-party mediation*, has focused on the reduction of modest acts of violence between the principal adversaries during their three *interstate crises*.

Crisis 1 (mid-March 1949–October 5, 1950) unfolded in two stages a year apart. It began in mid-March 1949 when Pakistan arrested Afghan infiltrators into its *North West Frontier Province* and rejected once more any Afghanistan claim to the disputed territory—on the ground of *ethnic identity*: the vast majority of the NWFP population and the largest single ethnic community in Afghanistan are *Pushtuns*. On March 27, there were reports of a substantial hostile Afghanistan non-violent military act, the dispatch of two divisions and part of its air force to the frontier with Pakistan. Six days later, Afghanistan recalled its diplomats from Pakistan. Violent escalation occurred on June 12, in the form of Pakistan's bombing of an Afghan village close to the border with Pakistan. *Crisis management* was swift and successful—investigation by a joint Afghanistan-Pakistan commission, Pakistan's acceptance of responsibility for an "unintentional flight," and its agreement on July 31 to pay compensation. *Political* escalation occurred on August 12, 1949, with the formation of a Pushtunistan Assembly in Pakistan's NWFP territory, its proclamation of Pushtunistan independence, and recognition by Afghanistan, but without a discernible Pakistan response. Propaganda and agitation for a separate Pushtunistan state maintained a moderate level of tension during most of 1950, until a brief violent skirmish in the second stage of this lengthy crisis: Afghan troops invaded Pakistani territory on September 30, 1950 and were repulsed by Pakistani forces on October 5, the ultimate effective crisis management technique in this low-severity crisis.

Crisis 2 (March 27–November 1955) was caused by a high-profile, controversial Government of Pakistan *political act*, a merger of its four western provinces, Baluchistan, North West Frontier Province, (West) Punjab and Sind, into a unified *West Pakistan*: the crisis trigger was Afghanistan's receipt of information on March 27, 1955 of Pakistan's "One Unit Scheme." It responded with firm protests, verbally by Prime Minister Daoud and in a formal government-to-government Note, which triggered a crisis for Pakistan. The crisis escalated on March 30, with an attack on Pakistan's embassy in Kabul. Pakistan's initial, immediate response was an undefined threat of retaliation. A month later, on 1 May, Pakistan responded with several severe hostile acts: the breaking of diplomatic relations; closing of the border with Afghanistan; and termination of economic relations, including the closing of all Afghan trade agencies in Pakistan. Threatened with grave economic consequences, because of its dependence on the use of Pakistan's ports for imports and exports, Afghanistan declared a state of emergency and a mobilization of forces. Pakistan dispatched troops to the border. However, successful conflict-crisis management was achieved, primarily by the role of several Middle East mediators (see below). An agreement was signed on September 9, 1955, in which Afghanistan pledged amends for an insult to Pakistan's flag. *West Pakistan* was inaugurated on October 14—without any further official Afghanistan protests against the "One Unit Scheme." And Pakistan's embassy in Kabul was re-opened in November, ending the crisis.

Crisis 3 (May 19, 1961–January 29, 1962) was triggered by reports on May 19, 1961 of the infiltration of 1000 Afghan troops into Pakistan's territory. Pakistan responded on the 21st by bombing areas along the border it claimed belonged to Pakistan. Three months later, on August 23, Pakistan demanded the closure of all Afghan consulates and trade agencies in Pakistan, triggering a crisis for Afghanistan, which responded with a threat to break diplomatic relations unless the Pakistan closure order was rescinded. Pakistan, in turn, issued a formal White Paper accusing its neighbor of "expansionism" and broke diplomatic relations with Afghanistan on September 6.

Initial attempts at third-party crisis management—by the UK and the U.S. in October 1961—failed. However, President Kennedy's offer of good offices and his special envoy, L.T. Merchant, a rare foray in this conflict by the U.S. at the presidential level until after "9–11" [2001], succeeded on January 29, 1962 in mediating a temporary agreement between the adversaries: goods were delivered from Pakistan to Afghanistan, and the border was re-opened, for 2 months, ending this interstate crisis. However, diplomatic relations were not re-established until May 28, 1963, facilitated by Iran's mediation role. The USSR provided economic aid and weapons to Afghanistan during this crisis, a then unrecognized prelude to the extension of the Cold War to this regional conflict almost two decades later—with the USSR invasion and occupation of Afghanistan in December 1979, lasting a decade.

Along with effective *conflict management* in these three Afghanistan/Pakistan crises, there were various attempts by the principal adversaries to achieve *conflict resolution* by direct negotiations, none fully successful. Some of these efforts are noted here.

Early 1948: A personal envoy of Afghanistan's king sought to negotiate a treaty of friendship with Pakistan, to include border, commerce and transit issues, and a commitment by each party to neutrality if 'the other' were attacked; unsuccessful.

1954–1955: There were lengthy negotiations by the two principal adversaries for trade agreements to remove existing bottlenecks, with the goal of a later replacement of the 1921 Afghanistan-UK treaty, with implications for revision of the status of the Durand Line, the long-term major bone of contention between Afghanistan and Pakistan, as noted earlier. Negotiations ended without agreement once Pakistan's controversial "One Unit Scheme" was announced in late March 1955.

1956: Tension eased with reciprocal visits by the two Heads of Government in August 1956 and mutual declarations of intent to improve their relations; no further development.

1957–1958: There was an exchange of goodwill visits by Pakistan's prime minister to Kabul in June 1957, welcoming the full resumption of diplomatic relations, and by King Zahir Shah to Karachi in January 1958; and the signing of an agreement in May 1958, calling for an improvement in relations; unfulfilled.

May 1970, and other years earlier and later: delegations were initiated by both governments and non-governmental organizations to seek expanded economic cooperation; they were occasionally successful, but without a consistent pattern.

May 1980: An Afghanistan-proposed negotiation for improved relations, based on mutual acceptance of the principle of non-interference in each other's domestic affairs, was aborted by the transformation of Afghanistan's political regime following the Soviet occupation of Afghanistan.

Afghanistan/Pakistan Conflict: Third-Party Conflict Management and Attempts at Conflict Resolution

November 6, 1950—After aloofness from this interstate conflict during its early years (1948–1950), the U.S. offered its *good offices* to the principal adversaries, in an attempt to overcome their unwillingness to discuss the Pushtunistan issue in direct negotiations until 'the other' changed its position on the status of the 1893 Durand Line, which had allocated the North West Frontier Province (NWFP) to British India. The first U.S. mediation offer focused on the value of an agreement to cease hostile propaganda, to persuade their supporters in the conflict zone to prevent tension-creating incidents, to exchange ambassadors, and to meet within 3 months for informal discussions of their conflicting positions. Pakistan demanded a prior U.S. statement supporting the validity of the Durand Line. Afghanistan demurred, and the attempt at mediation failed.

May–September 1955—Several Arab leaders and senior officials—Egypt's President Nasser, acting through his personal envoy and, later, successor, Anwar al-Sadat, Iraq ministers dispatched to Kabul and Karachi,

Saudi Prince Musaid Rahman, who was also sent to both cities—and officials from Iran and Turkey engaged in complementary mediation efforts between Afghanistan and Pakistan over the 'flag' controversy during their second crisis, noted above. The primary mediators in that crisis, Egypt's Sadat and Saudi Arabia's Musaid Rahman, succeeded in persuading the Afghanistan and Pakistan delegates to the Afro-Asian Summit Conference at Bandung in 1955 to express support for the Non-Aligned Movement's ideological mantra, the "Five Principles of Peaceful Existence." However, both adversaries renewed their commitment—Pakistan, to the "One Unit Scheme," which transformed the structure of Pakistan's political system, and Afghanistan, to non-recognition of the legality of the Durand Line and of the NWFP as an integral part of Pakistan. After months of uncertainty about the outcome of the "flag controversy," the lingering issue during Crisis 2, noted above, an agreement by the adversaries was signed on September 9. This outcome elicited Pakistan's thanks to the five Middle East mediating states but did not move this conflict closer to conflict resolution.

September 1961—When Afghanistan and Pakistan severed their diplomatic relations, after further border clashes and Pakistan's renewed blocking of economic traffic to and from Afghanistan, two Arab states assumed responsibility for their diplomatic interests—the United Arab Republic [Egypt], for Afghanistan's interests in Pakistan, and Saudi Arabia, for Pakistan's interests in Afghanistan.

Late September 1961-January 1962—As noted above, President Kennedy offered U.S. good offices in letters to the Head of Government in both Afghanistan and Pakistan, and he sent L.T Merchant as his personal envoy in October to attempt mediation. This mediation effort succeeded in producing a temporary solution to their third crisis—a re-opening of their closed border for 1 month in January 1962.

1962-1963—The Shah of Iran attempted personal mediation of the Afghanistan/Pakistan conflict by visiting both states for 6 days in July 1962. His initial effort was unsuccessful. However, after the Afghan royal family ousted Afghanistan's Prime Minister Daoud in March 1963, Iran's Foreign Minister succeeded in mediating a resumption of Afghanistan/Pakistan diplomatic relations in May 1963, via the Teheran Agreement.

1976–1978 Whether or not because of Iran's complex dual policy toward the Afghanistan/Pakistan conflict—support for Pakistan's claim to the disputed NWFP territory, along with support for Afghanistan's economic dependence on a reliable outlet for its external trade, both imports and exports—the Shah of Iran frequently sought to persuade these conflict adversaries to normalize their relations and resolve their protracted conflict. In 1976, 3 years after Daoud's return to power as President of a Republic, following his successful anti-monarchy coup in Afghanistan, he accepted an economic plan from Iran that was accompanied by a 2-billion-dollar aid package. Moreover, with the Shah of Iran's mediation, the adversaries seemed close to an agreement on Pushtunistan—that remains elusive.

1976–1979—Afghanistan's Daoud and Pakistan's President Bhutto held promising direct talks in 1976 and agreed to continue their negotiations toward a mutually acceptable resolution of their conflict. Apart from the direct benefit of a tranquil relationship between hostile neighbors in a volatile region, both perceived other geo-political gains: for Daoud, less dependence by Afghanistan on USSR military and political aid; for Bhutto, a weakening of the longstanding informal alignment between Afghanistan and India, always a nightmare scenario for Pakistan's leadership. However, Daoud could not muster sufficient support for his plan within Afghanistan's political elite, and Bhutto was assassinated. Although Bhutto's successor as Pakistan's leader, Gen. Zia-ul-Haq, supported the plan—they had an amicable meeting in March 1977—the plan proved premature. The *quid pro quo* was Daoud's pledge to forbid Pushtun and Baluchi fighters for Pushtunistan's independence from treating Afghanistan as a safe haven, and Bhutto's pledge to grant administrative autonomy to the Pushtuns in the NWFP, as well as the release from detention of leaders of the pro-Pushtunistan National Awami Party, notably their dominant figure, Wali Khan. However, Daoud too was assassinated. With the death of the two leading advocates for an amicable resolution of their conflict, the peace process dissipated. The following year, in December 1979, Afghanistan was occupied by the USSR for a decade; and its Communist governments, headed by Nur Mohammad Taraki and then Hafizullah Amin, who supported an independent Pushtunistan, lacked any incentive to normalize Afghanistan's relations with U.S.-allied Pakistan. So too did the Islamist *Taliban*, the hostile ideological successor to Afghanistan's Communist regime during the early and mid-1990s.

The UN has rarely performed the role of mediator in the *Afghanistan/Pakistan* conflict. An inconclusive exception was its sponsorship of proximity talks between the adversaries that began in June 1982, led by the UN Secretary-General's Special Representative, Diego Cordovez. They met infrequently during the 1980s, with no progress until the USSR's decision in February 1988 to withdraw its forces from Afghanistan within 9 months, beginning on May 15, 1988. The impending collapse of the Communist regime in Afghanistan re-activated the long-dormant talks between the two principal adversaries in this conflict. The result was another variation of the oft-designated "Geneva Accords," signed on April 14, 1988, with the U.S. and the USSR as guarantors. However, the agreement contained only oral expressions of good will and an intention to abide by the principle of non-intervention in each other's affairs, and a provision for the voluntary return of Afghan refugees. The core issue, control over the disputed territory of the North-West Frontier Province, was not included in the UN-sponsored agreement, and the conflict remains unresolved, though dormant for more than two decades.

Afghanistan/Pakistan: Causes of Non-Resolution

The relevant research question about the causes of non-resolution of the *Afghanistan/Pakistan* conflict, as for all *unresolved* interstate protracted conflicts, is the extent to which its most likely conditions for conflict resolution were-are *absent* in this conflict: specifically, were any, some or all of the six postulated conditions of resolution set out in the Conflict Resolution Model above absent from this on-going conflict?

Exhaustion—Neither of the principal adversaries has revealed acute fatigue, let alone exhaustion, as an intolerable collective pain created by their conflict. For Afghanistan, the historical record reveals an ability to withstand all foreign attempts by much greater Powers to conquer this land-locked state and subjugate its myriad of tribes—from Alexander the Great to Tsarist Russia and Great Britain in the nineteenth century 'Great Game,' to the Cold War and beyond, to one superpower, the USSR, in the twentieth century, and to the other superpower, the U.S., in the early twenty-first century: exhaustion does not seem to be part of the Afghan collective experience. For Pakistan, the historical record is much shorter. While it did reveal collective exhaustion as a result of the 1971 Bangladesh War against India and its consequence, the bifurcation of its territory, there is no evidence of exhaustion during, and as a consequence of, the 70-year-old conflict with Afghanistan. Moreover, for both principal adversaries, there have been few interstate crises and minimal violence, with few casualties. *In sum*, exhaustion has been absent from this conflict and from the behavior of the two neighbor-adversaries: this absence has facilitated their conflict being sustained at a low level of hostility and violence.

Changes in the Balance of Capability—In terms of a narrow-gauge bilateral calculus, Pakistan's military capability has long been markedly superior to that of Afghanistan. In 2013, the estimated size of their armed forces reveals a disparity of more than 3:1 in favor of Pakistan, 642,000–190,000. Moreover, Pakistan's acquisition of nuclear weapons in 1998 significantly enhanced the quantitative and qualitative difference in military power—but Pakistan has not threatened to use its 'absolute weapon' against Afghanistan, and the absence of large urban centers in Afghanistan, other than Kabul, would render a nuclear attack massive, counter-productive 'over-kill,' In any event, this bilateral calculus of military capability is misleading. Both adversaries have been the recipients of substantial weapons and funds to enhance their power to wage war. The U.S. has been Pakistan's generous provider of conventional military aid since their initial arms agreement in 1954, and the USSR was the primary source of military assistance for Afghanistan until the late 1980s. Moreover, India's longstanding role as a Pakistan-perceived reliable ally and protector of Afghanistan, confronting Pakistan with the high probability of a two-front war, has seriously diminished Pakistan's effective manpower and weapons superiority. So too has Afghanistan's reputation for effective defense against foreign invasion, noted above, and the presence of a very large Pushtun component from the disputed NWFP in Pakistan's army. Overall, the limited resort to violence by both of the principal adversaries in their three international crises has rendered an accurate balance of capability at any point in the lengthy conflict difficult to measure, except to note Pakistan's overall superiority in military manpower and conventional and unconventional weapons over the decades of this interstate conflict, along with a reluctance, for several reasons, to employ that superior military power against a weaker neighbor. Thus the *consistent imbalance of capability* cannot be identified as a cause of conflict persistence or a likely condition for resolution.

Domestic Pressures—There is no discernible evidence of internally generated pressure within Afghanistan or Pakistan to resolve their interstate protracted conflict. For most of this conflict, Afghanistan's political system was that of an authoritarian state—monarchical from 1948 until 1963, and long before, then Republican, with power concentrated in the presidency, 1963–1978, a Communist system modeled on that of the USSR (1978–1989) and Islamist rule by the Taliban (1992–2001). A Western-type democratic system, with elections for a president, a legislature, and local councils, has been in place since the U.S. invasion in 2001. The Pakistan political system was not uniformly authoritarian: there were several blocks of time in which democracy flourished, with decisional authority vested in elected officials and pivotal institutions—presidents, legislatures, and local councils. However, authoritarian rule by military leaders was widespread in Pakistan: Generals Ayub Khan, (October 1958–March 1969), Yahya Khan (March 1969–December 1971), Zia-ul-Haq (September 1978–August 1988), and Musharraf (June 2001–August 2008), all but Yahya Khan assumed power by means of a *coup d'état*. Moreover, even when civilian Governments were in place, the Pakistan Army was the dominant decision-making institution. Throughout this protracted conflict, since 1949, the media were a vital part of the political process in Pakistan. However, pressure on Pakistan's Government from its elites, non-governmental organizations, the media, intellectuals, and the attentive public to pursue a policy aimed at resolution of the conflict with Afghanistan was non-existent. As in the more traditional, civil authoritarian political system of Afghanistan, but more likely in Pakistan's quasi-democratic system part of the time, advocates of attempts to resolve this conflict may have existed in either or both of the conflict adversaries. However, they are not discernible as sources of influence on their rulers' behavior toward 'the other' on the core issue of the disputed NWFP territory, with one notable exception noted above, President Daoud's conciliatory meetings with Pakistan's Prime Minister Zulfikar Ali Bhutto in 1976 and with Bhutto's successor, Gen. Zia-ul-Haq, in 1977. There is no evidence to indicate that Daoud or his Pakistani counterparts in the late 1970s adopted the conciliatory path in response to domestic pressure. If those pressures existed, they were marginal in the decisions of the authoritarian leaders of both Afghanistan and Pakistan.

External Pressures—Unlike domestic pressures to seek resolution of this conflict, which, if they existed, were hardly, if ever, known and did not exert influence on the behavior of Afghanistan and Pakistan, external pressures in this protracted conflict were frequently exerted and, at times, influenced the behavior of both adversaries. Suffice it to note the major sources of such pressure. The most persistent and influential external source was *Iran*, specifically the Shah of Iran in the mid-1970s. Several Arab states and Turkey, especially the delegates from the *UAR (Egypt)* and *Saudi Arabia*, played an important role in resolving the 1955 Afghanistan/Pakistan crisis over the latter's integration of its four western provinces into one unit, 'West Pakistan'. Neither the USSR nor the U.S., despite their lengthy occupation of Afghanistan, each more than a decade, contributed to the resolution of this conflict.

Reduction in Discordance of Objectives—There is no evidence of a reduction in Discord between Afghanistan and Pakistan over their conflicting Objectives. For Afghanistan, their fundamental disagreement over conflicting claims to the territory of the North-West Frontier Province dates to 1947, during the months leading to the partition of India, culminating in the UK's allocation of the NWFP to Pakistan after a referendum that Afghanistan considered blatant discrimination: the predominantly Pushtun voters in the NWFP were given two options—integration with Pakistan or India. This was interpreted by Afghanistan as unconcealed UK bias because both of the Afghanistan-favored options, integration with Afghanistan or independence for the NWFP, were ignored. Afghanistan has never recognized the outcome of the 1947 referendum, and Pakistan has dismissed Afghanistan's claim to the disputed territory as totally lacking in substance and a rejection of a referendum in the NWFP prescribed by the UK as an integral part of the Partition of India. Neither adversary has manifested any change from their diametrically opposed, publicly declared objectives regarding the disputed territory since 1947.

Decline in Conflict-Sustaining Acts—The use of violence in this unresolved conflict, as noted, was moderate in the first and modest in the second and third international crises between Afghanistan and Pakistan, in

1950, 1955, and 1961. Moreover, while verbal hostility was frequently displayed by the leaders of the principal adversaries, there was no physical violence between them since their last crisis more than half a century ago. There was extensive violence in Afghanistan between *Mujahuddin* and the Soviet occupation forces from 1979 to 1989 and during the struggle for power between the Taliban and U.S. forces during the 1990s, continuing into the first decade of the twenty-first century; but these lengthy periods of violence did not derive from, or impinge upon, the Afghanistan/Pakistan conflict.

In sum, only one of the six conditions postulated in the Conflict Resolution Model as likely to lead to resolution of an interstate protracted conflict, *external pressures*, was present during the *Afghanistan/ Pakistan* conflict, spasmodically. The other five likely conditions—*exhaustion*, changes in the *balance of capability*, *domestic pressures*, *reduction in discordance of objectives*, and *decline in conflict-sustaining acts* were absent from this *unresolved* conflict, thereby supporting the negative causal link between the absence of these conditions and *non-resolution*, that is, long-term persistence of this interstate conflict.

Although the two principal adversaries in this Conflict share the belief system of virtually their entire population, Islam, substantively there are many sources of conflict between Afghanistan and Pakistan. One is *History*: the once pre-eminent Afghanistan Durrani empire over most of the residual territory of Pakistan, that is, the western half of Pakistan until 1971 and the entire state of Pakistan since the 1971 Bangladesh War; and the *Durand Line*, 1893,which, throughout this conflict, has provided the legal foundation of Pakistan's claim to the North West Frontier Province, a claim which Afghanistan has always rejected as illegal and illegitimate. Another source, the most crucial obstacle to conflict resolution, is *Territory*—the unresolved dispute over the NWFP, controlled by Pakistan since the onset of this protracted conflict in 1949 but claimed persistently by Afghanistan. A third source is *Ethnicity*, the fundamental ethnic differences between the multiple tribes and ethnic communities that constitute Afghanistan and the diverse ethnic groups in Pakistan—Baluchis, Punjabis, and Sindhis, an ethnic differentiation compounded by the ethnic identity of most of the population of one of the four initial provinces of West Pakistan, the NWFP, Pushtuns, with the largest ethnic community in Afghanistan. These profound differences continue to outweigh the shared belief system, Islam, in shaping the attitudes, perceptions, and behavior of the two adversaries in this conflict. Those differences, concentrated in the combined *ethnic and territorial conflict over the North West Frontier Province*, their *incompatible core objective*, have sustained this interstate conflict for seven decades. Although this conflict has long been dormant—their last interstate crisis ended early in 1962—it has not been resolved and is unlikely to attain resolution until one or both adversaries change(s) their rigid commitment to *control over this disputed territory*.

CHINA/VIETNAM CONFLICT (UNRESOLVED)

Behavior

Both of the principal adversaries in this age-old conflict, more than two millennia, made—and implemented—many *strategic* and important *tactical* decisions.

China: Decisions
Long before the onset of the post-World War II interstate conflict phase between the People's Republic of China (PRC) and the Democratic Republic of Vietnam (DRV), there was unmistakable evidence of tension and mistrust between these two ideologically kin Communist states. As early as 1954, PRC *Premier Zhou en-Lai* had taken the lead, at the Geneva Conference on Indo-China, in implementing the PRC decision, following North Vietnam's decisive victory over France's military forces in the *transforming* Battle of Dien Bien Phu, *to press the DRV not to insist on the immediate unification of North and South Vietnam and to accept a temporary two-state solution for 2 years*; it lasted 21 years, until the end of the Vietnam War in 1975. Ho Chi Minh, the charismatic DRV leader, did not conceal his and the Communist DRV's anger at the Communist PRC's pressure to deny its ideologically kin, the DRV, the fruits of its dramatic, history-shaping military triumph. Moreover, China made a *strategic* decision—the date is unknown, probably in the early 1970s, possibly earlier—*to support the Khmer Rouge in Kampuchea* (Cambodia), rather than *to accede to Vietnam's request to assist in crushing that Far-Left revolutionary movement*. That slow-to-evolve China decision was formalized, secretly, by *an agreement with the Khmer Rouge leader, Pol Pot, in 1975*.

The earliest known PRC decision in the post-WW II China/Vietnam conflict took the form of a *hostile verbal act* by China's Communist Party (CCP) Chairman, *Hua Guofeng*, around November 20, 1977—*accusing*

Vietnam, at a high-profile Beijing banquet for the visiting DRV leader, Le Duan, successor to Ho Chi Minh, of bullying Cambodia and trying to dominate it.

In another decision that was implemented as a verbal act, China's ambassador to Cambodia-Kampuchea *publicly expressed the PRC's "full support" for the weaker state in the Vietnam/Cambodia conflict*, on January 21 1978.

On May 12, 1978, in a tangible material decision, China *suspended* (part or all of) *its foreign aid to Vietnam because of Vietnam's alleged maltreatment of its ethnic Chinese minority*, followed by a severe public criticism on 24 May.

The two principal adversaries, the PRC and DRV, *held unsuccessful talks* on this issue from August 8 to September 24, 1978.

Nonetheless, China *declined a Cambodia request* in the autumn of 1978 for *a 'volunteer' PRC force to enhance Cambodia's security in the face of Vietnam's unconcealed hostility.*

A crucial *strategic* decision by China, 'to teach its little brother a lesson' was implemented by *the invasion of the DRV, Vietnam, on February 17, 1979.*

Eight days after its invasion, China publicly announced its decision *not to "extend its attack on Vietnam to the lowlands around Hanoi," Vietnam's capital*, though it was "still in the process of teaching Vietnam a good lesson."

On March 5, 1979, the PRC *announced that it had achieved the goals of its invasion and* began to implement its decision *to withdraw from northern Vietnam.*

China: Decision-Makers
In the most violent phase of this post-WW II interstate conflict—Vietnam's invasion of Cambodia in 1978 and China's invasion of Vietnam in 1979—the *two dominant leaders of the PRC were Hua Guofeng and Deng Xiaoping*. Hua was Mao's designated successor and held the three most important titles in China—Chairman of the Chinese Communist Party [CCP], Chairman of the Central Military Commission [CMC] (October 1976–June 1981), and Premier [Head of the State Council] (October 1976–1980). Deng re-emerged from a long period outside the PRC inner circle of decision-makers until after Mao's death in September 1976, serving as Vice-Chairman of the Communist Party and Chief of the People's Liberation Army [PLA] General Staff from July 1977 to

June 1981. In a December 1978 contest for the role of Leader, more important than all those formal titles, Deng, the advocate of a market-oriented economy, ousted Hua, the advocate of a revival of Soviet-style governmental economic planning. Thereafter, on the crucial PRC decisions to invade Vietnam (February 17, 1979) and to withdraw its forces from Vietnam (March 5, 1979), in fact, until his death in 1992, Deng was the highly respected *'paramount* leader' of China, that is, the preeminent decision-maker on all important policy issues.

China: Decision Process
Unlike the Mao era of charismatic leadership and absolute ultimate decision-making power, Deng was more than 'first among equals' but a leader who consulted his colleagues in China's pivotal decision-making institution since the PRC attained power in Mainland China in 1949, the Standing Committee of the Communist Party Politburo. The decision process in the Deng era was not transparent in the sense that decision-making in democratic political systems aspires to project and, may, on occasion, achieve. However, while Deng was China's pre-eminent decision-maker during more than a decade of this conflict with Vietnam (1978–1992), decision-making was not the sole prerogative of the 'paramount leader': the views of powerful interest groups—political, economic, bureaucratic, and military—were expressed, directly or indirectly, not entirely without influence, on important decisions on many issues of public policy, including Vietnam's behavior toward Cambodia and China. Moreover, in the post-Deng era, the concentration of decision-making power in an individual diminished during the presidency of both *Jiang Zemin* (1993–2003) and *Hu Jintao* (2003–2013), with a more important role for the most influential political institution, the Standing Committee of the CCP Politburo, than the 'paramount leader.' The preeminence of the current PRC leader, Xi Jinping (2013–2017), appears to be reversing this trend.

Vietnam: Decisions
Like the PRC, the other principal adversary in this interstate conflict, Vietnam, made—and implemented—many *strategic* and *tactical* decisions directed to the PRC leadership in 1977–1979.

Immediately after a Cambodia attack against its border villages on April 30, 1977, Vietnam responded with *retaliatory bombing raids*.

On 12 May, in a move perceived by China as hostile, Vietnam implemented a *strategic* decision *to proclaim an enlargement of its maritime border to 200 km*.

In May–June, Vietnam implemented another *strategic* decision perceived by China as extremely hostile, namely, *to increase ties with the USSR, by joining two international organizations of Soviet bloc member-states, dominated by the Soviet Union*—the *International Bank for Economic Cooperation (IBEC)* and the *International Investment Bank (IIB)*, both international financial organizations controlled by the USSR-dominated Council of Mutual Economic Assistance (COMECON).

At the same time, and later, Vietnam decided *in favor of a peaceful resolution of disputes with its neighbors*: it *proposed talks with Cambodia on June 7, 1977 and held meetings with China from October 3 to 7, 1977 to achieve this goal*, but neither initiative was successful.

Two months later, Vietnam exhibited another fundamental shift in policy toward Cambodia and, indirectly, China: it invaded the Fish Hook Parrot's Beak in southeast Cambodia on December 5, 1977, severely defeating Cambodia's forces and occupying considerable territory on the road to Phnom Penh. Even though Vietnam's forces stopped short of Cambodia's capital, its invasion was condemned by both Cambodia and China.

Vietnam also made and implemented major decisions during this conflict in 1978 and 1979.

At the beginning of January 1978, again on January 13, and on February 5 Vietnam offered *to negotiate its differences with Cambodia*, without success.

In the midst of these accommodating gestures, on January 6, Vietnam withdrew its combat forces, either entirely from Cambodia or part of the distance to their border.

At two meetings of its Communist Party Politburo from late January to mid-February, Vietnam made the *strategic* decision *to overthrow the Khmer Rouge regime in Cambodia* and *began to arm and train anti-Khmer Rouge insurgents*.

On March 24, Vietnam began to implement its decisions [date unknown] to deport ethnic Chinese residents of Vietnam and to increase its confiscations of their property.

On June 6, Vietnam revised its February 5, 1978 proposal for negotiations with Cambodia, calling for a mutual withdrawal of forces 5 km from their border and joint determination of a location for negotiations.

On June 29, Vietnam *formalized* its alignment with the USSR by becoming a full member of COMECON, the Soviet bloc's over-arching organizational integration of Communist states.

From August 8 to September 26, Vietnam and China held informal talks about their differences—without success.

On November 3, 1978, in a *strategic* decision, the growing bonds between Vietnam and the Soviet Union *crystallized into a treaty of friendship*.

On December 25, fortified by the security provision of its recent treaty of friendship with the USSR, Vietnam *invaded Cambodia*.

On March 4, 1979, Vietnam responded to China's invasion of its territory by *mobilizing its population to assist in the defense of their homeland*, but decided *not to withdraw its forces from Cambodia*.

On March 16, Vietnam *proposed peace talks with China in Hanoi, conditional on total withdrawal of China's forces from Vietnam*. The same day, China announced its withdrawal from Vietnam.

On April 4, Vietnam agreed to negotiations without complete withdrawal of PRC forces.

On April 6, China agreed to talks in Hanoi.

The withdrawal of China's forces from Vietnam did not resolve their conflict—it continues 38 years later (2017). Rather, attention of the two principal adversaries in this interstate conflict shifted to another major discordant issue, their dispute over territory in the South China Sea, the Spratly and Paracel Islands.

Vietnam: Decision-Makers
There were *three key Vietnam decision-makers* during the formative initial phase of this interstate conflict, continuing for almost a decade (1977–1986): Le Duan, who became First Secretary, later Secretary-General, of the Vietnam Workers Party in 1969, upon the death of the founder of that Communist Party, *Ho Chi Minh*, and held that position until his death in 1986; *Pham Van Dong*, who held the position of Premier as long as Le Duan was Party leader, and *Truong Chinh*, another long-serving DRV leader as Chairman of the State Council. Institutionally, the most influential body in Vietnam's decision-making process was the Politburo of Vietnam's Workers Party, though a consensus among the three leaders ensured institutional approval.

Vietnam: Decision Process
Other than the Ho Chi Minh era of charismatic leadership of Vietnam's Communist movement, even before he founded the Vietnam Workers Party in 1935, decision-making in the Democratic Republic of Vietnam

(DRV) has always been a collective process. Le Duan, who was Ho's principal aide for decades, lacked charisma and favored collective leadership, which he shared throughout his tenure with Van Dong and Chinh. Moreover, the most influential decision-making institution in the DRV was the Workers Party Politburo, with a remarkably stable composition: 8 of its 14 members at the onset of the twentieth-century *China/Vietnam* conflict (1977) had served on this pre-eminent body since 1960 and 3 others since 1953. Le Duan was a respected 'first among equals' throughout his years of party leadership. The Workers Party Central Committee, which was a much-larger group in 1977—101 full members and 32 temporary members, one-third of whom had been elected the preceding year—had limited influence on decision-making related to this interstate conflict. The bureaucracy's influence was limited to the implementation of decisions. *In sum*, long-time association and mutual respect among the Politburo's members, Le Duan's preference for collective leadership, and the legacy of Ho Chi Minh's disposition to consultation with his much younger Politburo colleagues, unlike Mao's decision-making behavior in the PRC's Politburo, ensured genuine collective participation in the framing of Vietnam's *strategic* and important *tactical* decisions aimed at China.

China/Vietnam Conflict-Sustaining Acts

Three of the four conflict-sustaining techniques (CST)—violence, political hostility, and verbal hostility-propaganda—have been used by both of the principal adversaries in this unresolved interstate conflict.

Violence had the greatest impact on the persistence of this conflict but violent acts were of relatively short duration, from its Onset in 1979 until 1988. The most important of three occurrences of substantial violence was the *China/Vietnam Border War* in 1979. The catalyst was Vietnam's successful 1978 invasion and occupation of Cambodia, which compelled the China-supported Khmer Rouge regime to seek asylum in neighboring Thailand and installed a pro-Vietnam regime in Cambodia. China responded with a large-scale invasion of Vietnam on February 17, 1979, declaring its intention 'to teach Vietnam a lesson' it would not soon forget. The war between the two Communist states, that had been allies against the U.S. from the France-Viet Cong War (1950–1954) until the end of the Vietnam War (1975), was very intense, with an estimated China invasion force of 320,000, the largest People's Republic of China (PRC) military operation since its involvement in the Korean War (1950-1953), and a Vietnam defending force of 75,000-100,000. Although a short war, from February 17 to March 16, 1979, there were very high casualties—an estimated 25,000 Chinese soldiers killed and 37,000 wounded, and 39,000 Vietnamese killed and wounded. Both adversaries claimed victory, but there was no victor, only the Chinese brief capture of 3 Vietnamese provincial capitals and several border villages in Vietnam before what appeared to observers an ignominious withdrawal of Chinese forces from Vietnam 28 days later. Vietnam remained in control of Cambodia, despite China's resort to minor violent clashes along the China/Vietnam border, from 1980 to 1984, and a second major incursion by China's People's Liberation Army (PLA) from April 28 to July 12, 1984, in another failed effort to compel Vietnam's withdrawal from Cambodia. The third phase of resort to violence relates to a longstanding competition between the claims of China and Vietnam, among others, to disputed territories in the South China Sea, dating to the mid-1970s. A notable instance of naval violence as a conflict-sustaining act was the controversial patrolling of waters surrounding the contested Spratly Islands in the South China Sea by the naval arm of China's PLA in May 1987, to which Vietnam objected. This resulted in a low-intensity naval battle between the two principal adversaries in this interstate conflict in March 1988, a precedent for threatening acts of violence in what has become the most active contentious issue in the China/Vietnam conflict in the second decade of the twenty-first century.

Political hostility has been evident throughout this interstate conflict. One type of hostile political act was the attempts by the PRC to maintain the exiled Khmer Rouge regime's retention of Cambodia's seat at the United Nations, long after its ouster from power. Two recent incidents highlight the political hostility dimension of the China/Vietnam conflict. In February 1992, China passed a Territorial Waters Law declaring its suzerainty over the South China Sea, reputed to contain very large natural gas and oil resources. And in May 2003, Vietnam belatedly responded by officially proclaiming its sovereignty over the two largest island clusters in the South China Sea, the Paracel and Spratly Islands. Moreover, both adversaries were accused of committing hostile acts with political implications: China was accused in May 2011 of severing the cables of a Vietnam vessel that was conducting a seismic survey in the South China

Sea, and, a month later, Vietnam ordered live-fire drills in the South China Sea, beyond its disputed territories. This territorial conflict is complicated by the competing claims of four other states with territory in the South China Sea. In 2013, a near-physical clash between China's and the Philippines' patrol boats near the Spratly Islands indicated that this multilateral conflict, of which competing claims by China and Vietnam are a part, might escalate in the future.

Verbal Hostility served to reinforce violent and politically hostile acts by both of the principal adversaries, mainly through officially sanctioned articles and editorials in the ruling party's newspaper, the People's Daily in China, and "the voice of the Party" in North Vietnam. Thus, in July 1979, a few months after the end of the *China/Vietnam Border War*, a PRC Vice-Premier threatened to teach Vietnam "a second lesson," a threat frequently uttered by senior China officials over the years, as in January 1985, in a message conveyed indirectly to Vietnam. Moreover, each of the adversaries accused 'the other' of hostile acts. For example, China, in a Beijing radio broadcast, accused Vietnam of 'ethnic cleansing,' in the expulsion of the *Hoa minority*, without using the highly charged term, and Vietnam accused "the Peking ruling circles," on the tenth anniversary of their naval clash in 1974—when China occupied several islands in the Paracel chain, then occupied by South Vietnam—of mobilizing large forces "to launch a massive attack" (on the Spratly Islands) and occupy it (article in Vietnam Communist Party newspaper, *Nhan Dan,* January 19, 1984).

CHAPTER 8

Select Case Study Findings on Interstate Conflicts: Europe and the Middle East

EUROPE

Finland/Russia-USSR Conflict (Resolved)

Behavior

Finland: Decisions
Finland made several *strategic* and important *tactical* decisions during this conflict with its great power, later superpower, neighbor, Russia-USSR (1919–1961). The first two Finland decisions occurred within the first year of this interstate conflict (1919). One was *to participate in the Western Powers' military intervention in Northern Russia*, in support of the 'White Russian' opponents of the Bolshevik regime. The second, near-simultaneous, decision was *to dispatch Finnish 'Volunteers' to 'liberate' Eastern Karelia*, a predominantly ethnic Finnish majority population that was an integral part of Tsarist Russia and its Communist successor. The first decision was only partly implemented because its primary advocate, then General, later Marshal, *Mannerheim*, acting as Regent of Finland in 1918–1919, was replaced by a moderate elected president, and because the 'White Russians', the intended beneficiary of that intervention, refused to recognize Finland's independence. The second decision, like all subsequent attempts to secure control of East Karelia, failed;

in fact, Finland was compelled *to abandon its claim to that disputed territory* in the 1920 Soviet Union-imposed Peace of Tartu, the third Finland decision in that initial phase of their conflict. There were no Finland decisions in the inter-World War period, the second peaceful phase (end 1920–beginning 1939).

The third phase of this protracted conflict (November 1939–1944) witnessed another cluster of important Finland decisions. One was *to accept the terms of the Soviet-initiated Peace of Moscow* in 1940 that ended their 'Winter War': it was less onerous for Finland than the preceding peace agreement (Tartu in 1920), as noted, because of the tenacious Finnish defense against vastly superior Soviet military power. The next Finland decision, in the autumn of 1940, was *to permit passage through its territory to German troops and their permission to establish supply bases, in exchange for military equipment*. This sharpened the hostility and mistrust of the USSR for its northern neighbor and led to the second major act of violence in their conflict, the 'Continuation War' (1940–1944), and the more demanding Moscow Armistice in 1944, because of the more emphatic Soviet military victory than during their 'Winter War'. Moreover, Finland had no alternative to accepting the severe terms of the 1947 Paris Peace Treaty which incorporated the harsh terms of the 1944 Moscow Armistice, for Finland was merely one of a group of lesser European enemy states that had supported Germany during WWII. The final, *strategic*, decision by Finland was *to change drastically its traditional attitude and policy to Soviet Russia*: in light of the transformation of world politics, especially, the emergence of the USSR as a superpower. Finland gradually decided to transform its historic image of the USSR as inveterate enemy to an overwhelmingly powerful peaceful neighbor that required of Finland a basic change of policy to that of a trusting, friendly neighbor. This found expression in the accommodative 1948 Finland-Soviet Union Treaty of Friendship, Cooperation and Mutual Assistance (FCMA). [See below.]

Finland: Decision-Makers
There were *three principal Finland decision-makers* during this Northern Europe interstate conflict. The first was Carl Gustaf Mannerheim, the commanding figure in Finland's political and military leadership during the first half of this conflict. He was the military leader of the 'Whites' in Finland's civil war (1918) and the Regent of Finland in 1918–1919. Then, after a 12-year semi-retirement, he served as Chairman of

Finland's Defense Council from 1931 to 1945 and, most important, was Commander-in-Chief of Finland's Defense Forces from 1939 to 1944, during the two Finland/USSR wars. He was elected President in 1944 and resigned in 1946 because of ill-health. Throughout his active public life, he was the most influential member of Finland's decision-making elite. Mannerheim adhered to the Realist paradigm until the end of WWII. However, he then became a primary and effective advocate of a fundamental change in Finland's attitude and policy toward the USSR during the formative years of the transition on that core issue of Finland's foreign and national security policy (1945–1948).

The second important Finnish decision-maker was *Juho Kusti Paasikivi*. He was Finland's representative in the crucial, unsuccessful negotiations with *Stalin* in 1939, leading to the 'Winter War' (1939–1940). After a withdrawal from the public arena during most of WWII, he served as President Mannerheim's Prime Minister (1944–1946) and was President from 1946 to 1956. He too advocated a positive change in Finland's policy toward the USSR, which became known as the 'Paasikivi Doctrine of Finlandization.'

The third and longest-serving Finland leader was *Urho Kekkonen*, who headed several Finnish governments as Prime Minister from 1950–1953 and 1954–1956 and then served as President from 1956 to 1982. He shared the Paasikivi policy of 'active neutrality', which became known as the 'Paasikivi-Kekkonen line', and forged friendly relations with the Soviet leader, Khrushchev (1955–1964), as well as with Western and NATO leaders. All three senior decision-makers for Finland contributed to the profound change in Finnish attitudes and policy toward its superpower neighbor from the mid–late 1940s.

Finland: Decision Process

The political system in which Finland's decisions in this interstate conflict were made and implemented was a Western-type democracy that combined a strong president, with some independent decisional powers, and a strong parliament: presidential decisions that were not ratified by parliament did not bind later governments or presidents. At the same time, the electoral principle of proportional representation made coalition government the norm, thereby introducing an obstacle to an efficient and stable decision process in all aspects of public policy. Another constraint was the deep-rooted and widespread antipathy of the Finnish nation to all aspects of Russian culture and politics from the period of Finland's colonial status *vis-à-vis* Tsarist Russia (1809–1918) until the end of WWII. Notwithstanding these constraints, Finland's respected and politically astute decision-makers succeeded in transforming a collective negative perception of Finland's powerful neighbor and people into a recognition that respect and accommodation were essential for the welfare of a small nation dependent on the goodwill of a major power for its survival in a complex, conflict-prone international system.

Russia-USSR: Decisions
The important decisions of Russia-USSR in this conflict can be presented more briefly, since almost all were the antithesis of Finland's core decisions. One, a *strategic* decision, was *to respond to the challenge and threat posed by Finnish 'Volunteers' to USSR control over East Karelia* in 1919. This took the initial form of successful military defense of Soviet territory against an intruding neighbor, followed by a demanding peace agreement (Tartu 1920), in which, as noted, Finland was compelled to yield its claim to rightful sovereignty over East Karelia (The Finnish 1919 decision to participate in Western military intervention in Northern Russia did not require a response because it was not fully implemented). The second important decision was *to resort to force* in late 1939, *the 'Winter War'*, after negotiation with Finland failed to secure its political goals. The third, closely related decision was *to initiate a peace proposal in 1940*, in order to end a very costly war, which led to the Peace of Moscow that year. The fourth major USSR decision was a replication of the third, namely, *to present a peace proposal in 1943, in an attempt to end the long, drawn-out 'Continuation War'*: this produced the 1944 Armistice, which effectively terminated that war; and its terms were formalized in the 1947 Paris Peace Treaty, the terms of which the USSR was a principal framer. The only major Soviet decision in this conflict that reflected a more cooperative than conflictive relationship was *to initiate the Treaty of Friendship, Cooperation, and Mutual Assistance* in 1948, which denoted a transformation of their longstanding hostile relationship.

Russia-USSR: Decision-Makers
The *dominant figure* among Russia's decision-makers in the first phase of this conflict (1918–1919) was *Lenin*, who often consulted two other senior members of the Communist Party Politburo, *Trotsky* and Stalin. In the second phase (1939–1945), Stalin stood alone as the most

powerful figure in the USSR regarding decisions on war and peace with Finland during the 'Winter War' (1939–1940) and the 'Continuation War' (1940–1944). The only other person who played an important role was *Molotov*, who held the USSR positions of Prime Minister or Foreign Minister during most of the period of Stalin's unfettered dominance after Lenin's death in 1922, Trotsky's banishment from the Soviet Union in 1929 and decimation of the Bolshevik 'Old Guard' by Stalin in the 'show trials' of the 1930s. Stalin remained the supreme decision-maker of the Soviet Union in all important aspects of its relations with Finland, as with all major USSR decisions in foreign policy and national security everywhere in the global system, until his death in 1953. For 2 years thereafter, the intra-party struggle for power, among the contenders for the succession to Stalin, generated instability and decisional uncertainty until the triumph of *Khrushchev* in 1955. His power was superior to that of his Politburo colleagues but less than absolute as in the brief tenure of Lenin and the much longer period of Stalin's pre-eminence as the unchallenged decision-maker in all issues of public policy, foreign and domestic, that he chose to address. The second phase of the protracted conflict with Finland (1939–1944), with both wars during this conflict, was one of those issues.

Russia-USSR: Decision Process

The political system in which decisions by Russia-USSR in this interstate conflict were made was a marked contrast to the democratic, parliamentary system of competing parties that characterized Finland. From the *Onset* of this conflict until its *Termination* and for 30 years beyond its resolution, the pivotal institution for *authorizing* decisions on all aspects of public policy was the Communist Party and, especially, its principal executive organ, the *Politburo*. For some decisions of lesser importance, an issue might be decided by the larger Party body to which, in theory, the Politburo was responsible, the *Central Committee*. In reality, however, all important decisions, *strategic* and *tactical*, were made by the General Secretary, later, the First Secretary of the Party. During the brief Lenin era, the decision process was largely confined to Lenin and a few senior members of the Politburo, notably Trotsky and Stalin, and sometimes the entire Politburo. During the first phase of the Finland/Russia-USSR conflict, the two major decisions in 1919 noted above were made by Lenin, in consultation with Trotsky and Stalin, as noted. In the crucial second phase (1939–1944), as well as on the crucial decision leading to the 1948 bilateral Treaty of Mutual Assistance, Stalin acted alone or in consultation with his subordinate Foreign Minister, Molotov. *In sum*, the decision process in Finland was more complex, involving more institutions, interest groups, and parties in a coalition government. The decision process in Russia-USSR was confined to the Communist Party elite decision-making body, the Politburo, but even narrower, to the incumbent Party leader for most of the important decisions in the Finland/Russia-USSR interstate conflict.

Finland/Russia-USSR: Conflict-Sustaining Acts
Violence was the most consequential, but not the most frequent, conflict-sustaining technique utilized by both of the principal adversaries. The first notable threat of violence was Finland's informal military intervention via the dispatch of 'Volunteers' to the southern part of East Karelia on April 20, 1919, in support of its attempt to secede from Russia and integrate into Finland. This dispatch of 'Volunteers' continued in 1921, despite Finland's formal renunciation of its claims to predominantly Finnish-speaking East Karelia in the 1920 Peace of Tartu (East Karelia had never been part of Finland). After almost two decades of non-violent hostility between the two principal adversaries, the USSR initiated a border incident on November 26, 1939, alleging the firing by Finnish artillery on Soviet forces across their frontier: this was accompanied by the USSR's renewed severance of diplomatic relations with Finland and renunciation of their 1932 non-aggression treaty, culminating in the invasion of Finland on November 30, the beginning of their 1940 'Winter War', which lasted for 3 months. Finland initiated another important non-violent military act in June 1941, granting free passage of German troops through its territory, thereby enabling Germany to launch the northern front of its 'Operation *Barbarossa*' on 22 June. During the following 6 months, Finland took advantage of the Soviet Union's pre-occupation with the siege of Leningrad and re-gained all of the territory that it had been forced to cede in the 1940 Peace of Moscow, after the 'Winter War'. Then Finland shifted to a defensive posture, until the massive Red Army attack on the Karelian front on June 9, 1944, which restored Soviet territorial gains at the end of the 'Winter War' (1939–1940), but had lost to Finland during the early months of Germany's attack on the USSR, that is, in the second half of 1941. Following a ceasefire in early September 1944, the Moscow Armistice agreement on September 19 ended the 'Continuation War', the second

major violent conflict-sustaining act during the *Finland/Russia-USSR* interstate conflict. As in 1920 (Peace of Tartu) and 1940 (Peace of Moscow), Finland was compelled to make territorial concessions in 1944—to cede parts of Finnish Karelia and several islands in the Gulf of Finland, as well as the northern Petsamo region, to the USSR. It also undertook to expel German forces from Finland, achieved in April 1945, near the close of WWII in Europe, to legalize the Communist Party in Finland, and to ban fascist, pro-Germany, organizations. There were no other violent conflict-sustaining acts in this conflict from 1944 to conflict termination in 1961.

Political Hostility—the second important conflict-sustaining technique in this Northern Europe conflict, with Finland its more frequent initiator, though sustaining the conflict was more often the consequence of its acts than their intent. Always insecure during its first 25 years as an independent state, Finland sought allies, sympathizers, and patrons to help compensate for its adversary's vastly superior military capability. At first, in the early 1920s, Finland sought the friendship and support of the Soviet Union's nearest neighbors—Estonia, Latvia and Lithuania, and Poland. Given their geographic location and complex relations with the USSR, their embrace by Finland was perceived by Moscow as hostile political acts. Then, Finland sought alignment with Scandinavia states, acts that also generated Soviet mistrust. Of greater concern to the Communist regime in the USSR were several domestic political acts by its Finnish adversary. One was the election of conservative, pro-German and anti-Communist presidents during the 1920s and 1930s, notably Svinhufsud (1931–1939), whose hostile attitude to the Soviet Union was unconcealed. Another related politically hostile act was Finland's ban on its Communist party in 1930. The USSR's most hostile political acts were its creation of a puppet regime in Finland at the beginning of their 'Winter War' (1939–1940) and its withdrawal of formal recognition of the internationally recognized, politically hostile Government of Finland, followed by the Soviet Union's attempt to interfere in Finland's domestic politics during the early months of WWII. This, in turn, contributed to Finland's unconcealed support for Germany's invasion of Northern Russia in 1941. Although less consequential than direct violent acts by both adversaries, acts of political hostility further enhanced mutual distrust of the other's intentions and objectives.

Verbal Hostility mostly in the form of propaganda attacks on Finland by the official Soviet media, and the disparaging images of Communism and Russian society, culture, politics and its economic system by Western-type private media and senior officials in Finland, from 1919 to 1944, reinforced the more significant and tangible negative consequences of violent and political conflict-sustaining acts.

Whatever acts of *Economic Discrimination* occurred between the adversaries did not contribute to the persistence of this conflict.

Finland/Russia-USSR: Conflict Management Evidence
Conflict management in this Northern Europe protracted conflict was virtually unique among post-World War I interstate conflicts, in the form in which it was manifested: three of the four major hostile episodes during the Finland/Russia-USSR 42-year interstate conflict (1919–1961) were characterized by violence, usually intense, serious clashes or full-scale war. All were ended by formal peace agreements, none of which led to *lasting peace*, or *a resolution of their conflict*. Rather, conflict management in this conflict generated finite periods of the suspension of violence between the two principal adversaries, each lasting for years; they were similar to periods of a lengthy truce, each of which was followed by a resumption of violence; and the third episode of violence was followed by 17 years without violence, until conflict resolution was achieved in 1961.

The first hostile episode in this conflict began on April 20, 1919, when Finnish soldiers, posing as "volunteers," backed by Finland's government, entered Russia-controlled East Karelia and seized a border town; this occurred even before Finland's independence was recognized by the UK and the USA, on 6 May; Russia's recognition came 1½ years later. There was sporadic fighting in May and through the summer and September. Finland/Russia negotiations began in June 1920, and the first peace agreement, the *Treaty of Tartu*, was signed on October 14. Conflict management was devoted to establishing a border between the two adversaries, in the form of a binding peace treaty. In essence, newly independent Finland ceded to Bolshevik Russia [the USSR was formalized in 1922] the eastern part of the Karelian Isthmus and two border districts, along with demilitarizing and neutralizing some islands in the Gulf of Finland, which Russia deemed vital for the defense of Leningrad; in return, Russia recognized Western Karelia and the northern region of

Petsamo as integral parts of Finland. An informal promise by Russia of a referendum in East Karelia, with the option of secession, which Finland believed would lead to integration with Finland, was never held.

The Treaty of Tartu maintained a 'cold peace' between mutually distrustful neighbors, accentuated by unconcealed hostility by Finland to every dimension of its giant neighbor—its political and economic system, ideology, culture, national behavior—until the outbreak of World War II. The cleavage was accentuated by Soviet Russia's creation of a rival, pro-Communist government, headed by Kuusinen, in the near-proximity of Finland, and the reluctance of Finland's recognized Ryti-Tanner government to respond favorably to the Soviet Union's offer of negotiations. The USSR, suspecting possible Western Powers' direct support to Finland, launched an offensive almost two decades later, designed to annex the rest of the Karelian Isthmus.

The result was the high casualty, 3-month, full-scale, bitter *Winter War* from December 1939 to early March 1940. As the much stronger power, the USSR emerged the victor, but Finland's defense against overwhelming odds evoked admiration from many Western and European states and respect from the Soviet Union. Once more, conflict management occurred in the form of a peace agreement, the *Peace of Moscow*, signed on March 13, 1940, which entailed even more far-reaching territorial concessions by Finland to the Soviet Union than the Peace of Tartu: the entire Karelian Isthmus, restoring the border set by Peter the Great; some islands coveted by the USSR in the Gulf of Finland, along with a 30-year lease of Hanko Cape and surrounding islands and water. It also prohibited either party from entering into an alliance with a third party to attack the other signatory. Like the Peace of Tartu, it produced a 'cold peace', along with intense grievances among the Finns, but for a much shorter period, 4 years.

The third phase of war and conflict management replicated the *Winter War* and the *Peace of Moscow* (1939–1940), with the *Continuation War* and its *Armistice*. By August 24, 1944, following another successful Soviet Union offensive in the Karelian Isthmus, and the awareness by Finland's leaders that their longstanding patron, Germany, would suffer defeat in WWII and, therefore, could not serve any longer as Finland's defender against further Soviet Union encroachments on its territory and, ultimately, its sovereignty, Finland decided to accept a harsh Soviet offer of peace. As conditions for negotiations, the USSR demanded a complete termination of Finland's relations with Germany and the withdrawal of all

German troops from its territory. Surprisingly, the Soviet Union's armistice terms were mild—no occupation of Finland's territory, a modest imposition of reparations, and a commitment by Finland not to enter an alliance with, or permit the transit of armed forces through its territory by, any potential Soviet enemy.

The Armistice in the Continuation War was signed on September 19, 1944 and served as a prelude to a formal peace agreement—the *Paris Peace Treaty* (September 15, 1947) between the victorious Four Powers in the European theatre of World War II (the UK, USA, USSR, and France) and the five allies or satellites of Germany (Italy, Bulgaria, Finland, Hungary, and Romania). Finland and the other four defeated states had no role in the drafting of this European Theatre peace treaty, unlike its formally equal role as a negotiator of the Peace of Tartu, the Peace of Moscow, and the Armistice in the Continuation War; they were invited to address the Paris Conference, attended by 21 states, but they were not permitted to participate in its discussions. Several provisions of the 1947 Peace Treaty related directly to Finland, though some were stated in terms applicable to the five defeated states. Two replicated provisions in the 1940 Peace of Moscow: an obligation to refrain from any attack on, or participation in an alliance directed against, another signatory; and a specific admonition against participation in the rearmament of Germany or in its military industries. Moreover, the Finland/USSR boundaries stipulated in the 1944 Armistice were re-affirmed; and the size of Finland's armed forces seriously limited, notably an army of 34,000 soldiers and 60 military planes. As for its contribution to *conflict termination*, the Paris Peace Treaty ended a *War*, World War II and Finland's participation in that war. However, it did *not* constitute *resolution of the Finland/Russia-USSR interstate conflict*. That did not occur until 14 years after the Paris Peace Treaty.

Finland/Russia-USSR: Conflict Resolution
The above discussion of conflict management in this conflict noted a unique trait—in three of the four major conflict episodes, management took the form of peace treaties between Finland and Russia-USSR, but lasting peace and conflict resolution were *not* achieved by any of their peace agreements! A second unique feature of this protracted conflict is that the path to conflict resolution was a de facto alliance between the principal adversaries, one year after the last of their peace treaties, the 1947 Paris Peace Treaty which, like its predecessors, did not constitute

conflict resolution: their alliance was entitled "Treaty of Friendship, Cooperation and Mutual Assistance" (FCMA), signed in April 1948. A third unique characteristic of the Finland/Russia-USSR conflict and relationship is that, while the formal wording of this treaty was identical to that used in other treaties that defined the relations between the Soviet Union and the East European states which became members of the Warsaw Pact, the USSR determined when the commitments of the alliance, affecting all signatories to FCMA treaties, took effect for all. By contrast, the activation of all FCMA commitments by Finland and the USSR required the approval of *both* signatories. Moreover, the Soviet Union accepted the proposed Finland wording, which significantly circumscribed the alliance commitments: in the Soviet proposal, Finland would have been committed to assist the USSR in defending its territory whenever necessary; the Finland counter-proposal would restrict military cooperation to a specific situation, an attack on the Soviet Union by Germany or its allies through Finnish territory; and Finland wished to include a clear statement of its desire not to be involved in great Power disputes.

The USSR accepted the Finland formulation, as evident in Article 1 of their FCMA treaty: its terms were to apply only to an armed attack on the Soviet Union through Finland's territory, and determination of the need for Finland's assistance was subject "to mutual agreement between the Contracting Parties." Article 2 reinforced the content of the first article by calling on the signatories to confer with each other on a course of action if the threat of an armed attack was considered genuine. This conciliatory Soviet behavior on the wording of their FCMA treaty, unique in the relations between the USSR and its other small-state neighbors, reflected the qualitative change in the *Finland/Russia USSR conflict*; and it contributed to a fundamental change in Finnish attitudes to its superpower neighbor, from hostility, mistrust, and hatred in the earlier decades of their conflict to growing mutual trust by the leaders of both adversaries, Stalin and Molotov for the USSR, Paasikivi and Kekkonen, who set the tone for an accommodation with the Soviet Union during their long tenure as presidents of Finland.

In essence, the former had achieved its primary goal, an assurance about Finland's future behavior in case of war between the USSR and one or more Western Powers, always a pre-occupation for Soviet leaders: Finland would not be a willing party to a military attack on the Soviet Union from its territory, land or sea, and Finland would provide military assistance to the USSR, however, limited it might be.

The Finnish leaders, in turn, felt reasonably secure that the Soviets would not attempt to occupy part or all of its territory and would not attempt to coerce it into accepting the demeaning status of the East European Communist-ruled states *vis-à-vis* the USSR, even before its dominance was formalized by the Warsaw Pact in 1955 and reaffirmed in 1956 by its suppression of the Hungarian Uprising, and by crushing the Prague Spring in 1968. Stated schematically, their Finland/USSR 1948 treaty, the FCMA, was a trade-off with high-value benefits for the principal adversaries: for Finland, a USSR commitment to accept Finland's independence and its neutrality regarding the Cold War between the superpowers; for the USSR, a Finland commitment to attempt to prevent a re-occurrence of an attack on Leningrad through its territory.

Nonetheless, in light of more than a century of Tsarist Russia rule over Finland and three decades of mistrust and hostility between Communist Russia and independent Finland, reinforced by four conflict episodes, three of them with violence, including one bitter and costly full-scale war, the 1939–1940 'Winter War', conflict resolution of the *Finland/Russia-USSR* conflict needed more time and more tests. One was a 1958 domestic political crisis in Finland, which aroused suspicion by Soviet leaders: they feared an abandonment of 'the Paasikivi-Kekkonen foreign policy Line', a conciliatory posture toward the USSR that had been sustained by two Finnish presidents. The Soviets made known their displeasure; and Finland's parliament attempted to form an alternative government. Finally, Kekkonen's Agrarian Party formed a minority government, terminating that crisis without a negative fall-out for Finland-USSR relations.

The second test of the authenticity of the mutual trust and conciliatory attitude of the two adversaries came in the form of their 1961 *Note Crisis*. The Soviet Union, concerned as always about Germany's re-emergence as a major power, was disquieted by its entry into NATO, re-armament, and the 1961 Berlin Crisis, along with the integration of Norway and Denmark into NATO's northern Europe command structure, perceiving these developments as possibly portending another Western attack on the USSR, via Finland. On October 30, reflecting these concerns and the possibility that, as in the 1958 crisis, Finland might discard the conciliatory 'Paasikivi–Kekkonen Line', the USSR sent a diplomatic Note to Finland, requesting consultations, in accordance with Article 2 of their 1948 FCMA Treaty. Finland responded a week later by sending its Foreign Minister to Moscow for consultations with Soviet Foreign Minister Gromyko. When that proved inconclusive, President Kekkonen met with Soviet leader Khrushchev on November 24 and convinced him that consultations on a declared military threat would cause fear in Norway and Denmark, leading to their military preparations; further, that by cancelling the request for consultations, the Soviet Union would indicate that it had no belligerent plans regarding its neighbors; and, perhaps most important, whoever won the pending Finland presidential election, Finland would remain committed to the 1948 Treaty. The Soviet leader was persuaded, and the military consultations were waived. This outcome of the 1961 Note Crisis crystallized the long-developing change from mistrust to trust by both adversaries and de facto resolution of their four-decade long conflict.

Finland/Russia-USSR Conflict: Causes of Resolution
Does the evidence on conflict-crisis management and conflict resolution of the *Finland/Russia-USSR* conflict support any, some or all of the likely basic causes of—favorable conditions for—conflict resolution postulated in the Resolution Model presented earlier?

Exhaustion—While the conflict episodes in this 42-year resolved conflict (1919–1961) were relatively few and scattered (1919–1920, 1939–1940, 1944, and 1958), the persistence of intense hostility and mistrust by both principal adversaries for 'the other' generated cumulative fatigue by both: it reached the level off exhaustion during the 'Winter War' (1939–1940) and the 'Continuation War' (1944). For Finland, the smaller, weaker state, a series of national challenges led to sustained collective fatigue, which escalated to exhaustion on several occasions. These developments began with a collective memory of Russian colonial rule (1809–1918). This was followed by a Communist-anti-Communist civil war in 1918, the former supported by Soviet Russian aid; military confrontation between Finnish and Soviet Union forces in three military campaigns; and the longstanding uncertainty about Soviet intentions. Uncertainty ranged from possible occupation and re-integration of Finland into a Russian state, to the frequent risk of unwanted involvement in major power conflicts and wars, notably between Western Powers and Communist Russia, as in the latter's civil war (1918–1921), and the war between Nazi Germany and Soviet Russia (1941–1945). The Finnish nation also confronted the geographic reality of permanent proximity to a major power, linked to a hostile historical relationship that continued as an *interstate* protracted conflict (1919–1961). All of these developments undoubtedly generated a desire for conflict termination, especially after the 'Winter War' and the 'Continuation War'. Although the available evidence is sparse, and Finnish culture is not favorably disposed to complaints about exhaustion, it is reasonable to assume that national fatigue-exhaustion made Finland aspire to a measure of tranquility and security that conflict resolution would provide.

While the combined pressures on Finland from conflict, war, and uncertainty about Soviet intentions were not shared to the same extent by Soviet forces beyond those engaged in battle with Finnish forces, or by Soviet society, which suffered from other sources of fatigue-exhaustion, the exhaustion of the Soviet defenders of Leningrad during a monumental 3-year siege, in a region where Soviet Russian and Finnish national interests collided directly, the Gulf of Finland, made the Finland dimension of conflict and war an important source of overall Soviet exhaustion. *In sum*, the role of exhaustion as a cumulative inducement to conflict resolution was more significant in Finland's behavior, especially after 1944, but it was not marginal as an inducement to the Soviet Union's wish for conflict resolution, especially because of the vulnerability of Leningrad to the influence of Finland in permitting or denying transit rights through its territory; this Soviet perception was evident in the USSR's conciliatory acts toward Finland on several occasions during their interstate conflict.

Changes in the Balance of Capability—For the leaders of Russia-USSR, the discovery that a small, weak state was capable of extraordinary feats in a military campaign against an enemy with overwhelming superiority in manpower and weapons, as displayed in the 'Winter War' and the 'Continuation War,' had a profound effect on their subsequent behavior. At the time, Western observers from afar expressed admiration for the tenacity and bravery of Finnish armed forces. During World War II, Stalin was reported as reluctant to expend more Soviet military power against the Finns in the 1944 'Continuation War' because of his respect for the quality of Finnish soldiers who might slow the advance of Soviet forces in 'the race for Berlin.' While the *material balance* of military capability clearly favored the USSR throughout this interstate conflict, the *non-material change in the balance of capability*—the display of an impressive Finnish defense capability in their two wars—and the vulnerability of Leningrad to invasion via the Gulf of Finland, if Finland were disposed to assist one or more major powers in an invasion of the Soviet Union, remained a pre-occupation of Soviet behavior in the protracted conflict with Finland. This link is most clearly evident in the wording of the two articles in the 1948 Finland-USSR FCMA Treaty, noted above, and in the Soviet decision to initiate its 1961 *Note Crisis* by attempting to persuade Finland to hold consultations about a Soviet-perceived military threat, referring to the danger of hostile, anti-Soviet, states trying to secure permission to use the Gulf of Finland as the path to an attack on the USSR. Thus, while the unequal military balance, per se, was not a condition to induce a USSR preference for conflict resolution, the profound concern for the security of Leningrad was a strong inducement to resolution, including a willingness to 'pay the price,' that is, to manifest a conciliatory, 'good neighbor' policy to the small state in geopolitical command of physical access to the Soviet Union's metropolis in the north.

Domestic Pressures—Within Finland's society the main source of pressure for a resolution of this conflict was the Communist Party and non-Party supporters of the Soviet Union. During the early years of Finland independence, the Communist movement was a substantial political force, which persistently advocated conflict resolution as a step toward closer relations with the USSR, to culminate in membership of USSR-led institutions. The Communist Party never achieved that ultimate goal but it remained a vocal, articulate exponent of peace and cooperation with the Soviet Union. More generally, support for conflict resolution in Finland emanated from *national fatigue* with a conflict, the benefit of which was virtually nil, politically, economically, socially, and culturally. Given this negative consequence, Finnish public opinion was favorably inclined to conflict resolution, after the 'Continuation War' (1944), as long as the most fundamental Finnish values were ensured—sovereignty, political independence, a democratic system of government, an economy free from external constraints or control, and guaranteed individual freedoms. Because of innate uncertainty as to the ability of any Finland Government to safeguard all of these values, the attitude to conflict resolution, while supportive, was more passive than active. Apart from exhaustion, as an independent cause, the presence of domestic pressures to induce a policy directed to conflict resolution was not strongly supported by the evidence—until after the end of World War II.

External Pressures—All of the available evidence on conflict-reducing acts in the *Finland/Russia-USSR* conflict, that is, successful conflict-crisis management, and on conflict-resolving acts, that is, successful conflict resolution, point to primarily *bilateral* processes. The three peace treaties, Tartu (October 1920), Moscow (March 1940), and the Armistice in the Continuation War (September 1944)—evidence of conflict management—resulted from direct negotiations between Finland and Russia-USSR; so too with the major acts leading to conflict resolution, notably the FCMA treaty (April 1948) and the termination of the Note Crisis (November 1961). Major Powers and a regional power were involved in some of these but none with a profound influence. In the 1919–1920 Karelia episode, Germany tried to mediate; France, the USA, and the UK issued statements supporting Finland, and the UK sent naval vessels to the Baltic at Finland's request to enhance Finland's bargaining position in the negotiations. During the 'Winter War,' Sweden's king refused to aid Finland; the UK and France pressed Finland to accept Allied armies in its territory, but Finland refused and negotiated an armistice with the USSR via Sweden. There was no external involvement in the Finland-USSR negotiations culminating in their 1948 'friendship' treaty or in the 1961 Note Crisis that led to conflict resolution of this conflict. Thus, external pressures for conflict resolution were minimal and insignificant.

Decline in Conflict-sustaining Acts—Interstate violence was intermittent in the *Finland/Russia-USSR* conflict, with three major episodes: the struggle over territory, East Karelia, in 1919–1920, with serious clashes between Finland Government-supported "volunteers" and Soviet forces, and two full-scale wars, the "Winter War" in 1939–1940 and the "Continuation War" in 1944, their last violent episode. While hostile Finnish attitudes and mutual mistrust continued, non-violent episodes of verbal hostility declined steadily from their April 1948 Treaty of Mutual Friendship, Cooperation, and Non-Aggression (MFCN), until the end of their conflict. Conflict resolution, without a formal document, emerged from successful negotiations between Finland's President Kekkonen and Soviet leader Khrushchev in November 1961 terminating the second "Soviet Note to Finland" crisis, which was treated by the two neighbors then and later as the end of their protracted conflict.

Reduction in Discordance of Objectives—The change from Finland-USSR acute discordance over objectives to mutual toleration of different social, economic, and political systems, and values, was the result of a slow process of changing perceptions of intentions of the adversary, mainly from Finland's political leaders, elites and mass public, from the end of the Continuation War in 1944 until 1961. After two costly wars, without any compensating benefits, along with a more compelling awareness of the massive difference in military power between the USSR and Finland, further enlarged by the USSR's emergence as a superpower, and possibly by a recognition of greater Russia-USSR security as a result of victory in World War II, the Finns began to view their former ruler as a potential 'good neighbor' which, despite their profound differences in ideology, system of government, economy, and values, no longer feared an invasion by a Western great power, via the traditional source of Russian and Soviet insecurity, the Gulf of Finland, with direct access to the highly vulnerable Soviet metropolis in the North, Leningrad. Thus, while ideological discordance over objectives (and values) remained, Finland's leaders made a choice to attempt to foster a 'good neighbor' relationship with the Soviet Union. For their part, the USSR leaders began to view Finland no longer as an agent of a hostile West determined to destroy their Communist rival but, rather, as a potential model of peaceful coexistence in a new conciliatory relationship. Whatever the reasons that prompted the leaders of both former adversaries to create a more positive, friendly, mutually beneficial relationship, the reduction in discordance of objectives became evident in the 13 years after the signing of their 1948 treaty of friendship, which differed fundamentally from treaties of friendship between the Soviet Union and other Communist states. In the absence of evidence to the contrary, that reduction in discordance over objectives continued long beyond resolution of the Finland/USSR conflict in 1961, and beyond the disintegration of the Communist Bloc and the USSR, in 1989 and 1991.

In sum, four of the six conditions that were postulated in the Conflict Resolution Model as most likely to lead to conflict resolution were present in the *Finland/Russia-USSR* protracted conflict. The most important condition—basic cause—of conflict resolution was collective *exhaustion*, especially in explaining Finland's behavior. *Change in the balance of capability* was relevant but only because the strategic vulnerability of Leningrad to grave damage if the Gulf of Finland were made available by Finland to potential invaders of the Soviet Union declined in relevance for Soviet attitudes to conflict resolution. Moreover, there was a *marked decline in conflict-sustaining acts*, specifically in state-organized and implemented violence from the end of the 'Continuation' War in 1944 to resolution of the Finland/USSR conflict in 1961. No less evident was the *reduction in discordance over objectives by the two adversaries*: both, especially Finland, made a conscious choice to build a 'good neighbor' relationship with its former ruler which, in turn, perceived the benefits of a positive relationship with a neighbor whose prevailing ideology, economic and political system differed fundamentally from that of the Soviet Union.

Overall, the four basic causes of conflict resolution in this conflict acquired policy significance by generating a fundamental shift in Finland's *perceptual calculus*. This was expressed in the change in its attitude to the Soviet Union, from an extremely negative perception of Communist Russia as Finland's hereditary enemy, a widely held view propagated by the nationalist wing of its political spectrum, toward a Realist view of Finland's need to adapt to a new configuration of power, specifically, to seek to transform Soviet mistrust of Finland's behavior to a relationship of mutual trust. This fundamental change in Finland's foreign policy was advocated by Finland's charismatic leader from the beginning of independence, Field Marshal Mannerheim, and his successor as Finland's President, Paasikivi. The change began at the end of the 1944 'Continuation War' and acquired widespread support, from the 1948 friendship (FCMA) treaty with the Soviet Union onwards.

Poland/Russia-USSR Conflict (Resolved)

Behavior

Poland: Decisions and Decision-Makers

Viewed in terms of *Poland's* behavior during this East European interstate conflict (1918–1981), there were six discernible phases, of unequal duration and frequency of decisions. In *Phase I* (1918–1922), Poland made two major decisions. The first was a *strategic* decision *to initiate a war against Communist Russia* in 1920, designed to restore Poland's pre-1772 border with Tsarist Russia, prior to the first partition of Poland by Hapsburg Austria, Prussia, and Russia that year. The second was an important *tactical* decision in 1920—to recognize Ukraine's independence, in exchange for a military alliance between these two neighbors against Bolshevik Russia. The military victory by Poland and Ukraine was reflected in the geopolitical outcome for Poland. The March 1921 *Peace of Riga* substantially enlarged Poland's territory by moving the frontier between Poland and Russia further to the east than the Curzon Line, which had been imposed as their border by the 1919 Treaty of Versailles. It was a major political achievement for Poland's *dominant* and *authoritarian decision-maker* during the first phase of this conflict, *President Josef Pilsudski*.

There were no major decisions by Poland related to this protracted conflict during *Phase II* (1922–1926), following Pilsudski's electoral defeat in 1922. However, soon after his return to power in 1926 via a *coup d'état*, Poland was actively engaged in the rivalry with Soviet Russia in *Phase III* (1926–1935). During that phase, another *strategic* decision by Poland was *to weaken the USSR* via *its Promethean program*—supporting independence movements of non-Russian nations in East Europe. This decision was implemented by a major *tactical* decision—*to foster good relations with Poland's neighbors*, a policy that was reflected in two non-aggression pacts with its two most powerful neighbors, Stalin's USSR in 1932 and Hitler's Germany in 1934.

The Pilsudski era of decision-making domination in Poland and Phase III of the *Poland/USSR* conflict ended with Pilsudski's death in 1935. *Phase IV* (1935–1939) was dominated by a power-sharing agreement between *General Felicjan* and *Slawoj-Skladkowski*, who continued Pilsudski's quest for alliances in attempts to counter Nazi Germany's military superiority. The most visible expression of this policy was Poland's *strategic* decision *to form military alliances* with the two major powers in Western Europe, both in May 1939—the Convention with France and the Defense Pact with the UK, in which the signatories pledged military assistance to each other in case of a military invasion of either party. Three months later Poland was engulfed by the German Army, followed by the partition and occupation of all of Poland by Germany and the USSR during most of World War II; that is, Poland ceased to exist as an independent state during the moribund *Phase V* of this conflict (1939–1944).

Its formal independence was restored in 1944, but throughout Phase VI of this conflict (1944–1981), Poland was under the control of a Communist regime, first by the Soviet-supported Polish Committee of National Liberation, the Lublin regime, and from the end of WWII until 1981 by a government dominated by the Polish Workers Party. While tensions existed between the USSR and Poland's Communist regime, the presence of a substantial Soviet military force in Poland and, since 1955, Poland's membership in the USSR-dominated Warsaw Pact deprived Poland of autonomous decision-making power *vis-à-vis* its principal adversary in their protracted conflict, the Soviet Union. During most of this lengthy *final conflict phase*, decisions and acts by Poland took the form of non-governmental civil protests and demonstrations hostile to the Polish Government's submissiveness *vis-à-vis* the decisions imposed by the Soviet Communist Party on the Polish Workers Party and by the dictates of the USSR regime on Poland's subservient government. To the extent that decisions by Poland relating to its conflict with the USSR were made, they were generated by non-governmental organizations hostile to Poland's Communist regime and the USSR, and took the form of popular movements and demonstrations. The Poland/USSR interstate conflict was substantively renewed only in its last 2 years, 1980 and 1981, when a new powerful Polish non-state actor, the *Solidarity* trade union, successfully challenged USSR domination of Poland's economic, political and military systems of power, leading to the termination of USSR control of Poland and the end of their conflict.

Poland: Decision Process
As indicated above, Poland's decision-making on issues relating to this lengthy conflict was highly authoritarian. For most of the pre-1944 years, 1918–1922 and 1926–1935, decisional power was concentrated in, and exercised by, President Pilsudski, virtually alone except for a small group of technical aides. From 1935 to 1939, decisional authority was shared by General *Felicjan* and *Slawoj-Skladkowski*, whose powers as president were greatly increased in a new constitution imposed by Pilsudski before his death in 1935. It was only in *Phase II* (1922–1926), after Pilsudski's electoral defeat by the National Democratic Party that decision-making approached the democratic model; but most decisions in that phase focused on the growing problem of domestic conflict, not the conflict with the USSR. With the coming to power of Polish Communists in 1944, the decision process in Poland resumed its authoritarian character—from the Left, not the Right, as in the Pilsudski era. In reality, the decision process on issues related to the USSR and Poland-Soviet Union relations moved to Moscow, with Poland's Communist regime acting primarily as the implementer of decisions made by the Soviet leader—Stalin (1944–1953), Khrushchev (1955–1964), and a Brezhnev-led 'troika' from 1964 to the end of the Poland/USSR

conflict—with Moscow decisions, especially from 1955 to 1981, authorized by the Soviet Communist Party Politburo.

Russia-USSR: Decisions, Decision-Makers, and Decision Process
As in other protracted conflicts in which Russia (from 1922 the USSR) was a principal adversary (Finland/Russia-USSR, Iran/Russia-USSR, Georgia/Russia-USSR, and USA/Russia-USSR), the Russia/USSR phases in this conflict reflected the changes in the composition of its key decision-makers, caused by death, expulsion, or dismissal: *Phase I*, 1920–1922, ending with the death of Lenin; *Phase II*, 1929–1953, ending with the death of Stalin; *Phase III*, 1955–1964, ending with the dismissal of Khrushchev; *Phase IV*, 1964–1972, ending with the illness of Brezhnev; and 1972–1981, ending with the termination of Brezhnev's tenure as First Secretary of the Soviet Communist Party.

In *Phase I* of this conflict, Russia made two major decisions. The first was an important negative *tactical* decision: *to accept its inability to avoid a war with Poland in 1920*, because Poland's President Pilsudski was determined to take advantage of Russia's pre-occupation with its civil war against the 'Whites' in 1919–1920, who were supported by military contingents from major powers—France, Japan, the UK, and the USA, providing him a unique opportunity to re-gain Poland's eastern frontier as it existed before the first Partition of Poland in 1772. The second important *tactical* decision by the Bolshevik regime in this phase—by Lenin, in consultation with his two most likely contenders for the succession to leader of the Bolshevik regime, Trotsky and Stalin—was *to make a significant territorial concession to Poland in their March 1921 Peace of Riga*: Poland's eastern border was extended 200 km east of the 1919 Versailles Treaty-sanctioned Curzon Line, enabling the Bolshevik regime to cope more effectively with the growing 'White Russian' threat.

In the first 7 years of *Phase II* of its conflict with Poland (1922–1929), the struggle for power between Stalin and Trotsky, the key rivals for succession to Lenin, was the major focus of attention within the Bolshevik leadership. Partly, perhaps, because of this pre-occupation, there were no major decisions by the USSR relating to the conflict with Poland during that *interregnum*. Then, having triumphed in the battle for succession to Lenin and, ideologically, in imposing his doctrine of 'Socialism in one Country', rejecting Trotsky's doctrine of 'Permanent Revolution', Stalin concentrated on domestic economic and political goals in the 1930s and the elimination of all other possible rivals to his leadership, via the 'Great Purge' trials in the mid- and late 1930s. In foreign policy, he sought alliances to cope with the emerging threat from a rising Germany. In that context, the Soviet Union (Stalin) made two major decisions relating to this conflict in the 1930s. One, already noted in the discussion of Poland's behavior, was *to prevent a feared Germany–Poland alliance by signing a non-aggression pact with Poland* in 1932. The other decision, with far-reaching consequences, including erasing the treaty with Poland, was *to sign an agreement with Germany in August 1939*, the Molotov-Ribbentrop *Pact*, which *committed the two great powers in Central and Eastern Europe, hitherto unconcealed enemies in the international politics of the 1930s, to the partition of Poland, the 4th partition since 1772*.

The USSR (Stalin) made two other *strategic* decisions relating to the conflict with Poland in the closing months of World War II. One was *to assert USSR hegemony over Poland*, which had long been, and was correctly perceived by Tsarist and Communist leaders of Russia to be, the gateway to invasion of Russia by West European and Central European Great Powers—Napoleonic France in the early nineteenth century, and Germany twice in the twentieth century. That decision was implemented by providing total support for the claim to primacy of the Polish Communist Lublin regime in 1944 and 1945, during its intense rivalry with the UK and US-supported London Polish Government-in-Exile, the successor to Poland's pre-WWII Government of Poland. This USSR policy was persistent in the negotiations among the leaders of the UK, the USA, and the USSR prior to and culminating at the Yalta Conference of *Churchill, Roosevelt,* and *Stalin* in February 1945. The stakes were very high for the USSR—control over the historic gateway to invasion from the West; and the outcome was a major triumph for the Soviet Union.

The second USSR *strategic* decision in 1945, more directly related to the Poland/Russia-USSR conflict, was the Soviet Union's insistence on territorial revision of the 1921 *Peace of Riga* award to Poland of substantial territory east of the Curzon Line, noted above. On this issue too, the outcome was a triumph for the USSR, a roll-back to the Curzon Line border between Poland and the USSR, with compensation to Poland of territory in the eastern part of Germany.

There were no other *strategic* or important *tactical* USSR decisions relating to this East Europe conflict during the last eight years of the Stalin era (1945–1953). During *Phase III*, 1955–1964, when

Khrushchev was the primary Soviet decision-maker, and for most of *Phase IV*, when Brezhnev was the leading USSR decision-maker (1964–1972) and the rest of this phase (1972–1981), when major decisions in foreign policy, including intra-Soviet bloc decisions, were made by the 'troika'—Brezhnev, *Kosygin,* and *Podgorny*—or small commissions acting as agents of the Communist Party Politburo, the Communist leaders of Poland role in the decision process was to *implement major decisions* on issues relating to Poland taken by the Soviet Communist Party leadership. It was only in the last year of Phase IV that the USSR Communist Party leadership was compelled to make another *strategic* decision—how to respond to the accumulating turmoil and mass criticism of both the Communist political system in Poland and the continuing pervasive Soviet domination of Poland, sustained by a USSR military presence and a compliant Communist government in Poland? The options were to suppress the anti-Communist and anti-Soviet Union upheaval, as the USSR had responded to comparable turmoil in East Germany (1953), Hungary (1956), and Czechoslovakia (1968), or to yield to the unmistakable expression of a widespread demand for the end of the Soviet Union's commanding presence. In 1981, the Soviet Communist Politburo correctly interpreted the national mood in Poland and chose the latter option, leading to the termination of this protracted conflict.

In sum, despite the fundamental differences in the *political system* and *ideology-belief system* of the two principal adversaries and their leaders, the *decision process* in both Poland and the USSR on issues relating to their protracted conflict, as distinct from the *content* of their *decisions,* reveal two shared characteristics: a *very small number of decision-makers,* for many decisions a *single person* and a shared *authoritarian style of decision-making.*

Poland/Russia-USSR: Conflict-Sustaining Acts
Violence there was one full-scale war in this protracted conflict (April–October 1920), initiated by an attack on Soviet-ruled Ukraine by Poland, which had been revived as an independent state in 1919 by the Treaty of Versailles. There were substantial casualties, killed and wounded, by both adversaries, approximately 60,000 Poles and 150,000 Russians. The next two decades were virtually without state-to-state violence. Then, following the partition of Poland by Germany and the USSR (the Molotov-Ribbentrop Pact, August 1939), an estimated

half million Poles were forcibly transported to Soviet Central Asia and Siberia, with large-scale mass killings (21,000) of Polish military officers, police, and civil servants in 1940–1941, highlighted by the later-discovered Katyn Massacre, and frequent clashes between Poland's 'Home Army' and Soviet forces during this transition from the outbreak of World War II (September 1939) to Germany's attack on the Soviet Union in June 1941. There were further deportations of thousands of Polish members of the 'Underground' during WWII, and minor clashes between the Soviet-dominated Communist regime in Poland and anti-Communist anti-Soviet groups in Poland from the end of WWII (1945) to the end of this protracted conflict in 1981. The cumulative effect of Soviet occupation, deportations, and mass killings was to reinforce the hostility and mistrust that resulted from more than a century of Russia's occupation of large parts of Poland (1772–1919) and the profound religious and cultural divide between Roman Catholic Poland and Eastern Orthodox Russia.

Political Hostility was rampant in Poland during the years of Soviet occupation of the eastern part of Poland (1939–1941), during WWII, when Poland was a continuous battleground between German and Soviet armies (1941–1944), and throughout the period of a Soviet-created and -sustained Polish Communist regime (1944–1981). From 1920 onwards, the pre-eminent theme of Poland's acts of political hostility toward the USSR was the demand for the restoration of its eastern border before the first partition of Poland (1772): this demand was raised in March 1920, soon after the state of Poland was restored by the Treaty of Versailles, and weeks before the onset of the Poland/Bolshevik Russia War in April 1920; and it remained the primary goal of Poland until vindication in the aftermath of WWII.

Among the many acts of political hostility during the *Poland/Russia* conflict, a dramatic illustration was the USSR's decision to halt the advance of the Red Army across the Vistula River, opposite Warsaw, in 1944 or to provide any material assistance to the Warsaw Uprising, which was then attempting to expel German forces from Poland's capital. Acts of political hostility during the long period of Communist rule in Poland reinforced the animosity between Poland and Russia, including frequent detentions of Poles critical of the Communist regime, the dissolution of Poland's Catholic Church in 1953, the cessation of religious instruction in the schools of an overwhelmingly Roman Catholic nation in 1961, and, in response, the creation of a large, well-organized trade union, *Solidarity*, which became the focus of strident opposition to Poland's Communist regime and its dominating patron, the Soviet Union, in 1981, The growth of political opposition within Poland, reinforced by acts of political and military hostility to the Polish Communist regime and its patron, the Soviet Union, generated violent outbreaks in Poland in 1970, 1976, and 1981, the last leading to the proclamation of martial law in Poland in December 1981 and the concentration of Warsaw Pact forces on Poland's borders. The 1981 upheaval was to lead, in turn, to the fall of Poland's Communist regime and the termination of the *Poland/Russia* interstate protracted conflict.

Verbal Hostility—was a secondary conflict-sustaining technique, as in many interstate conflicts. In the *Poland/Russia-USSR* conflict, propaganda in various forms (print, radio, later, TV) was utilized by both adversaries to reinforce national unity by emphasizing the ties that bind members of the nation and the differences, notably ideology (Poland's anti-Communism vs. Soviet Communism) and religious belief (Poland's Roman Catholicism vs. Russia's orthodoxy or the USSR's atheism) that separate each state from its adversary, often by demonizing the adversary's values and/or behavior.

Economic Discrimination—as in most aspects of public policy, the economic goals of Poland and Russia-USSR differed sharply, each attempting to retain and strengthen its economic system. Poland, primarily agricultural, and based upon private landholding until the USSR's imposition of its Communist regime (1944 ff.), opposed pressure by the USSR during the period of the Communist regime in Poland (1944–1981) to transform the foundations of Poland's economic system: this conflict became evident soon after WWII, when the USSR compelled Poland (and other East European states, recently absorbed into the Soviet Union's sphere of influence) to reject the US-offered membership in the Marshall Plan and to adopt the Soviet model of collectivized agriculture and state-planned economic growth generally. Poland's resistance to Soviet pressure was unsuccessful; but their conflict over economic policy and the economic consequences for a largely anti-Communist population in Poland reinforced the mistrust and hostility between the two adversaries that had been generated by the other types of conflict-sustaining acts during their protracted conflict—military, political, and propaganda.

MIDDLE EAST

Iran-Iraq Conflict (Unresolved)

Historical Roots

As with many other protracted conflicts that have been active since the end of World War I, the roots of the Iran/Iraq conflict are deep. Hostilities began as early as 632 Common Era (C.E.), the first phase culminating in 638 C.E., when Muslim Arab forces vanquished the Sassanian [Sassanid] Neo-Persian Empire. Violence between Arabs and Persians occurred periodically during the next millennium. Then, in the sixteenth century C.E., the Shiite Safavid dynasty emerged in Persia as a rival of the Turkish Ottoman Empire, which held sway over most of the Arab world in the Middle East and North Africa. The Safavid Shah, Ismail, conquered Iraq in 1510 but was defeated by the Ottoman Sultan in 1514. Several other wars between the two Middle East empires occurred soon after, in 1533–1535, 1548, and 1553, until the Treaty of Amasya in 1555 served as a peace settlement and defined the borders between the two rival major powers in the Middle East.

Their most significant agreement in the pre-modern era was the Treaty of Zuhab (1639), which "became the basis of all later treaties negotiated between the Ottoman and Persian states"; and, of special relevance to the later *Iran/Iraq* conflict, "formally incorporated Iraq into the Ottoman Empire and committed both nations not to interfere in the domestic affairs of the other" (Abdulghani 1984, p. 5).

With the collapse of the Ottoman Empire at the end of WWI and the introduction of the League of Nations Mandates system, the UK became the Mandatory Power for Iraq, along with Trans-Jordan and Palestine. Britain formally withdrew from Iraq in 1932 and transferred power to King Faisal, a member of the Hashemite royal family who had been placed on the Iraqi throne by the UK in 1920. Faisal died in 1933. In this context of domestic Iraq instability, Iran made demands the following year for changes in the informal rules governing the *Shatt-al-Arab* Waterway, which had long served as the de facto border between Iraq and Persia. Iraq appealed to the League of Nations in 1934 to resolve the boundary dispute. A *coup d'état* by Bakr Sidqi in Iraq, in 1936, during the negotiations, led to further instability and enabled Persia (Iran) to extract concessions from Iraq. These were incorporated in the 1937 Iraq-Persia treaty governing the *Shatt-al-Arab*. The dispute over this waterway, beginning in 1934, marked the onset of the *Iran/Iraq* conflict.

The historical roots of the *Iran/Iraq* conflict can be traced to the *Islamic Arab military triumph over the Sassanian (Neo-Persian) Empire in 638* C.E., 1296 years before the onset of this post-WWII *interstate* protracted conflict—the eruption, in 1934, of disputed claims by Iran and Iraq to the *Shatt-al-Arab* (Arab Waterway), which links/separates the two longstanding rival states, nations, belief systems, and contiguous neighbors.

Basic Causes
There were three basic causes of the onset of this modern Middle East protracted conflict—*territory, identity-religious* and *ethnic,* and *ideology.*

The overriding source of conflict between Iran and Iraq has been the territorial dispute over the *Shatt-al-Arab*, which dates to the sixteenth century. For Iraq, this Waterway has been its only viable access to the Persian/Arab Gulf, both during its long-imposed dependent status within the Ottoman Empire and since it acquired formal statehood in 1932, under a UK Mandate from the League of Nations in 1920. Thus sovereignty over the *Shatt*, which is crucial for the marketing of Iraq's oil, the most valuable element of its national economy and the primary source of its foreign exchange, has also been vital to Iraq's national security. For Iran, control over the *Shatt* was/is the key to its strategy for achieving hegemony in the Persian Gulf. In fact, territorial rivalry has long been closely linked to the struggle for its control. This Waterway also served as an important part of the boundary between the two competitors for primacy in the Gulf region.

Their 1937 treaty, as noted, framed a mutually accepted boundary in the middle of the *Shatt* for its entire length, an agreement that was in force for three decades. It was abrogated by both parties in 1968–1969 and then revived in their Treaty of Algiers in 1975. The Waterway then became 'fair game' for both Iran and Iraq in their high-casualty (one million killed), long war of attrition (1980–1988). From 1990 to the present, the Gulf region and the *Shatt* became enmeshed in the two wars between the US-led Coalition and Iraq (1991 and 2003). The years since the fall of Saddam Hussein in 2003 have witnessed a renewed *rapprochement* between Iran and Iraq, with restored diplomatic and trade relations: the process was facilitated by the coming to power in Iraq of Shia parties, religiously akin to Iran, after decades of Sunni domination in Iraq's politics.

The territorial dispute, as a basic cause of the *Iran/Iraq* conflict, has long been reinforced by two powerful intangible *identity* forces—differences in *ethnicity* and *religion*. The conflict between Persian and Arab civilization dates to antiquity. Within Islam, the conflict between Sunni and Shia began soon after the passing of the founder of the Muslim belief system in the seventh century C.E. Together, these potent intangible cultural identities have been the sources of deep-rooted hostility, which strengthened their conflict over territory: "real and imagined history, and traditional Iran-Arab and Shi'a-Sunni animosities," have been integral parts of their conflict relationship (Balkash et al. 2004, 22.). The fact that the Shia was an oppressed majority in Saddam Hussein's Iraq further embittered Shia Iran, as did frequent denial of access by Iranian Shia to some of their holiest sites in Iraq—in Najaf, Karbala, and Samarra.

During the last third of the twentieth century (CE), ethnic and religious differences were further reinforced by *ideology*. The political systems of Iraq and Iran were highly authoritarian. Saddam Hussein and Ba'ath Arab nationalism clashed with Ayatollah Khomeini and Iranian Islamism from 1979 onward. This ideological component of their conflict contributed "to its intensity and its prolongation, to its destructive force and to its terrible cost in human life," as evident in the savage Iran/Iraq War (ibid., 23).

The setting for the *onset* of their post-WWI *interstate* protracted conflict, in 1934, was twofold. One was the death in 1933 of Iraq's King Faisal, who was a source of stability in a highly factional society, with a Shia majority and a Sunni minority. The other was the decline of UK influence in the Gulf region, especially the port of Basra, after its transfer of de facto independence to Iraq's government in 1932. These events provided Iran with an opportunity to change their boundary in the *Shatt al-Arab*, and it pressed Iraq to agree.

Precipitating Cause
The *precipitating cause* of the *onset* of the post-WWI *Iran/Iraq* conflict was Iraq's appeal to the League of Nations in 1934 to resolve its boundary dispute with Iran. It took 3 years for the two adversaries to

conclude a basic and long-lasting agreement on their maritime boundary. However, their conflict was re-ignited in 1955, when the Shah of Iran proclaimed its sovereignty over the *Shatt*, and both parties sent troops to their land frontier.

Dormant since 2003, the *Iran/Iraq* conflict remains unresolved. However, in a marked shift from a conflict to a cooperative relationship after the departure of the last contingent of US troops from Iraq in 2011, the two Shia Muslim states began to move toward a potential alignment. In 2014, Iran expressed a willingness to provide military assistance to Iraq, if requested: Iraq was then confronted with an existential rebellion by an extremist Sunni movement, the *Islamic State of Iran and Syria* (ISIS).

Discordant Objectives
Iran's feeling of inequity in the division of the *Shatt al-Arab* (Waterway) can be traced to their agreement of 1937. With the increasing importance of Middle East oil to its economy, Iran's specific *objective* over the subsequent decades was the *revision of what it regarded as an imposed agreement*, in order to right the wrong by granting Iran a larger part of the Waterway, vital to both its exports of oil and imports of essentials for its economic development. Underpinning this objective was Iran's self-image as the pre-eminent Middle East civilization since antiquity, deserving of its recognition by neighbors, notably Iraq, of its claim to *regional primacy*. Iran's pursuit of hegemony in the Gulf seemed within its grasp following the UK withdrawal from the Middle East in 1971: only Iraq—continuing to experience political instability, generated by military coups and an on-going Kurdish secessionist movement confronting a newly emergent Ba'ath Party regime in Baghdad—was a potential weaker rival for dominance.

Iraq's *objectives* during the early years of this interstate conflict were *to maintain the favorable status quo in the Shatt-al-Arab (Waterway)*, as embodied in the 1937 agreement with Iran; *to enhance its claim to Pan-Arab leadership*; and *to establish its dominance in the Gulf region*. The first and third of these goals, related to its rivalry with Iran, remained unchanged until the fall of Saddam Hussein and the Ba'ath Party regime in Iraq in 2003, and its claim to leadership of the Arab world was overtaken by the coming to power in 1953 of a charismatic leader, Gamal Abdel Nasser, in Egypt, the largest, most populous and long recognized leader of the Arab world.

Perceptions
From the onset of their modern *interstate* conflict in the 1930s, the issues in contention between Iran and Iraq were the *location of their maritime border* in the *Shatt-al-Arab* (Waterway) and, more generally, their *competing goal of primacy* in the Arab/Persian Gulf.

Iran *perceived itself as stronger than Iraq until their devastating long war* (1980–1988): the heavy casualties and enormous material costs changed revolutionary Iran's perception in the direction of respect for Iraq's military capability. Iran's monarchy (to 1979) viewed Iraq's post-monarchical regime (1958 ff.), especially under the Ba'ath Party, as driven by a radical ideology and expansionist aims. However, it also recognized the growing military capability of Iraq under Saddam Hussein, with its strong ties to the USSR, the major supplier of modern weapons to Iraq.

Iraq *perceived* Iran's superior power until its military alliance with the USSR in 1972, and the consequent flow of arms enhanced Iraq's self-image regarding its military capability *vis-à-vis* Iran. The profound mistrust and rivalry between these Middle East powers shaped Iraq's view that Iran's primary goal was hegemony in the Gulf and, as such, the major obstacle to Iraq's claim to dominance in that region. Saddam Hussein's decision to initiate the Iran/Iraq War in 1980 represented an attempt by Iraq to establish its primacy in the Gulf against a new, vulnerable Islamist revolutionary regime in Iran. The effort failed, with enormous human and material losses suffered by both adversaries. Within 3 years of the end of the Iran/Iraq War, Iraq was further weakened in the first Gulf War (1991), a prelude to the collapse of the Ba'ath Party regime in the second Gulf War (2003) and years of instability and civil strife thereafter. The zero-sum perceptions by the adversaries in this conflict wreaked havoc for Iraq and severely weakened the Islamic Republic of Iran.

Behavior
Both of the principal adversaries in this currently dormant conflict made many *strategic* and important *tactical* decisions during several post-WWI periods of their longstanding conflict.

Iraq Decisions and Decision-Makers
There were four periods of Iraq's decisions and decision-makers in this conflict. In Period I (1921–1933), the two *key decision-makers* of Iraq

were *King Faisal* and the UK Representative to the British-created modern state of Iraq, which had long been part of the Ottoman Empire. (Another son of *Hussein*, a Hashemite ruler of Hejaz, part of what later became Saudi Arabia, was the first ruler of another British-created Middle East state, *Abdullah*, the Emir of Trans-Jordan, later, the King of Jordan.) While Faisal was the ultimate constitutional authority in Iraq, decisional influence was shared with the UK Pro-Consul. As noted, Iraq and Iran had long disagreed about governance of the *Shatt-al-Arab*. This first period of their post-WWI conflict was characterized by diplomatic engagement, not with frequent military clashes. Iraq made one *strategic* decision on this core territorial dispute. With an escalation of tension in 1934, Iraq decided *to submit a formal complaint to the League of Nations, alleging Iran's violation of existing treaty commitments on the Waterway.*

During a transition, following the death of King Faisal in 1933 and the succession of his weak son, *King Ghazali*, decision-making power shifted from Iraq's monarch to its Cabinet and, after a military coup, to the Iraq Army. However, the successor Iraq leadership abandoned Faisal's Pan-Arabism in favor of Iraqi national goals and domestic unity, leading to a policy of *détente* with Iraq's neighbors. This change found expression in two important 1937 Iraq decisions: *to sign a boundary agreement with Iran that granted it control of a larger share of the disputed Shatt-al-Arab Waterway*; and *to form a mutual defense pact with three other Middle East states, Iran, Afghanistan and Turkey, with commitments to non-interference in each other's domestic affairs, their territorial integrity, and the renunciation of force in their relations.*

The long Period II of Iraq's decision-making (1939–1958) began after two unrelated dramatic events—another military coup and the accidental death of King Ghazi. For nearly two decades, decision-making power was shared by a newly appointed prime minister, *Nuri al-Sa'id*, and the *Regent Prince Abd al-Ilah*, acting for Ghazi's infant son. Iraq's policy toward Iran continued to be moderate, pro-British, reverting to King Faisal's pro-Arab posture. The result was relative tranquility in relations between Iraq and Iran, with one *strategic* decision by both principal adversaries—*to sign a regional defense pact, with Turkey, Pakistan and the UK*, the Baghdad Pact, in 1955; Iraq perceived this pact as enhancing the influence of Arab nationalism.

Iraq's Period III (1958–1968) witnessed two military coups and several notable decisions that reflected a more intense Iraq (Arab) nationalism which, in turn, reinforced its distrust of, and hostility toward, Iran. It began with a military coup that overthrew the constitutional monarchy in July 1958 and struggles for power among the Army officers during the following 6 months, leading to the triumph of *General Abd al-Karim Qasim*, who served as president until February 1963. He, in turn, was ousted in another military coup, led by *Colonel Abdal Salam Aref*, who was even more committed to Pan-Arab nationalism than his military predecessor. It was during Aref's presidency that Iraq made three *strategic* decisions that sharply escalated the tension with its historic rival for domination of the Gulf region: (1) *to withdraw from the Baghdad Pact in 1959*, highlighting the growing chasm between Iraq's Arab nationalism and Iran's Western (Anglo-American) attachment; (2) *to reject the 1937 boundary agreement with Iran*, by re-affirming Iraq's ownership of the entire *Shatt-al-Arab* Waterway, along with the expulsion of thousands of Iranians from Iraq; and (3) *to claim the entire Gulf by renaming it* the 'Arabian Gulf'.

For Iraq, Period IV of Decisions and Decision-Makers was marked by the coming to power of the Ba'ath Party and *Saddam Hussein* in 1968–1969, and the overthrow of the Ba'ath, along with the capture of Saddam, by the USA in the second Gulf War, in 2003. This period represented a fundamental change from both its predecessors—the Constitutional Monarchy (1921–1958), especially the King Faisal era (1921–1933), and the decade of military coups and military authoritarianism (1958–1968). In Period IV, Iraq was governed by an ideologically committed Party, with clearly defined objectives and policies, and a much stronger attachment to Arab nationalism than King Faisal or any other Iraq ruler before 1968. This was evident in its aggressive posture on all matters related to the conflict with Iran: the call for 'liberation' of Arab *Khuzestan*; the evocative rhetoric about 'the Arab Gulf'' and its maximalist position on Iraq's maximum claim to total control of *Shatt-al-Arab*. However, the Ba'ath regime and Saddam Hussein in power shared with Qasim and Aref an authoritarian structure of government, with one dominant decision-maker, though Saddam's variant of authoritarian rule was more absolute than that of Iraq's military rulers. Moreover, he relied primarily on the Ba'ath Party elite, compared to their reliance on the support of military officers (Saddam did not assume Iraq's presidency until 1979 but dominated the major institutions of Ba'ath power—the Revolutionary Command Council (RCC), the Party, and Iraq's Cabinet as early as 1969).

Among the myriad of *Iraq decisions* during the Ba'ath-Saddam era, five were *strategically significant*.

- The first was a 1971 decision *to sever all diplomatic relations with Iran and the UK*, in reaction to Iran's occupation of three Gulf islands claimed by Iraq—Abu Musa, Greater Tunb, and Lesser Tunb. This act was accompanied by *the expulsion of Iranian diplomats and thousands of Iranians from Iraq*.
- The second *strategic* Iraq decision, not directly related to this conflict, was *to sign a Treaty of Friendship with the USSR* in 1972; this decision and act intensified the Iraq/Iran protracted conflict, since the latter perceived Iraq's alignment with the Soviet Union as gravely threatening to Iran's vital interests in the Gulf region.
- The third *strategic* decision by Iraq in this phase of their conflict conveyed a contradictory message to its principal adversary in 1975: Iraq decided *to sign the Algiers Agreement which, for the first time, granted Iran its longstanding goal in the dispute over the Shatt-al-Arab, namely, acceptance of the thalweg principle, which accorded equal control to Iran and Iraq in the Waterway.*
- The fourth of these *strategic* Iraq decisions was *to embark on a full-scale war with Iran* in 1980; the devastating destruction of the Iran/Iraq War, with at least a million dead, lasted until 1988.
- The final *strategic* decision in this phase, shared with Iran, was *to sign the armistice in 1988 that effectively ended this war in a stalemate*. During the next 30 years, this conflict remained unresolved but without a recurrence of war or even lesser degrees of military hostilities between the principal adversaries.

Iraq: Decision Process
The structure of Iraq's decision process during this interstate Middle East conflict underwent substantial changes since its onset. During Period I (1921–1958), the formal structure was *constitutional democracy*, with decisional power shared, initially (1921–1933) by the Monarch and the UK Pro-Consul; then, in the transition following King Faisal's death (1934–1938), by the Cabinet, followed by the Military; and thereafter (1939–1958), by a duumvirate, Prime Minister Nuri al-Sa'id and the Regent, acting for an infant monarch. In Period II (1958–1968), the structure was military dictatorship, dominated by two Army officers, Qasim (1959–1963) and Aref (1963–1968). The structure was civil

authoritarian in Period III (1968–2003), dominated by the Ba'ath Party, with Saddam Hussein as the charismatic leader. The US occupation controlled Iraq during a transition (2003–2007), followed by a Western-type democracy. In sum, the *structure of the decision process* varied—constitutional democracy, military dictatorship, and civilian dictatorship, but decisional power related to the conflict with Iran was highly concentrated until 2007, from one to a few decision-makers.

Iran: Decisions and Decision-Makers
Like Iraq, its arch-rival for primacy in the Persian/Arab Gulf region, Iran has made many decisions relating to their protracted conflict; ten of these were *strategic* or significantly *tactical* in content, scope, and or impact. These decisions occurred in three periods: the reign of *Reza Shah Pahlavi* (1921–1941); the reign of his son, *Mohammed Reza Pahlavi* (1941–1979); and the Islamic Republic (since 1979). Some were 'the other side of the coin'; that is, they addressed the same issue as Iraq, though from a diametrically contrasting perspective, sometimes with totally incompatible perceived objectives and/or consequences.

The first tangible evidence of modern Iran's hostile and condescending attitude to its smaller (in population and territorial size) and then less powerful state occurred before the Onset of their post-WWI protracted conflict in 1934: when the UK-created state of Iraq emerged from the disintegrating Ottoman Empire, soon after the end of World War I, Iran withheld recognition of Iraq in 1921, on the grounds that the existing boundaries with Iraq were unfair and did not accord with Iran's national interest. This unconcealed snub by Iran was not quickly forgotten by Iraq's political elite. Iran's second hostile act 5 years later also preceded the Onset of this conflict: in 1926, Iran decided *to establish a military presence in the Shatt-al-Arab*, thereby violating the extant 1914 Protocols, which recognized Iraq's exclusive ownership of this vital Waterway. A decade later, Reza Shah Pahlavi participated with Iraq in *the formation of a four-state Middle East Defense alliance—the 1937 Sa'adabad Defense Pact among Iran, Iraq, Afghanistan, and Turkey*; in terms of the *Iran/Iraq* conflict, it reinforced the positive atmosphere generated by the Iran/Iraq boundary agreement earlier the same year, as discussed above.

The first major Iran decision by Mohammed Reza Pahlavi was also shared with Iraq's decision—*to join the US-inspired, Cold War-oriented Baghdad Pact, along with Pakistan, Turkey and the UK, in 1955.* This further act of cooperation between long-term principal adversaries was facilitated by their shared political structure, a constitutional monarchy in both Iran and Iraq, and their alignment with the USA and the UK in the on-going Cold War with the Communist superpower, whose ideology and perceived hostility both Middle East monarchies, neighbor and near-neighbor, feared.

Four years later, the cooperative Baghdad Pact spirit gave way to another, initially verbal, deterioration in Iran/Iraq relations: Iraq's publicly expressed hostility to the construction of an Iranian port in what was deemed Iraq's sovereign territory led Iran's parliament, in 1959, *to accuse Iraq of violating treaty commitments on the disputed Waterway and aggressive behavior towards its neighbor*. This, in turn, led to an escalation of verbal hostility from Iran and its growing pressure to replace their 1937 boundary agreement with an equal division of rights in the Waterway.

Two *strategic* decisions by Iran in the 1960s accentuated the tension and rivalry with Iraq. One was to activate the 'Kurdish card': in 1966, Iran signed an agreement with the Kurds *to enlarge its supply of weapons and intelligence assistance to Iraq's Kurdish community, which was engaged in a long-term struggle for greater autonomy in Iraq*. The other decision, in response to an Iraqi rule in April 1969 that obliged Iranian ships to lower their flags and their crews to disembark before entering the Waterway, was *to abrogate their 1937 boundary treaty, unilaterally*. Nevertheless, the pendulum in Iran/Iraq relations swung to the cooperative dimension once more, in 1975: Iran and Iraq made a *strategic* decision, the Algiers Agreement, *to apply the thalweg principle to the Shatt-al-Arab, thereby granting Iran's long-sought goal of equal division of the Waterway*. The *quid pro qu*o was an Iran commitment to cease military aid to Iraq's Kurds.

Cooperation was short-lived. In 1980, Saddam Hussein, miscalculating the likely impact of the turmoil in Iran created by the Islamic Revolution a year before, launched the Iran/Iraq War: it caused enormous material damage and very high casualties for both of the principal adversaries, until exhaustion and stalemate led to termination of the human slaughter in 1988. One of the many consequences was pre-occupation of both Iran and Iraq with reconstruction of shattered economies and societies for a decade or more, leading to diversion of attention away from their protracted conflict. By then, Iraq became immersed in a conflict relationship with Kuwait and, more dangerous, an unresolved conflict with the sole superpower and the coalition arraigned against Iraq in the first Gulf War, 1991; persistence of the conflict with the USA and the UK in the 1990s, and then Gulf War II in 2003; the destruction of the Ba'ath regime and the capture of Saddam Hussein; and the long US occupation of Iraq. In Iran, the highest priorities of the Islamist regime were rehabilitation of a wounded society and economy, and the transformation of a secular society, under Pahlavi rule for almost 90 years, into the goal to which the Islamic Revolution aspired, an Islamist society, governed by Sharia law and re-shaped by Koranic principles. The protracted conflict with Iran was not resolved but it was dormant. Then, unexpectedly, perhaps wondrously for Iran, the long-suppressed Shiite majority in Iraq attained political power in Baghdad. The shared belief system by the overwhelmingly Shiite Iranian nation and the Shiite majority in Iraq, now politically empowered, created a new constellation of power and potential friendship between the two long-time adversaries. National interests and cultures were not easy to reconcile, and the scope of Islamist influence on the behavior of the two states differed. However, the core issues of their interstate protracted conflict did not generate hostile decisions or crises, with frequent escalating tension, as they did during the post-World War I era as independent states.

Iran: Decision Process
The political structure and decision-making process in Iran was highly authoritarian during the three periods in which its protracted conflict with Iraq unfolded. From 1921 to 1941, the structure and the process were dominated by the first Pahlavi Shah: the ultimate power of decision on all aspects of public policy, including the overriding domain of national security and foreign policy, rested with the Shah. Given his military background before he achieved the power of a Shah, his advisors, to the extent that, as an absolute ruler, he consulted specialists, were drawn from the Military.

His son and successor as Shah, Mohammed Reza, was no less authoritarian. However, he was more constrained by external and internal forces in the exercise of ultimate authority in Iran. Indebted to the USA and the UK for his assumption of the Persian throne in 1941, he relied heavily on Western advice on policy and government throughout the 38 years of his reign. The most dramatic illustration of that dependence relationship occurred in a context in which his authority was challenged by a popular prime minister, *Mossadegh*, who had the support of Iran's legislature, the *Majlis*, in 1953 and was challenging the Shah's economic, specifically petroleum policy, in which the Western Powers had a vital interest; the Shah survived the challenge only by the effective intervention of the US and UK Intelligence agencies.

In Period III of Iran's involvement in the conflict with Iraq, the political structure and decision process were dominated by Islamic authoritarianism, initially with *Ayatollah Khomeini* as the *ultimate authority in all issues of public policy*, from 1979 until his death in 1989, and thereafter, *Ayatollah Khamenei* as the *Supreme Ruler*. Islamist Iran has an elaborate set of institutions that perform governmental functions—a president, a legislature, the Military, the bureaucracy. However, on any major substantive issue of domestic and foreign policy, requiring a decision by Iran since 1979, authority and power have been concentrated in the Supreme Leader.

Discordant Objectives: Material Benefits and Power
The core issue of discord between these Gulf region rivals was control over their shared international waterway, the *Shatt-al-Arab*. Iran's objective for almost 40 years (1937–1975) was the revision of their formal 1937 agreement, which allocated most of the waterway to Iraq: Iran regarded the agreement as an inequitable imposition that led to disproportionate *material benefits* to Iraq because of the steadily increasing flow of oil-carrying ships through this waterway, which was indispensable for economic growth in many regions and states. Thus, the objective of Iraq, by far the main beneficiary of the constantly escalating worldwide export of oil from the Middle East, was to maintain the *status quo* embodied in the 1937 agreement on the *Shatt-al-Arab*. Iran benefited from the moderate revision of the 1937 agreement in 1975 (the Algiers Agreement), but this was short-lived: Saddam Hussein disavowed Iraq's commitment to the 1975 revised agreement on the *Shatt* (Waterway) in 1980, precipitating the mutually devastating carnage of the Iran/Iraq War (1980–1988).

The second persistent discordant objective of the two long-time Persian Gulf region and Middle East adversaries in this unresolved but dormant conflict was the closely related competing goal of *power*. For both Iran and Iraq, the extent of their control of the *Shatt-al-Arab* was not only a valued source of material benefit: it also enhanced Iraq's claim to leadership in the Arab world; and it was inextricably related to the

Iran/Iraq competition for primacy in the Gulf region and the Middle East as a whole.

Conflict Management and Conflict Resolution
The historical roots of this *interstate* protracted conflict date to 638 C.E., as noted, when the Muslim Arabs destroyed the four-century Sassanid (Neo-Persian) Empire. However, the modern, post-World War I phase of this *unresolved* conflict began in the second decade of the inter-world war period (1919–1939). Iraq accused Iran in 1930 of building dams that, it declared, illegally diverted water from the Iraq-controlled *Shatt-al-Arab*—their longstanding maritime conflict over the 'Arab Waterway'— which separated, and joined, the two regional major power Gulf rivals. This led to military incidents and the initial internationalization of a multi-faceted interstate conflict over *territory* (the *Shatt*-Waterway) and *power* (primacy in the Gulf region), superimposed on profound differences in *culture* and *ethnicity* (Persian-Iranian vs. Arab), *religion* (Shia vs. Sunni Islam), and the *historic rivalry* between Middle East empires (Mesopotamia vs. Persia). In 1934, Iraq complained to the League of Nations, whose Council attempted to mediate a seemingly minor material dispute. Iran, then the stronger Gulf power, made its acceptance of mediation conditional on Iraq's cession of territory—three miles of anchorage area, in accord with several earlier Iran/Iraq treaties, to enable Iran's use of the port of Abadan in the *Shatt*. Iraq rejected the demand, and the first of many mediation efforts by the global organization failed.

Despite this inauspicious attempt at *multilateral* conflict management, Iran and Iraq succeeded in reaching a *bilateral* agreement via *direct negotiations* three years later: the adversaries re-affirmed their adherence to the 1913 Constantinople Protocols in their 1937 Boundary Treaty, re-confirming Iraq's ownership of the *Shatt*, which had been established in several earlier treaties between the Ottoman Empire, of which Iraq was a part until 1920, and Persia, as well as the results of the 1914 Border Delimitation Commission. Moreover, reversing its rejection of Persia's minor territorial demand in 1934, Iraq ceded a four-mile anchorage area to Iran in the Waterway and agreed to establish a joint Iraq-Persia administrative commission to supervise all practical matters related to the *Shatt*. They also signed a symbolically relevant Treaty of Good Neighbor Relations in 1949. While disagreements about the *Shatt* administrative body caused tensions, the protracted conflict was relatively quiescent for three decades, except for a minor crisis over competing claims to the Waterway, with minimal border clashes (November 28, 1959–January 4, 1960).

A re-escalation of their protracted conflict was triggered in 1968 by the *Ba'ath* Party's assumption of power in Iraq and its imposition of stringent, humiliating rules for any Iran ship traversing the Waterway, e.g., the requirement that it lower its flag when entering the Waterway. This led to a sharp Persian response: on April 19, 1969, it abrogated the 1937 boundary agreement and demanded its re-negotiation. Iraq again sought mediation by the successor to the League of Nations, the UN, and proposed a joint Iran–Iraq submission of the issue to the International Court of Justice (ICJ) [World Court]. Iran, knowing Iraq's much stronger legal claims to the Waterway, refused both submission to the World Court and direct negotiations. Both adversaries sought UN support, to no avail. The crisis lasted 6 months (April 15–October 30, 1969). In that hopeful atmosphere, four Middle East states attempted to mediate the Iran/Iraq conflict—Saudi Arabia (in April 1969), Kuwait (May 1969), Jordan (May–June 1969), and Turkey (1960)—but, as often, they were rebuffed by Iran, aware, as always, of its weak legal position on matters relating to the Waterway.

During the early 1970s a very costly civil war, in casualties and material damage, raged in Iraq between the *Ba'ath* regime and the large Kurdish community in northern Iraq, supported with weapons and economic aid from Iran. On February 12, 1974, an exhausted Iraq, with an estimated loss of more than 60,000 soldiers and civilians, requested an emergency meeting of the UN Security Council. The Council appointed a Special Representative at the end of February to attempt to end the violence and to seek a more far-reaching political agreement between Iran and Iraq. In that setting, a skillful mediation effort by Algeria's *President Boumedienne*, acting on behalf of the UN, was highly successful in achieving both successful conflict management and near-conflict resolution, where so many earlier and later mediation efforts failed. A *ceasefire agreement* between the Iran and Iraq governments was signed on March 7, 1974, providing for a mutual withdrawal of forces along their joint frontier and a renewal of negotiations on the core issues in their protracted conflict. However, violent clashes continued along their border, largely because of Iran's continuing support for the Kurdish rebellion in Iraq: they ended only a year later.

On March 6, 1975, the two principal adversaries in this Middle East conflict signed the Algiers Accord, among the most significant advances in the quest for conflict resolution, as well as effective conflict management, during the entire Iran/Iraq protracted conflict. In April, they reinforced the general thrust to a relationship of peace and cooperation in the Accord by signing four implementing documents spelling out commitments on boundaries and on security measures to prevent the formation of subversive groups in the territory of both states. These preliminary agreements were formalized in their *Treaty on International Borders and Good Neighborly Relations*, signed on June 13, 1975.

What made possible this achievement of *conflict management* and near-conflict resolution, by a combination of skillful diplomacy and third party (UN) mediation? One crucial inducement was the perception by leaders of both states that the relative equality in their then-existing *balance of military capability* made a costly stalemate highly likely in a full-scale war; neither would benefit, both would suffer massively, from such a military escalation, as occurred later, during their long and bitter war from 1980 to 1988. The perceived likelihood of war in 1974 had approached high probability, with an additional shared perception that their oil production and income earned from the export of oil would be seriously undermined by a prolonged war. These perceptions were reinforced for Iraq by the drain on resources caused by the persistent Kurdish rebellion, abetted by Iran, and were reinforced for Iran by concerns about the potential spill-over from its support for the Kurds in Iraq to Kurdish irredentist claims in Iran. (Ironically, none of these perceptions served to deter Saddam Hussein from launching a full-scale war against Iran in September 1980, or served to deter Ayatollah Khomeini from rejecting several opportunities to end their war earlier: Saddam was persuaded that the dislocation in Iran attending the fall of the Shah and the Islamic Revolution in Iran in 1979 portended a profound shift in the balance of military power in Iraq's favor; and Khomeini was incapable of accepting termination of the war without Iraq's admission of responsibility from setting the war in motion. Thus, the promise of conflict resolution in 1975 was destroyed by the reality of full-scale war in September 1980.)

The UN role in attempted mediation pervaded the *Iran/Iraq* conflict from 1969 to 1988. In some instances, this was initiated by an Iraq appeal for intervention by the Security Council, as in 1969 and 1974, replications of Iraq's complaint to, and request for mediation by, the League of Nations at the onset of the modern phase of this protracted

8 SELECT CASE STUDY FINDINGS ON INTERSTATE CONFLICTS ... 251

conflict in 1934. In most cases, the UN, acting through the Security Council or the Secretary-General, took the lead. Resolutions by the former and interventions by Secretaries-General abound, among them the following, all but the first and last related to attempts to wind down the Iran/Iraq War (1980–1988):

Resolution 348 (March 7, 1974)	Called upon Iran and Iraq to adhere to the terms of their agreed-upon March 7 ceasefire, and offered the adversaries mediation by the Secretary-General.
Resolution 479 (September 28, 1980)	After *UN Secretary-General Waldheim's* offer of good offices to the principal adversaries was declined, he brought the matter to the Security Council; this resolution noted the beginning of the Iran/Iraq War and called upon Iran and Iraq "to refrain immediately from any further use of force and to settle their dispute by peaceful means and in conformity with principles of justice and international law."
Resolution 514 (July 12, 1982)	Called for an end to the Iran/Iraq War.
Resolution 522 (October 4, 1982)	Called for an end to the Iran/Iraq War and the withdrawal of the armed forces of both combatants to internationally recognized boundaries.

Resolution 540 (October 31, 1983)	Condemned violations of international law in the Iran/Iraq War.
Secretary-General Initiative (June 9, 1984)	Called upon the adversaries to agree to a truce, in order to protect civilians; this led to a truce in the 'war of the cities' that the combatants honored for nine months.
Resolution 582 (February 24, 1986)	"Deplores" the use of chemical weapons in the Iran/Iraq War.
Resolution 588 (October 8, 1986)	Called for implementation of Resolution 582.
Resolution 598 (July 20, 1987)	Demanded an immediate ceasefire by both combatants, the release of POWS by both adversaries, and the termination of military actions against neutral ships, and it requested the Secretary-General to begin an investigation to determine how the war started. Iraq accepted these terms; Iran demurred, declaring that it would not accept the resolution until Iraq's responsibility for starting the war was acknowledged. Iran formally accepted this resolution on July 17, 1988, marking

8 SELECT CASE STUDY FINDINGS ON INTERSTATE CONFLICTS ... 253

	the end of the Iran/Iraq War.
Resolution 612 (May 9, 1988)	Condemned the use of chemical weapons in the Iran/Iraq War—by implication, both adversaries, and offered mediation by the Secretary-General.
Resolution 619 (August 9, 1988)	The Security Council created the U.N Iran/Iraq Military Observer Group (UNIIMOG)—"to establish the ceasefire line, monitor compliance, investigate violations, confirm the withdrawal of forces, and seek agreement of the parties for other arrangements to help reduce tensions." This resolution was extended by a series of later Security Council Resolutions—631, 642, 651, 671, 674, and 685. The Observer Group functioned from 1988 to 1991.
Resolution 620 (August 26, 1988)	Renewed its condemnation of chemical weapons in the Iran/Iraq War.

As noted above, Algeria played a crucial role in mediating this conflict in 1974–1975, culminating in Iran's and Iraq's signing the Algiers Accord in 1975. In May 1983, the foreign ministers of Kuwait and the United Arab Emirates (UAE) offered to mediate the end of the Iran/Iraq War, and there was one attempt by the six-member Gulf Cooperation Council (GCC) to mediate, passively—a 1985 call for peace negotiations between

Iran and Iraq, based on UN Security Council Resolutions. Among these mediation episodes only the role of Algeria's President Boumedienne had a profound effect on this protracted conflict, for the years 1975–1980.

Assessing the *UN role* during the *Iran/Iraq* conflict, its contribution was notable for the *volume of attention* given to this protracted conflict from 1969 to 1991, especially during the Iran/Iraq War (1980–1988), and for the *persistence of attempts to achieve effective conflict management*, measured by the *plethora of Security Council resolutions* and *frequent mediation efforts by several Secretaries-General* on that war. In terms of *substantive* contribution to *conflict management*, there were three important episodes in which the UN performed a valuable service. One was its role in achieving a **ceasefire** in 1974, with a mutual withdrawal of forces. This, in turn, became a prelude to its second (indirect but most valuable) contribution: mediation by a *Special Representative of the UN Secretary-General* in producing the landmark *Algiers Accord* of 1974 and the follow-up treaty signed by Iran and Iraq in 1975.

The *third*, high profile, *contribution* was the *formula for ending the 8-year war*, embodied in Security Council Resolution 598, approved by Iraq in July 1987 and by Iran in July 1988. That UN achievement was the culmination of a long complex process because of Iran's traditional rejection of any form of mediation. However, because of sustained losses and costly military errors in 1982–1983, Iran began to search for a face-saving path to make war termination acceptable. It became more amenable to UN initiatives and reached out to other third parties, notably Persian Gulf states, and in 1986 entered into secret negotiations with the USA, Iraq's principal supporter in the Iran/Iraq War. In 1986, the UN produced a peace plan, as did the USA, favorable to Iraq, calling for a withdrawal of Iran and Iraq forces to their internationally recognized borders, which would have nullified Iran's territorial gains during the war. When the UN–USA plan was approved by the Security Council as Resolution 598 (July 20, 1987), Iran avoided acceptance or rejection. Only after another year of punishing casualties, Iran relented and accepted this resolution in July 1988. This was an impressive achievement in conflict management, formalized in Security Council Resolution 598. However, there was no *direct* UN contribution to the goal of conflict resolution, except for the role of a mediator appointed by the UN, a respected political leader of a Muslim state.

Causes of Non-resolution

The absence of conflict resolution in the *Iran/Iraq* conflict is evident, despite the end of their very-high-casualty and grave-damage war 30 years ago. There was no formal peace treaty, only a mutually accepted and respected ceasefire, signed in 1988 under UN Security Council auspices, actively supported by the USA. What then, were the basic causes of the failure to resolve the Iran/Iraq protracted conflict during the eight decades since the onset of its post-WWI phase? What explains the inability or unwillingness of the principal adversaries to resolve their conflict? Does the *absence* of any, some or all of the six postulated conditions for a likely achievement of conflict resolution, in the Resolution Model—**exhaustion, changes in the balance of capability, domestic pressures, external pressures, reduction in discordance of objectives** by the principal adversaries, and **decline in conflict-sustaining acts**—explain the non-resolution of this conflict, although it has been dormant since the overthrow of Saddam Hussein in 2003 and the replacement of a predominantly Sunni regime by the long-suppressed Shia majority in Iraq? Or does the presence of one or more of these conditions indicate partial, informal conflict resolution? Or are there other basic causes that perpetuate a passive interstate conflict?

Exhaustion—There is no doubt that both of the principal adversaries suffered grievously from the carnage of the Iran/Iraq War, with a million or more fatalities and massive material losses, along with profound psychological consequences in both societies, compounded by the absence of any human, political, or economic gains or compensation from a meaningless, purposeless mutual slaughter. Collective and individual exhaustion pervaded both nations, more than sufficient to induce a shared interest in resolving their conflict, on acceptable terms, far beyond a ceasefire agreement. Certainly this postulated basic causal condition of a favorable attitude to conflict resolution was evident in both nations during the eight-year war and for many years thereafter.

The **Balance of Capability** between Iran and Iraq experienced several changes during their conflict. Traditionally, before the 1980s war, Iran perceived itself, and Iraq acknowledged Iran, as the superior power: this was reflected in Iraq's frequent choice of UN intervention during their frequent disputes, and Iran's disposition to avoid commitments to such intervention. The balance shifted during the long war, but not fundamentally. By the end of the war, they had reached relative equality in military capability. These two conditions—acute exhaustion and mutually perceived relative equality in military capability after many years of punishing combat—were the basic causes of *war termination* in 1988, buttressed by an active UN peace-oriented posture throughout the war. However, *war termination* and *conflict resolution* are not synonymous, not conceptually nor in reality. (In the *France/Germany* conflict, *wars* ended in 1871, 1918, and 1945, but their *protracted conflict* thrived during that three-fourth of a century; so too in the *Arab/Israel* and *India/Pakistan* wars and *protracted conflicts*, among many other cases; *protracted conflicts often persisted long after wars ended.*)

Domestic Pressures—In contrast with exhaustion and relative equal military capability, there were no apparent domestic pressures for *conflict resolution* in either Iran or Iraq. Acute exhaustion and pain ultimately were crucial in persuading the leaders of both states to accept *war termination*, that is, *conflict management*, though Iran did so only a year after the Security Council ceasefire resolution had been approved and accepted by Iraq. Conflict resolution was not contemplated in 1988 or later, for the war had generated deep mistrust and hatred of the enemy. These negative attitudes were accentuated in Iran by the widespread conviction that they alone were the victims of Iraq's chemical weapons, from which, it was widely known, Iraq's Kurdish and Shia communities had suffered before and soon after the war. Thus, in the *Iran/Iraq* conflict, whatever domestic pressures existed, especially in Iran, were directed against, not in favor of, conflict resolution.

External Pressures—As indicated in the above presentation of evidence on conflict management and conflict resolution, there was persistent pressure from the UN Security Council and several UN Secretaries-General. However, most of that external pressure was verbal, especially calls for a cessation of hostilities by the combatants. Sanctions of any kind were avoided throughout—before, during and after the war. There were three tangible acts of successful UN pressure on Iraq and Iran— to acquiesce in conflict management by signing ceasefire agreements in 1974 and 1987, and a 1984 truce in the 'war of the cities' that lasted 9 months. There were also mediation attempts by UN Secretaries-General, individual Middle East states, and the Gulf Cooperation Council (GCC), as noted. However, only one had a profound effect on the quest for conflict resolution, the 1975 *Algiers Accord*. Most significant in this context was the *absence of external pressure from either of the superpowers*; rather, the USA supported Iraq during the long war, and the USSR supported Iran. Thus, while external pressure was abundant, *all of it was verbal*, mostly in the form of UN resolutions, which *never imposed any sanctions* and did not induce or constrain acts by Iran or Iraq that were favorable or unfavorable toward conflict resolution.

Decline in Conflict-Sustaining Acts—Since the end of the Iran/Iraq War nearly thirty years ago, state-organized, directed and implemented violence between the principal adversaries has ceased: the decline in hostile acts against the longstanding rival and enemy has been notable, especially after the overthrow of Saddam Hussein in 2003. A new era between Shia Iran and Shia majority Iraq was a notable consequence of the US's regime change in *Gulf War II*. However, that change, a muted, de facto resolution of this conflict has not yet translated into formal peace, normally a pre-requisite to conflict resolution.

Reduction in Discordance of Objectives—This change too has occurred but is more muted than the more visible decline in conflict-sustaining acts. Moreover, as with a decline in conflict-sustaining acts, reduced discordance does not guarantee conflict resolution, just as formal conflict resolution does not ensure reconciliation. This difference between *changes in behavior*—a decline in hostile acts—and *changes in attitudes* toward a long-time enemy is also evident in other interstate protracted conflicts. War termination is not synonymous with a transformation in attitudes to a former enemy; for example, Egypt and Israel signed a peace treaty in 1979, as did Jordan and Israel in 1994. In both relationships, a peace agreement led to a significant decline in conflict-sustaining acts, though it is doubtful that this has been accompanied by a marked reduction in discordance over objectives between the adversaries. Similarly, war termination in the case of Iran and Iraq has not automatically led to a reduction in discordance over objectives, not even to a formal peace agreement, the pre-condition to conflict resolution.

In sum, several basic conditions, postulated in the *Resolution Model* as likely to serve as basic causes of conflict resolution, were present in the *Iran/Iraq* conflict. The most notable was collective exhaustion, experienced by both principal adversaries during their devastating war, 1980–1988, with consequences for both societies and political elites long after the winding down of a very long, high-casualty-grave damage military catastrophe from which neither adversary benefitted. Moreover, as noted, external pressures from the United Nations were abundant. In addition, there emerged a considerable decline in conflict-sustaining acts decades after that war, including a cessation of military hostilities after 1988. And the coming to power of Iraq's majority Shia community provided an opportunity for a healing of wounds by both Iran's and Iraq's Shia societies, raising the possibility of active cooperation between the historical adversaries and competitors for primacy in the Gulf region. The hostile behavior between Iran and Iraq has clearly diminished during the last three decades. However, formal conflict resolution of this interstate conflict remains elusive, despite the presence of three conditions favorable to conflict resolution, even to reconciliation—exhaustion, a notable decline in conflict-sustaining acts, and a reduction in the level of hostility and discord of objectives.

This change in the political and military environment suggests a likelihood that conflict resolution of the *Iran/Iraq* conflict would ensue. However, the legacy of exhaustion persisted. Moreover, the impact of exhaustion was significantly enhanced, for both principal adversaries, by domestic pressures that were expressed as intense bitterness, distrust, hostility, and hatred for 'the enemy' by the leaders, elite, and population at large, especially in Iran, which had suffered the most from the relentless war. That domestic pressure would seem to offset whatever inducement to conflict resolution would normally be generated by mass exhaustion. Moreover, hatred for 'the other' was reinforced by deep-rooted *mistrust* and cumulative *hostility* based upon *several sources*: *conflicting narratives* of historic conflicts between Persian and Arab civilizations during more than a millennium; longstanding *rivalry for primacy* in the Gulf region; unrestrained *competition in religion*—the often explosive hostility between Shia and Sunni Islam, as long as Saddam Hussein and the Ba'ath Party held power in Iraq; *differences* in *ethnicity, culture and language*; and specific longstanding *sources of discord*, notably over the *Shatt* Waterway, *Iran's military support for Iraq's Kurds* in their perennial quest for greater autonomy, and memory of the long war. These material and psychological obstacles to conflict resolution of the Iran/Iraq protracted conflict remain.

Reconciliation
Conceptually, as noted, and in *practice* for the most part, *conflict resolution precedes reconciliation* between conflict adversaries. However, there are exceptions to this sequence; the *Iran/Iraq* protracted conflict is one of them, with evidence of accommodation and incipient reconciliation. Since the end of their disastrous war in 1988, relations have been correct—no full-scale crises or outbreaks of interstate violence. Iran's public reaction to Iraq's invasion of Kuwait in 1990 was muted—mild condemnation and support for all UN Security Council resolutions on that destabilizing event in the Gulf region. In the 1990s, many of the residual topics of their long war were dealt with amicably, notably the exchange of POWs and war reparations. A lingering border dispute was slowly being settled. The longstanding rivals in the Gulf region re-affirmed acceptance of their 1975 Algiers Agreement, which incorporated the *thalweg* principle (mid-point in the

Waterway) as their maritime boundary. The Waterway has been free of Iran-Iraq discord (though not free of discord between Iran and Western powers). Trade has grown considerably, even during, in part because of, the steady growth of economic sanctions imposed on Iran by the USA and other Western states since 2009.

Most important among the signs of *détente* were political changes in both states. Three reform presidents in Iran, *Akbar Hashemi Rafsanjani* (1989–1997), *Mohammad Khatami* (1997–2005), and *Hassan Rouhani* (since August 2013) contributed to the emerging détente between the two rival states. Most important for the beginnings of societal reconciliation has been the empowerment of the long-oppressed majority Shia Muslim community in Iraq, symbolized by the electoral victory and assumption of power in 2006 by Prime Minister Nouri al-Maliki, head of a Shia Coalition. Since then, many Iranians have flocked to Shia Holy Places in Iraq; and the shared attachment to the precepts and values of Shia Islam has generated a degree of mutual understanding between the overwhelming Shia majority population in Iran and the substantial Shia majority in Iraq, though such shared religious beliefs have not translated into shared policy preferences and decisions on many sources of Iran/Iraq discord.

The *ethnic, language,* and *cultural* differences between Iranian and Iraqi societies have not become submerged as a result of shared *religious beliefs* of the majority populations. Nor has the mutual inheritance of *historic rivalry* between Persians and Arabs, or the *interstate competition for domination of the Gulf region*, or *rivalry over the Shatt-al-Arab Waterway* yielded to the positive atmosphere created by their shared religious beliefs. Moreover, the memory of their long and bitter war in the 1980s has not been forgotten, especially in Iran, a national and individual memory accentuated by the grievous losses from Iraq's assaults of chemical weapons, a highly emotional obstacle to reconciliation by Iran's mass public. A formal peace treaty, that would mark the resolution of their protracted conflict, would be an important signal of a shared wish to enhance the process of reconciliation. Thus far, notwithstanding reports during 2013 that Iraq's government (informally) granted overflight permission to Iran, a major supplier of weapons and non-military aid to Syria's embattled government during its unresolved civil war, and an (informal) Iran offer of tangible support for the Iraq government's attempt to overcome the serious threat posed by the militant Sunni ISIS non-state actor to Iraq's continued existence as a Shia majority state, in 2014, the principal adversaries in this dormant conflict have not yet begun the arduous task of ascending any of the multiple stages of a Reconciliation Pyramid.

CHAPTER 9

Select Case Study Findings on Interstate Conflicts: Inter-Region

GEORGIA/RUSSIA-USSR CONFLICT (UNRESOLVED)

Historical Roots

The principal adversaries in this interstate conflict experienced a very close, unequal relationship for more than two centuries. Georgia was annexed by Tsarist Russia in 1800, at the request of Georgia's last monarch, who appealed for support against Persia, and it was an integral part of Russia until November 1917. In the turmoil attending the Bolshevik Revolution, Georgia became an independent state for 3 years (April 1918–February 1921). Along with Armenia and Azerbaijan, Georgia was merged into the Trans-Caucasian Soviet Socialist Republic, within the Soviet Union, from 1922 until 1936, when the three Caucasian entities became formally independent republics of the USSR until its dissolution at the end of 1991. Georgia, as well as its Caucasian neighbors, then resumed their independent statehood.

Behavior

Georgia and Russia-USSR: Decisions and Decision-Makers
This unresolved conflict between a major power, Russia, and Georgia, a former integral part of the Tsarist Empire, was preceded by a short-lived period of Georgia's independence soon after the Bolshevik attainment of

power in Russia in November 1917. Because that prelude to the current conflict, which began in 1991, remains a crucial element in the 'historical memory' of one of the principal adversaries, Georgia, it merits brief attention in an analysis of their *behavior* seven decades later and beyond.

The prelude began with a declaration of independence by Georgia in May 1918, at first with Lenin's promise to respect Georgia's right to independence, incorporated in the Georgia–Russia 1920 Moscow Treaty. The next year, the Bolshevik leader reversed course authorizing the Red Army to invade Georgia and re-integrate its territory into Russia. This *volte face* and the prelude to their interstate protracted conflict seven decades later ended with Russia's invasion and reincorporation of Georgia into Russia in February 1921, compelling the Georgian *Menshevik* government to depart for self-exile in France.

This interstate conflict began with Georgia's renewed declaration of independence from the recently dissolved USSR and the Russian Federation via a referendum in March 1991. However, it was not until 17 years later, highlighted by the successful Georgia 'Rose Revolution' in late 2003, that its new, youthful leader, *Saakashvili*, displayed an unconcealed bravado by mobilizing Georgia's army and attacking one of the two disputed Caucasian enclaves, South Ossetia, on August 7, 2008. Russia decided immediately *to expel the Georgian force* from its short-lived advance into South Ossetia, which was overwhelmingly successful in the four-day War that followed.

Georgia and Russia-USSR: Decision Process
The political system in which Georgia's two major decisions were taken was a Western-type democracy, in marked contrast to the authoritarian 'democratic centralism' that pervaded the Bolshevik regime, with Lenin as its unchallenged, commanding figure during the regime's first 4+ years. However, Lenin adhered to the Marxist-Leninist principle that important decisions, especially *strategic* decisions, required Communist Party authorization, acting through the Party's ultimate decision-authorizing body, the *Politburo*. In Period II, Georgia's regime continued to be a democracy of the Western type. However, all three of its early presidents—*Gamsakhurdia*, a respected Georgian nationalist leader, *Shevardnadze*, a former USSR Foreign Minister, and Saakashvili—displayed a considerable bent to authoritarianism, the first, of the traditional Caucasian ruler, the second, of the *Gorbachev* type, and the third, of a Western populist. The Georgia decision to attack

South Ossetia was made by President Saakashvili, with a small group of military advisors.

The Russian decision-making process in Phase II was also authoritarian, as in Georgia, without the veneer of participation by any democratic institutions. The principal decision-maker was President *Putin*, with a supporting role for Prime Minister *Medvedev* and some Russian military advisers.

Conflict-Sustaining Techniques

Violence several low-intensity violent incidents erupted between Georgia and two enclaves in the Caucuses, *Abkhazia* and *South Ossetia*, which had been claimed by Georgia since it regained independence from the Soviet Union in 1991, as well as by Russia-supported secessionists in these disputed territories. The first, in August 1992, was an *Abkhaz* attack on Georgian government buildings in Abkhazia's capital, Sukhumi. Russia terminated arms supplies to Georgia and, soon after, began arms shipments to Abkhaz separatists; strangely, it also facilitated a peace agreement and encouraged negotiations between Georgia and the Abkhaz rebels in December 1993, but these quickly led to stalemate. In May 1998, an attempt by Georgian guerillas to raise Georgia's flag on Abkhaz government buildings led to low-intensity violence for months and the forced withdrawal of the Georgians from the Abkhaz capital. Then, after several years of relative quiet, a plane flying Georgia's Defense Minister over South Ossetia in September 2006 was attacked by unknown assailants. In April 2008, a Russian jet fighter destroyed a Georgian Unmanned Aerial Vehicle in Abkhazian airspace. Then, unexpectedly, Georgia attacked South Ossetia on August 7–8, 2008. Russia responded at once, forced the much weaker Georgian invaders to withdraw and occupied considerable Georgian territory. The *four-day full-scale war* ended with a France-arranged cease-fire on the 12th, and 2 weeks later, Russia recognized the independence of the two contested enclaves. Since then the adversaries avoided another round of violence, but the uneasy calm masks Georgian hostility and fear and Russia's disdain.

Political Hostility—Conflict-sustaining political acts, too, began soon after Georgia regained its independence. Russia began to issue Russian passports to Abkhazia residents soon after a peace agreement was concluded between Georgia and the Abkhaz secessionists in 1993. After a long period of relative tranquility, Russia was reported by the BBC to have threatened in 2002 to bomb *Al-Qaeda* and *Chechen* bases in Georgia's Pankisi Gorge and to have threatened Georgia for not cooperating with Russia. In August 2004, Georgia's Premier warned Russian tourists not to travel to Abkhazia and threatened to fire on Russian ships bringing Russian tourists to Sukhumi. In the autumn of 2006, Russia began to deport ethnic Georgians illegally residing in Russia. After Kosovo's declaration of independence, in March 2008, recognized by many Western states, Russia lifted then-existing sanctions on Abkhazia, and in April it began to recognize documents issued by the local authorities in Abkhazia and South Ossetia. Although little-noticed elsewhere, the slow escalation of hostile political acts by both Georgia and Russia prepared the ground for the full-scale war 4 months later.

Verbal Hostility—Propaganda, too, was employed by the principal adversaries in this unresolved conflict, mostly in defense of their actions leading to, and during, the August 2008 War. In essence, Russia's arguments were as follows: first, Georgia, by its attack on South Ossetia, was the aggressor in this conflict; second, Russia had no alternative but to retaliate against Georgia's aggression; and third, Russia's actions in support of the enclaves were no different than NATO's actions in defense of Kosovo, an enclave of Serbia. Georgia's attempts to persuade onlookers from afar also focused on three arguments: first, its decision to dispatch troops to South Ossetia was legitimate and legal because the enclave had long been recognized by the USSR as an integral part of Georgia; second, Russia's hostile acts, challenging Georgia's sovereignty over the two enclaves, violated international law; and third, Russia's analogy between its behavior and NATO's UN-sanctioned behavior toward Kosovo was basically flawed. The arguments of neither adversary were convincing among a generally disinterested external audience.

Economic Discrimination—There were few openly hostile economic acts in this conflict, all by Russia, upon whose economy Georgia was almost totally dependent. One was its threat in 2006 to cut off Russia's monopoly supply of gas to Georgia, entirely; it did not resort to this draconian act, but *Gazprom* doubled the price of gas that it supplied to Georgia. The other hostile Russian economic act was to halt the import of Georgia's wine, accounting for 90% of Georgia's wine exports, and of its bottled water, Georgia's two largest exports. While a serious blow to Georgia's economy, this was the least important in sustaining the Georgia/Russia conflict. *Acts of political hostility* were the *most frequent*, but *acts of violence*, and the key security lessons for Georgia, reinforced by the August 2008 War, namely, the enormous difference in military power between the two adversaries, and the non-involvement of all the other major powers, especially the USA, had *the greatest impact* on sustaining this conflict, though without violence, in the future.

Conflict Management and Attempts at Conflict Resolution

During this *unresolved* conflict between a major power, Russia, and its small neighbor, Georgia, there have been several episodes of conflict management, especially during their first, year-long crisis, *Georgia–Abkhazia Civil War* (September 25, 1992–October 8, 1993) and their brief full-scale *crisis-war* (August 7–11, 2008). The other two crises were *Pankisi Gorge* (July 27–October 7, 2002) and *South Ossetia-Abkhazia* (June 10–November 5, 2004). All four crises within the on-going *Georgia/Russia* conflict focused on competing claims to territory, notably over two enclaves in the South Caucasus, Abkhazia and South Ossetia: Georgia claimed sovereignty over both entities, which aspired to independent statehood or merger with Russia, actively supported by Russia.

Georgia-Abkhazia Civil War (September 25, 1992–October 8, 1993): Fighting between Abkhaz separatists and Georgian troops began in August 1992—the anti-Georgia movement for separate status began in 1977 but had been suppressed by Soviet forces. It escalated to a Georgia–Russia crisis on September 25, when Russia's parliament, the *Duma*, condemned Georgia's resort to violence and suspended the delivery of weapons and equipment to its neighbor, triggering a crisis for Georgia. Despite its denial, Russia provided arms, humanitarian aid, and logistical support to the Abkhaz separatists. Serious clashes between Georgia and the Abkhaz separatists occurred periodically during the next year. Tension between Russia and Georgia escalated, with Georgia threatening to take control of all Russian weapons and equipment on Georgian territory—it seized a Russian arms depot in southern Georgia on November 2—and accusing Russia of bombing Georgian military positions in Sukhumi, the Abkhaz capital. In mid-December

1992 and again in mid-March 1993, during an Abkhaz separatist attack on Georgian forces then controlling the Abkhaz capital, Sukhumi, Georgia's President Shevardnadze, former Foreign Minister of Russia during Gorbachev's tenure as Russia's leader, and Georgia's parliament demanded the withdrawal of Russian troops from Abkhazia, while Russia denied involvement in the civil war.

Notwithstanding this 'war of words' between the two principal adversaries in this conflict, the major power in the conflict region also engaged in active mediation during the intermittent Abkhaz–Georgian violent clashes. Talks between Russia and Georgia were held in Georgia's capital in January 1993, aimed at a friendship and cooperation agreement, including the status of Russian troops in Georgia. Russia's foreign minister held talks in Moscow with Georgian and Abkhaz delegations from June 16 to 22, 1993. This led, on July 27, to a cease-fire agreement signed by Abkhaz separatists and Georgia, mediated by Russia, which agreed to provide peacekeepers; the conflicting parties agreed on the need for UN observers to monitor the cease-fire. The UN too became deeply involved. Georgia's president requested a UN peacekeeping force in January 1993. In April, UN Secretary-General Boutros-Ghali appointed a German diplomat as his Special Representative to assist in the quest for conflict resolution. Tangibly, following the cease-fire agreement, the Security Council decided on August 25 to send a UN Observer Mission in Georgia (UNOMIG), with 88 military observers, to the area of conflict. The next day, Georgia confirmed its withdrawal of all its heavy military equipment and some troops from the front line.

On September 16, an unexpected attack by Abkhaz separatists, following the withdrawal of Georgian forces after the cease-fire, led to their take-over of Sukhumi. A few days later, accused by Georgia's president of continuing to behave like 'an evil empire,' Russia imposed sanctions on Abkhazia. The crisis formally ended on October 8, 1993, when Georgia's President Shevardnadze agreed to join the Russia-created Commonwealth of Independent States (CIS), a loose successor to the USSR. In continuation of its active role in conflict management, Russia sent a peacekeeping force of 500 marines, formally from the CIS, to Georgia on November 4, 1993, to protect railway lines and main roads. On December 1, a fresh cease-fire agreement, mediated by the UN, was signed by Georgia and the Abkhaz separatists, who also agreed on the deployment of more international observers. In early February 1994, the presidents of Russia and Georgia signed a (symbolic) treaty of friendship and cooperation. Conflict management of the most important crisis in Phase 1 of this protracted conflict was consummated by the *Moscow Agreement*, signed by all the parties to this crisis on May 14, 1994 and formalized in a Security Council Resolution, extending the mandate of UNOMIG and calling for the deployment of more (Russian) observers.

A similar pattern of active conflict management is evident in the conflict over South Ossetia, the second disputed enclave in the South Caucasus. Violence began on January 5, 1991, when 6000 Georgian troops entered South Ossetia, and continued for several months in a stalemate. The presidents of Russia and Georgia, *Yeltsin* and *Gamsakhurdia*, held talks in March and signed an agreement in April aimed at stabilizing the situation in South Ossetia—via a newly created joint commission to inquire into the sources of the conflict, and the creation of a joint police unit to disarm illegally armed groups and to facilitate the return of refugees to their original homes. Russia also sent peacekeepers to wind down the fighting. A year later, in March 1992, a coup in Georgia led to the replacement of Gamsakhurdia by Shevardnadze, as noted. On June 10, Georgia's new leader and the leader of North Ossetia signed a protocol that included a cease-fire agreement. Two weeks later, the presidents of Georgia and Russia signed the Sochi Agreement, also known as the Treaty of Dagomys, which indicated the steps to end the Georgia/South Ossetia War, notably the entry of Georgian, Ossetian, and Russian troops into South Ossetia, which occurred in July 1992, ending that violent crisis-war. The two 'peace' agreements, Sochi (1992) and Moscow (1994), marked the end of Phase I of the Georgia/Russia interstate conflict, setting in motion a period of 8 years of tranquility; however, their conflict was far from resolved.

There were two additional Georgia/Russia crises early in the twenty-first century, both marked by considerable verbal threats and modest violence.

One was Pankisi Gorge (July 27–October 7, 2002), without any attempted mediation; it ended with a meeting between the two presidents at a CIS summit conference, an announced agreement on October 7 to create joint patrols of their common border, and a formal agreement on October 17.

The other crisis, South Ossetia-Abkhazia (June 10–November 5) was characterized by frequent verbal threats and little violence. It too ended without any third-party mediation: only Russia was present at the Georgia–South Ossetia negotiations that culminated in their crisis-ending demilitarization agreement on November 5.

The peak of conflict management in this interstate conflict occurred during and soon after the four-day **Georgia–Russia War (August 7–11, 2008)**. Tensions between the two contenders for control over Abkhazia and South Ossetia increased steadily after the Rose Revolution in Georgia in November 2003, when Shevardnadze was ousted from the presidency by the young, openly declared pro-American Saakashvili. Early in 2008, a concerned European Union dispatched its foreign policy leader, Javier Solana, to Abkhazia with an offer to mediate the conflict between Abkhazia and Georgia—and implicitly Russia as well—to prevent escalation to war; the Russian president—by then, Medvedev had succeeded Putin—declined.

The outbreak of full-scale war between Georgia and Russia, initiated by the former late at night on August 7, 2008, generated immediate attempts at conflict management, with the goal of an early cease-fire. The USA was the first to call for a cease-fire, with increasing intensity as Georgian troops were compelled to retreat from Georgia and Russian troops were advancing in Georgia's territory. However, the most active conflict manager was France's President Sarkozy, who was also head of the European Union in 2008. France's Prime Minister Kouchner was dispatched to Georgia and Abkhazia on August 10, accompanied by the head of the Organization for Security and Cooperation in Europe (OSCE), Finland's Foreign Minister Stubb, with an EU six-point plan to wind down the war: no further use of force; cessation of all military acts; complete access to humanitarian aid; immediate return of Georgia's troops to their bases; withdrawal of Russian troops to their pre-August 7 line; and to begin a discussion of the future status of Abkhazia and South Ossetia and their lasting security. Sarkozy carried the plan to Moscow and Georgia's capital, Tbilisi on the 11th. Georgia's President Saakashvili insisted—and Russia accepted—a meaningful change in the last point: "The territorial integrity of Georgia is not subject to discussion...and the future status of the disputed regions should be determined with help of an international process." This vague phrasing on future attempts to resolve this protracted conflict ensured a lengthy, continuing delay in resolution.

Georgia/Russia Conflict: Causes of Non-resolution

Does the absence of any, some or all of the six postulated conditions conducive to conflict resolution, noted in the Conflict Resolution Model earlier in this book, explain the absence of resolution of this dormant interstate conflict?

Exhaustion—Georgia experienced a severe defeat in the 2008 war, including Russia's occupation of much of its territory and high casualties, as well as the loss of Abkhazia and South Ossetia, the ostensible cause of its conflict with Russia. This undoubtedly led to exhaustion at the mass public level. Yet its leadership, notably President Saakashvili, insisted upon—and achieved—a significant change in the wording of the crucial last point in the EU Six Point Plan for a Cease-Fire in August 1998, cited above; that is, for Georgia, national exhaustion was not conducive to concessions on the future formal resolution of the conflict. As for Russia, there is no evidence of exhaustion as a result of the August 2008 war with Georgia or throughout this interstate conflict, in which it was the victor, achieving control over the two disputed enclaves.

Balance of Capability—The huge disparity in the military and economic capability of the two principal adversaries was not conducive to conflict resolution, and neither Georgia nor Russia pressed for resolution, though they were receptive to conflict management of specific episodes of crisis and war during their interstate conflict.

Domestic Pressures—These were present in Georgia's society, deriving from both the frequent eruption of threats of military incursions, including occasional occupation of Georgian territory, and economic pressure, including Russia's boycott or discrimination against vital Georgian exports. Yet these pressures did not lead George to make concessions for peace when issues considered vital national interests, such as the disputed enclaves, were at risk. There were no evident domestic pressures in Russia for an end to its conflict with Georgia except on terms that would benefit Russia's national interests.

External Pressures—As indicated above, there were abundant foreign pressures, in the form of attempted conflict management in both phases of this conflict, 1991–1994 and 2002–2008, manifested in efforts by individual states and international organizations to wind down threats, crises, and war. Pressures were directed to both of the principal adversaries, Georgia and Russia, and were conducive to termination of crises and war. *In sum*, foreign pressure was the sole postulated condition that was conducive to, and often effective, in conflict-crisis management, but not conflict resolution. This finding supports the basic thesis of the Resolution Model in negative terms, that is when all (or most) of the postulated conditions conducive to conflict resolution are absent, resolution is unlikely to occur.

In substantive terms, resolution of the *Georgia/Russia* conflict remains elusive because one of the principal adversaries, Russia, having triumphed in war, has no interest in further negotiations to resolve the conflict formally, which might involve Russian concessions, and the principal mediators, the EU, the UN, and France lacked the ability to impose negotiations for conflict resolution on either of the principal adversaries. Ironically, only Russia was a persistent and usually successful mediator—in violent and non-violent crises *between Georgia and the two enclaves*; in the interstate conflict with Georgia, it was a principal adversary, not a mediator.

Reconciliation
In the absence of formal conflict resolution, reconciliation between Georgia and Russia has not occurred. The immediate cause is that, since August 2008, Russia has steadily increased its de facto annexation of Abkhazia and South Ossetia: Russian passports have been provided to the inhabitants of the two enclaves, as have economic and financial aid to impoverished dependents, and physical security against a possible attempt by Georgia to re-assert its control of these enclaves by violence. Moreover, Georgia lacks the ability to undermine or reverse this process. A more fundamental obstacle to reconciliation is the lengthy period of Russian domination—control over Georgia by Tsarist Russia and Communist Russia for more than two centuries, alluded to earlier. This historical reality, which ended only two decades ago, overrides a potential conciliatory attribute, their shared belief system, Orthodox Christianity.

INTER-KOREA CONFLICT (UNRESOLVED)

Behavior

Decisions
The first significant decision in this Northeast Asia combined *civil war* and *interstate* conflict for mastery of the Korean Peninsula was the

launching of the Korean War by the Democratic People's Republic of Korea (DPRK) [North Korea] on June 25, 1950. The war, in which a very large contingent of People's Republic of China (PRC) 'Volunteers' later fought alongside North Korea, and the USA served as the main actively engaged ally of the Republic of Korea (ROK) (South Korea), ended in July 1953. Both Koreas, supported by their principal patrons, decided *to end the fighting* via *an armistice that has been sustained and largely respected by the two Koreas for 64 years*, though the DPRK verbally renounced the armistice on several occasions, most recently in March 2013.

North Korea: Decisions and Decision-Makers
The DPRK made several major decisions following the end of the Korean War. Its most important post-war *strategic* decision was *a general policy change*, not a choice on a specific conflict issue: in the mid-1960s, North Korea decided *to shift the emphasis in the allocation of its national resources from economic development to defense*, a policy change with profound consequences for its foreign policy, economic development, and the *Inter-Korea* conflict, because it remained in effect until recently. The next two North Korea major decisions related to the highly controversial issue of nuclear weapons, with implications for the persistence of both the *Inter-Korea* and *North Korean Nuclear* interstate conflicts. One decision occurred early in the Inter-Korea conflict: the DPRK decided in 1959 *to launch a nuclear weapons program by signing a nuclear cooperation treaty with the USSR*, following the USA–South Korea decision to introduce nuclear weapons into the Korean Peninsula in 1957. The other major decision by North Korea on nuclear weapons occurred 36 years later: in 1993, it declared that it was withdrawing from the Nuclear Non-Proliferation Treaty, which it had signed largely under Soviet pressure. This decision was a catalyst to the unresolved *North Korean Nuclear conflict* but it was also an important *conflict-sustaining act* in the *Inter-Korea* Conflict. *In sum*, North Korea's behavior toward its South Korea adversary and rival since their formation as independent states in 1948, largely at the behest of their patrons, the USSR and the USA, reflected a general, though not often proclaimed, decision to manifest hostility to, and mistrust of, its South Korea rival, though not without brief periods of cooperation in the shared goal of a re-united Korean Peninsula.

The principal North Korean decision-makers throughout this protracted conflict were the three members of the politically dominant family in the DPRK: *Kim Il Sung*, the founder and first ruler of this Communist state, 1948–1994; his son and successor, *Kim Jong Il*, 1994–2011, and his son, *Kim Jong-un*, the leader since 2011. Each had a small coterie of advisers, but only the first of the three Kim rulers was known to have rivals within the Korea Workers Party until the late 1960s. While their formal authority derived from their multiple roles as the central figure in all the key state institutions, the ruling Party, the military establishment, and the governmental regime, their power flowed, and continues, from an institutionalized three-generation family dynastic system of succession.

North Korea: Decision Process
Like most authoritarian, as well as democratic regimes, the governmental structure of North Korea comprises an executive branch headed by the President of the DPRK, a legislature, the Supreme People's Assembly, and a judiciary. However, power is concentrated in the ruling Workers Party of Korea (WPK) and, within it, the Politburo, as was the case in all ruling Communist parties. Ultimately, power has resided in the Supreme Leader, as enshrined in the DPRK 1972 constitution. Although little is known of its actual decision-making process, it is generally assumed that Kim Il Sung, his son, Kim Jong Il and, currently, his grandson, Kim Jong-un, is the supreme decision-maker on all important issues of public policy. Formally, this is legitimized by the Supreme Leader's multiple official roles: president of the DPRK, chairman of the People's National Assembly, First Secretary of the WPK Central Committee and Politburo, head of the Central Military Commission, etc. There are consultations with other Party leaders, military commanders, and technical specialists, including Foreign Ministry officials; but substantive decisions on all aspects of inter-Korea relations, as in all major policy issues, are made by the incumbent Supreme Leader.

South Korea: Decisions and Decision-Makers
Like the DPRK, the ROK made many *strategic* decisions relating to their conflict, some of great importance. The *first* was the *decision of its first President, Syngman Rhee*, on the day of North Korea's attack, June 25, 1950, *to seek instant USA military aid, both American forces and weapons*. The response was immediate, in the form of a USA-led UN Command, with a predominance of American troops and, over time, the contribution of military aid by many states. The ROK decision and the

USA response escalated during the next three years, generating an alliance between the two states that has been a crucial element in the power configuration of East Asia during the past six decades.

The next *strategic* South Korea decision, also made by President Rhee (1948–1961), was *to accept President Eisenhower's recommendation to introduce USA-controlled nuclear weapons into South Korea*, even though such an act violated a provision of the Korean War Armistice Agreement that prohibited the dispatch of new arms into the Korean Peninsula. The nuclear weapons were dispatched in January 1958 and remained in South Korea until 1991, long before the first DPRK nuclear test in 2006. (In light of the successful DPRK third nuclear test in February 2013 and further tests in 2014–2017, there has been a modest revival of South Korea interest in the re-acquisition of nuclear weapons to offset North Korea's impressive achievements in nuclear weapons technology.)

A third *major decision* by South Korea, with profound consequences for the DPRK/ROK rivalry and conflict, occurred soon after the ouster of President Rhee in a 1961 coup that brought General *Park Chung Hee* to power: the decision was to concentrate South Korea's material resources on economic development, especially industrialization, *the opposite of North Korea's policy decision later in the 1960s* to shift resources from economic development to national security. Among the consequences of this dual policy shift has been South Korea's impressive economic growth, achieving the status of a world-class economy, while North Korea became increasingly dependent on economic aid from China while vastly increasing its military power. A notable consequence for the inter-Korea conflict was an increasingly active debate in South Korea on the wisdom of persisting with the long-established governmental concentration on economic development, captured by the motto of South Korea's long-serving second president, Park Chung Hee, 'economic construction first, reunification later.' The growing evidence of North Korea's burgeoning nuclear weapons capability by 2017 reinforced this debate in South Korea, but without any decision.

Nonetheless, there were several *attempts by South Korean political leaders to initiate a dialogue with North Korea* on reunification, in 1972, 1992, 2000, and 2007. The *most notable* was South Korea's President *Kim Dae Jung*'s policy initiative, the 'Sunshine Policy.' His decision—*to reach out to* Kim Jong Il, then the DPRK Supreme Leader, in 1998—was *the tangible expression of a general policy decision* by South Korea's president, *to change South Korea's long-established 'hard line' of persistent conflict to a 'softer* line' of cooperation and persuasion. It had limited success: summit meetings between the two Koreas in June 2000 and October 2007, along with modest cross-border trade, a small number of family reunifications, and the opening of a tourist area in the southern part of North Korea. The ROK initiative ended abruptly in 2008, with the election of President *Lee Myungbak*, who restored the long-standing hardline prior to Kim Dae Jung's "Sunshine Policy." A reversion to the softer line was announced by the newly elected President of South Korea, Moon Jae-in, in 2017.

South Korea: Decision Process
The ROK [South Korea] political structure and its decision process were more complex than its counterparts in the DPRK [North Korea]. Three phases are evident in the changing character of South Korea's political system: Phase I, *civil authoritarian rule*, First and Second Republics (1948–1961); Phase II, *Military rule* (1961–1987); Phase III, *Western-style democracy* since 1987.

Syngman Rhee, who dominated the first phase as President of the Republic of Korea (ROK) , was a domineering religious-political leader who was actively engaged in foreign policy decision-making, including all issues relating to the inter-Korea conflict. No other ROK politician in that phase could rival or effectively challenge Rhee's control of decision-making on issues in which he had definite views. During the second phase, Park Chung Hee was the pre-eminent leader, no less authoritarian than Rhee, but more inclined to seek expert advice. The Director of the Korean Central Intelligence Agency (KCIA) and the Korean National Security Council (KNSC), both organizations modeled on their USA counterparts, were influential in the decision-making process on all foreign policy and Inter-Korean issues. Phase III witnessed a broadening of the decision-making group and process, with the bureaucracy, interest groups, the media and public opinion often active participants in shaping decisions on a wide range of issues, including those relating to, and impinging on, the Inter-Korean conflict. *In sum*, economic development, modernization, and urbanization transformed South Korea's economy, society, and political system in the 1990s and beyond, changing the decision process from a narrow, individual ruler-based process to a much broader, typical Western democratic political process. However, on major issues, among them, relations with the DPRK and the Inter-Korea conflict, the influence of an activist president has remained significant, as evident in the 'Sunshine Policy' initiative of President Kim

Dae Jung (1998–2003), continued by his successor, Roh Moo-Hyun (2004–2008), and the reversal of that policy by President Lee Myung-bak (2008–2013), in turn reversed by Moon Jae-in (2017).

Inter-Korea Conflict: Conflict-Sustaining Acts

Political Hostility This was the *most frequent* type of conflict-sustaining acts in the inter-Korea conflict. They began very soon after the independence of the two Korean states, the Republic of Korea (ROK), South Korea, and the Democratic People's Republic of Korea (DPRK), North Korea, in 1948. The ROK, under its long-time authoritarian, anti-Communist president, Syngman Rhee (August 1948–April 1960), denied recognition to North Korea (the DPRK) and, with USA support, secured UN recognition of the ROK as the sole Korea state. From November 1949 until June 1950, there were frequent ROK (President Rhee) statements of its intention to invade North Korea. Since the end of the Korean War (1953), the ROK refused formal relations with the DPRK and, in October 1953, it signed a Mutual Defense treaty with the USA, clearly aimed at North Korea. In 1968, during the North Korea/USA crisis created by the DPRK naval capture of the USS *Pueblo*, Rhee's successor-president, General Park Chung Hee, reiterated the ROK's longstanding commitment to unilateral military acts to overthrow the DPRK regime. From 1976 to 1992, and resumed after a 1-year suspension, the ROK engaged in an annual, high-profile, *non-violent military* act that contributed much to sustaining the inter-Korea conflict, the (often large-scale) joint 'Team Spirit' military exercise with USA forces stationed in South Korea. This ROK conflict-sustaining policy toward its North Korea Communist neighbor continued, with varying intensity of politically hostile statements, until 1998. A decade of 'Sunshine Policy' (1998–2008), introduced by President Kim Dae Jung (1998–2003) and continued by his successor, Roh Moo-Hyun (2003–2008), aimed at peaceful reconciliation with the DPRK. This accommodation policy was reversed by President Lee Myung-bak (2008–2013).

The DPRK reciprocated the ROK's (South Korea's) politically hostile acts, beginning with the assertion of its sole legitimacy as the custodian of Korea statehood, in 1948 and during the next 68 years. Like the ROK, it secured great power patrons, but somewhat later— Mutual Assistance treaties with the USSR and Mainland China (PRC) in 1961. In 1962, North Korea (DPRK) publicly abandoned the goal of peaceful unification with South Korea and reverted to violence as the DPRK preferred strategy to achieve Korean unity. Its long-time leader, Kim Il Sung, frequently contributed conflict-sustaining acts by proclaiming that revolutionary forces in both Koreas would achieve unification, without excluding the resort to violence. During the 'Poplar Tree' crisis with the USA in 1976, he termed war inevitable and placed DPRK armed forces on high alert. Moreover, North Korea frequently attempted to incite anti-government uprisings in South Korea. Long before the ROK's 'Sunshine Policy,' it rejected South Korea's proposals for summit meetings to pursue the goal of peaceful unification, to which both Koreas paid lip service. During the decade of 'Sunshine Policy' (1998–2008), a summit meeting of the leaders of the two Koreas was held in Pyongyang, the DPRK capital, in 2000, and economic aid from the much richer and economically developed South Korea to North Korea visibly increased. However, the accommodation was short-lived. Lee Myung-bak became the ROK president in 2008 and reversed the 'Sunshine Policy' of his two predecessors. In 2009, the DPRK conducted its second nuclear test (the first was in 2006). Two North Korea-related military incidents in 2010, the sinking of a South Korean naval vessel, with 46 casualties, and artillery fire on a South Korean island near North Korea's coast, contributed to the re-escalation of the hostile environment in the *Inter-Korea* conflict. As noted above, the election of a conciliatory president in South Korea indicated a return to the 'Sunshine Policy', *vis-a-vis* North Korea.

Violence—This dominated the conflict-sustaining activity in the early years of the Inter-Korea conflict, with enormous casualties by all of the participants in the 1950–1953 Korean War:

> According to the data from the US Department of Defense, the United States suffered 33,686 battle deaths, along with 2830 non-battle deaths during the Korean War and 8176 missing in action. Western sources estimate the PVA (PRC) had suffered between 100,000 to 1,500,000 deaths (most estimate some 400,000 killed); while the KPA (DPRK) had suffered between 214,000 and 520,000 deaths (most estimate some 500,000). Between some 245,000 to 415,000 South Korean civilian deaths were also suggested, and the entire civilian casualties during the war were estimated from 1,500,000 to 3,000,000 (most sources estimate some 2,000,000 killed).

Data from official Chinese sources, on the other hand, reported that the PVA had suffered 114,000 battle deaths, 34,000 non-battle deaths,

340,000 wounded, 7600 missing and 21,400 captured during the war. Among those captured, about 14,000 defected to Taiwan, while the other 7110 were repatriated to China. Chinese sources also reported that North Korea had suffered 290,000 casualties, 90,000 captured, and a "large" number of civilian deaths. In return, the Chinese and North Koreans estimated that about 390,000 soldiers from the United States, 660,000 soldiers from South Korea, and 29,000 other UN soldiers were "eliminated" from the battlefield. (Reported from multiple official sources by Wikipedia)

There were no other full-scale wars in the Korean Peninsula during this lengthy unresolved protracted conflict. Rather, frequent incidents of low intensity and short duration were the norm since 1953, for example, the attempted DPRK assassination of ROK President Park Chung Hee, modeled on January 21, 1968, the shooting-down of a USA reconnaissance plane in 1969 (EC-121 crisis), the axe-murder of two USA soldiers in 1976 (the Poplar Tree Crisis), and the 2010 DPRK firing on a ROK military installation near its border, noted earlier. The exception was the sinking of a ROK warship in 2010, with the death of 46 ROK sailors, but the immense human losses and material damage of the Korean War remained a profound memory and influence for the peoples of the two Koreas for a very long period.

Verbal Hostility—As in the unresolved *North Korean Nuclear* conflict, the two principal adversaries in this closely related conflict between the two Koreas engaged in a frequent and, often, intense exchange of hostile invective during almost all of the Inter-Korea conflict as well—anti-communism, on the part of the ROK, anti-capitalism and the ROK alliance with the USA, on the part of the DPRK. Propaganda from both sides was shrill, harsh, and condemnatory of 'the other,' each blaming its adversary for all of the failures to achieve a genuine accommodation and to facilitate the shared goal of unification of the Korean peninsula, along with intense hostility to the ideology and the economic and political systems of its irreconcilable enemy. However, notwithstanding the frequency and intensity of the verbal diatribes, the impact of an array of verbal hostility acts, while undoubtedly sustaining the conflict, was less influential than acts of political hostility and the traumatic memory of the Korean War. The latter intensified the consciousness of the havoc that would be wreaked by another Korean War, with the DPRK in possession of a growing stockpile of nuclear weapons, and both adversaries confronting an existential threat, with difficult-to-imagine consequences.

Economic Discrimination—In the absence of substantive inter-Korean economic relations during most of this Korean conflict, the scope for conflict-sustaining acts was very limited. It was non-existent as a technique for the DPRK to cause, or threaten to cause, economic damage to the ROK. However, the reverse flow, that is, the ability of the ROK to sustain—or reduce the intensity of—their Conflict with the DPRK was very considerable. On some crucial occasions, it did facilitate the temporary accommodation process between the two Koreas by meaningful economic gestures. A notable illustration was South Korea's offer to construct low-enrichment nuclear reactors that would provide North Korea with vitally needed electricity that would enable it to suspend its rapidly expanding nuclear enrichment program that was causing consternation for the USA and other Western states, as well as the ROK, thereby contributing to a rare agreement between the DPRK and its primary enemies, the USA and the ROK—the 1994 Agreed Framework (AF). Another notable example of economic cooperation as a means of achieving conflict reduction has been the ROK provision of food aid during periods of near or actual famine in North Korea. Still another illustration was the flow of ROK economic assistance to the DPRK during the decade of the former's 'Sunshine Policy' (1998–2008). And finally, the creation of a very large economic cooperation zone at the border between the two Koreas, facilitating employment for a large number of North Koreans, has assisted the tension reduction process. By contrast, an implied threat by the South Korea president to suspend the flow of food and to close the border economic zone at the height of the 2010 crisis over the sinking of a South Korean naval vessel with heavy loss of life, though not implemented, proved to be a sharp conflict-sustaining act in the economic domain. However, this type of conflict-sustaining acts has been the least important of the four techniques available to the *Inter-Korea* adversaries.

Inter-Korea: Conflict Management and Attempts at Conflict Resolution

Korean War
There have been many attempts to manage and resolve this Northeast Asia protracted conflict since its onset in 1948, when the two states in

the Korean Peninsula, the DPRK, North Korea, and the ROK, South Korea, were created by agreement between the USA and the USSR. The first major effort at *conflict management* took the form of a cease-fire and armistice negotiations and agreements, and battlefield outcomes, during the three lengthy phases of the Korean War (1950–1953), leading to temporary reductions of violence and, ultimately, virtual elimination of *major violence* between the two Koreas during the past 6 decades.

Korean War, Phase I (June 25–September 30, 1950): There were four conflict actors during this phase, the two Koreas (principal adversaries), the People's Republic of China (PRC), and the United States. The war began on June 25, when large-scale North Korean forces crossed the 38th Parallel, the unofficial border between the two Koreas since 1948. By the end of September, UN forces, commanded by USA General Macarthur, restored control of South Korea south of the 38th Parallel to the ROK government.

Korean War, Phase II (September 30, 1950–July 10, 1951): There were five conflict actors in this phase, the two Koreas, the PRC, the USA, and the USSR. This phase began with the crossing of the 38th Parallel by South Korea and USA forces. By June 1951, the battlefield stabilized around the 38th Parallel, and a cease-fire and armistice negotiations began on July 10.

Korean War, Phase III (April 16–July 27, 1953): There were four conflict actors in the third and last phase of the Korean War—the two Koreas, the PRC and the USA. This phase began with a new offensive by PRC-North Korean forces, in the midst of discussions about a cease-fire taking place at Panmunjom, in the Demilitarized Zone. An **Armistice Agreement** was signed on July 27, 1953, terminating the Korean War. That Agreement, despite frequent violations over the decades, continues to define the formal legal status of relations between North and South Korea 64 years later.

Inter-Korea Conflict: Further Attempts at Conflict Management and Conflict Resolution

Many of the efforts to manage and resolve the *Inter-Korea* conflict since the end of the Korean War were initiated in *bilateral negotiations* by the two Koreas. Among the agreements between the two principal adversaries in this protracted conflict, some oral, others followed by cooperative behavior, six merit attention for their promise and outcome: their *July 4 Joint Communiqué*, 1972–1973; their *Basic Agreement on Reconciliation, Non-Aggression, Exchanges and Cooperation*, 1991–1993; their *Joint Declaration on Denuclearization of the Korean Peninsula*, 1992–1993; their *Summit Meeting and June 15 Joint Declaration*, 2000; their *Summit Meeting and October 4 North-South Declaration*, 2007; and South Korea's '*Sunshine Policy*,' 1998–2008.

1972 Joint Communiqué—Talks by the dominant Korean leaders in 1971, *Kim Il Sung (DPRK)* and *Park Chung Hee* (ROK), who rarely met face-to-face and reportedly loathed each other, led to their Joint Communiqué on July 4, 1972. This formalized their verbal agreement on three principles designed to achieve their *goals*—*peaceful unification*, *tension reduction*, and *reconciliation* of their different *ideologies* and political systems. The guiding principles were as follows: *independent* achievement of *unification*, without any foreign involvement or constraints; its attainment *by peaceful means*; and the *shared objective* of *national unity as one people*. However, this attempt at conflict resolution, like all its successors, was aborted: North Korea withdrew from the follow-up negotiations on August 23, 1973, apparently because the two leaders held different interpretations of the Communiqué's three principles and were unwilling to make commitments to their implementation (Chang 1996, 246–247).

1991–1992 North-South Korea Basic Agreement—The prelude to this agreement was a declaration by South Korean President *Roh Tae Woo* in July 1988, at the beginning of South Korea's transition from an authoritarian to a democratic political system: he enunciated a more specific six-point Korean unification policy than the 1972 Communiqué which, after extensive negotiations, became the core of the Basic Agreement. Signed on December 13, 1991, with effect from February 19, 1992, this agreement re-affirmed the three principles set out in the 1972 Joint Communiqué; declared the intent of the two Koreas to end political and military confrontation and attain national reconciliation; agreed to reject armed aggression, to reduce tensions between them and to establish peace; and renewed their oft-stated commitment to the re-unification of families separated by the Korean War, and the promotion of common interests and the prosperity of the Korean people. Implementation of the Basic Agreement began but faltered and later failed, for several reasons. One was the revival of the annual South Korea–USA "Team Spirit" military exercises, always anathema to North Korea's leadership. Another reason was its timing: implementation of the Basic Agreement became enmeshed with the *first North Korea Nuclear Crisis* in 1993–1994, when the DPRK declared its intent to withdraw from the Nuclear Non-Proliferation Treaty (NPT). The third and most basic obstacle was the starkly different DPRK and ROK ideologies and their divergent conceptions of a desired outcome: for South Korea, the goals were a single and complete re-unified Korean state, with a democratic political system and a market economy; for North Korea, the objectives were a lower-stage federation of the two Korean states, in which the DPRK would retain its Communist political system and command economy. Thus, like most verbal agreements between the two Koreas, the ambitious Basic Agreement was aborted.

1992–1993 Joint Declaration on Denuclearization of the Korean Peninsula—Issued on January 20, 1992, with effect from February 19, it specified a commitment by the two Koreas not to manufacture, receive, store, deploy or use nuclear weapons and not to possess nuclear re-processing and uranium enrichment facilities. Verification of the implementation of these commitments and, more generally, denuclearization was to be achieved by a North-South Joint Nuclear Control Commission. However, this attempt at inter-Korea conflict management via a bilateral inspection regime was thwarted in 1993 by several developments: failed meetings between the two Koreas on the implementation of their Joint Declaration on Denuclearization the previous year; North Korea's refusal in 1993 to grant a request by the International Atomic Energy Agency (IAEA) for inspection of its suspected nuclear facilities; and North Korea's threat the same year to withdraw from the Nuclear Non-Proliferation regime, to which it was committed since it signed the Nuclear Non-Proliferation Treaty (NPT) in 1985, under USSR pressure—the Soviet Union no longer existed in 1993.

2000 North Korea–South Korea Summit Meeting and Their June 15 Joint Declaration—The DPRK (North Korea) leader, *Kim Jong Il* and the ROK (South Korea) president, *Kim Dae Jung,* held a Summit meeting in Pyongyang on June 13–15, 2000. In a Joint Declaration, they declared their agreement: to resolve the issue of reunification of the two Koreas on their own initiative; to permit an exchange of visits by members of Korean families that had been separated by the Korean War, on August 15, 2000; and to arrange an exchange of long-term prisoners in the two states. They also indicated a mutual recognition that both of their preferred constitutional-political solutions for a reunified Korean Peninsula—a lower-stage *federation* [*najundangueuiyonbangje-an*], for the DPRK, and a *federation* [*yonhapje-an*], for the ROK—contained common features and agreed to promote the shared goal of reunification that would be based on those common elements. The Declaration also called for greater economic cooperation between the two Koreas and proposed a dialogue among officials to implement the terms of their Declaration without delay. As with virtually all the preceding bilateral attempts at conflict management and conflict resolution noted above, the Joint Declaration of 2000 remained a conciliatory, vague verbal commitment by the two principal adversaries. More significant, Kim Jong Il's acceptance of Kim Dae Jung's reciprocal invitation in June 2000 to visit Seoul "at an appropriate time" was never implemented.

2007 North Korea–South Korea Summit Meeting and Their October 4 Joint Declaration

This Joint Declaration by Korea's then-leaders, *Kim Jong Il* (DPRK) and President *Roh Moo-hyun* (ROK), repeated the *general verbal commitments* expressed in the Joint Declaration 7 years earlier by Kim Jong Il and the then-President of South Korea, *Kim Dae Jung*, initiator of the ROK's "Sunshine Policy" in 1998, notably their shared goals—reunification, on their own initiative, greater economic cooperation, and an end to military hostilities. However, this Joint Declaration went beyond, with several specific commitments by the two Korea leaders. One was "to work together to advance the matter of having the leaders of the three or four parties directly concerned [the two Koreas, the PRC and the USA] to convene on the Peninsula and declare an end to the war," that is, to transform the Armistice regime since the end of the Korean War in 1953 to a formal peace agreement. This politically and symbolically significant provision of the Joint Declaration was not implemented. Nor were other commitments in the 2007 Joint Declaration: "to create a special peace and cooperation zone in the West Sea," in Haeju, a port town in southwestern North Korea, along with a joint fishing zone, maritime peace

9 SELECT CASE STUDY FINDINGS ON INTERSTATE CONFLICTS ... 283

zone, and a special economic zone, and "to work together to implement smoothly" two verbal agreements on the significant controversial issue of nuclear weapons in North Korea, their Joint Statement of September 19, 2005 and the February 13, 2007 Agreement framed at the Six Party Talks on North Korea's active nuclear weapons program. There were also verbal commitments on the construction of the *Kaesong Industrial Complex*, freight rail services between Munsan and Bongdong, shipbuilding facilities, and projects in agriculture, medical services, and environmental protection. Since South Korea's "Sunshine Policy" was still intact, optimism about a new era of cooperation between the two Koreas was reflected in the 2007 Joint Declaration. However, the optimism was short-lived—the election of Lee Myung-bak as South Korea President in 2008 led to the abandonment of its "Sunshine Policy," which made provisions of the 2007 Declaration irrelevant.

2000–2008 South Korea's "Sunshine Policy" The one partial success in Korean efforts to achieve conflict resolution was a South Korean (ROK) *unilateral* initiative to attain the positive goals expressed in the several agreements and declarations by leaders and regimes noted above. The tangible, innovative, high-profile "Sunshine Policy" by South Korea's President *Kim Dae Jung* (1998–2003) took the form of a dramatic 'opening' to the DPRK), with two dimensions—vitally needed economic aid to North Korea from South Korea, including the Hyundai Project of investment, and closer political relations. Kim Dae Jung's visit to Pyongyang in 2000 for a summit conference with the DPRK leader, *Kim Jong Il*, was an important *symbolic* element of the "Sunshine Policy," aimed at reconciliation and, ultimately, peaceful reunification of the two Koreas. Leaders of the DPRK and the ROK were long committed to these objectives, though they held fundamentally different conceptions of the preferred type of political system, economic system, and ideology that should prevail in a reunited Korean Peninsula. Although South Korea's "Sunshine Policy" toward North Korea proved to be of limited duration, it demonstrated promise and substantial fulfillment for a decade (1998–2008): this policy was sustained by Kim Dae Jung's successor, *Roh Moo-Hyun* (2003–2008). The policy led to four notable achievements. One was the initiation of a *successful summit meeting* between the leaders of the Korean adversarial states in 2000. Another was the *beginning of limited trade* between the DPRK and the ROK, after a half-century of economic isolation. A third was the *opening of* the Mt. *Kumgang* tourist area to South Korean visitors. And the fourth, which resonated among the aged segment of both North and South Korean populations, was the *beginning of a limited reunification of families* that had been separated by the Korean War.

In 2008, South Korea's policy toward the DPRK reverted to the predominant 'hard line' espoused and practiced by the Republic of Korea (ROK)'s political leaders during the first half-century of this protracted conflict (1948–1998), notably by its first two long-term authoritarian presidents—*Syngman Rhee* (1948–1960) and *Park Chung Hee* (1962–1979). The reversal from the "Sunshine Policy" to a hard-line policy occurred in 2008, with the election of a conservative political leader, Lee Myung-bak as President of the Republic of Korea (2008–2013), partly in response to the vigorous nuclear weapons program of the DPRK, highlighted by its first nuclear weapon test in 2006, followed by much more sophisticated nuclear weapon tests in 2009, 2013, 2014, 2016, and 2017. A return to the soft-line policy was pledged by the newly elected South Korean President in 2017.

In sum, the negative record of *bilateral* and *unilateral* attempts at conflict management and conflict resolution in the *Inter-Korea* conflict, with the partial exception of the "Sunshine Policy," was deeply rooted in the ideological conflict that dated to the creation of two Korean states in 1948. That enduring conflict between the two parts of a homogeneous nation re-escalated from 1993 onward primarily because of the DPRK's initially covert entry into the select group of nine nuclear weapon states—the USA, the USSR-Russia, the UK, France, China, Israel, India, Pakistan, and the DPRK—intensifying the longstanding rivalry between the two Koreas.

Inter-Korea: Third-Party Attempts at Conflict Management and Resolution

There have also been several notable *third-party* attempts at conflict management and conflict resolution focused on the Korean Peninsula, mainly by the two patrons of the principal adversaries in this conflict, the United States, patron of South Korea, and China, patron of North Korea. One of these efforts was ultimately successful—the lengthy process that led to the termination of the Korean War (1950–1953), noted above. The USA indicated its wish for a *cease-fire* in December 1950, six months after the outbreak of full-scale war. The USSR, not a direct participant in that war but the major initial supplier of arms to the

DPRK, did so six months later. The USA and China, the two major patrons of the two Korea belligerents, played the decisive role in *sustaining* the Korean War; but they were also instrumental in initiating and persisting in its *de-escalation*, culminating in the July 1953 Armistice Agreement, which ended the longest and most violent phase of this unresolved conflict. While many hostile acts—violent and non-violent— have occurred in the relations between North and South Korea during the past 6 decades, noted in the analysis of *conflict-sustaining acts*, the Armistice regime has been, and continues to be, an effective deterrent to a recurrence of *major* inter-Korea violence since 1953. As such, the third-party-engineered Armistice Agreement has been a highly successful achievement in conflict management.

A promising but only partly fulfilled development, four decades after the Korean War, combined *third party* and *bilateral* attempts at both conflict management and conflict resolution in the two unresolved conflicts that currently co-exist and reinforce each other, the *Inter-Korea* and the *North Korean Nuclear* conflicts: this was the October 1994 *Agreed Framework* between the DPRK and the USA, with other participants, the ROK and Japan, initiated and sustained by the USA (Clinton Administration) and North Korea (during Kim Il Sung's lengthy leadership). Like all the *bilateral* agreements between the two Koreas between 1972 and 2000 noted above, aimed at resolution of the *Inter-Korea conflict*, the 1994 Agreed Framework, *multilateral in form* but essentially a *bilateral agreement in content* between North Korea and the United States, became a terminal victim of escalating distrust between these two adversaries, consigned to 'what might have been' in 2002. Like the 1994 Agreed Framework, noted above, the primary focus at its 'on-again-off-again' high-profile successor in attempted conflict management and conflict resolution, the *Six Party Talks*, which unfolded in six Rounds from late August 2003 to mid-April 2009, when the DPRK announced that it would no longer participate in this forum and would not be bound by its previous agreements, was the controversial issue of North Korea's *nuclear weapons* program, *not* the *Inter-Korea conflict*.

Inter-Korea Conflict: Causes of Non-Resolution

The *Inter-Korea conflict*, like its close conceptual and empirical conflict relative, the *North Korean Nuclear Conflict*, has not been resolved. The *Model on Conflict Resolution* will be tested here by focusing on the following question: have any, some or all of the six postulated 'most likely' causes of interstate protracted conflict resolution been present in the *Inter-Korean conflict* during the 70 years since its onset in 1948?

Exhaustion—Although there was abundant evidence of acute exhaustion by the population of both the DPRK and the ROK at the end of the Korean War in 1953, that condition was sufficient for *partial* resolution only, in the form of the Armistice Agreement—which remains in force 64 years later, though occasionally under severe threat to its persistence, not *complete resolution* of their interstate conflict. Moreover, inter-Korean violence since 1953 has been episodic, mostly high-profile incidents initiated by North Korea, but minimal in intensity and casualties, except for the sinking of a South Korean naval vessel, with the loss of 46 South Korean naval personnel in 2010, the cause of, and responsibility for, that incident which remains formally unclear. The people of North Korea have endured several periods of exhaustion, but all resulted from famines and general economic privation resulting from governmental economic policy and foreign-imposed sanctions, not from the enduring conflict with South Korea. By contrast, the ROK, South Korea, enjoyed a 'qualitative leap' in economic development and prosperity from the 1970s onward. While its population has been subject to periodic increases in stress, especially since the DPRK demonstration of a nuclear weapons capability in its many nuclear tests (2006, 2009, 2013, 2014, 2016, and 2017) the largest test in September 2016, that triggered stiffer UN Security Council economic sanctions 2 months later), and other evidence of a missile capability superior to that of its South Korea rival (though vastly inferior to the nuclear weapon and missile capability of South Korea's patron, the USA), there is no evidence of collective exhaustion among the population of South Korea, deriving from a threat to survival or of grave damage from its adversary in this conflict. In sum, the *absence* of collective exhaustion by North or South Korea since the end of the Korean War contributed to its *non-resolution* thus far.

Changes in the Capability Balance—Throughout the *Inter-Korea* conflict, the principal adversaries have been relatively equally matched in war-making capability. The DPRK's armed forces were larger than those of the ROK, but the latter possessed superior conventional weapons, in both quantity and quality, provided consistently by its patron, the United States, since the beginning of the Korean War. During the last decade, since its first nuclear weapon test in 2006, North Korea acquired a modest nuclear weapon capability. However, in this domain, too, the longstanding USA 'boots on the ground' military presence in South Korea and the near-permanent military alliance between the USA and the ROK, with the significantly larger USA nuclear weapons capability, served as an effective deterrent thus far against North Korea's resort to nuclear weapons in a foreseeable future war with South Korea. This relative balance of military power on the Korean Peninsula made a full-scale war designed to unify the two Korean states by force since 1953 highly unlikely. Moreover, the ROK has possessed a vastly superior economic capability to sustain a war against its rival since the 1970s; and, as the more satisfied Korean state, the ROK is less likely to initiate a war of reunification. *In sum*, the absence of a decisive superiority in overall accessible military capability by the two Korean states also contributes to the persistence, that is, *non-resolution*, of the Inter-Korea conflict.

Domestic Pressures —There is no reliable evidence within the civil authoritarian Kim family political regime in the DPRK of internal pressures for a mutually acceptable resolution of the *Inter-Korea* conflict. The promise of several high-profile *verbal* agreements with the ROK, in favor of peaceful conflict resolution and re-unification—the 1972 Joint Communiqué, the 1992 Basic Agreement, and the 2000 Joint Declaration—was not fulfilled, as noted above. The sole indicator of a conceivable DPRK interest in a shared conflict resolution agreement was the reputed offer in 1980, by North Korea's 'founding father' and supreme leader from 1948 to 1994, Kim Il Sung, for a *federation* between the two independent Korean states. This would have been essentially a verbal, not a substantive, change, for it would permit both North Korea and South Korea to retain their distinctive political and economic systems, ideologies, and armed forces.

In South Korea, as noted above, there was one highly visible manifestation of domestic pressure in favor of genuine conflict resolution, a policy goal that was expressed in the 'Sunshine Policy' and implemented by two ROK presidents (1998–2008). Moreover, South Korea's political leaders frequently advocated re-unification in the form of a unified "one nation, one state, one system, and one government" in the final stage, a Korea *federal* state, with substantial autonomy for its two parts. This advocacy has long been the primary purpose of the ROK Government's Ministry of Reunification, accompanied by the expectation that the unified state would adopt the political system of democracy and a market economy, modeled on the United States, which have always been anathema to the DPRK leadership. *In sum*, the only significant manifestation of domestic pressure for peaceful conflict resolution was South Korea's 'Sunshine Policy,' pursued for a decade in a 70-year unresolved conflict. The absence of such pressures was an additional cause of its persistence.

External Pressures —There is considerable evidence of foreign pressures on the principal adversaries—the DPRK and ROK, North and South Korea—by the USA, China, and the UN, and by a group of states with diverse but substantive interests in conflict resolution in the Korean Peninsula, Japan and Russia, along with China and the USA. As indicated above, in the discussion of *Third-Party Efforts at Conflict Management and Resolution*, the most tangible expression of pressure by the patrons of the DPRK (China) and the ROK (United States) was their role in generating the Armistice Agreement that ended the Korean War in July 1953 and their role in initiating and sustaining the Six Party Talks from 2003 to 2009. Since 1993, most external pressures for conflict resolution of Korea-related conflicts have focused on the resolution of the *North Korean Nuclear conflict*, not the conflict between the two Koreas. This is evident in the UN–USA response to the first *interstate* crisis related to the North Korean nuclear weapons program (1993), culminating in the DPRK-USA Agreed Framework (1994), discussed above, as well as the Six Party Talks from 2003 to 2009, and the UN and US condemnation of North Korea's reported nuclear weapons tests thus far (2006, 2009, 2013, 2014, 2016, and 2017), joined by China's infrequent public criticism of the DPRK's third and fifth nuclear tests. Only one of these manifestations of external pressure, the 1994 Agreed Framework, registered (short-term) progress on the elusive path to conflict resolution of the *North Korean Nuclear* conflict (from 1994 to 2002); had this been sustained, it would have greatly assisted, but would not have been synonymous with, the resolution of the wider, multi-issue *Inter-Korea conflict*. Together, resolution of both Korea-based interstate conflicts would have brought peace to the Korean Peninsula.

Reduction in Discordance of Objectives—Notwithstanding several accommodative initiatives that led to cooperation by the principal adversaries in the *Inter-Korea conflict* for considerable periods—the USA role in the process that generated the Agreed Framework (1994–2002), that included cooperation between North and South Korea on the crucial issue of energy, the cooperative USA–China role, with the active participation of the two Koreas, in creating the Six Party Talks (2003–2009), and South Korea's "Sunshine Policy" toward North Korea (1998–2008), the two principal adversaries in the *Inter-Korea conflict have been consistently rigid on their core objectives.* For the DPRK, the primary goal has been the reunification of the two Koreas in a centralized Communist state modeled on the pre-1990 Soviet Union, with all aspects of public policy monopolized by the Communist Party, except for a brief indication by the DPRK's 'founding father,' Kim Il Sung, of a willingness to consider a *federation* [more accurately, a *confederation*] of two independent Korean states which would retain ultimate control over their economic and political systems, with a symbolic transfer of functions and authority to the confederation. This idea was never fully developed or seriously considered by either of the Korean states. For South Korea, both during its lengthy period of an authoritarian anti-Communist political system (1948–1987), and throughout its democratic phase, during the past 30 years, the objective has been unification of the two Koreas into a democratic political system, with a limited autonomy for its two constituents, and a market economy. There has been no reduction in discord on this core issue.

Decline in Conflict-Sustaining Acts—Despite infrequent gestures of concern for human rights, notably occasional episodes of limited family reunification visits, the norm in relations between North and South Korea has been deep-rooted mutual distrust of the other Korea's intentions and frequent displays of verbal and physical threatening acts. That norm clearly indicates the absence of a decline in conflict-sustaining behavior of the two Korea adversaries toward their rival for mastery of the Korean Peninsula. The conflict has been—and continues to be—profound 70 years after its onset.

In sum, only one of the six 'most likely' causal conditions favorable to conflict resolution of the *Inter-Korea conflict*, postulated in the *Conflict Resolution Model*, namely, *External Pressures*, was evident in the quest for resolution of that interstate protracted conflict. *The absence of five of the six 'most likely' conditions for resolution of the Inter-Korea conflict— Exhaustion by the principal adversaries*, the two Korea states, since the end of the Korean War, the *lack of qualitative change in their Balance of Capability, Domestic Pressures* for resolution, *Reduction in Discordance of their Objectives,* and *Decline in Conflict-Sustaining Acts*—indicates strong *negative* support for the theoretical rationale of the Resolution Model.

Substantively, three long-term significant incompatibilities for the principal adversaries, the DPRK and the ROK, have reinforced the absence of five 'most likely' conditions for conflict resolution as causes of the continuing persistence of this conflict. One is the profound *differences* in their *ideological* moorings, *Communism* and *Juché* (self-reliance) in North Korea, *anti-Communism* and *Democracy* in South Korea. Another source is the fundamental *differences in their political and economic systems,* an *authoritarian political structure,* dominated by a de facto monarchical family and an overwhelmingly *state-controlled economy* in North Korea, contrasting with a traditional authoritarian political regime during the first four decades of South Korea's statehood (1948–1987), transformed to a Western-type *democratic* political regime, and a USA-type *market* economy in South Korea. While the leadership in both Koreas has been committed to re-unification from the onset of their conflict in 1948, both have consistently envisaged a united Korea in which their ideology, political structure, and economic system would prevail. These *ideological* and *institutional* incompatibilities have been reinforced by *personal enmity* between some of the pre-eminent leaders of the two Koreas, especially the first dominant North Korea leader, Kim Il Sung, who ruled the DPRK from 1948 to 1994, and Syngman Rhee and Park Chung Hee, the ROK presidents from 1948 to 1960, and 1961–1979: their personal enmity, accentuated by ideological hostility and political rivalry, dated to the later years of Japan's colonial rule over Korea from 1910 to 1945.

Although impossible to verify, it is hypothesized here that, if all six 'most likely' conditions for protracted conflict resolution—collective *exhaustion, changes in the capability* balance, *domestic pressures* for resolution, *external pressures* for resolution, *reduction in discordance of objectives,* and a *decline in conflict-sustaining acts*—along with the three substantive incompatibilities—*ideology, political structure,* and *economic system,* discussed above—had obtained for the two principal state adversaries, the *presence* of the 'most likely' conditions would have triumphed over the incompatibilities, and conflict resolution would have been achieved. This hypothesis could be tested for the *Inter-Korea conflict* (and other *interstate* conflicts manifesting these or similar incompatibilities), if and when the six 'most likely' conditions existed *simultaneously* in a protracted conflict, along with the three incompatibilities. The likelihood of this pattern occurring is currently remote.

Reconciliation

Logically, *reconciliation* between-among adversaries in an interstate conflict *follows conflict resolution*, just as *resolution follows successful conflict management*. This three-stage process—*conflict management*—of specific hostile episodes, crises, or issues, followed by *conflict resolution*—of all the basic disputes—and then by *conflict reconciliation*—is discernible in very few post-World War I protracted conflicts, notably *France/Germany, Ecuador/Peru*, and, to some extent, *Egypt/Israel* and *Israel/Jordan*. As evident in the discussion of these cases elsewhere (Brecher 2016 L), these conflicts experienced conflict management of several crises and wars, notably: five interstate crises in the 1920s and 1930s, culminating in World War II, for the *France/Germany* conflict; four interstate crises from 1935 to 1991, culminating in the 1995 Cenepa War, for the *Ecuador/Peru* conflict; and 11 interstate crises from 1948 to 1973, culminating in the 1973 October-Yom Kippur War, for the *Egypt-Israel* segment of the Arab/Israel interstate conflict. In all three cases, successful *conflict management* led to peace agreements and *conflict resolution*, followed by varying degrees of *reconciliation*—active (France-Germany), moderate (Ecuador/Peru), and passive (Egypt-Israel and Israel-Jordan).

There are, however, exceptions to this three-stage linear process leading to conflict resolution. The *Inter-Korea conflict* is a prominent illustration. During most of this *unresolved* conflict, there have been unmistakable indicators of a mutual interest in, and acts of, *reconciliation* between North and South Korea, the principal adversaries, without *conflict resolution*. The quest for reconciliation took the form of *verbal* commitments to *peace, reunification*, and *reconciliation* by government leaders of the DPRK and the ROK, as evident in *their 1972 Communiqué, 1992 Basic Agreement, 2000 Joint Declaration, and 2007 Joint Declaration*. Moreover, the last of these expressions of amity was an integral part of the active implementation of *South Korea's "Sunshine Policy"* from 1998 to 2008, which included tangible acts of fraternal aid to the people of North Korea during and after a time of troubles, the famines and economic deterioration of the 1990s. These conciliatory acts occurred despite the absence of a formal peace agreement or other forms of conflict resolution during more than six decades after the costly, divisive, and stalemated Korean War, which ended with only an Armistice Agreement in 1953, still in force 65 years later. More significant, the frequent outbursts of verbal condemnations of alleged hostile acts by one or both of the principal adversaries, or of verbal threats of hostility against the adversary, were frequently accompanied or followed by conciliatory acts by one or both Korean adversaries. What seems to have made this possible was the special character of the adversaries in this conflict: their populations were members of the same nation, sharing a common history, language, and kinship. Thus, while experiencing a devastating interstate war (1950–1953) and a lengthy conflict between two independent states since 1948, it was also a civil war between two segments of the Korean nation. Thus, notwithstanding profound differences in ideology and political and economic systems, the population of the more prosperous and economically developed South Korea often contributed food and other forms of economic aid to the people of North Korea during periods of famine and other sources of distress. This kinship-driven behavior was often reflected in attempts, sometimes successful, to facilitate reunions of families that had been separated during the Korean War. A recent expression of this conciliatory behavior, after a lapse of more than 3 years in which these reunions were suspended by the DPRK (2010-early 2014), was a public appeal for improved relations by the North Korean leader on New Year's Day 2014, followed by his agreement in principle, in early February, to a resumption of family reunions between people in the two Koreas separated since the end of the Korean War, though without a specific date.

In the absence of *resolution* of the Inter-Korea protracted conflict, it is not surprising that full *reconciliation* between North and South Korea remains elusive: even among the vast majority of 20 *resolved* interstate conflicts that have been active for some or all of the years since the end of WWI, most with deep historical roots, very few have achieved genuine reconciliation, measured by Auerbach's imaginative but demanding seven-stage Reconciliation Pyramid (2009). Yet some progress in the *Inter-Korea conflict* is evident. The leadership and large segments of the elites in both North and South Korea, as well as the attentive public in South Korea, are well-acquainted "with clashing narratives" (Stage 1 of the Reconciliation Pyramid); that is, they "acknowledge the other's *narrative*..." more so in the post-1987 open society of South Korea than in the closed society of North Korea (Auerbach 2009, 304–305).

One can also infer, from the meetings and direct negotiations between leaders (Kim Il Sung and Park Chung Hee in 1971–1972, Kim Jong Il and Kim Dae Jung in 2000), and from their verbal and formal commitments and concessions to each other, that the Korean leaders "Acknowledge the Other's Narratives, Without Necessarily Accepting Them as True" [Ibid., 305] (Stage 2 of the Reconciliation Pyramid). In 1971–1972, the DPRK "Supreme Leader" for most of the period of this protracted conflict (1948–1994), Kim Il Sung, acknowledged that North Korea would no longer demand a complete withdrawal of USA forces from South Korea as a pre-condition of negotiations between the two Koreas. The same leaders also formally agreed on *peaceful unification of their states, tension reduction, and reconciliation of their ideologies and political systems*, with the shared objective of *national unity as one people*, and these principles were re-affirmed, as noted in the above discussion of the five communiqués and agreements by Korean leaders from 1972 to 2000. The fact that these formal agreements were not implemented does not nullify their "acknowledgement of the Other's Narratives…".

"Expressing Empathy for the Other's Plight" [Ibid., 307] (Stage 3 of the Reconciliation Pyramid) which is uncommon in identity conflicts, has been evident on frequent occasions by large segments of South Korea's population, in words and deeds, including the granting of material aid to North Koreans, especially during periods in which famines ravaged the North Korean economy and society, as noted. Little is known of the attitude of North Koreans to South Koreans. However, a strong feeling of kinship with the population of the other Korea can be inferred; that is, on both sides of their 'iron curtain' the population at large regards 'the other' as part of one Korean people. Thus, Stage 3 of the Pyramid seems to have been ascended by South Koreans and, likely, by the silent majority of North Korea's population.

There is no evidence that any of the other four stages of Reconciliation has been achieved: "Assuming (at Least) Partial Responsibility for the Other's Alleged Plights" (Stage 4); "Expressing Readiness for Restitution or Reparations for Past Wrongs" (Stage 5); "Publicly Apologizing and Asking for Forgiveness for Past Wrongs" (Stage 6); and "Striving to Incorporate Opposite Narratives into Accepted Mutual Accounts of the Past" (Stage 7) [Ibid., 307–311]. Are the two Korean adversarial states likely to ascend these advanced stages of reconciliation once *interstate* conflict resolution has been attained?

In the absence of any evidence, one must suspend judgment. However, except for the France/Germany protracted conflict, the states and peoples of North Korea and South Korea are probably the best prepared, psychologically and ethnically, to achieve the 'great leap' to Stages 5 and 6 of the Reconciliation Pyramid, with Stage 7—and genuine reconciliation—at some undefinable point in the post-conflict resolution phase of their complex relations.

NORTH VIETNAM/USA CONFLICT (RESOLVED)

Behavior

USA Decisions
The first of many important USA decisions during this interstate, inter-region conflict was *to issue a virtual declaration of war against the Communist-ruled Democratic Republic of Vietnam* (DRV, North Vietnam), in response to a perceived attack by North Vietnam torpedo boats on an American naval vessel in the Gulf of Tonkin on August 4, 1964. The decision, which took the form of an act by the USA Congress—overwhelming approval of the *Gulf of Tonkin Resolution* on August 10—was *strategic* in *content, scope,* and *impact*: President Johnson was granted far-reaching, virtually unlimited, authority to cope with what was designated a grave threat to USA security and interests. This act provided the legal basis (and perceived legitimacy) for all subsequent USA military acts during the 11-year war (1964–1975). [Informally, the USA participated in the broader Vietnam protracted conflict for a much longer period, as a major supplier of financial aid and weapons to France during its war with the DRV, North Vietnam, from 1950 to 1954, as well as the dispatch of military advisors to South Vietnam in the early 1960s, followed by massive direct military involvement in the Vietnam War for a decade].

The first USA *tactical* military decision relating to this emerging interstate conflict was *to respond quickly to the then-USA identified North Vietnam naval attack on August 4, 1964*: it took the form of *a retaliatory act against four North Vietnam torpedo boats (Operation Pierce Arrow) soon after Congress passed the Gulf of Tonkin resolution*. The next two *tactical* military decisions, *to launch air raids against Vietcong and DRV forces* in 1965, were more substantive and significant, for they led to direct American military involvement in the Vietnam War. One was the short *Operation Flaming Dart*, in response to a Vietcong attack on USA barracks in *Pleiku* on February 7. The other was a prolonged air campaign, *Operation Rolling Thunder*, from March 2 to November 2, 1965, which set the pattern for other lengthy American military acts during that war. A minor *tactical* military decision a week after the start of Operation Rolling Thunder—the deployment of 3500 Marines to provide more security for USA bases in Vietnam—was a hardly noticed signal of American participation in the ground war. The next USA military decision—President Johnson's acceptance, early in August 1965, of a Joint Chiefs of Staff (JCS) recommendation *to send 100,000 USA troops to Vietnam*—was much more significant, a *strategic* decision, for it marked the first substantive escalation of American involvement in that predominantly land war.

The contents of a significant *strategic* military-cum-political, peace-oriented USA decision were conveyed in President Johnson's *surprise announcement on March 31, 1968*, soon after the unanticipated large-scale North Vietnam-Viet cong *Tet* Offensive in February—of *the cessation of almost all USA bombing* and *a USA invitation to North Vietnam to engage in formal peace talks*. The importance of that announcement was greatly enhanced by the addition of Johnson's personal political decision which was bound to have far-reaching consequences for subsequent USA policy and behavior relating to the Vietnam War, that is, for the *North Vietnam/USA* conflict: he also indicated that he would not be a candidate in the USA presidential election scheduled for the next 8 months.

Almost certainly linked to this fundamental shift in USA policy toward American involvement in the Vietnam War, the year 1968 also witnessed the beginning of a prolonged American attempt to implement its *strategic* decision—*to achieve 'Vietnamisation.'* This *policy goal* had two complementary elements: steady, *stage-by-stage withdrawal of USA forces from Vietnam* and the *stage-by-stage transfer of responsibility for the continuing conduct of the war to the ARVN (Army of the Republic of Vietnam)*, along with an *escalation of USA airstrikes throughout Vietnam* to persuade the DRV to re-enter peace negotiations. This ambitious but unsuccessful program continued until 1973, the virtual end of USA active engagement in that long war.

The first substantive policy decision on the Vietnam War by the newly elected President *Nixon* in 1969 was *to attempt to entice North Vietnam to enter serious peace negotiations*; the attempt failed—it was premature.

In February 1971, once more with the active support of his principal adviser on the Vietnam War, as on USA foreign policy challenges generally, *Henry Kissinger*, the USA president made and implemented the highly controversial and much-criticized decision *to launch a massive secret bombing of Vietcong-North Vietnam military sanctuaries and the 'Ho Chi Minh' supply trail in Cambodia and Laos.* The magnitude of the Laos operation, castigated as grave war crimes by many, is evident in two awesome quantitative indicators. The USA dropped more bombs on Laos in 1971 than it did everywhere throughout World War II, killing 350,000, 10% of the Laos population. Another massive bomb decision by Nixon and Kissinger, the 'Christmas Bombing' of North Vietnam in December 1972, again designed to compel the DRV to re-enter peace negotiations, was successful. It led directly to the decision—by both of the principal adversaries—*to sign the Paris Peace Accord on January 13, 1973*, which marked the end of the formal USA involvement in the Vietnam War.

USA Decision-Makers

There were two clusters of crucial *USA decision-makers* in the North Vietnam/USA conflict and the Vietnam War, which were synonymous in duration. During the Lyndon Johnson phase (1964–1968), there were four 'principals'—President *Johnson, Robert McNamara,* Secretary of Defense, *Dean Rusk,* Secretary of State, *and McGeorge Bundy,* National Security Adviser. There was one notable dissenter from the 'hard line' propounded by the key decision-makers in *Phase I* of the Vietnam War, *George Ball,* Under-Secretary of State in both the *Kennedy* and Johnson Administrations (1961–1966): he was known, then and later, as 'Vietnam's Devil's Advocate.' During *Phase II* (1969–1973), there were two crucial USA decision-makers on the Vietnam War and the North Vietnam/USA conflict: President Nixon and his National Security Adviser, Kissinger, the principal USA negotiator with North (and South) Vietnam since the beginning of the Nixon presidency in January 1969.

USA Decision Process

The USA Constitution and political system generated an array of institutions and constraints on the exercise of authority by the USA President in the conduct of foreign policy: the role of Congress in creating a *state of war* by the United States and any other state; *supervisory control over all Departments in the Executive branch of Government;* the *vetting of presidential appointments to senior posts in the foreign service and the armed services*; and the *allocation of funds for all USA involvement in foreign wars*. Theoretically, these and other constraining powers by a non-cooperative or unfriendly Congress could seriously undermine the president's formal authority as commander-in-chief and head of the Executive branch of Government. In practice, however, as evident in the analysis of all interstate protracted conflicts in which the USA was/ is a principal adversary, the USA decision process is much less complex. The authority and power to make and implement *strategic* and *tactical* political and military decisions on issues relating to adversaries (and allies) in wars and military and political crises is highly concentrated in the president and his appointed aides. For example, this was evident in USA international crises within the USA/USSR interstate protracted conflict, such as the Berlin Blockade (1948–1949) and Cuban Missile crises (1962). So it was in the *North Vietnam/USA* conflict as well: all of the *strategic* and important *tactical* decisions by the USA in Phase I (1964–1968) were made by President Johnson and the small group of his appointees to the key national security positions in the USA government. During Phase II (1969–1973), the important decisions relating to North Vietnam and the Vietnam War were made by President Nixon and/or National Security Adviser Kissinger. This is not to dismiss or denigrate the advisory-pressure role of others whose input to these decisions, whether sought by the president or initiated independently by other senior officials, such as the Director of the Central Intelligence Agency, the Chairman of the Joint Chiefs of Staff, and the Chairs of the House and Senate committees on the armed forces and foreign affairs-relations, may influence, at times significantly, the decisions taken by the president and a core group of aides. There may also be influence exerted by pressure groups—the media, prominent political party leaders, interest groups, the media, and most broadly, public opinion. These were evident, for example, in President Johnson's announced decisions on March 31, 1968—the cessation of most bombing in Vietnam and the invitation to North Vietnam to enter peace negotiations. Thus the *decision process* may, and often does, extend far beyond the core *decision-makers* and influence their choices. However, the USA decisions on March 31, 1968 were made by President Johnson, not by any of the institutions or persons in the Executive or Legislative branches of the USA Government, or the leaders of the Armed Forces or the Intelligence agencies. *In sum*, the USA decision process on national security and foreign policy issues is complex at one level of analysis, namely, for advisory roles by select Congressional leaders and senior officials in relevant bureaucratic Departments—advisory or pressure roles; it is much less complex at the decision-maker level of analysis. In the North Vietnam/USA conflict, an atypical case, Kissinger played a dual role—National Security Adviser and decision-maker. Yet, as those who have analyzed this interstate conflict in depth have noted, and Kissinger himself acknowledged in his memoirs, his role as decision-maker, with few exceptions, was authorized and vetted carefully by President Nixon.

DRV-North Vietnam: Decisions
The overall *strategy* of North Vietnam for the achievement of its primary objective—the unification of North and South Vietnam in a Communist-ruled state—preceded the onset of its protracted conflict with the USA in 1964. A policy decision by the Politburo of the DRV Workers Party *to pursue the dau tranh (two-track) strategy—combining carefully planned military action with revolutionary zeal to counter superior USA weapons already made available to South Vietnam*—was communicated in a July 1962 letter from Le Duan, Secretary-General of the Workers Party, to the Communist organizations and cadres, notably the Vietcong, in South Vietnam. This dual strategy, which also called for continued adherence to the 1954 Geneva Accords that led to the 'temporary' creation of two Vietnam states, would facilitate the unhindered economic reconstruction of North Vietnam's damaged economy along communist lines and the achievement of unification of the two Vietnams, via continued resistance to USA plans to transform all of Vietnam to a USA-type capitalist dependency.

The first significant *strategic* DRV decision in the North Vietnam/USA protracted conflict, on November 22, 1964, soon after the USA Congress passed the Gulf of Tonkin Resolution (August 10, 1964), but before the initial display of superior USA military power in the Vietnam War—*Operation Rolling Thunder*, in January 1965—was *to accelerate the war against South Vietnam, with the goal of a total military victory before the beginning of large-scale USA military intervention.* (It took 11 years for North Vietnam to achieve total military victory over its southern adversary and the USA)

The most wide-ranging military decision by North Vietnam and its South Vietnam affiliate, the Vietcong, during this interstate-intrastate conflict was *to launch a "General Offensive and Uprising"* on January 31,

1968, the date of the official TET holiday; the date of the decision is not known. The scope of this operation was vast: 84,000 North Vietnam and Vietcong troops attacked simultaneously five of South Vietnam's major cities, 36 of 44 provincial capitals, and many district central towns. While there is disagreement about its degree of military success, the psychopolitical effects of this daring North Vietnam-Vietcong initiative on a totally surprised USA leadership were profound. A bipartisan group of former government officials from both American political parties advised President Johnson to set in motion steps to disengage from Vietnam. Most important, the TET Offensive was the catalyst to President Johnson's 31 March announcement noted above—declaring a cessation of almost all USA bombing and inviting the DRV to enter peace negotiations, the first meaningful step in a belated peace process, along with his no-less surprising statement that he would not stand for re-election in November 1968. As such, the TET Offensive can be termed the DRV's most decisive military-political decision during the prolonged Vietnam War-protracted conflict.

While there were many North Vietnam *tactical* decisions throughout the Vietnam War, they will not be discussed here. Two important DRV decisions in December 1972 and January 1973, both related to termination of this conflict and lengthy war, merit attention. The first was a quick response to the massive USA *Christmas Bombings* in late December 1972—the North Vietnam Politburo made the decision *to return to negotiations in Paris*, as demanded by President Nixon and Kissinger, his National Security Adviser.

The final North Vietnam *strategic* decision in this interstate conflict, also noted in the above discussion of USA behavior—since this decision was shared by the two principal adversaries—was *to sign the Paris Peace Accord*, the terms of which constituted a major triumph for the DRV. The USA made three major concessions in this peace agreement. It agreed to withdraw all its forces from Vietnam (at their peak, more than 500,000 troops). The USA also recognized the Provisional Revolutionary Government, the governmental arm of the Vietcong's National Liberation Front, in the areas under its control in South Vietnam. Thirdly, the USA acknowledged North Vietnam's demand that Vietnam be regarded as one country. The Paris Accord ended the USA formal involvement in the Vietnam War, though the war—between North and South Vietnam—continued until April 1975, when the Vietcong-North Vietnam forces occupied Saigon, later re-named Ho

Chi Minh City, the capital of the South Vietnam region in the unified Communist Democratic Republic of Vietnam (DRV).

North Vietnam Decision-Makers
During *Phase I* of the North Vietnam/USA conflict (1964–1969), as for the preceding three decades—since his creation of the Vietnam Workers Party in 1935—the *pre-eminent figure* in the DRV was its founding father, *Ho Chi Minh*. While comparable in stature to the other Communist luminaries of his generation, *Stalin* in the USSR and *Mao-tse-tung* in China—Stalin was 11 years older, Mao 2 years younger—Ho was more revered than feared by his colleagues and subordinates. He valued and considered carefully the views of members of the Workers Party Politburo, notably: *Le Duan*, his long-time principal aide and successor in 1969, who was to serve as Secretary-General of the Workers Party until his death in 1986; *General Nguyen Chi Thanh*; *General Vo Nguyen Giap*, the legendary victor in the decisive Battle of Dien Bien Phu (1954), which terminated France's empire in Indo-China and in the no-less decisive war of attrition against superior USA forces, in weapons and military manpower; *Pham Van Dong*, the DRV's long-time Prime Minister, and *Le Duc Tho*, later, North Vietnam's negotiator with Henry Kissinger from 1969 until their signing of the Paris Peace Accords in 1973. They, along with the other 8 members of the Party Politburo, were decision-makers, not subordinate Party officials.

North Vietnam: Decision Process
The most notable traits of the pivotal institution in the North Vietnam decision process, the Workers Party Politburo, were its *longevity* and *stability*. As noted in the discussion of the *China/Vietnam* conflict, as late as 1977, 8 of its 14 members had been appointed as early as 1960, and 6 in 1953. All had served as aides to Ho Chi Minh, and 6 had served on the Politburo in the climactic phase of the struggle against French colonial rule, culminating in the 1954 triumphant Battle of Dien Bien Phu. They also shared a commitment to Communist ideology. As comrades of long standing, who had been engaged in candid debates on issues that were often significant for the survival of their party and regime, they had developed a relationship of mutual respect and shared values. However, they did not always agree on policy.

Instructive evidence of the ability of the Communist leadership in North Vietnam to disagree sharply and openly was a profound disagreement on a crucial Party vote a few months after the USA Congress approved the Gulf of Tonkin Resolution on August 10, 1964. The militant faction in the Politburo, headed by Le Duan and *Nguyen Chi Thanh*, secured a majority over the faction, *including* Ho Chi Minh, that favored peaceful coexistence with South Vietnam: and they persuaded the Ninth Plenum of the Workers Party Central Committee, a much larger and, formally, a more authoritative Party body than the Politburo, to approve Resolution 9 on November 22, 1964, rejecting negotiation with the South Vietnam regime and decreeing full mobilization of North Vietnam's human and material resources *to accelerate the war effort*, with the aim of achieving a *total military victory* before the arrival of direct American military intervention. While some members of the Central Committee who openly expressed dissent later lost their seats, there were no known after-effects on membership of the Politburo.

North Vietnam/United States Conflict: Conflict-Sustaining Acts

Political Hostility by both of the principal adversaries in this conflict was visible from the beginning of the 1950s, long before the Onset of this protracted conflict. The USA was politically (and economically) active in support of France during its war against North Vietnam [later, the Democratic Republic of Vietnam (DRV)], from soon after the latter's proclamation of independence in 1946 until the traumatic defeat of France at the 1954 Battle of Dien Bien Phu, noted earlier. For the United States, the struggle between France and its former colony, North Vietnam, was part of the ongoing Cold War between the 'Free World' and international Communism, led by the Soviet Union. Thus, in March 1954, the USA publicly announced its intention to form a coalition against Communism in Southeast Asia, dramatically expressed by its refusal to endorse the Geneva Accord in July 1954, ending the France/North Vietnam War, and in September, the USA-initiated South East Asia Treaty Organization (SEATO) made a commitment to defend non-Communist (South) Vietnam, Cambodia, and Laos against a military attack. North Vietnam (the DRV), in turn, sought and received (primarily) verbal expressions of support from both the USSR and China in 1961 and thereafter.

Political hostility was also evident in the negative response by the USA to informal offers to negotiate an agreement to end the burgeoning conflict—by the USSR and North Vietnam in 1961, by the USSR, China and the UK in 1963, and even after the onset of North Vietnam-USA military hostilities, the August 1964 Gulf of Tonkin incident, by France's president, the UN Secretary-General, and the North Vietnam government, in 1965 (Hess 2010, 152, 153, 157). Thereafter, continuous military escalation dominated the North Vietnam/USA conflict, until long after the political shock generated by the large-scale Tet Offensive by North Vietnam and the Vietcong in January 1968. Prolonged negotiations led to an agreement to end the war, the Paris Peace Accords in January 1973, but the fighting continued until 1975.

Violence was the most frequent and most significant conflict-sustaining technique in this conflict, from the Gulf of Tonkin incident in early August 1964 until the ignominious evacuation of USA forces and diplomats from Saigon on April 29, 1975. Violence escalated with the February 7, 1965 Vietcong guerrilla night raid on the USA and South Vietnam Army barracks at Pleiku. The USA retaliated with an air attack on North Vietnam military targets, Operation Rolling Thunder, on February 19. Thereafter, violence was endemic for the next 10 years. The highlights were: the Tet Offensive, January 30–February 24, 1968, a decisive event in which 84,000 Vietcong troops attacked USA and South Vietnam military bases and cities throughout South Vietnam—a military setback for North Vietnam and the Vietcong, but politically significant because it demonstrated their determination to win the war and shocked the USA public and political leadership, notably President Johnson; the (North) Vietnam Spring Offensive, February 22–May 12, 1969; the (Vietcong-North Vietnam) Invasion of Cambodia, March 31–June 30, 1970; the (South Vietnam-USA) Invasion of Laos, February 8–March 25, 1971; the (USA) Vietnam Ports Mining, responding to another North Vietnam spring offensive, March 30–May 8, 1972; the (USA) Christmas Bombing, 14–December 26, 1972, leading to the Paris Peace Accords; and the Final North Vietnam Offensive, December 14, 1974–April 30, 1975, culminating in the completion of the USA withdrawal from Vietnam (Brecher and Wilkenfeld 1997, 189–198).

The estimated cost of the Vietnam War in casualties was enormous:

North Vietnam and Vietcong: 50,000–2 million civilians dead; 1,176,000 soldiers dead or missing; 600,000 wounded;
South Vietnam: 361,000–2 million civilian dead; 220,000 soldiers dead;
United States: 58,220 soldiers dead; 303,644 wounded;
Other states—Australia, New Zealand, Laos, Thailand, South Korea, small numbers.

Economic Discrimination USA economic sanctions against North Vietnam long preceded—and followed—their interstate conflict, which began with the Gulf of Tonkin Crisis in August 1964: they were part of USA support for France during its war with North Vietnam from 1947–1954 and after and they developed into a full trade embargo and the freezing of unified Vietnam's assets in the USA, following the end of the Vietnam War in 1975. The trade embargo remained in force until 1994. However, given the minimal economic relations between North Vietnam and the USA from long before the onset of their conflict, this conflict-sustaining technique was the least frequently used and the least influential of the four types of CST in this protracted conflict.

Verbal Hostility was more evident than the economic conflict-sustaining technique (CST) in this protracted conflict and was used by both of the principal adversaries as a supplement to the Violence dimension of their conflict, mainly to enhance the loyalty and commitment of their respective forces but in continuous attempts, by propaganda, to wean soldiers of their adversary to change their loyalty and thereby to change the balance of local military power in their favor. Defection flourished in the ranks of both North and South Vietnam, but, in the absence of reports on this dimension of their armed forces, the effectiveness of propaganda used by the two competing Vietnams cannot be meaningfully assessed. Because of its greater frequency than economic conflict-sustaining acts, verbal hostility can be ranked as a distant third type of CST, after violence and acts of political hostility in terms of its impact on the evolution of this conflict

Taiwan Strait Conflict (Unresolved)

Behavior: China [PRC] and Taiwan [ROC]

Decisions
There were three principal adversaries in this Inter-Region conflict—the People's Republic of China [PRC], Taiwan, Republic of China [ROC], and the United States. However, this discussion on conflict behavior will focus primarily on the decisions, decision-makers, and decision process of the 'two Chinas' that were the most directly engaged participants in this unresolved conflict, China (Mainland China, PRC) and Taiwan (ROC).

Moreover, since most of their major decisions were intertwined or impacted the target, as well as the initiator, they will be discussed together.

The first *strategic* decision was initiated by the People's Republic of China 5 years after its triumph in China's prolonged civil war: that triumph of the Chinese Communist Party (CCP) and its proclamation of the PRC on October 1, 1949 were accompanied by the expulsion of the forces of the Chinese Nationalist Party (*Kuomintang*) to the island of Taiwan, where it proclaimed the Republic of China (ROC) on December 8, 1949. The initial decisions of the "two Chinas" re-activated the *struggle for control of Taiwan, which both contenders for 'the Mantle of Heaven' agreed was an integral part of One China*. (Mainland China had terminated control of Taiwan [Formosa] by the Netherlands in 1662 and had ruled the island until its defeat in the first China/Japan War (1894–1895) and its enforced cession of Taiwan to Japan until September 1945 when, in accordance with several pledges by the victorious Powers in World War II—the 1943 Cairo Declaration and the July 1945 Potsdam Agreement—Taiwan was restored to China's sovereignty soon after Japan's surrender to the USA)

The initial PRC decision—the date is unknown, but 'liberation' of Taiwan was an oft-stated commitment by Communist China—was implemented by the *People's Liberation Army* (PLA) *artillery bombardment of one of the Nationalist-controlled 'off-shore' islands, Quemoy, on September 3, 1954*; these islands were the major land obstacles to an invasion of Taiwan by sea. The Nationalist Republic of China, on Taiwan, which, since its expulsion from the mainland, had often declared its intention of invading the mainland to regain control of historic China, implemented its first major responsive decision by *launching air strikes against the Chinese mainland opposite the 'off-shore' islands on September 7.*

The USA became an active conflict actor in this dispute soon after the outbreak of the 1954–1955 Taiwan crisis by several high-profile acts in support of Taiwan: its 7th Fleet was deployed to the Taiwan Strait; three USA aircraft carriers were repositioned in the East China Sea; and it authorized the Nationalist regime on Taiwan to use USA-provided jet planes against mainland targets. The 7th Fleet remained in the Taiwan Strait for 5 years. More important for the evolution of the balance of military capability in this conflict between the "two Chinas," the USA formalized its protector role for Taiwan 3 months later: *Taiwan (the ROC) and the US Mutual Defense Pact, incorporating a Missile Defense*

Treaty (*MDT*) *on December 2, 1954*. This qualitative escalation—the MDT formalized Taiwan's right to use USA-supplied air power against the Mainland without consulting the USA Military—led, in turn, to a major *tactical* decision by the PRC, namely, *to persist in its claim to all 'off-shore' islands and Taiwan*. The PRC implemented that decision by *heavy bombardment of the Nationalist-controlled Tachen Islands* on January 10, 1955. This tit-for-tat behavior by the principal adversaries continued with Nationalist-initiated battles on all these off-shore islands during January. Finally, USA material aid to Taiwan in fortifying Quemoy and Matsu ended the crisis for Taiwan on March 25. The crisis for the PRC (and the USA) ended on April 23, when PRC Prime Minister *Zhou Enlai* offered to negotiate its termination, and the PRC ceased military operations against those two islands. (Taiwan evacuated the Tachen Islands later.)

Another post-China Civil War cluster of decisions and implementing acts occurred during the second full-scale military-security crisis in the *Taiwan Strait* conflict: it too involved all three principal adversaries, after 3 years of relative tranquility, following the winding down of the 1954–1955 clashes over the off-shore islands. Once more the PRC was the triggering entity, on that occasion deciding *to test USA (and USSR) resolve in another dramatic assertion of its claim to Taiwan*, via *the dispute over the 'off-shore' islands*: it implemented this decision on July 17, 1958 when *it concentrated military forces near Quemoy and Matsu, triggering a crisis for Taiwan*. The PRC escalated the crisis by *another bombardment of those 'off-shore' islands* on August 23. Nationalist forces on these islands returned fire, as in 1954–1955. Once more, the USA played an active role, moving part of its Seventh Fleet into the conflict zone. This act triggered a crisis for the PRC, which responded on September 4, by extending its territorial waters to 12 miles off-shore, thereby blockading Quemoy and Matsu. (The USA, in turn, rejected the unilateral PRC extension of territorial waters and threatened military intervention, with the possible use of nuclear weapons, if Quemoy were invaded). The PRC backed off, with Zhou Enlai proposing a resumption of PRC-USA ambassadorial talks. These were resumed on September 14, ending the USA crisis. On the 30th, Secretary of State *John Foster Dulles* proposed a compromise solution, indicating that the USA favored the withdrawal of Nationalist forces from the "off-shore" islands if the PRC agreed to a cease-fire. The international crisis ended with a joint communiqué by *Chiang Kai-shek* the President of Taiwan and Dulles on 23 October, expressing their tacit understanding that a Nationalist invasion of Mainland China would not receive USA support. (The USSR also contributed to de-escalation of this crisis by a TASS news agency statement on October 5, 1958 that excluded Soviet military support for a PRC attempt 'to liberate' Taiwan).

Unlike the first two clusters of decisions and implementing acts (1954–1955 and 1958), the third was initiated by Taiwan. After another 3 years of relative tranquility in this conflict, the leader of Taiwan, President Chiang Kai-shek, revived a longstanding core Nationalist decision—*to attempt a restoration of Kuomintang power over all of China by force*. This was implemented by several acts, verbal and tangible: his *threat to invade the mainland*, during an Easter message to Chinese everywhere, on April 22, 1962; publicized conscription of more troops for Taiwan's army; a new tax, levied on 1 May, to support the "return to the mainland"; further statements about an invasion, from 22 May onward, and a claim by the PRC's Foreign Minister of a plan by Nationalist special agents from Taiwan and anti-Communists on the mainland to join forces, if Taiwan parachuted troops on to the mainland. This led to the PRC's first responsive decision in this cluster—*to mobilize more troops*, which was implemented by a *substantial troop build-up in Fukien Province, opposite the 'off-shore' islands*, beginning on 10 June. (Once more, the USA contributed to crisis de-escalation: on 27 June, President Kennedy reaffirmed USA policy in this conflict—*to defend Taiwan against a PRC threat*, clearly implying no support for a Taiwan attempt to invade the mainland.) This statement ended the 1962 crisis between the two China adversaries.

There were occasional upsurges of tension between the PRC and the ROC during the years that followed, but only one further cluster of hostile decisions and acts, in 1995–1996. Notwithstanding the USA renunciation of its 'Two Chinas' policy in 1971, which led to the ouster of Taiwan, the ROC, as China's representative to the United Nations and the formal recognition of the PRC as the legitimate representative of 'One China' at the UN, along with a USA commitment not to extend an invitation to any senior official of Taiwan's government to visit the USA, permission was granted to the Republic of China President, *Lee Teng-hui*, for a 'private visit' to his alma mater university, Cornell, in May 1995. No other decision and implementing act in this conflict, with the possible exception of the PRC bombardment of the "off-shore" islands in 1954, generated such a hostile reaction. The PRC was enraged, as evident in its (un-announced) decision—*to re-assert dramatically that it was determined, at some unspecified time, 'to liberate' Taiwan,* considered by the PRC a heretical province of China that must be restored to 'the Motherland,' *by negotiation, if possible, by force, if necessary.* That reactive decision was implemented by multiple acts that, together, conveyed rage and determination. The PRC ambassador to Washington was withdrawn for 5 months. High-level official visits to and from China were suspended. Most visible were 'show of force' naval maneuvers near Taiwan conducted during the summer and autumn of 1995. Later, in February–March 1996, intense, high-visibility military pressure was exerted by the PRC on Taiwan. However, largely in response to countervailing USA naval pressure, along with muted apologies, no violence occurred; and the crisis did not linger. However, this protracted conflict persists.

Decision-Makers
Both of the principal adversaries in this conflict were characterized by a pre-eminent decision-maker during all of the crises noted above, except the crisis in 1995–1996. For the PRC, the 'Paramount Leader' was Mao Tse-tung from 1949 until his death in 1976, as well as the commanding figure in the Chinese Communist Party since the mid-1930s. Similarly, Chiang Kai-shek was the dominant decision-maker of the Republic of China from 1949 until his death in 1975, as well as the Generalissimo of the *Kuomintang* and China's Government even longer, from the late 1920s until its collapse in the prolonged civil war that ended in 1949. As noted below, both pre-eminent figures consulted political and military aides but retained ultimate decision-making power on all major issues of public policy in their respective domain.

China [PRC] and Taiwan [ROC]: Decision Process
As in all Communist regimes, the People's Republic of China had an elaborate institutional structure. Formally, there were three crucial centers of decisional authority. One was-is the *Chinese Communist Party (CCP)*, with the *Political Bureau Standing Committee* of 9 or 7 members, headed by the Secretary-General, at the apex of the pyramid of decision-making power. A second key institution was-is the *Central Military Commission*, which controlled the Ministry of Defense and all of the armed forces, notably the *People's Liberation Army (PLA)*. The third was the elaborate State structure, headed by the *President*, assisted by a *State Council*, directed by the Prime Minister. In the Mao era (1949–1976), the 'Paramount Leader's power derived from his charismatic

leadership of the Party, the Military and the State, not from his positions in these structures: he held only two formal posts—Chairman of the National Committee of the Chinese People's Political Consultative Conference (NC CPPCC) [1949–1954] and President of China (1954–1959); but throughout his rarely disputed reign, no decision of consequence in the PRC was made without his approval. His principal aide and China's master diplomat, Zhou Enlai, was Premier of China (1949–1975) and Chairman of the NC CPPCC after Mao relinquished that post (1955–1975). Thus, on all matters relating to Taiwan, from 1949 to 1975 (both died in 1976), Mao consulted Zhou, among others, including military leaders, marshals of the People's Liberation Army (PLA) Directorate of Signal and Imagery Intelligence (DSII). He might have been persuaded by one or more of those consulted, but on any issue in which he was involved, including all important matters related to Taiwan, the final decision was made by Mao.

For much of the period after Mao there was also a commanding PRC figure, Deng Xiaoping, the acknowledged 'Paramount Leader' and primary decision-maker on important issues in both foreign and domestic policy (1978–1992). Like Mao, he too ruled China on the basis of acknowledged leadership qualities, rather than formal positions of authority in the Party and the State: he also held only two governmental posts for short periods—Chairman of the NC CPPCC, after Mao and Zhou en-Lai, (1978–1982) and Chairman of the Central Military Commission, one of the most powerful sources of power in the political system of the PRC. However, while he was more powerful than first among equals in the Standing Committee of the Communist Party Political Bureau, Deng was less authoritarian than Mao. He consulted more widely and more frequently than Chairman Mao, was more open to advice, sought to persuade his younger colleagues in the leadership, and was prepared to be outvoted, a situation that seemed inconceivable in the Mao era. Since the Deng era, there has not been a commanding figure in China's decision-making on issues related to Taiwan and their unresolved protracted conflict.

Rather, the three post-Deng leaders—Jiang Zemin (1993–2003), Hu Jintao (2003–2013) and *Xi Ping*, the current leader—all held/hold the three formal posts of decision-making authority and power in the PRC political system: President of the People's Republic of China, Chairman of the Central Military Commission, and Chairman of the Chinese Communist Party; none has exhibited political charisma. The only crisis in relations with Taiwan in the post-Deng era occurred during the leadership of Jiang Zemin; the decision-process in that case is not well known but would seem to have been the product of extensive consultation by the president with political, military, and bureaucratic colleagues and aides.

The Republic of China (ROC) on Taiwan also developed an elaborate formal structure of legislative, executive, and military institutions. As in the PRC, however, the period from 1949 to 1975 was dominated by its first and most authoritarian leader, Generalissimo Chiang Kai-shek: he held all three positions of decision-making authority—President of the Republic of China, Chairman of the ruling *Kuomintang* Party, and Commander-in-Chief of the ROC armed forces. In terms of their decision-making power and their authoritarian style of leadership, the commanding figures in the two China adversaries from 1949 to 1975 were remarkably similar. Thus, for most crises in this protracted conflict, the decision-making process was essentially the same: consultation with aides and colleagues at the will of the dominant decision-maker; decisions by Mao in the PRC, Chiang in the ROC. The process changed after their passing, with a more consultative process among political and military leaders in both China adversaries.

Taiwan Conflict: Conflict-Sustaining Acts

Political Hostility was the predominant type of conflict-sustaining act in this interstate–intrastate conflict. Both the People's Republic of China and the Republic of China claimed to be the sole legitimate representative of 'One China' from the beginning of this protracted conflict—the proclamation of the two regimes soon after the decisive Communist triumph over the Nationalists in China's civil war, the PRC on the mainland, October 1, 1949, and the ROC on Taiwan, December 7, 1949. Until 1971, the ROC was recognized by the UN and a majority of states as the representative of China, since then, the PRC has been recognized by the UN and the vast majority of states as 'China.' That political conflict over which regime represents 'China,' accompanied by violence in the first 13 years (see the discussion of *violence* below) remains formally unresolved.

Even in the Deng Xiaoping era as 'Paramount Leader' of the PRC (1978–1992), the political dimension of their conflict has resisted all attempts to reconcile these competing claims. For example, the PRC 'peace offensive,' from the beginning of 1979, elicited a 'three no response' from Taiwan (the ROC)—'no negotiations, no communications, no compromise.' Similarly, a later attempt to achieve agreement, the '1992 Consensus,' met with clearly opposed interpretations: for the PRC, Mainland China, that Consensus denoted agreement on it being the sole legitimate government of China, including Taiwan, whereas for the ROC, Taiwan, the Consensus meant that both sides agreed to disagree over 'One China.' So it was thereafter, with the two claimants reiterating their conflicting interpretations of the optimal formula for Cross-Strait relations. Thus ROC, Taiwan, President Chen rejected the PRC view of the 1992 'Consensus' as 'one China with different interpretations' and opted for 'one country on either side.' The PRC persisted in the attempt to secure from Taiwan (the ROC) acceptance of a legal status as an integral part of 'One China,' the PRC, while Taiwan persisted in attempting to secure Beijing's acceptance of Taiwan's distinctive status as a legal entity, not part of 'One China,' as interpreted by the PRC, though not, formally, an independent state. This political-verbal competition served as a near-permanent conflict-sustaining act, to which both adversaries contributed equally.

Verbal Hostility as noted above, a large part of conflict-sustaining acts that derived from *political* hostility between the PRC and the ROC took the form of *verbal* jousting by the two principal adversaries in the *Taiwan conflict*—over the meaning of 'One China,' regime legitimacy in representing 'China,' the legal status of Taiwan, and the correct relations between the two claimants to the designation, 'China.' As such, political hostility was often expressed as *verbally hostile acts*, in a prolonged, conflictive verbal contest, a major source of persistence of this conflict.

Perhaps the most cogent expression of verbally hostile behavior was the PRC pronouncement of five conditions in which it would resort to violence in this conflict: Taiwan's declaration of independence; political chaos within Taiwan; Taiwan's attempt to acquire nuclear weapons; its long-term (unspecified) refusal to negotiate the cross-border relationship; and an attempt by a third party [the USA] to resolve this conflict by unilateral acts. This formulation of a threat to use violence in any one of a wide-ranging set of circumstances served as an ultimatum on the limits of acceptable behavior by Taiwan. As such, it was a *pervasive conflict-sustaining act* by the PRC, with a potentially profound influence on the behavior of the two principal adversaries.

A less overt manifestation of hostile verbal behavior, framed as aimed at reducing the intensity of inter-regime conflict but which, objectively, served to sustain the protracted conflict, was the use of propaganda and collective memory in their verbal communication with an ethnic/national kin group. The PRC, acting through its principal state news agency, *Xinhua*, frequently distributed leaflets in Taiwan emphasizing the shared Han Chinese ethnic identity of the majority population in Taiwan and the mainland, their ancestral and cultural antecedents, their shared interest in restoring China's once-exalted status among the nations, and its economic prosperity for the benefit of all constituents of 'One China.'

Across the Strait, a 'Taiwan Sentiment' was gradually extolled by multiple elites on the island, who invoked Taiwan's long history of foreign rule, including the 'Middle Kingdom,' the Netherlands, Japan (from 1895 to 1945), and the oppression of the mainland's *Kuomintang* under Chiang Kai-shek (from 1949 to 1988). They portrayed the PRC as a Communist dictatorship, attempting to impose its will on a weak anti-Communist society, and were determined to remain separate from the mainland's political system and ideology, and the planned economy controlled by China's Communist Party until the liberalization of the PRC economy from 1978 onwards. The opposition in Taiwan to formal merger with the Mainland, even the Hong Kong formula of 'one state, two systems,' embraced a wide range of 'separatists': it included those who publicly favored full independence for Taiwan, and a much larger group who did so, privately, but were reluctant to identify openly with a political party that espoused the goal of an independent Taiwan. There were others who favored closer economic relations with the mainland—in fact, Taiwan's economic liberalization long preceded that of the PRC, and private investment from Taiwan played a notable role in the early years of Mainland China's economic growth in the 1980s and 1990s, with a continuing role as a source of foreign investment for the PRC. Political decision-makers and the attentive public in Taiwan are aware of China's vastly superior military and economic power and the need to adapt to that material reality. However, while PRC propaganda has persisted in its attempt to persuade the Taiwanese to accept its notion of 'One China,' it has failed thus far to achieve that goal. Rather, appeals to shared kinship and culture, and the lure of benefits of partnership in a renewed 'Middle Kingdom' seem to have aroused skepticism or outright opposition among the majority of Taiwan's people, more attracted to the 'Taiwan Sentiment.' *In sum*, the use of propaganda by the PRC has enhanced verbal hostility, thereby contributing to sustaining this protracted conflict, rather than to conflict termination.

Violence threats of violence occurred spasmodically during the near-7 decades of this conflict, notably in the fourth Taiwan Crisis, 1995–1996, with a dramatic 'show of force' by PRC naval and missile power. However, the *actual resort to violence*, by both adversaries, *was very infrequent*—only in the first three Taiwan crises.

Taiwan Strait I (early August 1954–April 23, 1955). The PRC bombarded Nationalist (Taiwan, ROC) held off-shore islands, Quemoy and Matsu, beginning on September 3, 1954. The ROC responded on the 7th with air strikes on the mainland. The exchanges continued until late November. On December 2, the USA and the ROC signed a Mutual Defense Pact. The PRC responded on January 10, 1955 with a heavy bombardment of the Taiwan-held Tachen Islands. Taiwan responded in January, and the exchanges wound down by March. The crisis ended on April 23, when the PRC Premier, Zhou Enlai, offered to negotiate a resolution of this crisis.

Taiwan Strait II (July 17–October 23, 1958). The violence began with a PRC bombardment of Quemoy and Matsu on August 23. The violence ended when the USA threatened to intervene militarily if Quemoy were invaded. The crisis continued until the USA intervened diplomatically, first with a statement by Secretary of State Dulles on September 30 that the USA favored evacuation of the off-shore islands by ROC forces if the PRC agreed to a ceasefire, and then with a joint communiqué by Dulles and ROC leader, Chiang Kai-shek on October 23, which served as a tacit understanding by the PRC and ROC that the USA would not support a ROC invasion of the mainland.

Taiwan Strait III (April 22–June 27, 1962). Taiwan's president, Chiang Kai-shek, threatened, on April 22, to invade the mainland, a threat repeated several times in May, along with the addition of manpower to Taiwan's army. The PRC responded on June 10 with a troop build-up in Fukien province, the closest mainland territory to the 'off-shore' islands. The USA made it clear, again, that it would not support a ROC invasion of the mainland, and the crisis ended.

Taiwan Strait IV (May 1995–March 1996). The PRC threatened resort to force and engaged in a provocative large-scale show-of-force, in the summer and autumn of 1995 and again in February–March 1996, with naval and missile power, thereby demonstrating its superior military capability to Taiwan's political and military leadership and people, along with its determination to integrate Taiwan into 'One China,' preferably by negotiation, but by force if necessary.

Economic Discrimination This type of conflict-sustaining act was virtually non-existent in the Taiwan protracted conflict. Rather, as noted above, during the first 3 decades of this conflict the more highly developed Taiwan economy was a major source of investment during the early phase of the People's Republic of China's economic modernization program (1980s and 1990s) and continues to play this role, with substantial economic cooperation between the two entities. As such, their *economic* relationship has contributed to successful conflict management and cooperation, not to conflict persistence.

CHAPTER 10

What Have We Learned About Interstate Conflicts?

What have we learned from this inquiry into the phenomenon of *interstate protracted conflicts*? Why do some conflicts among states emerge as, or develop into, *protracted conflicts* that is, their *Onset phase*? Why do some protracted conflicts persist and escalate beyond the onset phase to their second, *Persistence* phase, in fully developed interstate conflicts, while others do not—they atrophy or are aborted? Why are many interstate conflicts *Resolved*, but some only after almost a century, since the end of World War I, their *Resolution* phase, while other protracted conflicts persist into the twenty-first century, even a millennium or more from the beginning of their historical roots, e.g., *China/Vietnam*, more than two millennia? Two distinct but related paths have been pursued in this inquiry, in search for answers to these questions. One is *theory construction*, in the form of *models*—on conflict *onset*, *persistence*, and *resolution*. The other is extensive *empirical research* into *interstate* protracted conflicts that were-are *active in world politics since the end of World War I*. The answers to the three questions posed above are based upon findings from the testing of hypotheses on *Onset*, Persistence, and *Resolution for all 33 conflicts* that were active during the near-century, *since the end of World War I*.

Protracted Conflict Onset Model, Hypotheses and Evidence

The hypotheses on conflict *Onset* [Phase I of an *interstate* protracted conflict] derive from the Model on *Onset* and the *concept, Basic Causes of a Protracted Conflict*. This model postulates the existence of six *Basic Causes of Onset*. Three are *tangible* causal Conditions—*Disputed Territory, Power Rivalry,* and competition for *Economic Access*. Three are *intangible* causal Conditions—*competing Ideologies, Identity Conflict,* and *Rivalry among Political Leaders* [all six causal Conditions among conflict principal adversaries].

The central proposition of the theory of conflict Onset is captured by *Hypothesis 1* [hereafter H1]: the *presence* of one or more of the six Basic Causes of conflict *Onset* contributes to—and is *sufficient* to explain—the onset of an *interstate* protracted conflict.

This hypothesis is *very strongly supported*: more than one of the six Basic Causes were present in 31 of the 33 analyzed conflicts, the full dataset; the two cases in which these Basic Causes were absent were single-cause phenomena.

H3 which postulates that disputed *Territory* is the most likely Basic Cause of the Onset of an *interstate* protracted conflict, is *strongly supported* by empirical research in this inquiry: disputed territory was a Basic Cause in 25 of the 33 active post-World War I conflicts—and the most important Basic Cause in 16 of the 25 conflicts.

H4 postulating that the most likely cluster of Basic Causes of conflict Onset is one in which disputed *Territory* is the primary cause, is also *strongly supported*. Among the 31 conflicts with more than one Basic Cause, Territory ranked first in 16 conflicts. The other Basic Causes occurred much less frequently: *Identity, Ideology, Political and Economic Systems*, 5 conflicts each.

H5 postulates that the trigger to an *interstate* conflict is most likely to be a *hostile physical and/or verbal Military or Political Acts*. This hypothesis is *very strongly supported: Political Act(s)*, 8 cases, e.g., *North Korean Nuclear; Military Act(s)*, 8 cases, e.g., *Greece/Turkey; Political and Military Act(s)*, 15 cases, e.g., *Ethiopia/Somalia*.

H6 postulates that an *Identity* conflict, accompanying a *territorial dispute*, will occur at both intrastate and interstate levels simultaneously. This hypothesis is *modestly supported*: there were 18 conflicts in which both identity and territorial disputes occurred; among these, 7 cases operated at both levels simultaneously, e.g., *Yugoslavia*. In *sum*, two hypotheses on the Onset phase of a conflict (H5) is *very strongly* supported by the evidence; two others (H3 and H4) are *strongly* supported, and H6 is *modestly* supported. Hypothesis 1 and 2 was not testable.

PROTRACTED CONFLICT PERSISTENCE MODEL, HYPOTHESES AND EVIDENCE

The intermediate phase of an interstate protracted conflict, following conflict *Onset* and, often, followed by conflict *Resolution*, was elaborated in the *Model on conflict Persistence*. Three *Basic Causes* of conflict Persistence, postulated as the Independent Variables of this Model, are as follows: *Discordant Objectives* [disputes among the conflict principal adversaries] *over Territory, Power, Ideology, and/or Material Benefits*; the *Balance of Capability among the principal adversaries*; and *Conflict-Sustaining Acts*, the third Basic Cause serving as the Intervening Variable, unfolding as acts of *violence, political hostility, economic discrimination*, and *verbal hostility*. What does the evidence from the full dataset of 33 conflicts reveal about the extent of support for/rejection of hypotheses on the Basic Causes of conflict Persistence?

H7 *Persistence* of interstate protracted conflicts is the consequence of one or more causal *Conditions* in the relations between adversarial states within a conflict and one or more types of *Conflict-sustaining Acts*. The presence of any one or more of these causal *Conditions* in the Onset phase of a conflict is *sufficient* to cause its persistence.

All 33 interstate conflicts persisted beyond the onset phase [and 20 of the 33 conflicts have been resolved].

In sum, the extensive evidence provides *very strong support* for the hypothesis that all three independent variables in the conflict Persistence Model served as Basic Causes (causal Conditions) of the persistence of the 33 conflicts in the full dataset set beyond their Onset phase.

H8 Among the two clusters of sources of conflict Persistence—causal *Conditions* and types of *Conflict-Sustaining Acts*—the most frequent in generating persistence beyond the Onset phase is on-going *disputes over Territory,* involving *Violence* between the principal conflict adversaries. A set of indicators, designed to compare the *impact* of *conflicts over Territory* and *Power* generates the postulate that *violent conflict* over *Territory* will be the *most significant Discordant Objective* (D.O.) and the *most frequent source of Persistence of conflicts.*

Territory was a persistent, highly visible and significant discordant objective in 21 of the 33 active protracted conflicts during the years since the end of World War I. Moreover, it was-is the *exclusive, more important or most important* discordant objective in 17 protracted conflicts, that is, in 80.9% of those 21 conflicts. Its *primacy* as a cause of conflict persistence is further evident in the fact that, among the 33 conflicts in the full dataset for this project, Territory was the sole discordant objective in 3 of 5 conflicts with one discordant objective (60%), a discordant objective (D.O.) in 11 of 18 cases with two D.Os. (61%), and ranked first in importance in 8 of those 11 conflicts (72.7%). It was also a D.O. in 7 of the 10 conflicts with 3 discordant objectives (70%), and ranked first in 6 of those 7 cases (85.7%).

In sum, disputes over territory were pervasively present in *interstate protracted conflicts* during a near-century (late 1918–2017).

H9 *Discordance* over *Power,* too, was prominent as a contributor to the *Persistence* of interstate conflicts: it was a *discordant objective* in 26 of the 33 conflicts, 5 more than Territory. However, Power was the *exclusive, most important* or *more important* discordant objective in only 9 of those 26 conflicts (34.6%), compared with 17 of 21 conflicts for Territory (80.9%). As with Territory, disputes over Power were visible in all categories of conflicts to which they contributed to persistence: in 2 of 5 conflicts with one discordant objective (D.O.); in 14 of 18 conflicts with two D.O.s, but the more important discordant objective in only 6 conflicts of that cluster (42.8%), compared to 72.7% of D.O.s with two discordant objectives in which Territory was a more important Discordant Objective. A similar difference in *scope of impact* by disputes over *Territory* and *Power* is evident in conflicts with three discordant Objectives. Thus, on this dimension of interstate protracted conflicts— their contribution to conflict Persistence, as with many others, *Territory* ranks first and *Power,* second, in significance-impact.

The same indicators were employed to assess the contribution of the two other discordant objectives to conflict Persistence, namely, *Ideology* and *Material Benefits-Economic Discrimination.*

Both were-are much less visible than Territory and Power, with a *much more limited presence and impact*. Material Benefits have been very slightly more visible than *Ideology* in the Persistence phase of post-World War I interstate protracted conflicts; they were present in 11 conflicts and 10 conflicts, overall, respectively. However, the evidence on impact points to *Ideology* as more significant: it was the *most important* Discordant Objective in 5 of the 10 conflicts in which it occurred, compared to 2 of 11 cases in which *Material Benefits* served as a discordant objective. Moreover, the five conflicts in which Ideology ranked first in importance exhibit a much broader scope than the 2 conflicts in which *Material Benefits* ranked as most important. The USA and the USSR were the principal adversaries in 2 of the 5 conflicts—Russia-USSR in *Iran/Russia-USSR*, and the USA in *Iraq Regime Change*. No less noteworthy, *middle powers* in the global system were principal adversaries in all five of the conflicts in which Ideology ranked first in importance. The evidence, though limited, indicates that *Ideology* had a greater impact on conflict Persistence than *Material Benefits*.

In sum, the empirical findings reveal a rank order for *presence* and *impact*, as anticipated in the *Model on conflict Persistence*—two clusters of Discordant Objectives, *Territory* and *Power*, followed by *Ideology* and *Material Benefits*.

H10 The larger the number of *Discordant Objectives* in the relations between–among principal adversaries in the *Persistence* phase of an interstate conflict, the more likely it is that a conflict will persist beyond that phase. Further, any *addition* to the *number* of Discordant Objectives during that phase will exacerbate the tension between the principal adversaries which, in turn, will extend the duration of an existing conflict.

The evidence on Discordant Objectives among 13 conflicts (a subset of a total of 33 post-World War I active interstate conflicts explored for this hypothesis) that continue to elude conflict resolution is instructive in assessing this hypothesis. Only one persisting conflict, *Western Sahara* (since 1975), exhibited a *single Discordant Objective* between its principal adversaries, Morocco and Polisario-SADR, the independence movement of Western Sahara's African Arab Muslim majority population—the contested control over governmental Power in the former colony of Spain and, through governmental power, control over the territory of Western Sahara. There are eight persisting conflicts with *two Discordant Objectives*: two conflicts in Africa., e.g., *DRC/Rwanda* over Power and

Material Benefits (since 1996, with deep historical roots); two in Asia, e.g., *India/Pakistan*, a conflict over Territory (Kashmir) and competition over Ideology (since 1947); one in the Middle East, *Iran/Iraq*, over Material Benefits and Power in the Gulf region (since 1934, with deep historical roots); and three Inter-Region conflicts, e.g., *Inter-Korea*, over Ideology and Power (since 1945). There are also four persisting conflicts with *three Discordant Objectives*, e.g., *Arab/Israel*, over *Territory*, Power, and National Identity.

In sum, all but one of the 13 persisting unresolved conflicts, among the full dataset of 33 post-World War I cases, exhibited two or three *Discordant Objectives*, indicating substantial support for the postulated link between the number of discordant objectives in a conflict and the likelihood of a conflict's continuing persistence.

H11 Whether an interstate protracted conflict will follow the path leading to *resolution or* extended *persistence* also depends, in part, on the *Volume* and *Impact* of *Conflict-Sustaining Acts* (CSAs) by a conflict's principal adversaries.

The evidence on the distribution of Conflict-Sustaining Acts among the four types, *Violence, Political Hostility, Material Benefits-Economic Discrimination,* and *Verbal Hostility-Propaganda*, is instructive.

Violence exhibited the highest frequency of *Conflict Sustaining Acts*, with the greatest impact, in 21 of the 33 Post-World War I conflicts. In 5 of these cases, Violence shared frequency and impact with Political Hostility, e.g., *Ethiopia/Somalia* (persisting), *Ecuador/Peru* (resolved 1998). Among the 21 cases, Violence was the primary Conflict-Sustaining Technique (CST) in 13 resolved conflicts and 8 cases that persist.

Political Hostility was the second most-frequently employed and consequential CST—in 15 of the 33 interstate protracted conflicts, including 5 conflicts shared with Violence. Among the 15, Political Hostility was the most frequent and consequential CST in 10 cases, e.g., *Costa Rica/Nicaragua* (resolved 1955) and *Greece/Turkey* (unresolved) and among the five shared cases of primary CST role of Violence and Political Hostility, e.g., *Chad/Libya* (resolved) and *Western Sahara* (unresolved).

Material Benefits-Economic Discrimination was the primary CST—frequency and impact—in only two conflicts, *Iraq/Kuwait* (resolved 1994) and *Afghanistan/Pakistan* (unresolved).

Verbal Hostility-Propaganda was not frequently employed and did not achieve highest frequency or greatest impact on the Persistence of any protracted conflict since the end of WWI.

In *sum*, the evidence on the two most frequent and consequential types of CSA and the prospect of conflict resolution or persistence points to a strong association: the larger the number of acts of *Violence* and of *Political Hostility*, the greater the likelihood that a conflict will continue to persist beyond the *Onset* and *Persistence* phases of a conflict, rather than achieve *Resolution*.

H12 The *Balance of Capability* between/among conflict principal adversaries, notably military power, constitutes another causal Condition that contributes to decision-makers' choice of a preferred outcome— extended *persistence* or *resolution* of a conflict.

Findings on the relationship between the *Balance of Capability* among conflict adversaries and the *outcome* of an *interstate* protracted conflict reveal a strong association between *four Balance of Capability clusters of conflict adversaries*, assessed in global system terms, and conflict outcomes during the past near-century:

Equality or near-equality of middle powers—five *persisting* conflicts, two in Asia (*India/Pakistan, Inter-Korea*), two in the Middle East (*Arab/Israel, Iran/Iraq*), and one Inter-Region (*Greece/Turkey*);

Equality or near-equality of power between small powers—a less clear pattern, with an outcome of five *resolved* conflicts and three *persisting* cases; the three persisting conflicts are located in Africa (*DRC/Rwanda, Ethiopia/Somalia*, and *Western Sahara*); the five resolved cases were-are located in three regions—Africa (*Angola* and *Rhodesia*), America (*Costa Rica/Nicaragua, Honduras/Nicaragua*), and Middle East (*Yemen*);

Unequal or Mixed Powers: Super Powers-Middle Powers—a *clear majority of conflicts in this cluster* (4-1) led to *resolution;* the USA was the superpower in three of these conflicts (*Iraq Regime Change, North Korean Nuclear*, and *North Vietnam/USA);* the USSR was the superpower in the other two cases (*Iran/Russia-USSR, Poland/Russia-USSR*);

Middle Power-Small Power—this cluster too reveals a *clear majority* (6-1), leading to *resolution* (*Chad/Libya*, Ecuador/Peru, Indonesia, Lithuania/Poland, Iraq/Kuwait, and Yugoslavia); the sole unresolved conflict in this cluster is *Afghanistan/Pakistan*).

In sum, three of the 10 clusters of conflicts, classified in terms of changes in the Balance of Capability and conflict Outcome among principal adversaries, comprise one conflict or none. Thus, the pairs in the four meaningful clusters comprise a large proportion of the full dataset, 25 of the 33 conflicts (75.8% of all Post-World War I cases). While *association* does not constitute *cause–effect linkage* between changes in capability of adversaries and conflict outcome, continued persistence, or resolution, this finding, combined with findings on discordant objectives and conflict-sustaining acts reported above, facilitates probabilistic prediction on three important dimensions of interstate protracted conflict.

Hypotheses and Findings on Conflict Resolution

As with the Conflict Onset and Persistence Models, six Basic Causes—Conditions likely to contribute to conflict resolution—were postulated as the Independent Variables in the Resolution Model: they are *Changes in the Balance of Capability, Decline in Conflict-Sustaining Acts, Domestic Pressures on decision-makers to pursue Resolution, Exhaustion, External Pressures for Resolution, and Reduction in Discordant Objectives* [by the principal adversaries].

H13 According to the underlying theory of conflict resolution, developed in the Resolution Model, the presence of one or more of the six causal *Conditions* is *sufficient* to generate a causal chain leading to conflict resolution. Moreover, when more Basic Causes of resolution are present in a conflict, the likelihood of conflict resolution will increase; and when all six causal conditions are present in a conflict, conflict resolution will be virtually certain.

The *first general observation* in a test of this hypothesis is that *all of the six postulated* Causes of Resolution, discussed earlier, *have been present in one or more stages of the process shaping the Outcome of 13 protracted conflicts*, the matching subset of the full dataset of 33 conflicts for this part of the inquiry into "International Crises and Interstate Conflicts." More precisely, the six postulated causes were present 42 times [of a theoretically possible 78 times] among 13 conflicts in this part of the inquiry, providing moderate support (53.8%) of H13, which postulates that *conflict resolution* is likely to occur when one or more of the six causal Conditions characterize at least one of the principal adversaries in a protracted conflict.

The *frequency of occurrence* of the six Conditions varies considerably. Two Conditions (Basic Causes) occurred very frequently in the cluster of 13 conflicts—*External Pressures on conflict principal adversaries to seek conflict resolution*, in 11 of 13 post-World War I protracted conflicts and *Changes in the Balance of Capability* in 10 conflicts. At the other extreme, *Domestic Pressures* occurred in 4 conflicts and the other 3 conditions, *Reduction in Discordance of Objectives, Decline in Conflict-Sustaining Acts*, and *Exhaustion* are discernible in 5, 6, and 6 conflicts, respectively. Thus, *overall presence* of the postulated *Basic Causes of Resolution* is evident *in these 13 conflicts* but the frequency distribution among the six causal Conditions is unequal.

H14 The larger the number of Basic Causes [causal Conditions] that are present in a protracted conflict, the more likely is a conflict to be resolved—the most relevant evidence is the *number of Basic Causes* experienced by *resolved* and *persisting interstate protracted conflicts*.

Among the 8 *resolved* conflicts in the matching subset of 13 protracted conflicts explored for this phase of the inquiry, two conflicts experienced all six postulated Basic Causes of Resolution, *Ecuador/Peru* and *USA/USSR;* and two conflicts experienced five Basic Causes, *Angola* and *Yugoslavia*. Moreover, there were no resolved conflicts with only one Basic Cause, and only two resolved conflicts with two Basic Causes, *China/Japan* and *Iraq Regime Change*. By contrast, among the five of 13 *persisting* conflicts, two experienced one Basic Cause, e.g., *North Korean Nuclear,* one experienced two Basic Causes, *India/Pakistan*, and two experienced three Basic Causes, e.g., *Arab/Israel*. There were no persisting conflicts with more than three Basic Causes of Resolution, that is, with a majority of causal conditions. Thus, the findings on the very different distribution of the number of Basic Causes of Resolution among resolved and persisting conflicts in a matching subset of conflicts support Hypothesis 14.

H15 and H16 focus on the role of *External Pressure* on conflict principal adversaries to seek conflict resolution. H15 postulated that foreign pressure on at least one principal adversary in a conflict is the *most likely single Basic Cause* of interstate conflict resolution. This hypothesis is strongly supported by several strands of evidence: External Pressure was present in 7 of the 8 resolved conflicts (87.5%), among a total of 11 resolved and persisting conflicts that experienced *External Pressures*. As evident below, *Changes in the Balance of Capability* occurred in all 8 resolved conflicts, that is, with a higher proportional frequency than

External Pressures; however, it ranked lower than External Pressure in *impact* on the outcome of resolution.

The findings on the *presence* of the other four postulated likely Basic Causes of Resolution in the Resolution Model supplement the finding on the *presence* of the two noted high-frequency Basic Causes. *Exhaustion* and *Domestic Pressure* were experienced only in resolved conflicts, in 6 and 4 cases, respectively. *Reduction in Discordance of Objectives is evident* in 4 (of 5) *resolved conflicts* (80%). *Decline in Conflict-Sustaining Acts* occurred in 3 (of 6) resolved conflicts (50%).

The findings on H16, which postulates the primacy of External Pressure in the most likely cluster of *Basic Causes of conflict Resolution*, also illuminate the *presence* and *relative importance* of the six postulated Basic Causes of conflict Resolution. The operational indicator of importance is the rank order of the Basic Causes that were evident in the resolution of the 8 resolved conflicts among the subset of 13 cases that were explored for this assessment, with a focus on Rank 1 and Rank 2 *in resolved* conflicts, as follows:

Changes in Balance of Military Capability—Rank 1 in 4 of 8 resolved conflicts, Rank 2 in 3 resolved conflicts, together in 7 of 8 resolved conflicts (87.5%).
External Pressures—Rank 1 in 2 of 8 resolved conflicts, Rank 2 in 4 resolved conflicts, together in 6 of 8 resolved conflicts (75%).
Exhaustion—Rank 1 in 2 of 8 resolved conflicts, Rank 2 in 0 resolved conflict, together in 2 of 8 resolved conflicts (25%).
Domestic Pressures—Rank 1 in 0 of 4 resolved conflicts, Rank 2 in 0 resolved conflict, together 0 in 4 conflicts (0%).
Decline in Conflict-sustaining Acts—Rank 1 in none of 3 resolved conflicts, Rank 2 in none of 3 resolved conflict, together 0%.
Reduction in Discordant Objectives—Rank 1 in none of 4 resolved conflicts, rank 2 in none, rank 1 + 2, 0%.

The results of this probe reinforce the earlier finding on the *presence* and *significance* of the six postulated Basic Causes of interstate protracted conflict resolution since the end of World War I.

In sum, Changes in the Balance of Military Capability of, and *External Pressure* on, the conflict principal adversaries clearly constitute the apex of this assessment. They rank first and a very close second overall as contributors to conflict resolution of a matching subset of the full dataset of 33 conflicts active during the near-century since the end of World War I:

10 WHAT HAVE WE LEARNED ABOUT INTERSTATE CONFLICTS? 325

a difference of only 1 conflict in the number of cases in which they rank 1 or 2 overall—7 of 8 and 6 of 8 resolved conflicts, respectively.

Collective *Exhaustion* ranks a distant third in both *presence* and *importance of contribution* to conflict resolution—only 2 of 8 resolved conflicts in which it ranked 1 or 2 in importance of contribution.

In terms of contribution to *conflict resolution*, the other three postulated causal conditions did not rank 1 or 2 in the contribution to resolution in any of the 8 resolved conflicts (among the 13 in the matching subset).

One further aspect of the findings is the light that they cast on the most frequent combination of causal Conditions most likely to lead to the resolution of interstate protracted conflicts. The most frequent formula is the presence of three of the postulated six Conditions in the *Model on Resolution: External Pressures, Changes in the Balance of Military Capability,* and collective *Exhaustion* in at least one of the principal adversaries. In four of six cases of successful conflict resolution, in the matching subset since the end of World War I, these conditions rank 1, 2, and 3, though the ranking varies within the 1-2-3 combination.

Ecuador/Peru conflict: Exhaustion Rank 1, External Pressures Rank 2, Changes in Military Capability Rank 3.

France/Germany conflict: Exhaustion Rank 1, Changes in Military Capability Rank 2, External Pressures Rank 3.

Iraq/Kuwait conflict: Changes in Military Capability Rank 1, External Pressures Rank 2, Exhaustion Rank 3.

Yugoslavia conflict: External Pressures Rank 1, Changes in Military Capability Rank 2, Exhaustion Rank 3.

The other two resolved conflicts, in which this combination of conditions appears, with a different ranking, are as follows:

Angola conflict: Changes in Military Capability Rank 1, External Pressures Rank 2, Exhaustion, present but unranked.

USA/USSR conflict: Changes in Military Capability Rank 1, External Pressures Rank 2, and Exhaustion, present but unranked.

H17 postulates the predominance of two of the six Basic Causes identified in the Resolution Model as most likely contributors to the resolution of interstate protracted conflicts. The evidence presented here is far from definitive, because of the unavailability of most primary sources on a complex process that often succeeded, but also failed, in the quest for conflict resolution. However, the evidence provides persuasive support for this hypothesis on the crucial roles of *External Pressures* on conflict principal adversaries to seek conflict resolution and on the more elusive changes in the *Balance of Military Capability* between principal adversaries.

In sum, the evidence presented here indicates that the presence of three of the six postulated Basic Causes in the *Conflict Resolution Model*—*External Pressures, Changes in the Balance of Capability,* and with notably less frequency of occurrence, *Exhaustion*—were-are most likely to lead to the resolution of interstate protracted conflicts. *Domestic Pressures* for conflict resolution, *Decline in Conflict-Sustaining Acts,* and *Reduction in Discordant Objectives* of a conflict's principal adversaries merit continuing attention but no longer merit recognition as 'most likely conditions' to generate conflict resolution. Their reduced *explanatory status* would enhance the parsimony of the *Resolution Model,* without detracting from its *explanatory power* regarding a complex phenomenon in world politics during, and possibly beyond, the rest of the twenty-first century.

CHAPTER 11

Critique of International Studies

Shortcomings

As with most academic disciplines or fields of study, **International Relations (IR)**, **World Politics (WP)**, and **International Studies (IS)** have been the *object of many assessments* during the past half-century. An ambitious predecessor, comprising the views of 44 scholars, was presented in the Millennial Reflections project (1999–2002) earlier in this book. To conclude this volume, I present my own thoughts on the topic, based upon a wide-ranging critique, "International Studies in the Twentieth Century and Beyond: Flawed Dichotomies, Syntheses, Cumulation" (International Studies Quarterly 1999).

The **shortcomings** are as follows:
Intolerance of competing paradigms, models, methods, and findings;
closed-mind mentality;
tendency to **research fashions**;
retreat from science in IR, WP, IS; and
low value placed on cumulation of knowledge.

The **flawed dichotomies** are as follows:
Theory vs. **History** as approaches to knowledge;
Deductive vs. **Inductive** paths to theory;
Horizontal (breadth) vs. **Vertical** (in-depth) focus of inquiry;
Aggregate data (quantitative) vs. **Case study (qualitative)** methods of analysis;

Large 'N' vs. **Small 'N'** clusters of data;
System vs. **Actor** as the optimal level of analysis; and closely related,
Unitary vs. **Multiple** competing actors;
Rational calculus vs. **Psychological constraints** on choice; and the related divide
Reality vs. **Perceptions** as the key to explain state behavior; and
Neo-Realism vs. **Neo-Institutionalism** vs. **Constructivism** as the correct paradigm for the study of world politics.

These shortcomings and dichotomies are elaborated immediately below.

The 'state of the field' of International Studies, International Relations, World Politics remains chaotic, generating a need to break out of what seems an intellectual-academic morass.

Where have we gone wrong? The question is not new but it continues to perplex. The answers, unfortunately, are as numerous as our contentious 'schools,' which are divided by epistemology, methodology, and ideology, along with idiosyncratic elements such as personality. Realism and Neo-Realism, Institutionalism and Neo-Institutionalism, Critical Theory, Post-Modernism, Post-Positivism, Rational Choice Theory, Cognitive Psychology, the English School, Neo-Marxism, World System, Feminist IR, and Constructivism offer different reasons for the *malaise* of International Studies. Most would agree, I think, that the promise evident in the work of the modern founders of International Relations, notably E.H. Carr (1939, 1946), Quincy Wright (1942, 1955), Hans J. Morgenthau (1946, 1948), Martin Wight (1946), and Raymond Aron (1957, 1966), has not yet been fulfilled.

As someone who has learned from many of the pioneers and later 'schools' but is a prisoner or apostle of none, I present another answer to this elusive question. In particular, I will examine why this field of knowledge, using the terms, **International Relations (IR)**, **World Politics (WP)**, and **International Studies (IS)** interchangeably, has not yet crystallized into a mature social science discipline.

IR, WP, IS scholarship, as noted schematically above, is replete with shortcomings.

The first is **intolerance** of competing paradigms, models, methods, and findings. From a Classical Realism perspective, Hedley Bull (1966) launched a "shotgun attack upon a whole flock of assorted approaches," specifically the work of Morton Kaplan, Karl Deutsch and Bruce Russett, Thomas Schelling, Richardson, Riker, and other contributors to the IR field. One of the most pungent assaults on one IR paradigm by another was made by Post-Modernism's Richard Ashley: in "The Poverty of Neorealism" (1984), he decried "Neorealist structuralism" as "an orrery of errors... structuralism, statism, utilitarianism, and positivism [which] are bound together in machine-like, self-enclosing unity." Another blunt critique—of Neo-Institutionalism—came from Kenneth Waltz, the creator of Neo-(Structural) Realism in IR theory: "A theory's a theory. It has to meet certain standards whether it's a natural science theory or a social science theory. Beyond that, I would call it [Neo-Institutionalism] interpretation, philosophy, history.... Keohane... says that the core of the theory [of Neo-Institutionalism] is structural realism. That's the only theory that there is in liberal internationalism: the rest is application" (1998). Waltz's verbal assault was in response to a much more muted claim to primacy for Neo-Institutionalism by its leading proponent, Robert O. Keohane: "To analyze world politics in the 1990s is to discuss international institutions: the rules that govern elements of world politics and the organizations that help implement those rules" (1998). *In sum*, prominent advocates of contending approaches in International Studies have not been immune to crass intellectual intolerance.

A second weakness in IR-IS-WP is a **closed-mind mentality**, humorously captured by Dina Zinnes's comment at a 1997 conference on "What Do We Know About War": "I think it's kind of intriguing that everybody who was asked to contribute to [this conference] loves their variable, nobody was willing to stand up and say, 'I give up my variable'."

A third shortcoming is the tendency to research **fashions**, as evident in the shifting sands of the IR topical agenda during the twentieth century: legal and formal-structural aspects of international institutions, notably the League of Nations, in the 1920s; the Realism-Idealism debate in the 1930s and 1940s; decision-making and Neo-Functionalism in the 1950s and 1960s; Neo-Realism, Neo-Institutionalism, Comparative Foreign Policy, and Political Psychology in the 1970s; Critical Theory, Post-Modernism, and Feminism in the 1980s; and Constructivism in the 1990s. Many of these topics remain active in 2017. While change is a necessary condition of intellectual progress and a desirable response to changing world reality, many of these topic changes took on the appearance of a fad or fashion. Rather than contributing to cumulation of knowledge, they tended to create a myriad of debates that generated more heat than light and often polarized the community of IS, IR, WP scholars.

A fourth shortcoming, apparent from a reading of the evolution of the field, is an increasingly visible **retreat from science** in International Studies, most recently evident in the extreme version of the constructivist critique.

A fifth shortcoming, accentuated by the retreat from science, is the **low value** placed by an increasing number of IR scholars on **cumulation of knowledge**.

Some of these shortcomings—intellectual intolerance, a closed-mind mentality, and a penchant for fads and fashions—can be viewed as part of the human condition and act as constraints on scholarly progress. Other shortcomings—the retreat from science and inadequate attention to cumulation of knowledge—are grave intellectual weaknesses. Together, for they reinforce each other's negative influence and have helped to thwart efforts to attain the three objectives of a fully developed social science discipline: accurate **DESCRIPTION**, convincing **EXPLANATION**, and high probability **PREDICTION** of the multiple strands that compose world politics.

The negative impact of these shortcomings has been even more extensive, for they spill over to the second, more fundamental source of the *malaise* in **IR**, **IS**, and **WP**, in my view. In fact, they have facilitated the creation, persistence, and accentuation of a set *of flawed dichotomies* that continue to pervade this field of knowledge.

Flawed Dichotomies

One way of framing the concept of *flawed dichotomies*, as noted above, is in terms of the **thesis/antithesis** syndrome:

- **Theory vs. History** as approaches to knowledge;
- **Deductive vs. Inductive** paths to theory;
- **Horizontal (breadth) vs. vertical (in-depth)** focus of inquiry, based upon;
- **Aggregate data (quantitative) vs. Case Study (qualitative) methods of analysis**, using **large 'N' vs. small 'N'** clusters of data;
- **System vs. Actor** as the optimal *level of analysis* and, closely related, **unitary vs. multiple competing actors**;
- *Rational Calculus* by authorized decision-makers vs. *Psychological Constraints* on choice, and the related divide over *Reality* vs. *Image* as the key to explaining state behavior; and, perhaps, the most sweeping dichotomy of all;

(Neo)-Realism vs. (Neo)-Institutionalism as the correct paradigm for the study of world politics.

It has long been my conviction that each of the competing strands in approaches to knowledge, paths to theory, foci of inquiry and methods, levels of analysis, explanations of choice, and paradigms has merit. However, intolerance has been the prevailing tone of debates on what seem to me to be flawed dichotomies, often with disdain for alternative paths. Whichever organizing device is used to frame these cleavages, the central point remains that there is a plethora of dichotomies in the field of International Studies and these are all flawed.

Many years ago I set out the case for "many paths to knowledge" and made a plea for pluralism in International Studies (1989, 1995). In this spirit, I turn to what I consider the flawed dichotomies.

Theory vs. History

The adherents of both theory and history claim that theirs is the superior *path to knowledge* in International Studies–International Relations–World Politics. This cleavage is generally framed in either/or, correct/incorrect terms, and protagonists of both persuasions (broadly, social science vs. the humanities) have, for the most part, yielded to the thesis–antithesis syndrome.

I have always been a *pluralist* in the matter of research strategy: there are, it seems to me, many paths to knowledge; no single path has a monopoly of truth. In this I was influenced by my South Asia experience, especially the Hindu adage that no religion has a monopoly of the truth; all can claim to know only a part of the whole. Translating this to the enduring issue of the optimal path to knowledge, I became committed, very early, to pluralism in methodology. Deductive logic generates models and hypotheses which must be tested with empirical evidence. From inductive research one can derive generalizations, both from comparative case studies, a small N, and from aggregate data analysis, a large N; these can be framed as hypotheses and tested with evidence from other cases.

Theory clearly occupies a central place, whether deductively or inductively derived. Although the former is accorded higher status in the natural and social sciences, the evidence thus far in the study of world politics is mixed and, in any event, the choice depends upon a researcher's disposition. Stated differently, the issue of whether formal theory must precede—and take precedence over—empirical investigation remains unresolved. My own disposition has always been in favor of an iterative process—pre-theory, in the form of a framework to guide empirical inquiry, followed by the creation of models and hypotheses, testing, their refinement as the evidence dictates, further testing and so on.

The stimulus is often a puzzle. In my long research experience, the most complex puzzle has been the ubiquitous phenomenon of inter-state crisis. I began by framing what seemed to me core questions. What is a **crisis**? How does it differ from, and how is it related to, **conflict, war, dispute**, and **incident**? Does it unfold at one or more levels? What are the defining conditions of an international (macro-level) crisis and of a foreign policy (micro-level) crisis? What is the logical relationship between them? What triggers an external crisis for a state? How do decision-makers cope with the stress of crisis? How do crises wind down and terminate? Are there differences in international crises in diverse configurations of polarity, geography, economic development, political regime, etc.? How does one explain its core dimensions such as crisis outbreak, actor behavior, major power activity, the involvement of international organizations, crisis outcome, its intensity, and consequences?

This, in turn, led to a related puzzle: what path should be followed in order to answer these questions? My choice from the outset was a two-track strategy, flowing from a conviction about the inherent merit of pluralism. One path is ***in-depth case studies*** of perceptions and decisions by a single state, using a micro-level model of crisis that I designed to guide research on foreign policy crises for individual states and to facilitate rigorous comparative analysis of findings about state behavior under varying stress. This approach, which I termed "structured empiricism," gathers and organizes data on diverse cases around a set of common questions, permitting systematic comparison.

Comparative case study alone, however, cannot uncover the full range of findings about any phenomenon in world politics. For this purpose, a second path was necessary, namely, ***studies in breadth of aggregate data*** on crises over an extended block of time and space. The result was a selection of a large-scale empirical domain, all military-security crises of all states, across all continents, cultures, and political and economic systems, initially from 1929 to 1979, extended back and forward in time, to late 1918 and, at present, to the end of 2015, and on-going. In the shaping of this aggregate data dimension of the ICB project and in the many volumes and papers that presented the data and the findings, Jonathan Wilkenfeld and I have been academic collaborators in the best sense of the term, for 40 years. Stated in terms of paths to knowledge, we and our associates and assistants sought *conceptual clarity* and a rich *empirical base*, simultaneously, in order to achieve the goal of illuminating the causes, evolution, termination, and consequences of interstate crises and protracted conflicts.

It is important to emphasize that the plethora of questions noted above emerged both from thinking about the puzzle (*theorizing*) and from initial research on twentieth-century cases (*empirical investigation*), which the questions were designed to guide. Over time—the main data-gathering phase lasted 40 years thus far and continues—the puzzle became more, rather than less, complex, and the body of questions grew, for we sought to tap every attribute of interstate crises.

Was this research program shaped by theory or by history, that is, by a priori reasoning or by empirical evidence? It was, in reality, a synthesis of the two, and consciously so. In fact, at the same time that the initial set of variables was being created, a preliminary set of cases was being generated for the period 1929–1979. With the advice of specialists on international conflict in all regions of the world, a revised set of cases became the basis for our research, all guided by the same questions, as noted earlier in this book. In short, the assumed dichotomy between theory and history seemed flawed: in fact, theory and history served as our joint disciplinary guides.

Deductive vs. Inductive Theory

The cleavage between theory and history spills over to **deductive** *vs.* **inductive** reasoning as **paths to theory**, the second flawed dichotomy in my view.

Hedley Bull, a *guru* of the English School in IR, rejected both deductive and inductive paths to theory. In fact, theory seemed anathema to him: "...in *framing* hypotheses in answer to these empirical questions we are dependent upon intuition or judgment...; [and] in the *testing of* them we are utterly dependent upon judgment, also upon a rough and ready observation" (1966).

The exemplar of the **inductivist** approach to IR knowledge was David Singer: from the outset of his Correlates of War (COW) project (1963), he urged concentration on the generation of data and the search for correlates of war. Causation and theory were eschewed by him.

The **deductivist** view was stated with admirable clarity by Bruce Bueno de Mesquita. On the one hand, he acknowledged the virtue of pluralism: "Does it matter whether our research proceeds inductively or deductively, so long as we... satisfy the requirements of rigorous theory construction and rigorous empirical investigation? I think not, at least in terms of the value of the final product. The logic of discovery apparently is not laid out along a single, neat path. However, the two paths are less than equal: while "observation is useful to falsify theory.... [It] is not particularly useful for confirming theories.... [P]roof must come from axiomatic logic." Moreover, "... *formal, explicit theorizing takes intellectual, if not temporal, precedence over empiricism*" (1985).

In this view, empirical findings cannot validate theory; they can only falsify. There is, however, an alternative path to theory 'from the top down,' namely, theory 'from the bottom up.' In this perspective, theory is the end-point of an intellectual process, not the starting-point; that is, theory is the highest step on a *four-step* ladder designed to create, organize, and validate knowledge, following the initial task, concept definition. The initial task takes place in some kind of theory-driven environment, as noted by Popper, Lakatos, and other philosophers of social science.

A **taxonomy**, or classification of variables, is the most rudimentary but often the most appropriate technique to *begin* a scientific research enterprise, for it brings together variables that identify relevant attributes about a topic, even though relations among the variables have not yet been specified. It is the first pre-theoretical step. The next step in the bottom-up strategy of theory-creation is to group variables in *a* **conceptual map** based on logical links among the variables. Hypotheses are derived deductively from **models**, the third step in the bottom-up strategy.

For the pure theorist, a model does not merit the accolade, **theory**, since its primary function is to guide research. For others, however, theory is generated from a model and its hypotheses. A model goes far beyond both taxonomy and conceptual map in specifying cause–effect linkages between independent and dependent variables, often with intervening variables as well. Such postulates are the essence of explanation. When tested with, and supported by, empirical data, these postulates merit the designation **theoretical propositions**. Thus, in my view, a rigorous model, qualifies as contingent theory.

What theoretical functions have been performed by the **Unified Model of Crisis (UMC)**, presented earlier in this book? First, it provided the intellectual rationale for the phase models, noted earlier in the discussion of the UMC. Second, it presented the logic for the inferences derived from these models. And third, it specified these in the form of propositions and hypotheses. As such, it made possible the testing of theoretical expectations with the abundant evidence on interstate crises, facilitating the crucial confrontation between theory and reality. In so doing, the Unified Model serves as the core of a **scientific research program** (Lakatos 1970) on crisis, for it aims to discover which logically derived assumptions about crises and state behavior are falsified and which are confirmed.

Aggregate Data vs. Case Study

This dichotomy is framed in terms of *breadth* vs. *depth*, that is, a *horizontal* vs. a *vertical* focus, which translates into *aggregate data* vs. *case study*. And this, in turn, is linked to the number of cases—a *large* vs. *small N*—to be used in testing deductively derived hypotheses or to serve as the empirical basis of theory-type generalizations.

The issue of **methods** is no less contentious than the debates between theory and history, and over paths to theory. Most of the debates on IR methods have focused on the merits and limits of case study. The alternative—quantitative, aggregate data analysis—and the optimal number of cases have received little attention.

I know all the arguments of the proponents of one or the other approach. But I have always found them flawed and counter-productive, for they are based on the fundamentally faulty premise that one of these methods is RIGHT, and the other, WRONG. Rational actor theorists rarely undertake case studies; they view the findings as unproductive in theory-testing, let alone theory construction. Political psychologists attach great importance to case studies but they often err in their analyses of why decision-makers did or did not initiate war. After engaging in many case studies of crisis, conflict, and war, and the behavior of states in various regions, at diverse levels of power and economic development, with different cultures and historical legacies, I have concluded that, in some cases, rational calculus is the primary path to illuminating choice on war initiation; in other cases, the decision is a product of complexity, incomplete information, miscalculation, fear, etc. In almost all cases, both rational calculus and psychological constraints operate.

Is the impasse over IR methods merely another indicator of an underdeveloped academic discipline? Must we choose rigidly between a qualitative, small N, in-depth case study research program and quantitative, large N, aggregate data analysis? I do not think so. Rather, my experience of research on crisis, conflict, and war for decades demonstrates that the dead end of clinging to one's preferred method and the thesis/antithesis wrangling can be overcome through the adoption of a *dual strategy of research*—**case studies and aggregate data analysis**. However, this is not accomplished mechanically by fusing the two methods. Rather, multi-method analysis is the optimal path to progress in International Studies.

Levels of Analysis
A fourth flawed dichotomy in **IS, IR, WP** relates to the **level of analysis** problem. Variations in the number of levels of analysis were suggested over the years—ten levels, five, and three. However, the consensus in support of two IR levels—the state and the system—has been sustained. Scholars sang the praises of one or the other level. The core question posed earlier about other dichotomies comes to mind once more: are the levels of analysis mutually exclusive, as implied by the protagonists of system determinism and state decision-makers' autonomy? The answer, based upon a prolonged inquiry into twentieth and early twenty-first century crises and protracted conflicts, is emphatically 'no.'

The **International Crisis Behavior (ICB)** Project focuses on both *international crises* (the *system* level) and *foreign policy crises* (the *actor* level), and treats them as parts of an *integrated whole—interstate crises*. Moreover, while the models designed to guide research at the two levels differ, with respect to independent, intervening, and dependent variables, they are not mutually exclusive: they are complementary.

Rational Calculus vs. Cognitive Constraints
Another dichotomy that has bedeviled International Studies is that between **rational choice theory** and **political psychology**: it focuses on the actor level of analysis, specifically, on how foreign policy decision-makers choose.

The concept of *rational choice* and expected utility theory derive from the social science tradition of neo-classical microeconomic theory and from game theory, but it was slow to penetrate IR. Notable early works by Brams (1975) and Bueno de Mesquita (1981) were followed by a plethora of books and articles in The Journal of Conflict Resolution and other journals. The focus on *perceptions* (images) in International Studies can be traced to an economist, Boulding (1956, 1959) and, even more visibly, to the Stanford-mediated stimulus response model in the 1960s. But it was not until the mid-1970s that the psychological dimension— the importance of cognitive constraints on decision-making—attained high visibility with books by Jervis 1976, Axelrod 1976, and Janis and Mann, 1977.

The rational choice school has created a parsimonious and rigorous theory of political behavior. In the subfield of international conflict, it contends that decision-makers choose to initiate or not to initiate war solely on the basis of a rational calculus of costs and benefits. Several assumptions underpin this theory: first, that the decision-making process can be equated with one or a few leaders, with the roles of civil and military bureaucracies, legislatures, interest groups, and, in democracies, the media and public opinion being inconsequential; second, that human decision-makers are capable of pure rationality, a view that psychologists, political and other, have vigorously challenged, as in Simon's (1957) concept of "bounded rationality"; and third, that choice can be examined solely in terms of the behavior of the chooser, that is, of a single state, rather than as a product of hostile interaction among state adversaries.

All of these assumptions have been challenged. In particular, critics have argued that the concept of pure rationality is an ideal type which does not conform to reality. They also emphasized the role of constraints on choice, in Jervis's words, "cognitive limitations on information processing" and "motivated biases," as well as constraints on rational decision-making flowing from domestic politics and organizational behavior (1976, 1989).

There is merit in both of these contending approaches. The motivations of foreign policy decision-makers are varied and complex. Not all are pure rational actors. Nor are all driven by fear. Some will respond to a strategy of deterrence, others to a strategy of reassurance. And in still other cases neither strategy nor a mix will be effective. Once more the either/or contention is flawed. Deterrence and reassurance are complementary strategies; each explains part of state behavior in the military-security issue-area of foreign policy; together they explain much but not all about the decision process attending the initiation of violence.

To explain a decision to initiate war solely in terms of a subjective expected utility calculus may satisfy a penchant for parsimony, but does such a model do justice to the complex process attending a decision to go to war? I am profoundly skeptical, based upon decades of in-depth research on the decision-making process leading to war. Similarly, to focus exclusively on the cognitive constraints on decision-makers and to argue that a calculus of utility is either not made or plays a marginal role in the choice process is also flawed. The vigorous debate between rational choice theory and political psychology theory goes on.

Paradigms Lost

Academic disciplines are slow to mature. One of the indicators of maturity is a consensus frame of reference that shapes the intellectual tone, the research agenda, and the methods of inquiry of a community of scholars. Competition among paradigms is not unique to International Studies–International Relations–World Politics or the social sciences generally. And the concept of "paradigm shift" is one of the major unresolved controversies in the philosophy of science.

In the years before World War I, continuing through most of the inter-World War period (1919–1939), **Idealism** or **Utopianism** held sway, with international law and its institutional nexus, the League of Nations, as the main focus of research in International Studies. It was only with the weakening of the Versailles system and the increasing visibility of conflict, crisis, and war attending the spread of Fascism, Nazism, and Japanese militarism in the 1930s that Idealism as the dominant paradigm in International Studies came under criticism by Realism.

Classical Realism, which had dominated International Studies and international practice for more than two millennia, continued its primacy for 3 decades after World War II: Vasquez's designation, in his The Power of Power Politics (1983), "color it Morgenthau" (the 1st edition of Morgenthau's Politics Among Nations 1948), captured the essence of Realism's pre-eminence. Then, in a substantial revision by Waltz (1979), Neo-Realism (Structural Realism) held sway through most of the 1980s.

So awesome was Realism's stature in IR—for almost 2500 years—that the first serious intellectual challenge to its primacy avoided a frontal attack. In their initial formulation of the new antithesis, Neo-Institutionalism, Keohane and Nye (1977) tried to assert equality, not hegemony: "We do not argue...that complex interdependence faithfully reflects world political reality. Quite the contrary: both it and the realist portrait are ideal types. Most situations will fall somewhere between these two extremes." Later, with increasing confidence in Neo-Institutionalism as the superior paradigm, they and the rapidly growing

International Political Economy (IPE) community of scholars staked a claim to hegemony.

The clash of paradigms in International Studies has generated more heat than light. The initial dichotomy, Idealism vs. Realism, dominated the first three-fourths of the twentieth century. Since the late 1970s, the thesis/antithesis syndrome was expressed by Neo-Realism vs. Neo-Liberalism/Institutionalism. Other claimants to the 'true path' have staked their claim with increasing fervor and visibility: the global system paradigm, in its Neo-Marxist and long-cycle varieties; several strands of Post-Positivism, including Post-Modernism and Constructivism; the English school of Neo-Idealism, and Feminism.

The most assertive challenge to the two competing mainstream paradigms emanates from Constructivism. As Checkel noted (1998): "Constructivism...is not a theory but an approach to social inquiry [that] question[s] the materialism and methodological individualism upon which much contemporary IR scholarship has been built." In a thoughtful attempt to build a bridge between Constructivism and mainstream IR, Adler remarked: "Constructivism is the view that *the manner in which the material world shapes and is shaped by human action and interaction depends on dynamic normative and epistemic interpretations of the material world*" (1997). Moreover, "Constructivism also challenges empiricist and realist assumptions of working science" (Onuf 1989).

Early in the twenty-first century, IR–IS–WP is, I think, the skeptical beneficiary of a plethora of competing paradigms. While pluralism is a virtue, cleavage and confrontation, and ensuing confusion, are not. The paucity of serious attempts at synthesis, or at least complementarity, among contending paradigms is an indicator of deep malaise.

Perhaps the most enduring reflection about International Studies is that *'plus ca change, plus c'est la meme chose.'* World politics have changed drastically during the past three-quarters of a century—the structure of the international system and subordinate state systems, the number of member-states, the emergence of transnational and sub-national actors, the increasing importance of the economic dimension in state behavior, and many other far-reaching changes.

What has not changed, I think, is the enduring divisiveness within IR–IS–WP, which reflects a persistent immaturity. Sometimes the conflict between 'schools' is wrapped in the superficially civil discourse of a 'debate,' sometimes not. Debate, especially when it is based upon mutual respect, is healthy, even necessary in the growth of any branch

of knowledge. But confrontation that is cast in terms of a hostile we/
they syndrome, right and wrong, scientific rigor versus historical description, is an indicator of a deep malaise. This was captured with insight by
one of the major contributors to the field and, more broadly, to political
science.

"...the various schools and sects of political science now sit at separate
tables, each with its own conception of proper political science, but each
protecting some secret island of vulnerability.... We are separated along
two dimensions: an ideological one and a methodological one" (Gabriel
Almond 1990).

Where do I stand on all of the contentious matters discussed above?

1. I remain convinced that, despite the critique of Post-Modernism, **Positivism** is still a valid basis for creating and accumulating knowledge about state behavior and international system change.
2. I recognize that **nation-states** are no longer the virtually exclusive actors in the international system, the status they enjoyed during the three centuries of the Westphalia system (1648–1945). Non-state and transnational actors have come to play an increasingly important role in world politics, especially in non-military-security issue-areas. But the state is far from dead and is not likely to disappear in the foreseeable future. It is still the central actor in the important military-security issue-area, as the crises and wars of the post-Cold War world clearly demonstrate—in the Middle East, including the Persian Gulf, Yugoslavia, North Korea, Iran, and the cluster of upheavals on the periphery of the extinct Soviet Union.
3. The end of the Cold War has not ushered in the 'Nirvana' of cooperation, as evident in the ubiquity of **conflict, crisis, and war** between and within states, though the domain of cooperation has dramatically expanded during the past 25 years.
4. **Violence** played an important part in world politics in the 1990s and the early years of the new century, as in previous decades, centuries, and millennia, and is likely to continue to do so.
5. **Nationalism** has re-emerged as a primary force in world politics—in a new form, **Ethnicity,** which is manifested in the widespread demand for self-determination and secession. Ethnicity is, in fact, a late twentieth-century variation of the Goddess of Nationalism that shaped the history of Europe in the aftermath of the French Revolution and the Napoleonic Wars and, later, Asia and Africa, in

the anti-colonial Revolution that swept the world from the mid-nineteenth to the late-twentieth centuries.
6. **Parsimony** is undoubtedly a high scientific value, and, *wherever possible*, it should be sought, but it should not be forced on to the data. The *primary goal of all* **IR–IS–WP** *research* is not *parsimony* but *accuracy* in both the ***description and explanation*** *of reality*. The subject matter of crisis, conflict, and war, and, more generally, of world politics, is extraordinarily complex. To force this complexity into a single-factor explanation may be satisfying in terms of parsimony, but is it an accurate explanation of the process leading to war? The answer, in my judgment, is, No. And I would rather forego parsimony than accuracy in the explanation of any complex issue in world politics.

It would be unproductive to enter into a disquisition on who is 'right' and who is 'wrong,' for this is precisely the kind of evaluation that has been the bane of our intellectual endeavor. Suffice it to express the view that none of the contending 'schools' is wholly right or wholly wrong.

FINAL WORDS

There seems to me to be an inner logic in the metaphor of three 'hats,' and there has been a kind of natural evolution of focus throughout my Intellectual Odyssey, all guided by an enduring interest in the **Conflict** domain of world politics: I devoted 2 decades to crisis, war, and protracted conflict, as well as nation-building, in South Asia; 2 decades on crisis, war, and protracted conflict in the Arab/Israel domain of the Middle East; and 4 decades on the perennial effort to illuminate, and construct valid theory about, interstate crises and protracted conflicts. It has been an illuminating and rewarding journey, and one I would happily make again.

Appendix:
Reviews of Michael Brecher's Books

The Struggle for Kashmir (1953)

"Of the three books under review [the others were George Fischer's Soviet Opposition to Stalin and W. Macmahon Ball's Nationalism and Communism in East Asia] the most interesting and suggestive is the one which from its title might appear the least important in the general field of current international relationships. Dr. Michael Brecher's The Struggle for Kashmir is a fine piece of research. Lucidly and attractively written, it offers a penetrating analysis of the course of the Kashmir dispute, of the reasons for the intense interest of both India and Pakistan in the disposition of the state, and of the opposed points of view of the governments of the two countries which remain as yet unreconciled. In particular, the Indian case has nowhere been so clearly and persuasively presented.... Pakistan contests the validity of the original accession [of the princely state, Jammu and Kashmir, to India in October 1947] on the ground of Indian conspiracy and pressure on the Maharaja [of Jammu and Kashmir], but Dr. Brecher's careful evaluation of the evidence suggests that this thesis is unfounded....

The heart of the Kashmir dispute lies in the fact that it strikes at the foundation of the very existence of Pakistan and India alike.... If it be admitted that predominantly Muslim Kashmir may be included in India, then the reason for Pakistan's existence disappears. For India, on the other hand, to admit this communal argument would be to forswear the inter-communal, secular structure of the Indian state: it would give strength to the Hindu extremists...and would therefore endanger the foundation of the Indian state as it is at present constructed and would gravely threaten the lives of the 40 million Muslims who at present [1954] live within India's frontiers." [In 2011, there were approximately 172 million Indian Muslims, 14% of India's population].

"It is the great merit of Dr. Brecher's study that he has not merely given us a careful and detailed analysis of the niceties of the dispute, but he has been able to stand back from its complexities and place it in its broad international and philosophical setting. In so doing he has achieved his object of contributing to an understanding of this 'grave problem in contemporary Asian and Commonwealth affairs' (p. x), but he has in addition thrown much light on the problems and difficulties of the sub-continent as a whole and therefore on the part it plays on the world stage. This book should be widely read." (**P.A. Reynolds**, University College of Wales, **The Canadian Journal of Economics and Political Science**, 20, 3, August 1954, 386–388)

"This book is by a young Canadian student of international affairs...now lecturing at McGill University.... The combination of diverse experience, enthusiasm and application has produced a valuable work, which all concerned with the Kashmir problem should have for reference. The author is thorough in his collection of material and lucid in his arrangement; he displays a notable desire to be fair and conveys the impression that nothing has been deliberately suppressed or distorted on either side....

The main body of the book is concerned with the history of the dispute before the United Nations and the various attempts to reach a solution.... This part is objectively written and carefully documented. There is a most interesting chapter on Kashmir in transition...which I think one of the best in the book. The book explains clearly the issues involved, the main arguments and principal moves on either side.... Dr. Brecher rightly minimizes Mr. Nehru's personal feelings as a Kashmiri by race.... Kashmir is to Mr. Nehru a symbol of the secular political idea even more than of Indian nationalism or prestige; that is why he fights so hard for it...." (**Percival Spear**, Selwyn College, Cambridge University, **Pacific Affairs**, 27, 4, December 1954, 384–385)

"Mr. Michael Brecher has performed a very useful service in collecting the available data and giving us a clear and detailed account of the Kashmir problem. He has also furnished us with important background information...The author has been scrupulously fair.... the care and consideration with which he records the points of view of both sides.... He...supports arguments with copious references to other sources.... We are grateful to the author for a careful account of the laborious course of international negotiation. In particular, UNCIP's [the U.N. Commission on India and Pakistan's] failure to get to grips with the problem is clearly revealed.... Mr. Brecher convincingly exposes this weakness in the Commission's activities." (**Lord Birdwood** [author of a book on Kashmir in 1956], **International Affairs**, 30, 2, April 1954, 257)

"...this excellent and scholarly study of the Kashmir dispute.... The reader closes it with the conviction that he has been given an unprejudiced account of relevant historical facts and of the arguments by which both India and Pakistan have sought to justify their actions and substantiate their conflicting claims. Mr. Brecher has sifted the mass of government and United Nations documents and the books and periodical literature on the subject and has interviewed politicians and officials in India, Pakistan and Kashmir.... His book admirably meets the needs, down to April 1953, of those who wish to become acquainted with the story of the conflict." (**J.R. Aitchison, The Dalhousie Review**, 34, 1, Spring 1954)

"We are indebted to a young Canadian scholar for this useful guide through the many ramifications of the Kashmir question—the central problem in dispute between India and Pakistan and one of the great uncomprehended controversies in contemporary international relations.... Dr. Brecher has written an intelligent and objective book, based on a careful study of the pertinent documents and on first-hand observations in Kashmir, and in India and Pakistan...." (**Norman D. Palmer**, University of Pennsylvania, **The Annals of the American Academy of Political and Social Science**, vol. 294, July 1954, 166–167)

"An exhaustive review of the documentation, especially by the U.N., on this subject, plus eight months of investigation in Kashmir, Pakistan, and India, have produced a handy guide to developments within and the protracted negotiations over this contested region." (**The American Political Science Review**, XLVIII, 2, June 1954)

"Brecher concludes that this [the failure to 'bring about a solution of the conflict'] was due partly to inept handling by the international organization; but he feels that the deeper causes of the conflict make a solution possible only through an effort at direct political settlement between the contestants. The events subsequent to the writing of this book seem to bear out this conclusion.... This is a scholarly investigation of a touchy subject whose complex and emotional nature the author has succeeded in reducing to an understandable and reasonably clear study." (**Werner Levi**, University of Minnesota, **Middle East Affairs**, February 1955, 58–59)

"Among the studies of the Kashmir problem, four books stand out as the major works on the subject—The Struggle for Kashmir by Michael Brecher [1953], Danger in Kashmir by Joseph Korbel [1954], Two Nations and Kashmir by Lord Birdwood [1956], and The History of Struggle for Freedom in Kashmir by Prem Nath Bazaz [1954]. Brecher's is a doctoral dissertation and hence largely based on an objective analysis of the various documents on the subject.... The special merit of the book lies in two of its chapters—one on the internal developments in Kashmir and another on the cost of the Kashmir dispute.... It is in this book again that the ideological aspects of the Kashmir question are brought out in sharp relief.... With its objectivity and its great accuracy in the presentation of facts, Brecher's work on Kashmir deserves the closest study by anyone who attempts to understand the problem in all its aspects." (**Sisir Gupta**, Indian Council of World Affairs, "The Kashmir Question 1947-60," **International Studies**, New Delhi, III, 2, October 1961, 187)

"In this well-documented, definitive study...the author has delved deep into the source material to give an objective and penetrating analysis of 'the greatest and the gravest single issue in international affairs'." (**Narendra Kumar**, **Seminar**, No. 58, New Delhi, June 1964, 60–61)

Nehru: a Political Biography (1959)

"Any new book has to be very good indeed to justify its claim upon the attention of serious students.... It is therefore high praise of Mr. Brecher's book to state, quite plainly, that it makes a really notable contribution to the understanding both of Nehru himself and of the work which he has done for his country.... He writes with an ease which cloaks a clear perception of essentials.... The merits of the book are of a most uncommon order." (**The Times**, London, 2 July 1959)

"To draw the portrait of such a man is a tantalizingly difficult task. Mr. Nehru once attempted it himself, and only partially succeeded.... Mr. Brecher's portrait of a weaker, more human, more attractive Nehru is more complete and detailed than the self-portrait; and it is perhaps as nearly final as anything that can be done in a great man's lifetime." (**The Times Literary Supplement**, London, 3 July 1959)

"In his careful and subtle indication of how British policy and a mistaken British state of mind turned Nehru into an opponent, not always a reasonable one, of the country he could still admire, in his astute application of personal and general matter, Dr. Brecher shows himself a writer in a high class.... what he says about the career of this singular man and of the political actions in which he was involved, is entirely convincing.... the man, the predicament, the amazing story are all there...." (**Christopher Sykes**, in <u>The Spectator</u>, London, 10 July 1959)

"It is Mr. Brecher's achievement to have written a book which, despite the existing mass of material, will carry the average reader a long way forward in the understanding of both the man and his surging age.... Mr. Brecher gives us this portrait...freshly and perceptively renewed.... The second half provides an unequalled study of India's first and only Prime Minister in the years of power.... This is excellent contemporary history.... Mr. Brecher's intelligent speculations about the way ahead make up one of the most interesting sections of an unusually interesting book." (<u>The Economist</u>, London, 18 July 1959)

"...enormously exciting to read and intellectually provocative." (**Max Beloff** in <u>Encounter</u>, London, January 1960, 85–86)

"Every major British politician—and the Washington State Department experts—must read this book. I know Nehru, and Brecher's picture of him is excellent. An intensely human and humane person, his character and integrity shine out from the pages. But his many faults and failures and his dangerous indecisiveness are not glossed over." (<u>The Daily Herald</u>, London, July 1959)

"...the author has succeeded in giving us a book that...will be the definitive account of Nehru's life for some time to come. Mr. Brecher's admiration of Nehru never blinds him to his faults. His sympathy with India never leads him to underestimate the seriousness of the problems which the country faces." (**MHF**, in <u>The Financial Times</u>, London, 20 July 1959)

"Mr. Brecher has accomplished the notoriously difficult feat of writing a good biography while the subject is still alive." (**Altrincham**, in <u>The National and English Review</u>, July 1959)

"This book is a long one..., full of information which is well-documented. But it is written in an easy and attractive style and should be read by everyone interested in India's recent past. It should also be read by those who are interested to speculate regarding India's future..." (**Sir Francis Mudie**, <u>The Listener</u>, London, 1959)

"Prof. Brecher probes deeply into these and other facets of this strange political character.... It would be useful as required reading for everyone in authority at the Foreign Office." (**The Glasgow Bulletin**, 1959)

".... a valuable life of a great nationalist..., an array of interesting detail marshalled with scholarship and lucidly presented." (**John Biggs-Davison**, in **Journal of the Royal Central Asian Society**, vol. 46, issue 3–4, July–October 1959, 306)

"This large and rewarding book deserves acclaim for what it is—a welcome and valuable contribution to a fuller understanding of a complex man who governs a very complex country. The tyro in Indian affairs will find here perhaps the most complete, and certainly the most readable, panorama in a single volume of the Ages of Gandhi and of Nehru; the veteran will appreciate how masterfully the complicated story of Jawaharlal Nehru and modern India unfolds in new perspectives. Professor Brecher of McGill University has discharged a difficult task with rare skill, with an authority derived from thorough exposure to source materials and his subject and with a style unusual to a study so documented and detailed." (**Washington Post**, 28 June 1959)

"It is always a risky business to attempt a definitive biography of a living statesman.... In the case of Jawaharlal Nehru...the task becomes truly Himalayan.... Dr. Brecher boldly makes the assault on Everest.... The result is a monumental biography – well-written, carefully documented, giving as complete a picture of India's leader as anyone could hope for at this time.... Whatever the future may bring, Dr. Brecher's study will always be valuable...." (**Christian Science Monitor**, Boston, 2 July 1959)

"His authoritative biography now takes precedence over all its predecessors and even over the [Nehru] autobiography of the 1930s ("Toward Freedom"). Almost the most interesting aspect of the biography is the new light cast on Nehru's mental processes.... It is scholarly, a bit too scholarly...." (**Louis Fischer**, in **The Saturday Review**, New York)

"Both supporters and detractors will be considerably better informed from a reading of this masterful, 640-page portrait. Exhaustive research, intensive travel and hundreds of interviews have been compiled to shed considerable new light on Nehru and India.... Prof. Brecher is by no means a Nehru apologist; the Nehru weaknesses of character and manner, in fact, are clearly sketched in every instance in which the author concludes they have been a factor in history. Brecher's 'Nehru' brings both the man and his foreign policy to life. More than that, it is a meticulously detailed history of India in modern times. The author's narrative is told with skill and clarity.... The concluding assessment of India's future is valid and well-documented.... This book should be a standard work of reference in Washington." (Carter Davidson, in **Chicago Sun-Times**, 1959)

".... It is the definitive, panoramic story of India's long fight for independence.... Dr. Brecher's painstaking research seems as patient as the erosive campaign of non-violence that dissolved British rule in the Indian subcontinent.... His writing of sober and often tragic history races along like an adventure story – this one peopled with names that drop easily." (**Associated Press**)

"Judging it from the standpoint of one who has had some little knowledge of Nehru over many years [from Nehru's student days at Cambridge; moreover, 'I was with Nehru in Switzerland at the beginning of 1936, when {Nehru's wife,} Kamala, died'], I can testify that it is a scholarly and serious work. It is written with sympathy and knowledge of the Indian political background – admittedly from the viewpoint of an admirer of Nehru and the Congress, but not the less valuable for that." (**R. Palme-Dutt,** in **Daily Worker**, New York, 25 June 1959)

"With a truly remarkable grasp of detail and documentation the author gives as full a picture of the man and his time as we have seen, as indeed it is perhaps possible to reconstruct while the hero is still alive.... To read this work is to see afresh how complex the struggle [for independence] was.... Mr. Nehru comes out of it all with something akin to glory although Mr. Brecher is not to be taken as a blind admirer.... Not the least of Mr. Brecher's achievements is to remind us how Mr. Nehru, without ever fully controlling the party machine, has yet exerted unmistakable and perhaps enduring influence on the thinking process of the Congress. Mr. Brecher also provides a full portrait of the man with his many diversities, not to say contradictions.... As an analysis of some aspects of the Indian ethos...Mr. Brecher's book is admirable." (**The Sunday Statesman**, Calcutta, 5 July 1959)

"It is a monumental work.... Dr. Brecher has produced a work which does credit not only to his scholarship but also to his 'fascinating subject'.... In many ways this is an outstanding work. It is not only an impressive study of Nehru's political career but also a penetrating analysis of the currents and cross-currents of Indian politics.... Those who want to understand Nehru must read this book; it is as important a work as his autobiography itself." (**The Illustrated Weekly of India**, New Delhi)

"Dr. Brecher's is an important book. It is scholarly, erudite, critical. The illustrations...are illuminating; they bring out Mr. Nehru's dual personality in a most striking fashion.... However, Dr. Brecher's book is too long...." (**Taya Zinkin**, in **The Economic Weekly**, Bombay, 24 October 1959)

"...this informative and thought-provoking biography.... The author gives all the facts, writes quietly and justly, and succeeds brilliantly in sketching...in every significant detail the life and character of a great national leader.... It is on the whole a fair assessment, covering every aspect of Mr. Nehru's life and of his domestic and foreign policy...." (**The Times of India**, Bombay, 30 July 1961; review of the abridged edition)

"It is an indispensable book to read in order to understand modern India." (**Le Monde Diplomatique**, August 1959)

"This very substantial and scholarly biography...is probably the best single work presently available on the political career of Nehru." (**Foreign Affairs**, New York, October 1959)

".... undoubtedly the most objective and comprehensive political history of India from 1920 to 1948 at present available.... His beginning and concluding chapters on 'Portrait of the Man' and 'Portrait of a Leader' could be read separately as masterly interpretations of one of the half-dozen leading figures of our day.... Brecher deserves our gratitude for his immense job of research and his objective and skillful handling of many controversial subjects. His book will certainly stand for many years as the definitive historical account of Nehru's political career.... It should be added that Brecher writes well and organizes his chapters clearly." (**Charles H. Heimsath**, in **Yale Review**, Autumn 1959)

"This voluminous biography by a Canadian professor of political science is...an admiring one, though not unduly so. Dr. Brecher...is aware of Nehru's shortcomings but correctly dismisses them as minor in a balanced appraisal of the man.... The book offers some revealing glimpses of the man himself.... On the whole, this is an admirably documented biography...." (**The Saturday Review Syndicate**)

"Dr. Brecher has conferred credit on McGill, at which he is a professor, and his country by writing such an enormously authoritative work on the prime minister of another Commonwealth member." (**The Toronto Telegram**, 1959)

"This may well be the definitive biography of the Indian prime minister, at least for years to come.... It is the most detailed political record available. Despite its weight of material, it is not ponderous; the writing is smooth and easy to read." (**The Montreal Gazette**, 1959)

"One of the excellences of Dr. Brecher's book lies in his lucid and logical account of the mental and emotional development of a personality.... Dr. Brecher's character study is subtle, clever and completely convincing. Another excellence is the ordering of the vast amount of material, so much of it of an exceptionally complex nature.... Finally, Dr. Brecher's ability to write of Nehru and not to lose sight of India, to write of India and not to lose sight of Nehru, stamps his book with some of the greatness of its subject." (**The Saskatoon Star-Phoenix**, 1959)

"This biography is an important book for many reasons. First, its subject has attained a unique place in history.... This book gains importance also from its scope.... As a narrative of events, [it] deserves high praise for careful scholarship. As interpretation, the book bears the stamp of courage and honesty throughout...." (**Margaret W. Fisher**, in **The Annals of the American Academy of Political and Social Science**, 328, March 1960, 189–190)

".... certainly the most exhaustive examination of Nehru's life and lifetime yet to appear. At times Brecher probes even more deeply into the elusive centers of Nehru's patterns of thought and character than has been done in Nehru's own autobiographical musings.... Both Nehru and Brecher can be proud of this book.... without doubt the best biography of Nehru." (**Richard L. Park**, University of California at Berkeley, in **Pacific Affairs**, 33, 1, March 1960, 76–77)

"Dr. Brecher's book is an achievement.... The account of the period 1920–1945 is ably done.... On the second and, even more perhaps, on the third [of his stated aims – 'to make Nehru more intelligible to his admirers and critics alike' (and) to give 'some insight into the role of the outstanding individual in history'] Dr. Brecher has succeeded brilliantly.... later on will come perhaps an outstanding artistic portrait of the man; but in the probably long interval we shall be grateful for this impressive volume." (**W.H. Morris-Jones**, Durham University, in **The Journal of Asian Studies**, 19, no. 3, May 1960, 369)

"...undoubtedly the best biography of Nehru yet to appear. His book reveals a truly remarkable grasp of the main outlines, as well as of the intricate byways, of India's history during the past 40 years.... a major achievement in the art of political biography.... Brecher writes well, often with distinction.... There are remarkably few inaccuracies...." (**F.G. Carnell**, Institute of Commonwealth Studies, Oxford University, in **Political Studies**, 8, 2, June 1960, 207)

"...as a history of modern India since 1920, the work provides a highly readable and at times almost gripping narrative. The author has undoubtedly performed a most valuable service to India and to history.... He is exemplary in avoiding bias in almost every controversial issue." (**Elmer H. Cutts**, Northeastern University, in **The American Historical Review**, 65, 2, Winter 1960, 385–386)

"...the first biography which really does justice to the subject. As such, its appearance is a major publishing event. It is certainly the best life of Nehru...and it is perhaps the most readable and comprehensive single volume on modern India.... This book is a physical as well as intellectual *tour de force*." (**Norman D. Palmer**, in **The Political Science Quarterly**, 1960)

"This is a masterful biography of one of the great figures of the twentieth century.... No review can do justice to the fascinating account developed in this book. Based on meticulous research, it bears the imprint of superlative scholarship.... This is biography at its best...unlikely to be improved upon." (**Alvin Z. Rubinstein**, in **Current History**, 1960)

"...the best biography of Nehru this reviewer has read.... and [there is] probably also no better introduction to contemporary India." (**Merrill R. Goodall**, Claremont Graduate School, in **The Journal of Politics**, 22, 3, August 1960, 583)

"As for the interpretative portions of the book, a large part of them is stimulating.... In all probability Brecher's book will remain *the* biography of Nehru." (**Anthony J. Parel**, in **The Review of Politics**, 22, 4, October 1960, 581–583)

"Brecher's work is an admirable example of sensitivity, impartiality and understanding." (**M. Mujeeb**, in **India Quarterly**, New Delhi, January–March 1961)

"Up to 1959, no single book gave as adequate an impression of Indian politics as Brecher's biography.... Brecher's name for this [the Nehru-Patel] relationship, the 'duumvirate' and his insight that it is a foundation stone of constitutionalism in India are likely to become standard elements in the future literature of Indian politics and modern history.... to one who feels...that Nehru is...the living politician deserving to be called great, the book catches the grandeur and fatefulness of his role." (**Henry C. Hart**, University of Wisconsin, in **Midwest Journal of Political Science**, 5, 4, November 1961, 410–411)

"The standard work on Nehru, which is also a penetrating study, is Michael Brecher's NEHRU.... [It] is very valuable from the time of the appointment of the Simon Commission [1927]. [It] is an important source based on original material [for the national struggle, 1929–34]. [It] has great authority for the World War II period...The inner Congress history [during the transfer of power] is best given by M. Brecher in his NEHRU.... For these years as a whole ['Independence and Consolidation'] Brecher's NEHRU is a primary authority." (**Percival Spear**, **India: A Modern History**, Ann Arbor, MI: University of Michigan Press, 1961)

Among the personal communications, direct or indirect, two merit notice:

Lord Mountbatten "I have not yet had time to read your book, but I have glanced at it, and what I have seen so far leads me to feel that you have done a very fine job in writing an objective political biography of one of the greatest of Statesmen." (**letter to the author** 6 July 1959)

Lord Casey, former Governor of Bengal: "I think it [the Nehru book] is very good indeed. I have got more out of it than any book or books on India or on Nehru that I've read before." (**personal communication to the editor of Oxford University Press**, London, August 1960)

Some—but not Nehru—undoubtedly thought that my 1959 assessment was too harsh. **Nehru** did not indicate his view directly, in his brief, gracious note to me on June 27, 1959:

"Thank you for your letter of May 15 and your book which you have been good enough to send me and on which you laboured for long. I shall certainly read the book, but I fear this will have to wait for some time. One of the major disa dvantages of my present profession or calling is that it prevents me from reading much. Or, rather I should say, from reading worthwhile books. With all good wishes, Yours Sincerely, Jawaharlal Nehru."

Nehru read the book sometime in the next few months, as evident in his comments conveyed during an interview with **Taya Zinkin**, then correspondent in India for **The Economist** and **The Manchester Guardian**:

"He realizes that Dr. Brecher's criticisms are devastating, the more devastating because he is such a friendly and admiring critic; yet he feels that every criticism is justified." "The Lonely Man," (a review of NEHRU: A Political Biography), (**The Economic Weekly**, Bombay, 24 October, 1959, 1464)

A more illuminating version of Nehru's reaction to my book, as conveyed to Zinkin, was presented by her in a book on India 3 years later:

"I had been reading Brecher's Political Biography of Nehru while I was waiting, and still held the book in my hand. Nehru flopped on a sofa and apologized for being late."

"So you are reading this book. It is a good book. The only good book written about me," he sighed.

"I looked at him amazed. The book was excellent, but contained the severest indictment of the Prime Minister so far written. I said so."

'I suppose it is true,' said Nehru wearily. 'It is all fair criticism you know, and I must accept it. The only thing which really hurt me when I read the book was that Brecher made no mention of the one thing which I consider to have been my greatest contribution to India: getting the [reform] Hindu Code Bill passed into Law.'

Nehru also provided insight into his total reliance on Gandhi's leadership.

"Turning back to Brecher, I [Zinkin] said that he had criticized Nehru for letting Subhash Bose [the Bengali Congress leader and colleague/rival of Nehru in the 1930s] down in his fight against Gandhi, and asked him whether...the criticism was fair. 'It is true I did let Subhash down. I did it because I had realized that, at that stage, whatever one's views might be about the way India should develop, Gandhi was India. Anything which weakened Gandhi weakened India. So I subordinated myself to Gandhi, although I was in agreement with what Subhash was trying to do. I suppose it is right to say that I let him down. India had to come before either of us. But I think he should have mentioned the part I played in the reform of Hindu Law'."

The interview with Zinkin ended with a typical gracious Nehru gesture:

"On a sudden impulse I asked him to autograph my copy of Brecher. He looked amused: 'But I did not write it, how can I autograph it? I have never done such a thing before. 'All right, if it gives you pleasure,' and he signed his name on the fly leaf." (**Reporting India**, London: Chatto & Windus 1962, 216, 217 and 219)

"So far, Jawaharlal Nehru has been fortunate in his biographers. Perhaps Professor Brecher's great 'political biography,' written while its subject was still alive, has put the memorialists on their mettle...." (**The Times Literary Supplement**, London, in a review of Tyson's Nehru: The Years of Power, 1966)

Four decades later, a respected historian of modern India, **Leonard A. Gordon**, who received the **Watumull Prize** of the **American Historical Association**—in 1974, for his book, **Bengal: The Nationalist Movement (1876–1940)**—responded to a review by Marina C. Nussbaum of two recent biographies of Nehru:

"Nussbaum does not name any good biography of Nehru, so let me do so. *Nehru, A Political Biography* is still the most compelling biography, even though it was written in 1959, while Nehru was still alive and while the author, Michael Brecher, lacked access to some of the papers that later biographers have had." (**New Republic**, New York, 28 March–4 April, 2005)

The New States of Asia (1963)

"Asia, an area which is bound to affect world politics so seriously that we had better *not* remain as ignorant of it as most of us are, is illuminated by the first-rate 'political analysis' of Michael Brecher, whose last book was the biography of Nehru. His new collection of essays includes the clearest short survey I know of Western imperialism in Asia and the nationalist reaction it produced; also an explanation of the political instability\of many of the new Asian States; studies of several international aspects of Asian politics, including a sympathetic account of neutralism as the logical foreign policy for a newly-independent state;... Mr. Brecher's book provides an admirable short guide to the forces shaping the future of Asian and, in fact, world politics." (**Roger Morgan**, **Tribune**, London, 21 February, 1964)

"Some perceptive comments on neutralism...and the role of the states of South and South-East Asia in world politics generally are to be found in Professor Brecher's book, The New States of Asia. His conclusions... will, I hope, serve to encourage people to undertake a careful reading of the rest of the book." (**Malcolm Caldwell**, **Peace News**, London, 27 March, 1964)

"...concise and well presented. Brecher's analysis of the general causes of political instability is especially good.... He writes with authority and obvious sympathy on India, without, however, doing less than justice to Pakistan.... a crisply written volume for which many readers may well be thankful." (**The American Historical Review**, 1965, 70, 2, 499–502)

Nehru's Mantle/Succession in India (1966)

"This is a courageous book for an academic to write.... It is of absorbing interest and will provide the historian with a wealth of material which might otherwise have been lost forever." (**The Times Literary Supplement**, London, 1966)

"Ever since he wrote his massive biography of Nehru, Professor Brecher has taken an almost proprietary interest in the survival of Indian democracy.... [His sanguine enthusiasm] overrides all the impediments Delhi puts in the way of anyone looking for political truth. His inquisitorial function is now accepted...by most Indian leaders. With these advantages, Mr. Brecher has written a marvelous book about the two occasions on which India has had to choose a new Prime Minister. It is by no means addressed exclusively to the author's brother political scientists....and should be found absorbing by anyone at all interested in the nature of the world's biggest democracy and its prospects." (**The Observer**, London, 1966)

"*Succession in India* is a fascinating work..." (**International Affairs**, London, 1966)

"Dr. Brecher is always stimulating to read and this latest book of his by and large justifies the publishers' claim that it is a unique contribution to the understanding of decision-making and change at the summit of government.... it is superbly well-informed and very acutely written." (**Royal Central Asian Review**, London, 1967)

"This book offers a more detailed and accurate picture of the interrelationships between the upper levels of the Indian political establishment than has ever before appeared in print. It is a major achievement." (**Richard L. Park, The Annals of the American Academy of Political and Social Science**, 371, 1967, 238–239)

"This vivid, incisive account of the Nehru and Shastri successions is without doubt the best single account of Indian politics at work in a crisis situation. More than that, it provides insights into the functioning of the

Congress Party, both as an institution and as an arena for a remarkable collection of political leaders from all areas of the country that are lacking in some of the more recent studies of politics in India." (**Asian Survey**, University of California, Berkeley, 6, 12, December 1966)

"Brecher succeeds in reconstructing in a fascinating manner, at times minute by minute, the unfolding of events following Nehru's death and those leading to a selection of a new leader... an important landmark in contemporary Indian political history." (**The American Political Science Review**)

"An important contribution by a mature scholar.... A good portion of his materials comes directly from interviews with the leading participants, so there is an authenticity and vitality so often lacking in such a contemporary work." (**The Asian Student**)

"The story is not only admirably told but the learning, perceptiveness and analytical skill brought to bear on the subject are truly exceptional.... Indispensable for every student of Indian politics.... Mr. Brecher...has once again demonstrated that he is unrivalled as a learned commentator on the Nehru era." (**Choice**)

"This book contains some of the most perceptive and insightful analyses yet written on the post-independence political system of India, and includes a substantial amount of new data.... a most important and valuable volume." (**Ralph H. Retzlaff**, **The Journal of Asian Studies** 26, 4, 1967, 722–724)

India and World Politics: Krishna Menon's View of the World (1968)

"The principal source for this excellent new book by Professor Brecher is the record of an extended talk between the author and Mr. Krishna Menon, dated November 1964 and May 1965. These lively and informative exchanges have an admirable edge.... Most of this fascinating and tremendously readable book consists in the tape-recorded dialogue. The subjects dealt with are those which anyone interested in the history of India since 1947 must consider important." (**The Times Literary Supplement**, London, 1968)

"Whenever the storm-clouds of the past darken Mr. Krishna Menon's recollection...his hatred of the American leaders he knew flashes out like lightning. It lividly illuminates this long and fascinating dialogue between the Canadian biographer of Nehru and the most articulately embittered of all Modern India's discarded political giants. For 17 hours Mr. Brecher examined Mr. Menon over the rotating tapes. Perhaps nobody but Mr. Brecher could have pulled off this scoop.... He has studied Indian affairs for years and is now accepted by most of the Indian hierarchy as a friend of the family. He shows no evident fear of Mr. Menon's notoriously short temper. He probably knows more about the first two decades of India's independence than anyone except Mr. Menon, with the result that this record of their exchanges is both revealing and dramatic." (**The Observer**, London, 1968)

"One of the exciting but as yet uncharted areas of study is the personality and perceptions of top level decision makers.... there are almost no systematic studies primarily devoted to this problem. The book under review here is an attempt to move in this direction.... That the book is not entirely successful should not detract from the significant fact that Mr. Brecher has blazed new paths for further investigation.... The character of Menon emerges in sharp and distinctive outline.... Once begun, I found the book impossible to put down. This is clearly the principal contribution of the study: an indispensable insight into the mind of a major world leader...." (**Dina Zinnes**, **The American Political Science Review**, 56, December 1969, 192–193)

Almost 40 years later, an Indian commentator marked the approaching 110th [really, the 111th] anniversary of Menon's birth and recalled my Menon book as follows: "I have read no more remarkable exposition of the mindset of the first generation of India's nationalist leaders than Krishna Menon's magisterial interviews with the Canadian political scientist, Michael Brecher, published in 1968 as a book entitled India and World Politics: Krishna Menon's View of the World. It is difficult to think of an Indian leader other than Nehru who would have been capable of the extensive discourse on world affairs, human history and international politics that Menon so magisterially managed." (**Shashi Tharoor**, "An Unusual Life," **The Hindu**, New Delhi, 29 April 2007)

The Foreign Policy System of Israel (1972)

Winner of the Woodrow Wilson Foundation Book Award of the American Political Science Association in 1973, for "the best book on politics, government and international relations published in the United States during the preceding year."

"...his monumental analysis of *The Foreign Policy System of Israel*.... Professor Brecher is one of the rare contemporary theoreticians who maintains a full interest in real life and applies his theories and models to it. His book...is not only a case-study of decision-making analysis but also the fullest and most comprehensive book on the actual making of Israel's foreign policy." (**J. Frankel**, University of Southampton, in **Political Studies**, 20, 3, 1972, 375–377)

"...a combination of meticulous research, comprehensive use of documentary sources and interviews, and impressive marshaling of data guarantees the author that his effort will endure as a standard for future researchers and as a starting point for subsequent study or debate.... Perhaps the best chapters in the book are those devoted to penetrating character studies of Israel's foreign policy elite...." (**A.S. Klieman**, Tel Aviv University, in **The Middle East Journal**, 27, 1, 1973, 84–86)

"This is a seminal work by an outstanding political scientist who has constructed an exquisite model and tested it in the study of the experience of a small new state with an unusually pervasive foreign policy system and baffling problems of external relations that stubbornly resist positive normalization. If sound, the model should have general application; and whether sound or not, it cannot help but excite foreign-policy theorizers. Nothing like it has ever been attempted for Israel or indeed for any other...state.... The model will doubtless spark other case studies.... The thumbnail biographies are truly brilliant. The process of foreign policy formulation and execution is also elucidated with enviable precision." (**J. C. Hurewitz**, Columbia University, in **The American Political Science Review**, 67, 2, 1973, 705–707)

"In the context of Israel's sometimes morbid proclivity towards secrecy, his range of inquiry and his accumulation of primary evidence are impressive.... In brief, this is not a book for weekend reading. Nevertheless, it does break new paths and should be examined by all who seek to contribute to the development of an inclusive model for the study of foreign policy in motion." (**J. C.Hurewitz**, Columbia University, in **Survival**, London, May–June 1973, 151–152)

"Michael Brecher has undertaken a mammoth and most original task – to analyze, down to what seems to be very minor detail, the foreign policy 'system' of a single state.... the book makes fascinating reading, for it contains a vast accumulation of knowledge which is never dead or even dull. The author combines freshness of outlook with depth of knowledge and sureness of judgment. Especially good are his studies of the Israeli leaders who have made, and are mostly still making, a major contribution to the formulation and conduct of foreign affairs...." (**T. Prittie** in <u>International Affairs</u>, London, 49, 2, 1973, 294–295)

"Already an established scholar on India and the politics of Asia, Professor Brecher...has firmly established the parameters within which Israeli foreign policy must take form.... In the light of his painstaking scholarship, once these parameters have been outlined, it is difficult to fault them. If one were only interested in the substantive findings of the book, it would be most useful. However, it is also a significant attempt to be conceptually consistent and methodologically rigorous in an area of discourse that is marked by ambiguous and speculative thinking...." (**R. H. Pfaff**, University of Colorado, **The Journal of Politics**, 34, February 1973, 1295–1296)

"Of outstanding interest in...this fascinating and detailed study...are the studies of the Israeli leaders who have made, or are still making, the crucial decisions in the formulation of foreign policy – Ben-Gurion..., Golda Meir..., and Moshe Sharett in the past, Dayan, Eban, Allon, Sapir and Peres today." (**International Relations**, London, May 1973, 320–321)

"Among the nation-states of the world, Israel is unique.... Approximately paralleling the uniqueness of the subject, we now have a unique book.... The conceptual basis of the study is systems analysis.... Brecher makes use of an impressive variety of research techniques.... He is refreshingly candid and impartial in his analysis and evaluations.... The evidence of a decade of scholarship is manifest.... Aside from sheer comprehensiveness, this study has many strengths. The analysis highlights the tensions and polarities of Israeli foreign policy.... These are relatively minor flaws in a work that I recommend as not only highly competent, but exceptionally informative and incisive." (**Frank Tachau**, University of Illinois at Chicago Circle, **The Western Political Quarterly**, 26, 1, March 1973, 183–186)

"In the constant underlying debate between social scientists and humanists.... Professor Brecher has made a valuable contribution toward bridging the two approaches. His large work presents a rigorous research design which uses input-output systemic analysis.... The study is a *sine qua non* for any scholar who is involved in Israeli politics and institutions, and for Middle East specialists in international relations.... The book, long and detailed, has become the cornerstone of scholarship in this field." (**A. Avi-Hai**, Hebrew University of Jerusalem, <u>The Political Science Quarterly</u>, September 1973, 537–539)

"...an indispensable handbook for studying the Palestine conflict, as well as a good case study in FP (foreign policy) analysis.... Brecher has rendered a great service to students of the conflict. It is to be hoped that studies of this quality and scope will be conducted concerning Arab policy, at which time this book will be invaluable as a model." (**D.W. Littlefield**, Library of Congress and Georgetown University, in <u>The Journal of Palestine Studies</u>, 1, 3 (1972), 110–113)

"A monumental 10-year study, an information-packed, well-documented handbook, and a model for studies on other countries." (**Littlefield**, in <u>Library Journal</u>, May 1972)

"This new book [by Michael Brecher] is an inquiry on a grand scale. It is indeed nothing less than a total dissection of a Foreign Policy System.... The result of the investigations of the author is a very valuable book for our understanding of Israel and her foreign policy. Every scholar working on the modern history of the Middle East has to handle this important book day after day." (<u>Bibliotheca Orientalis</u>, XXIX, 1–2, Jan–March 1972, 111)

"Apart from its contribution to the recent history of the Middle East, this excellent book provides a method that can be applied, with profit, to other cases of foreign policy," (<u>Revue Francaise de Science Politique</u>, Paris, June 1972)

"...the study of foreign policy tends to be deficient in theoretical content and analytical rigor. The book under review represents a commendable attempt to overcome these deficiencies...The result is a definitive study which is original in conception and brilliant in execution..., this stupendous inquiry.... Professor Brecher's is a monumental work which merits serious attention of students of Israel politics and of foreign policy in general." (**M.S. Agwani**, Jawaharlal Nehru University, in <u>India Quarterly</u> [New Delhi], October–December 1972, 389–391)

"This book presents information on the internal political elite of Israel which has never before been published.... For the political scientist... the book represents a virtual breakthrough in foreign policy analysis, a coherent, clearly detailed, new mode of political analysis...This, then, is an undeniably crucial book in the literature on Israel. This writer can only encourage others to study this volume and attempt to utilize both its insights and its methodology...." (**H. S.**, **Genesis 2**, 18 May 1972)

"This first volume of a projected two-volume work (the second will scrutinize specific foreign policy decisions) is in itself a tour de force that has emerged from many years of research and interviewing in Israel. It is a thorough, comprehensive, scholarly probing of the policy-making process (and its matrix) as it has functioned during the first 20 years of Israel's existence. No serious discussion of the topic today can ignore the rich store of data and analyses Prof. Brecher has afforded us." (**New Outlook** [Tel Aviv], 16, 2 (139), February 1973, 42–46)

"This is so excellent a book that I regret to have to draw attention to its one irritating defect.... If it were not for this methodological screen it would be immediately clear that Professor Brecher has made a profound and perceptive study of the makers and executants of Israel's foreign policy, of the influences contributing to their attitudes and of the ideas which have inspired their domestic critics.... It is to be hoped that this book will find an audience among the makers of opinion and of policy in the Arab countries.... he promises a second volume in which the more important of those [Israeli] decisions will be explored in depth. I trust we shall not have long to wait." (**Harold Beeley**, **Middle East International**, March 1973, 34)

"This book is one of the modern books dealing with Israel's foreign policy within a systemic framework. This book according to our knowledge is the first one written in English.... This book is a new addition to the system of research in international relations. Nevertheless, the author tends to get the Israeli view." (**International Politics**, Cairo, March 1973)

"A massive, monumental, disturbing and very worth-while book," (**C. Alpert**, Executive Vice-Chairman, the Haifa *Technion* Board of Governors, in **Jewish Bookland**, March 1973)

"The work is the first major scholarly analysis of Israel's foreign policy system.... Much of Professor Brecher's work consists of an extremely original and far-ranging analysis of the environment in which decisions relative to foreign policy are made and the processes by which decisions are reached.... Brecher's ['pioneering'] study concludes with some trenchant criticisms of Israeli foreign policy decisions." (**David Shermer**, a Research Student at the London School of Economics, in **Millennium**, London, 11, 2, 1973, 113–117)

"…. Brecher…has now presented us with the first volume of his profound work…. Prof. Brecher has broken new ground, and for that alone he deserves to be commended, though, naturally enough, such a deviation from the beaten track ['a historical narrative"] is bound to evoke justified criticism as well…. an excellently written chapter on the global system in which Israel had to develop her foreign policy…. In an excellent chapter, he describes Jewishness as the dominant factor in the attitudinal prism of Israel's foreign policy decision-makers…. The chapter on Ben-Gurion and Sharett makes fascinating reading…. My main critical remark…pertains to its time-limits ['the first two decades of Israel's existence']. Finally, the book is overloaded with details…. In spite of these shortcomings, Prof. Brecher's study deserves high commendation. The patient and critical reader will be highly rewarded by the host of information, well-documented, as well as stimulated by the author's analytical and critical approach." (**Chaim Yahil**, a former Director-General of Israel's Foreign Ministry, in **The Jerusalem Post**, 13 July 1973)

"Another pioneering contribution in this and other respects ['an analytical prism of a universal application'] was…Michael Brecher's monumental study of *The Foreign Policy System of Israel*…. Brecher's theoretical endeavor was met with mixed reactions. But the importance of his substantive contribution was widely acclaimed. After two decades of partial, patchy, parochial and often amateurish descriptions of the Israeli experience the intellectual reader at last had a comprehensive, painstakingly detailed and exceedingly systematic analysis." (**I.S. Lustick**, Dartmouth College, "The Study of Israel's National Security," in **Books on Israel**, Vol. I, The Association for Israel Studies, 1988, p. 67)

Decisions in Israel's Foreign Policy (1974, 1975)

"…the case studies [provide] a lucid and fascinating account of actors, motives and events…. In the detailed account of the history of each crisis decision, the language is clear…and the lay reader will find himself both gripped and instructed. For me, having lived through that period as a diplomat, much is revealed by Professor Brecher's detailed and painstaking research which was hitherto new…. Brecher's obviously impartial account…. Brecher deals with the various crises facing Israel's decision-makers with great sympathy and understanding. Any serious student of Middle East affairs will profit greatly by a thorough study of his book – not least the experts of the [British] Foreign Office who could learn a lot about the likely behavior of Israel's decision-makers in the many and complex decisions to be faced in the future." (**Michael Hadow**, a former British Ambassador to Israel, <u>The Jewish Observer and Middle East Review</u>, London, 20 December 1974)

"...the essential character of this masterful book [is] the tracing, the delineation, the analysis of external and internal forces, playing on one another, that have led Israel's decision-makers into the directions they have taken since the formation of the state....What he has to say, for instance, about the decision to make Jerusalem Israel's capital in 1949 – despite objection from the United Nations, the United States and much of the world – and later to annex East Jerusalem, is a chapter that by itself serves as a guide to help us understand present-day decisions.... The general public...will benefit enormously from the fresh material, Brecher's erudition, clarity of expression and his insight from long residence in Israel.... But insight alone, without systematic analysis, is a fickle guide. Brecher's analysis is brilliant, as he proved earlier in his companion volume, <u>The Foreign Policy System of Israel</u>.... Basically this is an objective study of why and how Israel confronts crucial issues. But Brecher is not unsparing when he sees the need, to criticize. At times he finds shortcomings in Israeli foreign policy due to a lack of long-range planning or, worse, no planning at all...An understanding of contemporary Israeli attitudes is incomplete without <u>Decisions in Israel's Foreign Policy</u>." (**Gerald Clark**, "Analytical Erudition," **The Montreal Star**, 22 March 1975, D3)

"A monumental work in which six major foreign policy decisions taken by the Israeli government between 1949 and 1970 are analyzed. A thorough, well-documented volume that brings to light hitherto unpublished materials." (**Frank X.J. Homer**, "A Spring Bookmark," **America**, 26 April 1975, 327)

"Brecher clearly substantiates his thesis that the key to dissecting state behavior is the analysis of the decision makers' perceptions.... his massive, meticulous, and sometimes exciting presentation.... Foreign policy theorists and close students of Israeli politics will doubtless enjoy here an intellectual treat of the highest order, and...the general reader will find a feast of factual information.... A pioneering achievement in both foreign policy theory and contemporary history, this seminal work (along with its companion volume) should be in all advanced undergraduate and graduate libraries." (**Choice**, July–August 1975, pp. 667–668)

"...the comprehensive synthesis and profound insights offered by Professor Brecher, along with his massive documentation, bibliographies, indices, and appendixes, are extremely valuable and seemingly definitive.... By whatever judgment, this work is an encyclopedic piece of scholarship...and written with wisdom and expertise...." (**Herbert Rosenblum**, Hebrew College, **The Annals of the American Academy of Political and Social Science**, 421, September 1975, pp. 157–158)

"The first part of his [Brecher's] objective ["to illuminate a particular issue"] he achieves with remarkable precision. Military readers will especially value his dissection of the Six-Day War decision.... The book should become an invaluable tool for understanding the Middle East, and Israel's position in it." (Col. **Donald J. Delaney**, **Military Review**, LV, 10, October 1975, p. 103)

"Brecher's work...is the most complete study yet made of the personalities and forces at work in the determination of Israeli foreign policy. It is particularly welcome since it lays open to examination the multitudinous groups and attitudes that comprise the Israeli state of mind." (**Melvin I. Urofsky**, Virginia Commonwealth University, **Midstream**, October 1975, p. 80)

"Michael Brecher has produced a scholarly tour de force.... The case studies...also illuminate the internal decision making process.... The book is a model of scholarship in international relations.... It is praiseworthy for its painstaking and fully documented research, the multiple streams of evidence – both written and oral – and its presentation of the evidence within a dynamic framework.... No other work exists in the field which is as comprehensive and as successful in providing a framework and then utilizing it." (**Jewish Social Studies**, 1975, pp. 352–353)

"Using an elaborate theoretical framework for studying the making of foreign policy, the author examines in detail the domestic and external considerations that went into seven key decisions during Israel's first 25 years as a state. A richness of detail and insight, a thoroughness of investigation, and a soundness of judgments make this a valuable study." (**Alvin Z. Rubinstein**, University of Pennsylvania, **Current History**, January 1976, p. 30)

"...Michael Brecher's erudite and meticulous study...represents a valuable effort to dissect the sources of conflict in the region.... Professor

Brecher's evaluations, based on some of the most advanced social science research techniques are exemplary. In addition, he handles the problems head-on and makes no effort to hide behind political exegeses... [He also provides] a fascinating portrayal of the conceptual world of Israeli decision makers...." (**Amos Perelmutter**, American University, **Times Literary Supplement** (London), 29 October 1976, p. 1369)

"...two years later [after *The Foreign Policy System* volume] Brecher proceeded to publish a sequel focusing on the genesis of a whole series of critical decisions in Israel's foreign and national security policy. This second volume, *Decisions in Israel's Foreign Policy*, was for the author a systematic application of the theory which had been proposed in the previous [1972] volume. But for his readers it was also, and perhaps primarily, a series of breathtakingly documented monographic studies showing how Israel conducted its relations with the rest of the world, chief of all with its neighbors." (**I.S. Lustick**, Dartmouth College, "The Study of Israel's National Security," in **Books on Israel**, Vol. I, the Association for Israel Studies, 1988, 68)

Israel, The Korean War and China: Images, Decisions, and Consequences (1974)

One review of **Israel, the Korean War and China**, by an Israeli specialist on China, was drawn to my attention years later:

"Although some details of Israel's exchanges with China have been revealed and published elsewhere, this study is indubitably the most thorough, detailed and penetrating to date. It relies heavily on the Israeli Foreign Ministry archives...and on elaborate interviews and communications with most of those who had taken part in the decision-making." (**Yitzhak Shichor**, **The China Quarterly**, vol. 66, 1975, pp. 388–390)

Decisions in Crisis: Israel, 1967 And 1973 (1980)

When **Decisions in Crisis** was published, it received the assessment of two renowned scholars in International Relations. One was a pioneer in the neo-functionalist theory of international organization and a mentor of the creators of neo-institutionalism as a paradigm in IR, *Ernst Haas*, of the University of California at Berkeley:

"Case studies of international crises are usually written as history or biography; they rarely reflect theoretical perspectives of studies in social psychology, organizations, and decision-making. This book combines the best of all. It gives us the most complete insight into how Israel copes with crises. More important, it provides a sophisticated method for the comparative study of crises. The book is a major achievement."

The other commentary was by *Robert C. North*, a pioneer in the study of international crises, creator of the Stanford Studies in Conflict and Integration in the 1960s and 1970s:

"This book is a landmark in the literature on international crisis. In illuminating the perceptions and behavior of a particular state in crisis, Brecher has also made a major contribution to the fields of foreign policy, decision-making, and the broad dynamics of conflict and war. *Decisions in Crisis* will be required reading for all persons interested in international relations and contemporary world politics."

"…an impressive array of sources, although the primary ones are mostly Israeli…. The theoretical construct is provocative and worthy of serious debate…. All academic levels." (**Choice**, vol. 18, p. 308, October 1980)

"The work is engaging and fascinating. A number of startling revelations give some insight into the most sensitive decisions that led to war… The guts of international diplomacy, bargaining and negotiations are laid bare here. *Decisions in Crisis* will prove to be a touchstone for further research in crisis decision making."(S.R. Silverburg."(**Library Journal**, vol. 105, p. 514, February 15, 1980)

The Qualitative, Case Studies Segment of the ICB Project

The most comprehensive assessment was **J. L. Richardson**'s review article, "New Insights on International Crises" in the **Review of International Studies** (London), 1988, 14, pp. 309–316:

Michael Brecher…is not the only scholar who has recently sought both to extend the data base and to deepen the theoretical understanding of international crises, but his is the project of greatest scope—indeed, it must rank as one of the major social science undertakings of the present decade….

The five volumes [by Brecher-Geist, Shlaim, Dowty, K. Dawisha, and Jukes] provide an example of a rare phenomenon, a group of distinguished scholars working with a common concept, organizing their studies in accordance with a common format, and addressing the same central research questions....

Brecher formulates the central question for his own book, and thus for the series as a whole, as follows: 'What is the impact of changing stress, derived from changes in the perceptions of threat, time pressure, and the probability of war, on (a) the processes and mechanisms through which decision makers cope with crisis; and (b) their choices, [specifically] the effects of changing crisis-induced stress: on information..., on consultation..., on decisional forums, on alternatives....'

If the format and questions are the same, the crises covered in the five volumes are of strikingly different types.... The answers to the questions on cognitive performance, information and alternatives...are of the greatest significance for the theoretical understanding of crises....

When the conclusions of the five works are placed together, they point to the need for a radical revision of previously accepted hypotheses, which Brecher refers to as the 'consensus findings,' on the effects of stress on crisis decision making.... The five case studies offer a resounding disconfirmation of this [Holsti-George 1975] view of the effects of stress in crises...None of the authors finds that there was a *general* increase in cognitive rigidity during the crises.... The authors find very frequent recourse by decision makers to the lessons of past experience, but much less evidence that this adversely affected their decisions...There was no *general* tendency for decision makers to overlook options.... The analysis of options...more often than not was characterized by the author as careful, reasonable or responsible, viewing the crisis as a whole.... Implicit in Brecher's conclusions, and explicit in those of Shlaim and Dowty, is the suggestion that, contrary to the received view, stress may have positive effects on crisis decision-making....

The central finding of the early volumes of the ICB series, then, is that crisis-induced stress did not have the pervasive, adverse consequences for coping which one of the more prominent theories of crisis decision-making would lead one to expect.... The 'effects of stress' theory may well amount to over-generalization from a single crisis, the July 1914 crisis, in much the same way as many contemporary notions of crisis management can plausibly be seen as over-generalizations from a different case, the Cuban missile crisis. It will be ironic if the principal outcome of the ICB series should be the final discrediting of the theory which provided its central research hypotheses, but so decisive an empirical finding, albeit of a negative kind, would also be a tribute to the power of the methodology of the ICB Project....

...one may conclude that, *in general*, decision-makers cope with crises more satisfactorily than psychological theories of decision-making under stress have postulated.... Disaster is not typical, but it is possible....

Over and above their immediate contribution to the ICB Project, comprehensive and insightful studies of decision-making, such as these five volumes, offer much material for researchers interested in exploring further questions as well. Thus they may contribute to the larger ambition of the ICB Project, "to facilitate the avoidance of crises or their effective management so as to minimize the adverse effects on global order."

Crises in the Twentieth Century: Vol. I, Handbook of International Crises (1988), Vol. II, Handbook of Foreign Policy Crises (1988), Vol. III, Crisis, Conflict and Instability (1989)

On the first two volumes: "This set will become a standard reference work for studies of crisis in the 20th century. Although aimed primarily at the research needs of graduate students and faculty, advanced undergraduates engaged in research will find it valuable, especially the narrative summaries of the individual crises." (**R.J. Stoll**, Rice University, <u>Choice</u>, November 1988, p. 565)

"After more than 20 years of work, M. Brecher and his colleagues have finally erected the monument to quantitative knowledge of international politics. Those who have always differentiated between political science and international relations, based on the experimental nature of the former and the evaluative nature of the latter should finally change their minds as a result of this impressive research in the field.... This monumental work could truly be, if correctly utilized, representative of a grand historical occasion for the growth of theory, and not only empirical research, of international relations." (**Luigi Bonanate**, University of Turino, <u>Teoria Politica</u>, No. 2, 1988)

On the third volume, <u>Crisis, Conflict, and Instability</u>, Choice commented: "An important addition to any collection on international crises and war" (July–August 1990)

And on the three-volume set, Crises in the Twentieth Century: "These three volumes form one of the two tiers of a monumental research project on international crisis behavior. The International Crisis Behavior (ICB) project supplies the most comprehensive and complete Dataset...on the phenomenon of international crises for the period 1929-1979.... The project has succeeded remarkably in bridging the gap between aggregate data-based research and case studies oriented research and integrating their results ...no competition in available data banks.... The data is organized in a user-friendly form that is easy to read and comprehend.

It would be impossible to summarize here the enormous amount of systematic descriptive information that is presented. Two things are worth noting... the innovative and sophisticated measurement of crisis severity.... And the concise summaries of each crisis case....

The ICB Project is without doubt one of the most ambitious and important research enterprises of the last decade in the social sciences and perhaps the most impressive research project of its kind in the field of international relations. The magnitude, significance and quality of the present three volumes testify to this..., an indispensable contribution to significantly extending the boundaries of our knowledge of the critical phenomenon of international crisis behavior." (**Yaacov Vertzberger**, Hebrew University of Jerusalem, **Jerusalem Journal of International Relations**, vol. 12, no. 4, December 1990)

CRISES IN WORLD POLITICS (1993)

"Michael Brecher's work on international crises is the closest that international relations get to a Lakatosian scientific research program. For over 25 years, he has worked on international crises.... This book represents his attempt to synthesize the findings from that work..., no easy task given the fact that ICB has involved some ten detailed case-studies, based on what Brecher terms 'structured empiricism,' and Brecher and associates have undertaken several major studies of aggregate data on crises.... In this book Brecher not only attempts to pull together the work undertaken by the ICB project, but also wants to use it to develop a unified theory of crisis behavior.

Brecher's structure is admirably clear....

This is a most impressive book. Brecher's conclusions tend to support a realist account of international behavior, since internal differences seemed to have little effect on foreign policy in crises. However, it is impossible to do justice to the wealth of his findings in a short review. In truth, there are questions over whether or not he can succeed in uniting the two models since they are based on such distinct and perhaps incommensurable views of the social world. But these worries must not be allowed to detract from what is a definitive work on crisis behavior which does a superb job of synthesizing a mass of aggregate data and ten separate case-studies. This is both a fitting tribute to Brecher's pioneering role in the study of crisis and an exemplary piece of scholarship. This book is absolutely required reading for anyone interested in crisis behavior, and contains enormous insights for policy-makers as to how they actually cope in crises." (**Steve Smith**, University of Wales, **International Affairs**, London, 70, 3, July 1994, p. 520)

"*Crises in World Politics* is a major contribution to the understanding of international crises in several respects. First, its conception of crises as multi-phase processes is very important to the understanding of this phenomenon....

Second, the study offers a wealth of empirical findings on the various factors that are involved in the initiation, escalation, termination, and consequences of international crises....

Third, at each stage of the study, the analysis and discussion are sensibly related to the extant literature, and thus we get a good sense of what we know that is new, what is confirmed, and what is disconfirmed in terms of previous research on crises.... Overall, we are now in a much better position to evaluate empirical knowledge on crises than we were in the past....

This book is must reading for anyone interested in understanding international crises in the twentieth century. The conception of crisis, the wealth of evidence and the case studies make this study one of the most comprehensive sources on this important phenomenon.... No serious student of international relations can afford to overlook this important work." (**Zeev Maoz**, Tel Aviv University, **Mershon International Studies Review**, 38, 2, October 1994, pp. 332–337)

"That question [can the 'enormously varied episodes reveal any patterns about the conditions under which crises escalate and become violent'] drives this ambitious work. To conduct the inquiry, Brecher constructs and tests separate models for crises at both the state and the international-system levels and then merges them into a unified model. The result is a general model designed to explain twentieth-century crises that involved a risk of war or expansion of an existing violent conflict....

The conceptualization of crises at two levels—international and state—is one of the many innovative features of this volume....

For multiple reasons, Brecher's book will be an essential touchstone for the study of crises for years to come. It provides a comprehensive review of much relevant scholarship and case material. It offers an impressive interplay of insights from both crisis case studies and findings presented as descriptive statistics from a major aggregate dataset. It advances an inventive multilevel and multistage approach that includes the often-neglected deescalation and impact phases; and the latter stage makes the case for why crises can be critical for both states and the international system. Finally, it presents a number of findings, including puzzles and unconfirmed expectations, that should stimulate considerably more research" (**Charles F. Hermann**, Ohio State University, **The American Political Science Review**, 89, 3, September 1995, pp. 796–797)

"Michael Brecher's overview and analysis of the findings from the International Crisis Behavior (ICB) project is the most ambitious attempt so far to integrate the multitude of approaches in all the subfields of crisis research.... Brecher admirably brings together the various aspects of crises covered in the ICB project.

However, "*Crises in World Politics* is more than a mere summary of this project. It is also a masterful interweaving of theoretical approaches, datasets and methods. This work is certain to become a classic for scholars in all areas of crisis research" (**Mats Hammarstrom**, Uppsala University, **The Journal of Peace Research**, 32, 2, 1995, pp. 233–238)

"The author's primary objective is 'to create a theory of crisis and crisis behavior.'" He is secondarily concerned with enhancing policy-makers' abilities to cope with decision-making under stress. Consequently, this work contributes to both the literature on conflict management and on crisis decision-making.... [It] makes some important contributions to the study of crisis decision-making....

Brecher's findings support the rational school. He found that despite tremendous variation in the causes of the crises and the actors involved, and despite large cultural, political and historical differences, policy-makers reacted to crises in a strikingly similar pattern. Brecher explains these findings with the concept of 'commonality,' in which he argues that all states seek survival, and that all humans act comparably in situations of impending harm. During crises, these fundamental similarities outweigh all other differences.

Of even greater interest is Brecher's finding that these policy-makers responded to crises in roughly the way the rational actor school predicts they would.... Under increasing levels of stress...they were more active in their search for more information..., consulted a wider circle of sources. Leaders also tended to develop and carefully evaluate alternative policy options.... This work, therefore, challenges one of the central tenets of crisis decision-making literature: the assumption that policy-makers perform poorly under stress. Brecher's tome is a significant step toward 'making order out of chaos'" (**Beth A. Fischer**, University of Toronto, **Political Psychology**, 16, 2, June 1995, pp. 437–439)

A STUDY OF CRISIS (1997, 2000)

"This book not only provides an important data resource that will be used by many researchers, but breaks new theoretical ground, especially in the use of its strong empirical base. Theoretically this book is important, not only in its substantive findings, but in the central issues dealt with." **Manus Midlarsky**, Rutgers University (Assessment to the publisher)

"This volume makes available to scholars the most comprehensive dataset on international crises in the 20th century.

This dataset is a great asset for scholars who intend to do basic research in crises. In addition, a description of each crisis is provided, which is of immense value to scholars working with the dataset." **Paul Huth**, University of Michigan (Assessment to the publisher)

"...the many scholars with a taste for large N studies seeking major relationships through standard forms of analysis will find the book a godsend. This volume is the most comprehensive survey we have of international crises..., an enormous amount of detailed research that should prove invaluable to other students of international politics..., a superb source book and a prod to further research" (**Robert Jervis**, Columbia University, **The Canadian Journal of Political Science**, 31,4 1998, pp. 826–827)

"The ICB project has been one of the most important in international relations. The project has published significant quantitative studies and in-depth case studies. Much of this work has been reviewed and built-upon in Brecher's *Crises in World Politics: Theory and Reality*, which is probably the project's theoretical magnum opus.

ICB data. now represent one of the two most important data collections scholars have for testing hypotheses about crises and war...This book is an exemplar for current and future data collectors on how to present their data.

The book is a milestone in crisis research that other projects should strive to equal.... The book also provides new findings on the factors associated with crisis escalation to war and the role played by third parties in bringing about the non-violent resolution of crises....

Given the scientific rigor with which the data have been assembled and the care that has been taken in the case summaries, this book should be in most reference libraries (public and academic...)" (**John Vasquez**, Vanderbilt University, **International Studies Review**, 1, 1, 1999, p. 126)

"This is surely the definitive reference book on international crises The extraordinary breadth and detail of the information in this massive volume is impressive and the effort no less than heroic" (**Fen Hampson**, Carleton University, **International Journal**, 53, 4, 1998, p. 797)

"The late Karl Deutsch was fond of describing data collection as 'the Lord's work' in social science. Expensive, frustrating, tedious, and thankless, it nevertheless is the foundation on which cumulative findings are built. The material in this massive work is worthy of several hosannas" (**Russell Leng**, Middlebury College, **The American Political Science Review**, 93, 3, 1999, p. 746)

"A quantitative empirical study of international crises using a large N and a carefully constructed dataset, it fully deserved the favorable reviews it received at the time [hard-cover edition, 1997]. Both versions contain a rich source of information about 412 international crises that occurred between 1918 and 1994. With their data, the authors test a number of hypotheses involving the following seven attributes of the international system and its member states: polarity, geography, ethnicity, democracy, protracted conflict, violence, and third-party intervention. In short, this is an outstanding quantitative, empirical study of a key aspect of international conflict." (**J.M. Scolnick Jr.**, University of Virginia, <u>Choice</u> (May 2001)

MILLENNIAL REFLECTIONS ON INTERNATIONAL STUDIES (2002)

"This gargantuan volume represents perhaps the most comprehensive compendium of international relations scholarship ever assembled between two covers.... The contributors are a virtual Who's Who of Anglophone scholars in the field of international studies, including scholars whose reputations were made any time from the 1950s to the 1990s.... this astounding volume... Summing up—highly recommended." (**J.F. Clark**, Florida International University, <u>Choice</u>, June 10, 2003, p. 02)

INTERNATIONAL POLITICAL EARTHQUAKES (2008)

"This is a highly original study that makes a major and enduring contribution to the scientific study of crisis and foreign policy decision making. It is of immense importance and will be seen as the capstone work of Brecher's International Crisis Behavior (ICB) project." **John A. Vasquez**, Thomas B. Mackie Scholar in International Relations, University of Illinois, Urbana-Champaign (Assessment to the publisher)

"Brecher makes a significant contribution to our knowledge about international crises and about the relationships among crisis, conflict, and system structure." **Zeev Maoz**, Professor of Political Science and Director of the International Relations Program, University of California, Davis (Assessment to the publisher)

"This authoritative study represents a point of culmination for three decades of research. It is essential reading in International Relations." **Patrick James**, Professor of International Relations and Director of the Center for International Studies, University of Southern California (Assessment to the publisher)

REFERENCES

GENERAL

S. J. Andriole, 'The Levels of Analysis Problems and the Study of Foreign, International, and Global Affairs: A Review Critique, and Another Final Solution' in *International Interactions* 5 (1978), pp. 113–133.

R. Aron, *Peace and War* (Garden City, NY, 1966).

K. J. Arrow, 'Economic Equilibrium', in David L. Sills (ed.), *International Encyclopedia of the Social Sciences*, Vol. 4 (New York, 1968), pp. 376–389.

W. R. Ashby, *Design for a Brain: The Origin of Adaptive Behavior* (New York, 1952).

E. E. Azar, 'Conflict Escalation and Conflict Reduction in an International Crisis: Suez, 1956' in *Journal of Conflict Resolution* (June) 16 (1972), pp. 183–201.

E. E. Azar, R. Brody and C. A. McClelland, 'International Events Interaction Analysis: Some Research Considerations' in *Sage Professional Papers in International Studies*, 02-001 (Beverly Hills, 1972).

E. E. Azar et al., 'A System for Forecasting Crisis: Findings and Speculations about Conflict in the Middle East' in *International Interactions* 3 (1977), pp. 193–225.

L. Binder, 'The Middle East as a Subordinate International System' in *World Politics* (April) X (1958), pp. 408–429.

K. E. Boulding, 'General Systems Theory—The Skeleton of Science' in *Management Science* (April) 2 (1956), pp. 197–208.

L. W. Bowman, 'The Subordinate State System of Southern Africa' in *International Studies Quarterly* (September) 12 (1968), pp. 231–261.

M. Brecher, 'International Relations and Asian Studies: The Subordinate State System of Southern Asia' in *World Politics* (January) XV (1963), pp. 213–235.
M. Brecher, with B. Geist. *Decisions in Crisis: Israel, 1967 and 1973* (Berkeley and Los Angeles, CA, 1980).
P. M. Burgess and R. W. Lawton, 'Indicators of International Behavior: An Assessment of Events Data Research' in *Sage Professional Papers, International Studies Series*, Vol. 1 (Beverly Hills, 1972).
L. J. Cantori and S. L. Spiegel, *International Politics of Regions* (Englewood Cliffs, NJ, 1970).
W. H. Corson, *Conflict and Cooperation in East-West Crises*, Ph.D. dissertation (Harvard, 1970).
P. D. Dean and J. A. Vasquez, 'From Power Politics to Issue Polities' in *Western Political Quarterly*, 29 (1976), pp. 7–28.
K. W. Deutsch, *Politics and Government*, 2nd Ed. (Boston, 1974).
K. W. Deutsch and J. D. Singer, 'Multipolar Power Systems and International Stability' in *World Politics* (April) XVI (1964), pp. 390–406.
J. E. Dominguez, 'Mice that do not Roar' in *International Organization* (Spring) 25 (1971), pp. 175–208.
W. Eckhardt and E. E. Azar, 'Major World Conflicts and Interventions, 1945-1975' in *International Interactions* 5 (1978), pp. 75–110.
R. Gilpin, *War and Change in World Politics* (Cambridge, 1981).
E. B. Haas, *Beyond the Nation State* (Stanford, 1964).
M. Haas, *International Conflict* (Indianapolis, 1974).
M. Haas, 'International Subsystems: Stability and Polarity' in *American Political Science Review* (March) 64 (1970), pp. 98–123.
W. F. Hanrieder, 'The International System: Bipolar or Multibloc?' in *Journal of Conflict Resolution* (September) 9 (1965), pp. 229–307.
S. Hoffmann, 'Discord in Community' in *International Organization* (Summer) 17 (1963), pp. 521–549.
S. Hoffmann, 'International Systems and International Law', in *World Politics* (October) XIV (1961), pp. 205–237.
K. J. Holsti, *International Politics*, 2nd Ed. (Englewood Cliffs, 1972).
O. R. Holsti, 'Historians, Social Scientists and Crisis Management: An Alternative View' in *Journal of Conflict Resolution* (December) 24 (1980), pp. 665–682.
G. W. Hopple and P. J. Rossa, 'International Crisis Analysis: Recent Developments and Future Directions', in P. T. Hopmann, D. A. Zinnes, J. D. Singer (eds.), *Cumulation in International Relations Research* (University of Denver Monograph Series in World Affairs, 1981), Vol. 18, Book 3, pp. 65–97.
K. Kaiser, 'The Interaction of Regional Subsystems' in *World Politics* (October) XXI (1968), pp. 84–107.

M. A. Kaplan, *System and Process in International Politics* (New York, 1957).
R. O. Keohane, Letter to the author (1981); and J. S. Nye, *Power and Interdependence* (Boston, 1977).
S. D. Krasner (ed.), *International Regimes*, special issue of *International Organization* (Spring) 36 (1982).
D. E. Lampert, 'Patterns of Transregional Relations', in Werner J. Feld and Gavin Boyd (eds.), *Comparative Regional Systems* (New York, 1980), pp. 429-81.
G. Liska, *International Equilibrium* (Cambridge, Mass., 1957).
C. A. McClelland, 'Comments', pp. 6-7 in C. Hermann, *International Crises* (New York, 1972).
——. 'Access to Berlin: the quantity and variety of events, 1948–1963', in J. D. Singer (ed.), *Quantitative International Politics: Insights and Evidence* (New York, 1968), pp. 159–186.
——. *Theory and the International System* (New York, 1966).
——. 'Systems and History in International Relations: Some Perspectives for Empirical Research and Theory', in *General Systems*, Yearbook of the Society for General Systems Research, Vol. Ill (1958), pp. 221–247.
——. 'Applications of General Systems Theory in International Relations' in *Main Currents in Modern Thought* (November) 12 (1955), pp. 27-34.
J. M. McCormick, 'International Crises: A Note on Definition' in *Western Political Quarterly* (September) 31 (1978), pp. 352–358.
G. Modelski, 'International Relations and Area Studies: The Case of Southeast Asia' in *International Relations* (April) II (1961), pp. 143–155.
R. C. North, 'Research Pluralism and the International Elephant' in *International Studies Quarterly* (December) 11 (1967), pp. 394–416.
S. Peterson, 'Research on Research: Events Data Studies, 1961–1972' in Patrick J. McGowan (ed.), *Sage International Yearbook of Foreign Policy Studies*, Vol. 3 (Beverly Hills, 1975).
W. C. Potter, 'Issue Area and Foreign Policy Analysis' in *International Organization* (Summer) 34 (1980), pp. 405–427.
D. G. Pruitt, 'Stability and Sudden Change in Interpersonal and International Affairs' in *Journal of Conflict Resolution* (March) XIII (1969), pp. 18–38.
R. N. Rosecrance, 'Bipolarity, Multipolarity, and the Future' in *Journal of Conflict Resolution*, X (1966), pp. 314–327.
R. N. Rosecrance, *Action and Reaction in World Politics* (Boston, 1963).
J. N. Rosenau, 'The External Environment as a Variable in Foreign Policy Analysis' in J. N. Rosenau, V. Davis and M. East (eds.), *The Analysis of International Politics* (New York, 1972), pp. 145–165.
B. M. Russett, *International Regions and the International System* (Chicago, 1967).
J. D. Singer, *A General Systems Taxonomy for Political Science* (New York, 1971).

J. D. Singer, 'The Level-of-Analysis Problem in International Relations' in *World Politics* (October) XIV (1961), pp. 77–92.

J. D. Singer and M. Small, *The Wages of War, 1816-1965: A Statistical Handbook* (New York, 1972).

R. Tanter, 'International Crisis Behavior: An Appraisal of the Literature' in *Jerusalem Journal of International Relations* (Winter-Spring) 3 (1978), pp. 340–374.

R. Tanter, *Modelling and Managing International Conflicts: The Berlin Crises* (Beverly Hills, 1974).

———. 'Dimensions of Conflict Behavior Within and Between Nations, 1958–1960' in *Journal of Conflict Resolution*, X (1966), pp. 41–64.

W. R. Thompson, 'The Regional Subsystem' in *International Studies Quarterly* (March) 17 (1973), pp. 89–117.

K. N. Waltz, *Theory of International Politics* (Reading, Mass., 1979).

———. 'International Structure, National Force, and the Balance of World Power' in *Journal of International Affairs*, XXI, 2 (1967), pp. 215–231.

———. 'The Stability of a Bipolar World' in *Daedalus* (Summer) XCIII (1964), pp. 881–909.

———. *Man the State and War* (New York, 1959).

A. J. Wiener and H. Kahn (eds.), *Crisis and Arms Control* (New York, 1962).

J. Wilkenfeld et al., 'Conflict Interactions in the Middle East, 1949–1967' in *Journal of Conflict Resolution* (June) 16 (1972), pp. 135–154.

O. R. Young, *A Systemic Approach to International Politics* (Princeton, 1968a).

———. 'Political Discontinuities in the International System' in *World Politics* (April) XX (1968b), pp. 369-92.

———. *The Politics of Force* (Princeton, 1968c).

I. W. Zartman, 'Africa as a Subordinate State System in International Relations' in *International Organization* (Summer) XXI (1967), pp. 545–564.

W. Zimmerman, 'Hierarchical Regional Subsystems and the Politics of System Boundaries' in *International Organization* (Winter) 26 (1972), pp. 18–26.

D. A. Zinnes, 'Prerequisites for the Study of System Transformation', Chapter 1 in O. R. Holsti, A. L. George and R. M. Siverson (eds.), *Change in the International System* (Boulder, Col., 1980).

WORKS CONSULTED: SELECTED INTERSTATE CONFLICTS: AFRICA

Chad/Libya Conflict

Azevedo, Mario J. *Roots of Violence: A History of War in Chad*. The Netherlands: Gordon and Breach Publishers, 1998.

Bearman, Jonathan. *Qadhafi's Libya*. London: Zed Books, 1986.

Brecher, Michael, and Jonathan Wilkenfeld. *A Study of Crisis*. Ann Arbor, MI: University of Michigan Press, 1997, 83–95.

Buijtenhuijs, Robert. *Le Frolinat et les révoltes populaires du Tchad*, 1965–1976. The Hague: Mouton Publishers, 1978.

Decalo, Samuel. "Regionalism, Political Decay, and Civil Strife in Chad." *Journal of Modern African Studies* 18, 1 (1980): 23–56.

_____. *Historical Dictionary of Chad*. London: Scarecrow Press, 1987.

Joffe, E. G. H. "Libya and Chad." *Review of African Political Economy* 21 (1981): 84–102.

Lemarchand, René (ed.). *The Green and the Black: Gadhafi's Policies in Africa*. Indianapolis, IN: Indiana University Press, 1988.

Pollack, Kenneth M. *Arabs at War: Military Effectiveness, 1948–1991*. Lincoln, NE: University of Nebraska Press, 2002.

Qaddhafi, Muammar. *The Green Book Part One: The Solution of the Problem of Democracy "The Authority of the People."* London: Martin Brian & O'Keeffe Ltd, 1976.

Ronen, Yehudit. *Qaddafi's Libya in World Politics*. Boulder, CO: Lynne Rienner, 2008.

Vandewalle, Dirk (ed.). *Libya Since 1969: Qadhafi's Revolution Revisited*. New York: Palgrave MacMillan, 2008.

Ethiopia/Somalia Conflict

Adejumobi, Saheed A. *The History of Ethiopia*. Westport, CT: Greenwood Press, 2007.

Brayton, Abbot A. "Soviet Involvement in Africa." *Journal of Modern African Studies* 17, 2 (1979): 253–269.

Brecher, Michael, and Jonathan Wilkenfeld. *A Study of Crisis*. Ann Arbor, MI: University of Michigan Press, 1997, 96–102.

Brind, Harry. "Soviet Policy in the Horn of Africa." *International Affairs* 60 (Winter 1983–1984): 75–95.

Brownie, Ian. *African Boundaries: A Legal and Diplomatic Encyclopedia*. Berkeley, CA: University of California Press, 1979.

Day, Alan J. *Border and Territorial Disputes*. 2nd ed. Burnt Mill, Harlow, Essex, UK: Longman, 1987.

Drysdale, John. *The Somali Dispute*. New York: Praeger, 1964.

Farer, Tom J. *War Clouds on the Horn of Africa: The Widening Storm*. 2nd rev. ed. New York: Carnegie Endowment for International Peace, 1979.

Gorman, Robert F. *Political Conflict on the Horn of Africa*. New York: Praeger, 1981.

Haile, Getatchew. "The Unity and Territorial Integrity of Ethiopia". *Journal of Modern African Studies* 24, 3 (1986): 465–487.

Harkavy, Robert E., and Stephanie G. Neuman (eds.). *The Lessons of Recent Wars in the Third World: Approaches and Case Studies.* Toronto, ON: Lexington Books, 1985.

Hoskyns, Catherine. *Case Studies in African Diplomacy: The Ethiopia-Somalia-Kenya Dispute 1960–1967.* London: Oxford University Press, 1969.

Jackson, Donna R. "The Ogaden War and the Demise of Détente." *Annals of the American Academy of Political and Social Sciences*, 632 (2010): 26–40.

Kendie, Daniel D. "Toward Northeast African Cooperation: Resolving the Ethiopia–Somalia Disputes." *Northeast African Studies* 10, 2 (2003): 67–109.

Laitin, David D. "The War in the Ogaden: Implications for Siyaad's Role in Somali History." *Journal of Modern African Studies* 17, 1 (1979): 95–115.

Laitin, David D., and Said S. Samatar. *Somalia: Nation in Search of a State.* Boulder, CO: Westview Press, 1987.

Lefebvre, Jeffrey A. *Arms for the Horn: U.S. Security Policy in Ethiopia and Somalia.* Pittsburgh, PA: University of Pittsburgh Press, 1991.

Legum, Colin, and B. Lee. *Conflict in the Horn of Africa.* New York: African Publishing Company, 1977.

Leogrande, William M. *Cuba's Policy in Africa, 1959–80.* Berkeley, CA: Institute of International Studies, 1980.

Levine, Donald Nathan. *Greater Ethiopia: The Evolution of a Multiethnic Society.* Chicago: University of Chicago Press, 2000.

Lewis, I.M. *A Modern History of the Somali: Nation and State in the Horn of Africa.* Oxford: James Currey, 2002.

———. *Understanding Somalia and Somaliland: Culture, History, Society.* New York: Columbia University Press, 2008.

Lewis, William H. "Ethiopia–Somalia." In Robert E. Harkavy and Stephanie G. Neuman (eds.), *The Lessons of Recent Wars in the Third World*, 1, 99–116. Toronto, ON: Lexington, 1985.

Mariam, Mesfin Wolde. "The Background of the Ethio-Somalia Boundary Dispute." *Journal of Modern African Studies* 2, 2 (1964): 189–219.

Markakis, John. *National and Class Conflict in the Horn of Africa.* Cambridge: Cambridge University Press, 1987.

Metz, Helen Chapin. *Somalia: A Country Study.* Washington, DC: Federal Research Division, Library of Congress, 1993.

Napper, Larry C. "The Ogaden War: Some Implications for Crisis Prevention." In Alexander L. George (ed.), *Managing U.S.–Soviet Rivalry: Problems of Crisis Prevention*, 225–254. Boulder, CO: Westview Press, 1979.

Ofcansky, Thomas P., and LaVerle Bennette Berry. *Ethiopia: A Country Study.* Washington, DC: Federal Research Division, Library of Congress, 1993.

Ottaway, Marina. *Soviet and American Influence in the Horn of Africa.* New York: Praeger, 1982.

Patman, Robert. *The Soviet Union in the Horn of Africa: The Diplomacy of Intervention and Disengagement.* Cambridge: Cambridge University Press, 1990.

Porter, Bruse D. *The USSR in Third World Conflicts: Soviet Arms and Diplomacy in Local Wars, 1945–1980.* Cambridge: Cambridge University Press, 1984.

Selassie, Bereket H. *Conflict and Intervention in the Horn of Africa.* New York: Monthly Review Press, 1980.

Tareke, Gebru. "The Ethiopia-Somalia War of 1977 Revisited." *International Journal of African Historical Studies* 33, 3 (2000): 635–667.

———. *The Ethiopian Revolution: War in the Horn of Africa.* New Haven, CT: Yale University Press, 2009.

Touval, Saadia. *Somali Nationalism: International Politics and the Drive for Unity in the Horn of Africa.* Cambridge, MA: Harvard University Press, 1963.

———. "Somalia, Ethiopia, and Kenya." In Steven L. Spiegel and Kenneth N. Waltz (eds.), *Conflicts in World Politics.* Cambridge, MA: Winthrop Publishers, 1971.

———. *The Boundary Politics of Independent Africa.* Cambridge, MA: Harvard University Press, 1972.

Woodward, Peter. *The Horn of Africa: State Politics and International Relations.* London: I.B. Tauris, 1996.

Zartman, I. William. *Ripe for Resolution: Conflict and Intervention in Africa.* rev. ed. New York: Oxford University Press, 1989.

Western Sahara Conflict

Batia, Michael. "The Western Sahara under Polisario Control." *Review of African Political Economy* 28, 88 (2001): 291–298.

Brecher, Michael, and Jonathan Wilkenfeld. *A Study of Crisis.* Ann Arbor, MI: University of Michigan Press, 1997, 118–131.

Damis, John. *Conflict in Northwest Africa: The Western Sahara Dispute.* Stanford, CA: Hoover Institution Press, 1983.

Encyclopedia of Nationalism: Fundamental Themes. s.v. "Western Sahara." http://www.credoreference.com/entry/estnationala/iv_western_sahara.

Hodges, Tony. *Western Sahara: The Roots of a Desert War.* Connecticut: Lawrence Hill & Company, 1983.

———. *The Western Saharans.* London: Minority Rights Group, 1984.

International Court of Justice (ICJ). *Summary of the Summary of the Advisory Opinion of 16 October 1975.*

Jensen, Erik. *Western Sahara: Anatomy of a Stalemate?* Boulder, CO: Lynne Rienner, 2012.

Maghraoui, Abdeslam. "Ambiguities of Sovereignty: Morocco, The Hague and the Western Sahara Dispute." *Mediterranean Politics* 8, 1 (2003): 113–126.

Mercer, John. *Spanish Sahara*. London: George Allen & Unwin, 1976.
Mundy, Jacob A. "Seized of the Matter: The UN and the Western Sahara Dispute." *Mediterranean Quarterly* 15, 3 (2004): 130–148.
Shelley, Toby. *Endgame in the Western Sahara: What Future for Africa's Last Colony?* London: Zed Books, 2004.
United States Central Intelligence Agency. *The World Factbook.* "Western Sahara." Washington, DC.
Zunes, Stephen, and Jacob Mundy. *Western Sahara: War, Nationalism, and Conflict Irresolution*. Syracuse, NY: Syracuse University Press, 2010.

WORKS CONSULTED: SELECTED INTERSTATE CONFLICTS: AMERICAS

Costa Rica/Nicaragua Conflict

Ameringer, Charles D. *Democracy in Costa Rica*. Stanford, CA: Hoover Institute Press, 1982.
———. *Don Pépé*. Albuquerque, NM: University of New Mexico Press, 1978.
Atkins, G. Pope. *Encyclopedia of the Inter-American System*. Westport, CT: Greenwood, 1997.
Bermann, Karl. *Under the Big Stick: Nicaragua and the United States since 1848*. Boston, MA: South End Press, 1986.
Bethell, Leslie. *The Cambridge History of Latin America*. Cambridge: Cambridge University Press, 1990.
———. *Central America since Independence*. Cambridge: Cambridge University Press, 1991.
Brecher, Michael, and Jonathan Wilkenfeld. *A Study of Crisis*. Ann Arbor, MI: University of Michigan Press, 1997, 132–135.
Brysk, Alison. "Global Good Samaritans? Human Rights Foreign Policy in Costa Rica." *Global Governance*. 11, 4 (2005): 445–466.
Busey, James L. "Foundations of Political Contrast: Costa Rica and Nicaragua." *Western Political Quarterly* 11, 3 (1958): 627–659.
———. "Central American Union: The Latest Attempt." *Western Political Quarterly*. 14, 1 (1961): 49–63.
Cruz, Consuelo. *Political Culture and Institutional Development in Costa Rica and Nicaragua: World-Making in the Tropics*. Cambridge: Cambridge University Press, 2005.
Foreign Relations of the United States. Costa Rica 1917. 302–349.
———. Costa Rica 1918. 229–275.
———. Costa Rica 1919. 803–876.
———. Nicaragua 1919. 819–849.
———. Costa Rica 1948. 488–542.
———. Costa Rica 1955. 2–32.

Harrison, Benjamin T. "Woodrow Wilson and Nicaragua." *Caribbean Quarterly* 51, 1 (2005): 25–36.
Hoivik, Tord, and Solveig Aas. "Demilitarization in Costa Rica: A Farewell to Arms?" *Journal of Peace Research* 4 (1981): 333–351.
International Court of Justice. "Certain Activities Carried Out by Nicaragua in The Border Area." Costa Riva v. Nicaragua (2013).
Longley, Kyle. "Peaceful Costa Rica, the First Battleground: The United States and Costa Rica Revolution of 1948." *The Americas* 2 (1993): 149–175.
Orlander, Marcia. "Costa Rica in 1948: Cold War or Local War?" *The Americas* 4 (1996): 465–493.
Pact of Amity between the Governments of the Republics of Costa Rica and Nicaragua. February 21, 1949.
Rankin, Monica A. *The History of Costa Rica.* Santa Barbara, CA: Greenwood, 1972.
Rosset, Peter, and John Vandermeer. *Nicaragua: Unfinished Revolution.* New York: Grove Press, 1986.
Salisbury, Richard V. "Domestic Politics and Foreign Policy: Costa Rica's Stand on Recognition, 1923–1934." *The Hispanic American Historical Review* 3 (1974): 453–478.
Sandoval Barcia, Carlos. *Threatening Others: Nicaraguans and the Formation of National Identities in Costa Rica.* Center for International Studies Ohio University, 2004.
Stansifer, Charles L. "Application of the Tobar Doctrine to Central America." *The Americas* 3 (1967): 251–272.
Staten, Clifford L. *The History of Nicaragua.* Santa Barbara, CA: Greenwood, 2010.
Wilson, Bruce M. *Costa Rica: Politics, Economics, and Democracy.* Boulder, CO: Lynne Rienner, 1998.
Woolsey, L. H. "Boundary Disputes in Latin-American." *American Journal of International Law* 25, 2 (1931): 324–333.
Yashar, Deborah J. *Demanding Democracy: Reform and Reaction in Costa Rica and Guatemala, 1870s–1950s.* Stanford, CA: Stanford University Press, 1997.

WORKS CONSULTED: SELECTED INTERSTATE CONFLICTS: ASIA

Afghanistan/Pakistan Conflict

Akhtar, N. "Pakistan, Afghanistan, and the Taliban." *International Journal on World Peace* 25, 4 (2008): 49–74.
Barfield, Thomas. *Afghanistan: A Cultural and Political History.* Princeton, NJ: Princeton University Press, 2010.

Brecher, Michael, and Jonathan Wilkenfeld. *A Study of Crisis*. Ann Arbor, MI: University of Michigan Press, 1997, 147–150.

Burke, S. M. *Pakistan's Foreign Policy: A Historical Analysis*. London: Oxford University Press, 1973.

———. *Mainsprings of Indian and Pakistan Foreign Policies*. London: Oxford University Press, 1974.

Dalrymple, William. *Return of the King: The Battle for Afghanistan, 1839–1842*. New York, Vintage, 2013.

Duprée, Louis. "A Note on Afghanistan: 1960." *American University Field Staff Reports Service: South Asia Series* 4, 8 (1960): 143–171.

———. "'Pushtunistan': The Problem and its Larger Implications, Part I." *American University Field Staff Reports Service: South Asia Series* 5, 2 (1961): 31–46.

Emadi, Hafizullah. "Durand Line and Afghan–Pak Relations." *Economic and Political Weekly* 25, 28 (1990): 1515–1516.

Ewans, Martin. *Afghanistan: A Short History of its People and Politics*. New York: HarperCollins, 2002.

Franck, Dorothea S. "Pakhtunistan: Disputed Disposition of a Tribal Land." *Middle East Journal* 6, 1 (1952): 49–68.

Fraser-Tyler, W. K. *Afghanistan: A Study of Political Developments in Central and Southern Asia*. London: Oxford University Press, 1967.

Grare, Frédéric. *Pakistan: In the Face of the Afghan Conflict 1979–1985 at the Turn of the Cold War*. New Delhi: India Research Press, 2003.

———. "Pakistan–Afghanistan Relations in the Post 9/11 Era." *Carnegie Papers* 72 (2006): 1–22.

Hasnat, S. F. "Pakistan's Strategic Interests, Afghanistan and the Fluctuating U.S. Strategy." *Journal of International Affairs, Columbia University* 63, 1 (2009): 141–156.

Johnson, Thomas H., and M. Chris Mason. "No Sign until the Burst of Fire: Understanding the Pakistan–Afghanistan Frontier." *International Security* 32, 4 (2008): 41–77.

Kaur, Kulwant. *Pak–Afghanistan Relations*. New Delhi: Deep & Deep Publications, 1985.

Khan, Azmat H. *The Durand Line: Its Geo-Strategic Importance*. Peshawar, Pakistan: Area Study Centre, 2000.

Misra, Amalendu. *Afghanistan: The Labyrinth of Violence*. Cambridge: Polity Press, 2004.

Newell, Richard S. *The Politics of Afghanistan*. Ithaca, NY: Cornell University Press, 1972.

Omrani, Bijan. "The Durand Line: History and Problems of the Afghan–Pakistan Border." *Asian Affairs* 40, 2 (2009): 177–195.

Qassem, Ahmad Shayeq. *Afghanistan's Political Stability*. Burlington, VT: Ashgate, 2009.

Qureshi, S. M. M. "Pakhtunistan: The Frontier Dispute between Afghanistan and Pakistan." *Pacific Affairs* 39, 1–2 (1966): 99–114.
Razvi, Mujtaba. *The Frontiers of Pakistan: A Study of Frontier Problems in Pakistan's Foreign Policy.* Karachi: National Publishing House, 1971.
Roberts, Jeffrey J. *The Origins of Conflict in Afghanistan.* Westport, CT: Praeger, 2003.
Rubin, Barnett R., and Abubakar Siddique. "Resolving the Pakistan–Afghanistan Stalemate." *United States Institute of Peace Special Report* 176 (2006): 1–20.
Saikal, A. "Afghanistan and Pakistan: The Question of Pashtun Nationalism?" *Journal of Muslim Minority Affairs* 30, 1 (2010): 5–17.
Schofield, Julian. "Diversionary Wars: Pashtun Unrest and the Sources of the Pakistan-Afghan Confrontation." *Canadian Foreign Policy Journal* 17, 1 (2011): 38–49.
Weinbaum, Marvin G. *Pakistan and Afghanistan: Resistance and Reconstruction.* Boulder, CO: Westview Press, 1994.
Ziring, Lawrence. *Pakistan: The Enigma of Political Development.* Boulder, CO: Westview Press, 1980.

China/Vietnam Conflict

An, T.S. "Turmoil in Indochina: The Vietnam-Cambodian Conflict." *Asian Affairs: An American Review* 5, 4 (1978): 245–256.
Brecher, Michael, and Jonathan Wilkenfeld. *A Study of Crisis.* Ann Arbor, MI: University of Michigan Press, 1997, 158–164.
Brocheux, Pierre. *Ho Chi Minh : A Biography.* Cambridge: Cambridge University Press, 2007.
Chandler, D.P. *Brother Number One: A Political Biography of Pol Pot.* Boulder, CO: Westview Press, 1999.
Chang, Pao-min. *The Sino-Vietnamese Territorial Dispute.* New York: Praeger, 1986.
Chen, Hung-Yu. "The PRC's South China Sea Policy and Strategies of Occupation in the Paracel and Spratly Islands." *Issues & Studies* 36, 4 (2000): 95–131.
Chen, King C. *Vietnam and China, 1938–1954.* Princeton, NJ: Princeton University Press, 1969.
———. *China's War with Vietnam: 1979, Issues, Decisions, and Implications.* Stanford, CA: Hoover Institution Press, 1986.
Duiker, William J. *China and Vietnam: The Roots of Conflict.* Berkeley, CA: Institute of East Asian Studies, University of California, 1986.
———. "China and Vietnam and the Struggle for Indochina." *Postwar Indochina: Old Enemies and New Allies.* US Department of State, Foreign Service Institute, Center for the Study of Foreign Affairs, 1988, 147–191.

Elleman, Bruce A. "China's 1974 Naval Expedition to the Paracel Islands." In Bruce A. Elleman and S.C.M Paine (eds.), *Naval Power and Expeditionary Warfare: Peripheral Campaigns and New Theatres of Naval Warfare.* New York: Taylor & Francis Group, 2011.

Emmers, Ralf. "The Changing Power Distribution in the South China Sea: Implications for Conflict Management and Avoidance." *SAGE* 62, 2 (2010): 118–131.

Gilks, Anne. *The Breakdown of the Sino-Vietnamese Alliance, 1970–1979.* Berkeley, CA: Institute of East Asian Studies, University of California, 1992.

Globe and Mail (Toronto). "'Teaching Vietnam a Good Lesson', China will not Extend Drive to Hanoi Area, Official Says." 26 February 1979: 1.

Guan, Ang Cheng. *Vietnamese Communists' Relations with China and the Second Indochina Conflict, 1956–1962.* Jefferson, NC: McFarland, 1997.

———. "The South China Sea Dispute Revisited." *Australian Journal of International Affairs* 54, 2 (2000): 201–215.

Lacouture, Jean. *Ho Chi Minh: A Political Biography.* New York: Random House, 1968.

———. *Pierre Mendés France.* New York: Holmes & Meier, 1984.

Lawson, Eugene. *The Sino-Vietnamese Conflict.* New York: Praeger, 1984.

Leighton, M.K. "Perspectives on the Vietnam-Cambodia Border Conflict." *Asian Survey* 18, 5 (1978): 448–457.

Lemon, Daniel W. *Vietnam's Foreign Policy Toward China since the 1970s.* Thesis. Naval Post Graduate School, Monterey, CA, 2007.

Lescaze, Lee and Jay Mathews. "China Declares Withdrawal Completed." *Washington Post,* 16 March, 1979.

Marr, David G., and Christine Pelzer White. *Postwar Vietnam: Dilemmas in Socialist Development.* Ithaca, NY: Southeast Asia Program, Cornell University, 1988.

Mohan, J. "Why Vietnam Invaded Kampuchea." *Economic and Political Weekly* 16, 4 (1981): 448–457.

Nguyen-yo, T. *Khmer-Viet Relations and the Third Indochina Conflict.* Jefferson, NC: McFarland, 1992.

O'Dowd, Edward C. *Chinese Military Strategy in the Third Indochina War: The Last Maoist War.* Abingdon, Oxon: Routledge, 2007.

Pouvatchy, J.R. "Cambodian-Vietnamese Relations." *Asian Survey* 26, 4 (1986): 440–451.

Pribbenow, M.L. "A Tale of Five Generals: Vietnam's Invasion of Cambodia." *Journal of Military History* 70, 2 (2006): 459–486.

Ray, Hemen. *China's Vietnam War.* New Delhi: Radiant Publishers, 1983.

Ross, Robert S. *The Indochina Tangle: China's Vietnam Policy, 1975–1979.* New York: Columbia University Press. 1988.

Scobell, Andrew. *China's Use of Military Force: Beyond the Great Wall and the Long March.* New York: Cambridge University Press, 2003.

Segal, Gerald. *Defending China*. New York: Oxford University Press, 1985.
Sharkey, John. "China Agrees to Discuss Peace; China Agrees to Peace Talks with Vietnamese; Tough Talks with Hanoi Expected." *Washington Post* 7 Apr. 1979: A1.
Thayer, Carlyle A. "Vietnamese Perspectives of the 'China Threat.'" In Ian Storey and Herbert Yee (eds.), *The China Threat: Perceptions, Myths and Realities*. Routledge, 2002, 265–278.
Ton That Thien. *The Foreign Politics of the Communist Party of Vietnam: A Study of Communist Tactics*. New York: Taylor & Francis, 1989.
Tretiak, Daniel. "China's Vietnam War and its Consequences." *China Quarterly* 80 (Dec. 1979): 740–767.
Turley, William S. "Origins and Development of Communist Military Leadership in Vietnam." *Armed Forces & Society* 3 (1979): 219–247.
Turley, William S, and Jeffrey Race. "The Third Indochina War." *Foreign Policy* 38 (1980): 92–116.
Van Canh, Nguyen. *Vietnam Under Communism, 1975–1982*. Stanford, CA: Hoover Institution Press, 1983.
Vogel, Ezra E. *Deng Xiaoping and the Transformation of China*. Cambridge, MA: Harvard University Press, 2011.
Vuving, Alexander L. "Grand Strategic Fit and Power Shift: Explaining Turning Points in China-Vietnam Relations." In Shiping Tang, Mingjiang Li and Amitav Acharya (eds.), *Living with China: Regional States and China through Crises and Turning Points*, 229–245. New York: Palgrave Macmillan, 2009.
Westad, Odd Arne, and Sophie Quinn-Judge (eds.). *The Third Indochina War: Conflict Between China, Vietnam and Cambodia, 1972–1979*. New York: Routledge, 2006.
Womack, Brantly. *China and Vietnam: The Politics of Asymmetry*. New York: Cambridge University Press, 2006.
Woods, L Shelton. *Vietnam: A Global Studies Handbook*. Santa Barbara, CA: ABC-CLIO, 2002.
Zhang, Xiaoming. "Deng Xiaoping and China's Decision to go to War with Vietnam." *Journal of Cold War Studies* 12, 3 (2010): 3–29.
"75 Years of the Communist Party of Vietnam (1930–2005): A Selection of Documents from Nine Party Congresses." Hanoi, Vietnam: Gioi Publishers, 2005.

WORKS CONSULTED: SELECTED INTERSTATE CONFLICTS: EUROPE

Finland/Russia-USSR Conflict

Alapuro, Risto. *State and Revolution in Finland*. Berkeley, CA: University of California Press, 1988.

Allison, Roy. *Finland's Relations with the Soviet Union, 1944–1984.* New York: St. Martin's Press, 1985.
Berner, Örjan. *Soviet Policies Toward the Nordic Countries.* Lanham, MD: University Press of America, 1986.
Brecher, Michael, and Jonathan Wilkenfeld. *A Study of Crisis.* Ann Arbor, MI: University of Michigan Press, 1997, 231–236.
Browning, Christopher S. *Constructivism, Narrative and Foreign Policy Analysis: A Case Study of Finland.* Oxford: Peter Lang, 2008.
Cohen, Yohanan. *Small Nations in Times of Crisis and Confrontation.* New York: New York University Press, 1989.
Jakobson, Max. *Finland Survived.* Helsinki: Otava Publishing Co., 1961.
———. *Finnish Neutrality.* New York: Frederick A. Praeger, 1968.
Luostarinen, Heikki. "Finnish Russophobia: The Story of an Enemy Image." *Journal of Peace Research* 26, 2 (1989): 123–137.
Meinander, Henrick. *A History of Finland.* New York: Columbia University Press, 2011.
Moisio, Sami. "Finland, Geopolitical Image of Threat and the Post-Cold War Confusion." *Geopolitics* 3, 3 (1998): 104–124.
Novikova, Irina. "The Provisional Government and Finland: Russian Democracy and Finnish Nationalism in Search of Peaceful Coexistence." In Jane Burbank, Mark Von Hagen and Anatolyi Remnev (eds.), *Russian Empire: Space, People, Power*, 398–421. Bloomington, IN: Indiana University Press, 2008.
Polvinen, Tuomo. *Between East and West: Finland in International Politics, 1944–1947.* Minneapolis, MN: University of Minnesota Press, 1986.
Puntila, L.A. *The Political History of Finland 1809–1966.* London: Heinemann, 1975.
Singleton, Fred. *A Short History of Finland.* Cambridge: Cambridge University Press, 1989.
Smith Jr, C. Jay. *Finland and the Russian Revolution, 1917–1922.* Athens, GE: University of Georgia Press, 1958.
Sundbäck, Esa. "A Convenient Buffer between Scandinavia and Russia." *Jahrbücher für Geschichte Osteuropas* 42, 3 (1994): 355–375.
Zubok, V.M., and Konstantin Pleshakov. *Inside the Kremlin's Cold War: From Stalin to Khrushchev.* Cambridge, MA: Harvard University Press, 1996.

Poland/Russia-USSR Conflict

Aras, Bulent, and Faith Özbay. "Polish–Russian Relations: History, Geography, and Geopolitics." *East European Quarterly* 1 (2008): 27–42.
Bethell, Nicholas. *Gomulka: His Poland and His Communism.* New York: Holt, Rinehart & Winston, 1969.
Brecher, Michael, and Jonathan Wilkenfeld. *A Study of Crisis.* Ann Arbor, MI: University of Michigan Press, 1997, 256–261.

Brzezinski, Zbigniew K. *The Soviet Bloc: Unity and Conflict*. Cambridge, MA: Harvard University Press, 1967.

Crankshaw, Edward. *Khrushchev: A Biography*. London: Collins, 1966.

Davies, Norman. *White Eagle, Red Star: The Polish–Soviet War, 1919–1920*. London: Macdonald, 1972.

———. *Heart of Europe: A Short History of Poland*. London: Oxford University Press, 1984.

———. *Heart of Europe: The Past in Poland's Present*. London: Oxford University Press, 2001.

———. *God's Playground: A History of Poland*. London: Oxford University Press, 2005.

Dunn, Dennis J. *The Catholic Church and Russia: Popes, Patriarchs, Tsars and Commissars*. Aldershot, UK: Ashgate, 2004.

Dziewanowski, Marian K. The Communist Party of Poland. Cambridge, MA: Harvard University Press, 1959.

Gibney, Frank. *Frozen Revolution; Poland: A Study in Communist Decay*. New York: Farrar, Straus, 1959.

Gluchowski, L. W. "Poland, 1956: Khrushchev, Gomulka, and the 'Polish October.'" CWIHP *Bulletin* 5 (1995): 1, 38–49.

Kennan. George F. *Russia and the West under Lenin and Stalin*. Boston, MA: Little, Brown, 1960.

Khrushchev, Nikita S. *Khrushchev Remembers: The Last Testament*. Trans. and ed. Strobe Talbott. Boston, MA: Little, Brown, 1974.

Korbonski, A. *Politics of Socialist Agriculture in Poland, 1945–1960*. New York: Columbia University Press, 1965.

Kramer, Mark. "Poland, 1980–1981: Soviet Policy during the Polish Crisis." CWIHP *Bulletin* 5 (1995a): 1, 116–126.

———. "Declassified Soviet Documents on the Polish Crisis." CWIHP *Bulletin* 5 (1995b): 116–117, 129–139.

Langer, William L., ed. *Encyclopedia of World History*. 5th ed. 2 vols. New York: Harry N. Abrams, 1974.

Leslie, R. F., and Antony Polonsky. *The History of Poland since 1863*. Cambridge: Cambridge University Press, 1980.

Lewis, Flora. *The Polish Volcano: A Case History of Hope*. London: Secker & Warburg, 1959.

Lukowski, Jerzy and Hubert Zawadzki. *A Concise History of Poland*. 2nd ed. Cambridge: Cambridge University Press, 2006.

Mikolajczyk, Stanislaw. *The Pattern of Soviet Domination*. London: Low, Marston, 1948.

Tatu, Michel. "Intervention in Eastern Europe." In Stephen S. Kaplan (ed.), *Diplomacy of Power: Soviet Armed Forces as a Political Instrument*, 205–264. Washington, DC: Brookings, 1981.

Ulam, Adam B. *Expansion and Coexistence: A History of Soviet Foreign Policy, 1917–1973*. 2nd ed. New York: Praeger, 1974.
———. *The Rivals—America and Russia since World War II*. New York: Viking, 1971.
Ullman, Richard H. *Anglo-Soviet Relations, 1917–1921: The Anglo-Soviet Accord*. Vol. 3. Princeton, NJ: Princeton University Press, 1972.

Iran/Iraq Protracted Conflict

Abdulghani, Jasim. *Iraq and Iran: The Years of Crisis*. London: Croom Helm, and Baltimore, MD: Johns Hopkins University Press, 1984.
Amin, S. H. "The Iran-Iraq Conflict: Legal Implications." *International and Comparative Law Quarterly* 31, 1 (1982): 167–188.
Bakhash, Shaul. "The Troubled Relationship: Iran and Iraq, 1930–1980." In Lawrence G. Potter and Gary G. Sick (eds.), *Iran, Iraq, and the Legacies of War*, 11–28. New York: Palgrave Macmillan, 2004.
Brecher, Michael, and Jonathan Wilkenfeld. *A Study of Crisis*. Ann Arbor, MI: University of Michigan Press, 1997, 300–312.
———. *International Political Earthquakes*. Ann Arbor, MI: University of Michigan Press, 2008.
Chehabi, H E. "The Pahlavi Period." *Iranian Studies*, 31 (1998): 495–502.
Chubin, Shahram, and Charles Tripp. *Iran and Iraq at War*. London: I.B Taurus, 1988.
Cordesman, Anthony H., and Ahmed S. Hashim. *Iraq: Sanctions and Beyond*. Boulder, CO: Westview Press, 1997.
Dawisha, Adeed. *Iraq: A Political History from Independence to Occupation*. Princeton, NJ: Princeton University Press, 2009.
Ehteshami, Anoushiravan. "The Foreign Policy of Iran." In Raymond A. Hinnebusch and Anoushiravan Ehteshami (eds.), *The Foreign Policies of Middle East States*, 283–310. Boulder, CO: Lynne Rienner, 2002.
———. "Iran–Iraq Relations after Saddam." *Washington Quarterly* 26, 4 (2003): 115–129.
Farhi, Farideh. "The Antinomies of Iran's War Generation." In Lawrence G. Potter and Gary Sick (eds.), *Iran, Iraq, and the Legacies of War*, 121–140. New York: Palgrave Macmillan, 2004.
Fatemi, Khosrow. "Leadership by Distrust: The Shah's Modus Operandi." *Middle East Journal* 36, 1 (1982): 48–61.
Fürtig, Henner. "Conflict and Cooperation in the Persian Gulf: The Interregional Order and Us Policy." *The Middle East Journal* 61, 4 (2007): 627.
Gause, F. Gregory III. 2002. Iraq's Decisions to Go to War, 1980 and 1990. *The Middle East Journal* 56 (1): 47–70.
Hilterman, Joost R. "Outsider as Enablers: Consequences and Lessons from International Silence on Iraq's Use of Chemical Weapons during the Iran-Iraq

War." In Lawrence G. Potter and Gary Sick (eds.), *Iran, Iraq, and the Legacies of War*, 29–70. New York: Palgrave Macmillan, 2004.

Hiro, Dilip. *The Long War: The Iran-Iraq Military Conflict*. London: Grafton Books, 1989.

———. *Neighbors, Not Friends: Iraq and Iran After the Gulf Wars*. London: Routledge, 2001.

Ismael, Tareq Y. *Iran and Iraq: Roots of Conflict*. Syracuse, NY: Syracuse University Press, 1982.

Karsh, Efraim. "Geopolitical Determinism: The Origins of the Iran-Iraq War." *Middle East Journal* 44, 2 (1990): 256–268.

Khadduri, Majid. *The Gulf War: The Origins and Implications of the Iran–Iraq Conflict*. New York: Oxford University Press, 1998.

Kheli, Shirin, and Shaheen Ayubi (eds.). *The Iran–Iraq War: New Weapons, Old Conflicts*. New York: Praeger, 1983.

Nasr, Seyyed V. R. *The Shia Revival: How Conflicts Within Islam Will Shape the Future*. New York: Norton, 2006.

Post, Jerrold M. "Saddam Hussein of Iraq: a Political Psychology Profile." *Political Psychology* 12, 2 (1991): 279–289.

Potter, Lawrence G. and Gary G. Sick (eds.). *Iran, Iraq, and the Legacies of War*. New York: Palgrave Macmillan, 2004.

———. "Introduction." In Lawrence G. Potter and Gary G. Sick (eds.), *Iran, Iraq, and the Legacies of War*, 1–11. New York: Palgrave Macmillan, 2004.

Iran/Iraq Protracted Conflict (2)

Saikal, Amin. *The Rise and Fall of the Shah*. Princeton, NJ: Princeton University Press, 1981.

Schofield, Richard. "Position, Function and Symbol: The Shat Al-Arab Dispute in Perspective." In Lawrence G. Potter and Gary G. Sick (eds.), *Iran, Iraq, and the Legacies of War*, 29–70. New York: Palgrave Macmillan, 2004.

Shahram, Chubin, and Charles Tripp. *Iran and Iraq at War*. London: I.B. Tauris, 1988.

Sirriyeh, Hussein. "Development of the Iraqi-Iranian Dispute, 1847–1975." *Journal of Contemporary History* 20, 3 (1985): 483–492.

Takeyh, Ray. "Iran's New Iraq." *Middle East Journal* 62, 1 (2008): 13–30.

Tomasek, Robert D. 1976/77. The Resolution of Major controversies between Iran and Iraq. *World Affairs* 139 (3): 206–230.

Tripp, Charles. *A History of Iraq*. Cambridge: Cambridge University Press, 2002.

———. "The Foreign Policy of Iraq." In Raymond A. Hinnebusch and Anoushiravan Ehteshami (eds.), *The Foreign Policies of Middle East States*, 167–192. Boulder, CO: Lynne Rienner, 2002.

INTER-REGION: GEORGIA/RUSSIA-USSR CONFLICT

Antonenko, Oksana. "Frozen Uncertainty: Russia and the Conflict over Abkhazia." In Bruno Coppieters and Robert Legvold (eds.), *Statehood and Security: Georgia after the Rose Revolution*, 83–116. Cambridge, MA: MIT Press, 2005.

Bank, Stephen. "From Neglect to Duress: The West and the Georgian Crisis Before the 2008 War." In Svante E. Cornell and Frederick Starr (eds.), *The Guns of August 2008: Russia's War in Georgia*. New York: M.E. Sharpe, 2009, 104–121.

Broers, Laurence. "'David and Goliath' and 'Georgians in the Kremlin': A Post-Colonial Perspective on Conflict in Post-Soviet Georgia." *Central Asian Survey* 28, 2 (2009): 99–118.

Cheterian, Vicken. *War and Peace in the Caucasus*. New York: Columbia University Press, 2008.

———. "The August 2008 War in Georgia: From Ethnic Conflict to Border Wars." *Central Asian Survey* 28, 2 (2009): 155–170.

Coppieters, Bruno. "Conclusion." In Bruno Coppieters and Robert Legvold (eds.), *Statehood and Security: Georgia after the Rose Revolution*, Cambridge, MA: American Academy of Arts and Science, 2005, 339–387.

Cornell, Svante E. "Autonomy as a Source of Conflict: Caucasian Conflicts in Theoretical Perspective." *World Politics* 54, 2 (2002): 245–276.

Cornell, Svante E, and Frederick Starr (eds.). *The Guns of August 2008: Russia's War in Georgia*. Armonk, NY: M.E. Sharpe, 2009.

Darchiashvili, David. "Georgian Defense Policy and Military Reform." In Bruno Coppieters and Robert Legvold (eds.), *Statehood and Security: Georgia after the Rose Revolution*, Cambridge, MA: American Academy of Arts and Science, 2005, 117–151.

Devdariani, Jaba. "Georgia and Russia: The Troubled Road to Accommodation." In Bruno Coppieters and Robert Legvold (eds.), *Statehood and Security: Georgia after the Rose Revolution*, Cambridge, MA: American Academy of Arts and Science, 2005, 153–203.

Felgenhauer, Pavel. "After August 7: The Escalation of the Russia-Georgia War." In Svante E. Cornell and Frederick Starr (eds.), *The Guns of August 2008: Russia's War in Georgia*. New York: M.E. Sharpe, 2009, 162–180.

Filippov, Mikhail. "Diversionary Role of the Georgia–Russia Conflict: International Constraints and Domestic Appeal." *Europe–Asia Studies* 61, 10 (2010): 1825–1847.

Gahrton, Per. *Georgia: Pawn in the New Great Game*. London: Pluto Press, 2010.

Goble, Paul. "Defining Victory and Defeat: The Information War Between Russia and Georgia." In Svante Cornell and Frederick Starr (eds.), *The Guns of August 2008: Russia's War in Georgia*, 181–195. Armonk, NY: M.E. Sharpe, 2009.

Goltz, Thomas. "The Paradox of Living in Paradise: Georgia's Descent into Chaos." In Svante E. Cornell and Frederick Starr (eds.), *The Guns of August 2008: Russia's War in Georgia*. New York: M.E. Sharpe, 2009, 10–27.

Gordadze, Thornike. "The Georgian-Russian Relations in the 1990s." In Svante E. Cornell and Frederick Starr (eds.), *The Guns of August 2008: Russia's War in Georgia*. New York: M.E. Sharpe, 2009, 28–48.

———. "Georgia-Russia Conflict in August 2008: War as a Continuation of Politics." In Annie Jafalian (ed.), *Reassessing Security in the South Caucasus: Regional Conflicts and Transformation*. Burlington, VT: Ashgate, 2011, 11–31.

Helly, Damien, and Giorgi Gogia. "Georgian Security and the Role of the West." In Bruno Coppieters and Robert Legvold (eds.), *Statehood and Security: Georgia after the Rose Revolution*, Cambridge, MA: American Academy of Arts and Science, 2005, 271–305.

Illarianov, Andrei. "The Russian Leadership's Preparation for War, 1999–2008." In Svante Cornell and Frederick Starr (eds.), *The Guns of August 2008: Russia's War in Georgia*, 49–84. Armonk, NY: M.E. Sharpe, 2009.

King, Charles. *The Ghost of Freedom: A History of the Caucasus*. New York: Oxford University Press, 2008.

Lapidus, Gail W. "Gorbachev's Nationalities Problem." *Foreign Affairs* 68, 4 (1989): 92–108.

Markedonov, Sergey. "Unfreezing conflict in South Ossetia: Regional and International Implications." In Annie Jafalian (ed.), *Reassessing Security in the South Caucasus: Regional Conflicts and Transformation*. Burlington, VT: Ashgate, 2011, 33–46.

Mitchell, Lincoln. "Georgia's Rose Revolution." *Current History* 103, 675 (2004): 342–348.

Mouritzen, Hans, and Anders Wivel. *Explaining Foreign Policy: International Diplomacy and the Russo-Georgian War*. Boulders, CO: Lynne Rienner, 2012.

Niedermaier, Ana K. (ed.). *Countdown to War: Russia's Foreign Policy and Media Coverage over the Conflict in South Ossetia and Abkhazia*. Minneapolis, MN: East View Press, 2008.

Nilson, Niklas. "Georgia's Rose Revolution: The Break with the Past." In Svante Cornell and Frederick Starr (eds.), *The Guns of August 2008: Russia's War in Georgia*, 85–103. Armonk, NY: M.E. Sharpe, 2009.

Nodia, Ghia. "Georgia: Dimensions of Insecurity." In Bruno Coppieters and Robert Legvold (eds.), *Statehood and Security: Georgia after the Rose Revolution*. Cambridge, MA: American Academy of Arts and Science, 2005, 39–82.

Pain, Emil. "The Russian-Georgian Armed Conflict." *Russian Politics and Law* 47, 5 (2009), 10–25.

Popjavesnki, Johanna. "From Sukhumi to Tskhinvali: The Path to War in Georgia." In Svante Cornell and Frederick Starr (eds.), *The Guns of August 2008: Russia's War in Georgia*, 143–161. Armonk, NY: M.E. Sharpe, 2009.

Tuathail, Gearoid O. "Russia's Kosovo: A Critical Geopolitics of the August 2008 War over South Ossetia." *Eurasian Geography and Economics* 49, 6 (2008): 670–705.

Wheatley, Jonathan. *Georgia from a National Awakening to Rose Revolution: Delayed Transition in the Former Soviet Union.* Aldershot, UK: Ashgate, 2005.

Zürcher, Christoph. "Georgia's Time of Troubles, 1989–1993." In Bruno Coppieters and Robert Legvold (eds.), *Statehood and Security: Georgia after the Rose Revolution.* Cambridge, MA: American Academy of Arts and Science, 2005, 83–115.

Inter-Korea Conflict

Armstrong, Charles K. "Inter-Korean Relations: A North Korean Perspective." In Samuel S. Kim (ed.), *Inter-Korean Relations: Problems and Prospects,* 39-56. New York: Palgrave Macmillan, 2004.

Brecher, Michael, and Jonathan Wilkenfeld. *A Study of Crisis.* Ann Arbor, MI: University of Michigan Press, 1997, 212–221.

Byun, D-H. *North Korea's Foreign Policy: The Juche Ideology and the Challenge of Gorbachev's New Thinking.* Seoul: Research Center for Peace and Unification of Korea, 1991.

Carpenter, Ted G., and Doug Bandow. *The Korean Conundrum: America's Troubled Relations with North and South Korea.* New York: Palgrave Macmillan, 2004.

Cha, Victor D. "The U.S. Role in Inter-Korean Relations: Container, Facilitator, or Impeder." In Samuel S. Kim (ed.), *Inter-Korean Relations: Problems and Prospects,* 139-157. New York: Palgrave Macmillan, 2004.

———. *The Impossible State: North Korea, Past and Future.* New York: Harper & Collins, 2012.

Chang, Keung Ryong. "Foreign Policy Decision–Making in a Protracted Conflict: Korea, 1948–1993. PhD Dissertation, McGill University, Montreal, QC, 1996.

Connor, Mary E. *The Koreas: A Global Studies Handbook.* Santa Barbara, CA: ABC–Clio, 2002.

Correlates of War Project. "National Material Capabilities. Data Documentation Version 4.0." Michael Greig and Andrew Enterline. *Correlates of War Project.* Pennsylvania State University, June 2010.

Cumings, Bruce. *The Origins of the Korean War, Vol. I: Liberation and the Emergence of Separate Regimes, 1945–1947.* Princeton, NJ: Princeton University Press, 1981.

———. *The Origins of the Korean War, Vol. II: The Roaring of the Cataract, 1947–1950.* Princeton, NJ: Princeton University Press, 1990.

Curtis, G.L., and S-J. Han. 1983. *The U.S-South Korean Alliance.* Lexington, MA: Lexington Books.

Eberstadt, N. *The North Korean Economy: Between Crisis and Catastrophe*. New Brunswick, NJ: Transaction Books, 2007.

Gabroussenko, T. "From Developmentalist to Conservationist Criticism: The New Narrative of South Korea in North Korea Propaganda." *Journal of Korean Studies* 16, 1 (2011): 27–62.

Haggard, S., and M. Noland. "North Korea's External Economic Relations." *Peterson Institute for International Economics: Working Paper Series* 7, 7 (2007): 1–45.

Hahm, Song Deuk, and L. Christopher Plein. *After Development: Transformation of the Korean Presidency and Bureaucracy*. Washington, DC: Georgetown University Press, 1997.

Halliday, J. "The North Korean Model: Gaps and Questions." *World Development*, 9, 9–10 (1981): 889–905.

Hong, Y-P. *State Security and Regime Security: President Syngman Rhee and the Insecurity Dilemma in South Korea, 1953–1960*. New York: St. Martin's Press, 1999.

Jager, Sheila Miyoshi. *Brothers at War: The Unending Conflict in Korea*. New York: WW Norton, 2013.

Kaufman, Burton I. *The Korean War: Challenges in Crisis, Credibility, and Command*. Philadelphia, PA: Temple University Press, 1986.

Kim, Abraham. "The Challenges of Peacefully Reunifying the Korean Peninsula." In Samuel S. Kim (ed.), *Inter–Korean Relations: Problems and Prospects*, 197–218. New York: Palgrave Macmillan, 2004.

Kim, H-A. *Korea's Development under Park Chung Hee: Rapid Industrialization, 1961–1979*. London: RoutledgeCurzon, 2004.

Kim, H-K. *The Division of Korea and the Alliance-Making Process*. Lanham, MD: University Press of America, 1995.

Kim, M. "The Cheonan Incident and the East Asian Community Debate: North Korea's Place in the Region." *East Asia* 28 (2011): 275–290.

Kim, Y. *North Korean Foreign Policy: Security Dilemma and Succession*. Plymouth, MA: Lexington Books, 2011.

Kim, Y. J. *Toward a Unified Korea*. Seoul: Research Center for Peace and Unification of Korea, 1987.

Kim, Samuel S. (ed.). *Inter–Korean Relations: Problems and Prospects*. New York: Palgrave Macmillan, 2004.

Kirk, D. *Korea Betrayed: Kim Dae Jung and Sunshine*. New York: Palgrave Macmillan, 2009.

Koh, Byung Chul. *The Foreign Policy Systems of North and South Korea*. Berkeley, CA: University of California Press, 1984.

Koo, B., and C. Nam. "South Korea's Sunshine Policy and the Inter-Korean Security Relations." *Korean Journal of Defense Analysis* 13, 1 (2001): 79–102.

Kwak, T-H., and W. Patterson. 1999. The Security Relationship between Korea and the United States, 1960–1982. In *Korea –American Relations*,

1866–1997, eds. Y-B. Lee and W. Patterson, 83–99. Albany, NY: State of New York University Press.

Kyung-suk, C. "The Future of the Sunshine Policy: Strategies for Survival." *East Asian Review* 14, 4 (2002): 3–17.

Landsberg, M. H. *Korea: Division, Reunification, and U.S. Foreign Policy.* New York: Monthly Review Press, 1998.

Lankov, Andrei. *The Real North Korea: Life and Politics in the Failed Stalinist Utopia.* New York: Oxford University Press, 2013.

Levin, N. D., and Y-S. Han. *Sunshine in Korea: The South Korean Debate over Policies toward North Korea.* Santa Monica, CA: RAND Center for Asia Pacific Policy, 2002.

Merrill, John. "Internal Warfare in Korea, 1948–1950: The Local Setting of the Korean War." In Bruce Cumings (ed.), *Child of Conflict: The Korean-American Relationship, 1943–1953.* Seattle, WA: University of Washington Press, 1983.

Myers, R. J. *Korea in the Cross Currents: A Century of Struggle and the Crises of Reunification.* New York: Palgrave Macmillan, 2001.

Paige, Glenn D. *The Korean Decision: (June 24–30, 1950).* New York: Free Press, 1968.

Sigal, L. "Primer—North Korea, South Korea, and the United States: Reading between the Lines of the Cheonan Attack." *Bulletin of Atomic Scientists* 66, 5 (2010): 35–44.

Snyder, Scott. "Inter-Korean Relations: A South Korean Perspective." In Samuel S. Kim (ed.), *Inter-Korean Relations: Problems and Prospects,* 21–37. New York: Palgrave Macmillan, 2004.

Son, Key-young. *South Korean Engagement Policies and North Korea: Identities, Norms and the Sunshine Policy.* New York: Routledge, 2006.

Srivastava, M. P. *The Korean Conflict: Search for Unification.* New Delhi: Prentice Hall, 1982.

Stuek, W. *The Korean War: An International History.* Princeton, NJ: Princeton University Press, 1995.

———. *Rethinking the Korean War: A New Diplomatic and Strategic History.* Princeton, NJ: Princeton University Press, 2002.

Yahuda, Michael B. *The International Politics of the Asia–Pacific, 1945–1995.* London: Routledge, 1996.

Yang, Sung Chul. *The North and South Korean Political Systems: A Comparative Analysis.* Boulder, CO: Westview Press, 1994.

North Vietnam/U.S. Conflict

Anderson, D. L. *The Columbia Guide to the Vietnam War.* New York: Columbia University Press, 2002.

———. "The Vietnam War." In Robert D. Schulzinger (ed.), *A Companion to American Foreign Relations.* Oxford: Blackwell, 2005.

REFERENCES

Anderson, D. L. (ed.). *The Columbia History of the Vietnam War*. New York: Columbia University Press, 2010.
Ang, C. G. "The Vietnam War, 1962–1964: The Vietnamese Communist Perspective." *Journal of Contemporary History* 35, 4 (2000): 601–618.
———. *Ending the Vietnam War: The Vietnamese Communists' Perspective*. London: Routledge-Curzon, 2004.
Asselin, Pierre. *A Bitter Peace: Washington, Hanoi, and the Making of the Paris Agreement*. Chapel Hill, NC: University of North Carolina Press, 2002.
Austin, Anthony. *The President's War: The Story of the Tonkin Gulf Resolution and How the Nation Was Trapped in Vietnam*. Philadelphia, PA: Lippincott, 1971.
Berman, Larry. *Lyndon Johnson's war: The Road to Stalemate in Vietnam*. New York: Norton, 1989.
Brecher, Michael, and Jonathan Wilkenfeld. *A Study of Crisis*. Ann Arbor, MI: University of Michigan Press, 1997, 179–198.
Duiker, W. "In Search of Ho Chi Minh." In M. Young and R. Buzzanco (eds.), *A Companion to the Vietnam War*. Oxford: Blackwell, 2002.
Gardner, L. "Richard Nixon and the End of the Vietnam War, 1969–1975." In M. Young and R. Buzzanco (eds.), *A Companion to the Vietnam War*. Oxford: Blackwell, 2002.
———. "Lyndon Johnson and the Bombing of Vietnam: Politics and Military Choices." In D. L. Anderson (ed.), *The Columbia History of the Vietnam War*, 168–190. New York: Columbia University Press, 2010.
Gelb, Leslie H., and Richard K. Betts. *The Irony of Vietnam: The System Worked*. Washington, DC: Brookings, 1979.
Gravel, Senator Mike. *The Pentagon Papers*. Senator Gravel Edition. 5 vols. Boston, MA: Beacon Press, 1971–1972.
Halberstam, David. *The Best and the Brightest*. New York: Random House, 1972.
Herring, George C. *America's Longest War: The United States and Vietnam 1950–1975*. New York: Wiley, 1979.
———. *LBJ and Vietnam*. Austin, TX: University of Texas Press, 1994.
Hersh, Seymour M. *The Price of Power: Kissinger in the Nixon White House*. New York: Summit, 1983.
Hess, G. "South Vietnam under Siege, 1961–1965: Kennedy, Johnson and the Question of Escalation or Disengagement." In D. L. Anderson (ed.), *The Columbia History of the Vietnam War*, 143–167. New York: Columbia University Press, 2010.
Ho Chi Minh. *On Revolution*. Ed. Bernard B. Fall. New York: Praeger, 1967.
Immerman, R. H. "Dealing with a Government of Madmen: Eisenhower, Kennedy and Ngo Dinh Diem." In D. L. Anderson (ed.), *The Columbia History of the Vietnam War*, 120–142. New York: Columbia University Press, 2010.
Isaacson, Walter. *Kissinger: A Biography*. New York: Simon and Schuster, 1992.
Johnson, Lyndon B. *The Vantage Point: Perspectives of the Presidency 1963–1969*. New York: Henry Holt, 1971.

Kahin, George McT. *Intervention: How America Became Involved in Vietnam.* New York: Knopf, 1986.

Kahin, George McT, and John Wilson Lewis. *The United States in Vietnam.* New York: Dial, 1967.

Kail, F. M. *What Washington Said: Administration Rhetoric and the Vietnam War: 1949–1969.* New York: Harper & Row, 1973.

Karnow, Stanley. *Vietnam: A History.* New York: Penguin Books, 1984.

Kearns, Doris. *Lyndon Johnson and the American Dream.* New York: Harper & Row, 1976.

Khong, Yuen Foong. Analogies at War: *Korea, Munich, Dien Bien Phu and the Vietnam Decisions of 1965.* Princeton, NJ: Princeton University Press, 1992.

Kimball, J. "Richard M. Nixon and the Vietnam War: The Paradox of Disengagement with Escalation." In D. L. Anderson (ed.), *The Columbia History of the Vietnam War,* 217–246. New York: Columbia University Press, 2010.

Kissinger, Henry A. *Years of Upheaval.* Boston, MA: Little Brown, 1982.

———. *The White House Years.* Boston, MA Little, Brown, 1979.

Kolko, Gabriel M. *Anatomy of a War: Vietnam, the United States, and the Modern Historical Experience.* New York: Pantheon Books, 1985.

Lacouture, Jean. *Ho Chi Minh: A Political Biography.* New York: Random House, 1968.

———. *Pierre Mendes France.* New York: Holmes & Meier, 1984.

McMahon, R. "Turning Point: The Vietnam War's Pivotal Year, November 1967–1968." In D. L. Anderson (ed.), *The Columbia History of the Vietnam War,* 191–216. New York: Columbia University Press, 2010.

McNamara, Robert S. *In Retrospect: The Tragedy and Lessons of Vietnam.* New York: Times Books, 1995.

Nguyen, L. T. "The War Politburo: North Vietnam's Diplomatic and Political Road to the Tet Offensive." *Journal of Vietnamese Studies* 1, 1–2 (2006): 4–58.

Nixon, Richard M. *RN: The Memoirs of Richard Nixon.* New York: Simon and Schuster, 1978.

O'Ballance, Edgar. *The Wars in Vietnam, 1954–1973.* New York: Hippocrene, 1975.

Rusk, Dean. *As I Saw It.* Edited by Daniel Papp. New York: Bantam, 199.

Shapley, Deborah. *Promise and Power: The Life and Times of Robert McNamara.* Boston, MA: Little, Brown, 1993.

Smith, R. B. *An International History of the Vietnam War.* London: MacMillan, 1985.

Steinberg, Blema S. *Shame and Humiliation: Presidential Decision-Making on Vietnam.* Montreal and Kingston: McGill-Queen's University Press, 1996.

Rusk, Dean. *As I Saw It.* Edited by Daniel Papp. New York: Bantam, 1990.

Tucker, Spencer. *Encyclopedia of the Vietnam War: A Political, Social, and Military History.* Santa Barbara, CA: ABC Clio, 1998.

Taiwan Strait Conflict

Barnett, Arthur D. "Problems and Issues: Multiple Factors." *The Kuomintang Debacle of 1949.* Boston, MA: D.C. Heath, 1966.
Bercovitch, Jacob, and Kwei-Bo Huang. *Conflict Management, Security, and Intervention in East Asia: Third–Party Mediation in Regional Conflict.* London: Routledge, 2008.
Bush, Richard C. *Untying the Knot: Making Peace in the Taiwan Strait.* Washington, DC: Brookings, 2005.
Chen, Chien Kai. "China and Taiwan, A Future of Peace? A Study of Economic Interdependence, Taiwanese Domestic Politics, and Cross-Strait Relations." *Josef Korbel Journal of Advanced International Studies*, 2009, 14–25.
Chen, Guo, and Ringo Ma. *Chinese Conflict Management and Resolution.* Westport, CT: Ablex Publishing, 2002.
Chow, Peter C. Y (ed.). *The "One China" Dilemma.* New York: Palgrave Macmillan, 2008.
Clough, Ralph N. *Cooperation or Conflict in the Taiwan Strait.* Lanham, MD: Rowman and Littlefield, 1999.
Cooper, John F. *Playing with Fire: The Looming War with China over Taiwan.* Westport, CT: Praeger, 2006.
Friedman, Edward. "The Prospects of a Larger War: Chinese Nationalism and the Taiwan Strait Conflict." Suisheng Zhao (ed.), *Across the Taiwan Strait: Mainland China, Taiwan, and the 1995–1996 Crisis.* London: Routledge, 1999.
Garver, John W. *Faceoff: China, The United States, and Taiwan's Democratization.* Seattle, WA: University of Washington Press, 1997.
Hickey, Dennis. *Foreign Policy Making in Taiwan: From Principles to Pragmatism.* New York: Routledge, 2007.
Hua, Shiping. *Reflections on the Triangular Relations of Beijing–Taipei–Washington since 1995: Status Quo at the Taiwan Straits?* New York: Palgrave Macmillan, 2006.
Hungdah, Chiu. "Taiwan in Sino-American Relations." In Chiu Hungdah (ed.)., *China and the Taiwan Issue*, 147–198. New York: Praeger, 1979.
Jacob, J. "Taiwan's Colonial History and Postcolonial Nationalism." In Peter Chow (ed.), The "One China" Dilemma, 37-56. New York: Palgrave Macmillan, 2008.
Kissinger, Henry. *On China.* New York: Penguin Press, 2011.
Lijun, Sheng. *China's Dilemma: The Taiwan Issue.* London: I.B. Tauris, 2001.
Matsumoto, Haruka. "The First Taiwan Strait Crisis and China's 'Border' Dispute Around Taiwan." *Eurasia Border Review* 3 (2012): 77–91.

Myers, Ramon H., and Jialin Zhang. *The Struggle Across the Taiwan Strait: The Divided China Problem*. Stanford, CA: Hoover Institution Press, 2006.

Shirks, Susan. *China: Fragile Superpower*. Oxford: Oxford University Press, 2007.

Swaine, Michael D. "Chinese Decision–Making Regarding Taiwan, 1979–2000." In David M. Lampton (ed.), *The Making of Chinese Foreign and Security Policy in the Era of Reform*, 289–336. Stanford, CA: Stanford University Press, 2001.

Tanner, Murray Scot. *Chinese Economic Coercion Against Taiwan: A Tricky Weapon to Use*. Santa Monica, CA: RAND Corporation, 2007.

Taylor, Jay. *The Generalissimo: Chiang Kai-shek and the Struggle for Modern China*. Cambridge, MA: Belknap Press of Harvard University Press, 2009.

Tsang, Steve. *In the Shadow of China: Political Developments in Taiwan since 1949*. Honolulu, HA: University of Honolulu Press, 1993.

Tse-tung, Mao. *Mao Zedong on Diplomacy*. Beijing: Foreign Languages Press, 1998.

Tucker, Nancy B. *Strait Talk: United States–Taiwan Relations and the Crisis with China*. Cambridge, MA: Harvard University Press, 2009.

Whiting, Allen. "China's Use of Force." *International Security* 26, 2 (2001): 103–131.

Wu, Hsing-hsing. *Bridging the Strait: Taiwan, China, and the Prospects for Reunification*. London: Oxford University Press, 1994.

Names Index

A
Abd al-Ilah, 241
Abd al-Karim Qasim, 242
Abdul-Aziz, Mohammed, 161
Acheson, Dean, 99
Acosta, Julio, 176
Agwani, M.S., 361
Aitchison, J.R., 345
Allon, Yigal, 16
Almond, Gabriel, 340
Alpert, C., 362
Altrincham, Lord, 347
Amin, Hafizullah, 196
Andriole, S.J., 52n8
Anglin, Douglas, 7, 122
Annan, Kofi, 169, 172
Aref, Abdal Salem, 242, 243
Aron, Raymond, 49n1, 51n4, 328
Arrow, K.J., 32, 51n4
Asaad, Riad al, 103, 115
Ashby, W.R., 30, 50n4
Ashley, Richard, 329
Attlee, Clement, 15
Auerbach, Y., 292–3
Avi-Hai, A., 360
Axelrod, R., 337

Khamenei, Ayatollah, 247
Khomeini, Ayatollah, 238, 247, 250
Ayub Khan, Muhammad, 39, 186, 188, 199
Azar, E.E., 30, 33
Azar, E.E. et al. (1977), 24, 30, 33

B
Baker, James, 160, 169
Balkash et al. 2004, 238
Ball, George, 296
Beeley, Harold, 362
Beloff, Max, 347
Ben-Gurion, David, 15
Ben-Yehuda, Hemda, 19
Bhutto, Zulfiqar Ali, 184, 185, 186, 187, 196, 199
Biggs-Davison, John, 348
Binder, L., 17, 50n2
Birdwood, Lord, 344, 345
Bobrow, Davis B., 10
Bogra, Mohammad Ali, 186
Bonanate, Luigi, 369
Boulding, K.E., 52n8, 337
Boumedienne, Houari, 253

© The Editor(s) (if applicable) and The Author(s) 2018
M. Brecher, *A Century of Crisis and Conflict in the International System*, DOI 10.1007/978-3-319-57156-0

Boutros-Ghali, Boutros, 266
Bowman, L.W., 50n2
Brady, H.E. and Collier, D., 86, 88, 89
Brams, Steven J., 9, 336
Brecher, M., 6, 19, 22, 50n2, 52n7, 54, 76, 115, 131, 343
Brecher, M. and Ben-Yehuda, 52n12
Brecher, M. and Geist, B., 6
Brecher, M. and Harvey, F.P., 10, 14
Brecher, M. and James, P., 27
Brecher, M. and Wilkenfeld, J., 7, 22, 26, 51n6, 76, 131, 132, 302
Brezhnev, Leonid, 231, 233
Bueno de Mesquita, Bruce, 9, 334, 336
Buhutto, Z.A., 92
Bull, Hedley, 328, 333
Bundy, McGeorge, 296
Bunge, M., 53
Burgess, P.M. and Lawton, R.W., 34
Bush, George, 104
Bush, George W., 105, 107

C
Caldwell, Malcolm, 355
Cantori, L. and Spiegel, S.L., 50n2
Carnell, F.G., 351
Carr, E.H., 11, 124, 328
Carter, Jimmy, 175
Casey, Lord, 353
Castillo Armas, Carlos, 98
Chamberlain, Neville, 97
Chamorro, Pedro, 177
Checkel, J.T., 339
Chen Shui-Bian, 310
Cheney, Dick, 104
Chiang Kai-shek, 305, 306, 307, 309, 311, 312
Churchill, Winston, 232
Clark, Gerald, 363, 364

Clark, J.F., 374
Clay, Lucius D., 92
Clinton, Bill, 105
Cordovez, Diego, 197
Corson, W.H., 33
Cox, Michael, 9
Cox, Robert W., 9
Croci, O., 121, 122
Cutts, Elmer H., 352

D
Daoud Khan, Muhammad, 182, 185, 192, 195, 196, 199
Davidson, Carter, 348, 349
Dawisha, Adeed, 6, 122
Dawisha, Karen, 7
Dayan, Moshe, 16
Dean, P.D. and Vasquez, J.A., 50n2
Delaney, Donald J., 365
Deng Xiaoping, 203, 204, 308, 309
Desai, Morarji, 15
Deutsch, K.W., 52n8, 328
Deutsch, K.W. and Singer, J.D., 50n4, 51n4
Dominguez, J.E., 50n2
Dowty, Alan, 7
Dulles, J.F., 305, 312

E
Easton, David, 18
Eban, A., 16
Eckhardt, W. and Azar, E.E., 34
Eisenhower, Dwight, 273
Eshkol, L., 15

F
Fahd, King of Saudi Arabia, 166
Faisal, King of Saudi Arabia, 236, 238, 241, 242, 243

NAMES INDEX 405

Faqir of Ipi, 189
Figueres, Jose, 174, 175, 177
Fischer, Beth A., 372, 373
Fischer, George, 343
Fischer, Louis, 348
Fischer, Margaret W., 351
Fox, W.T.R., 11
Frankel, J., 358, 359

G
Gadhafi, Muammar, 148, 149, 150
Gamsakhurdia, Z., 262, 267
Gandhi, Mathatma, 101, 102, 179
George, A.L. and Bennett, A., 89
Géró, Erno, 99
al-Ghazali, Mohammad, 241
Gilpin, R., 51n4, 51n5, 124
Goodall, Merrill R., 352
Gorbachev, Mikhail, 262
Gordon, Leonard A., 355
Goukouni Oueddei, 149, 150
Grieco, Joseph M., 8
Gromyko, Andrei, 223
Gupta, Sisir, 346

H
Haas, Ernst B., 9, 49n1, 366
Haas, M., 29, 50n2, 51n5
Habré, Hissene, 150
Hadow, Michael, 363
Haile Selassie, 92, 95, 96, 155, 156
Hammarstrom, Mats, 372
Hampson, Fen, 374
Hanrieder, W.F., 50n2
Hart, Henry C., 352
Harvey, Frank, 8
Hashim, Muhammad, 182
Hassan II, King of Morocco, 161, 166, 167, 168, 170
Heimsath, Chalres H., 350

Hermann, Charles F., 371, 372
Hitler, Adolf, 97, 229
Ho Chi Minh, 202, 206, 207, 300
Hobbes, Thomas, 124
Hodgkin, T., 17
Hoffman, S., 7, 49n1, 50n2, 51n4
Holsti, K.J., 8, 28, 50n2
Holsti, O. R., 10, 44, 120, 122
Holsti, O.R. and George, A.L., 122
Homer, Frank X.J., 364
Hopple, G.W. and Rossa, P.J., 44
Hu Jintao, 204, 308
Hua Guofeng, 202, 203, 204
Hurewitz, J.C., 359
Hussein, King of Jordan, 101
Huth, Paul, 373

I
Idris, King of Libya, 148
Ismail, Shah of Iran, 236

J
James, Patrick, 2, 8, 81, 375
Janis, I. and Mann, L., 337
Jervis, Robert, 337, 373
Jiang Zemin, 204, 308, 309
Jinnah, Mohammed Ali, 185, 186, 187
Johnson, Lyndon, 100, 107, 175, 295, 296, 297, 299
Jukes, Geoffrey, 7

K
Kaiser, K., 50n2
Kaplan, Morton, 34, 49n1, 50n4, 51n4, 328
Kaunda, Kenneth, 100
Kautilya, 124
Kekkonen, Urho, 213, 222, 226

Kennedy, John F., 99, 193, 195, 296, 306
Keohane, R.O., 8, 32, 329
Keohane, R.O. and Nye, J.S., 28, 50n1, 50n2, 338
Khatami, Mohammad, 259
Khrushchev, Nikita, 99, 215, 223, 226, 230, 231, 233
Kim Dae Jung, 273, 274, 275, 281, 282, 292
Kim Il Sung, 272, 276, 280, 287, 289, 290, 292, 293
Kim Jong Il, 272, 281, 282, 292
Kim Jong-un, 272
King, G., Keohane, R.O. and Verba, S., 86, 87–89
Kissinger, Henry, 295, 296, 297, 298, 299, 300
Klieman, A.S., 359
Kolodziej, Edward A., 10
Kosygin, Alexei, 39, 233
Kouchner F.R., 268
Krasner, S.D., 50n2
Krishna Menon, V.K., 15, 92
Kudrle, Robert T., 10
Kumar, Narendra, 346
Kuusinen, O.W., 219

L

Lakatos, I., 334, 335
Lake, David A., 8
Lampert, D.E., 50n2
Lapid, Yosef, 9
Le Duan, 203, 206, 207, 298, 300
Le Duc Tho, 300
Lee Myung-bak, 274, 275, 276, 283
Lee Teng-hui, 306
Leng, Russell J., 10, 374
Lenin, Vladimir, 214, 215, 231, 262
Levi, Werner, 345, 346
Levy, Jack S., 10

Liaquat Ali Khan, 185, 186, 187
Ling, L.H.M., 9
Liska, G., 51n4
Littlefield, D.W., 361
Lustick, I.S., 363, 365, 366

M

Machiavelli, Niccolò, 124
MacMahon Ball, W., 343
al-Maliki, Nouri, 259
Malloum, Felix, 150
Mannerheim, Carl Gustaf, 211, 212, 213, 228
Mao Tse-tung, 203, 207, 300, 307, 308, 309
Maoz, Zeev, 10, 371, 375
Marshall, George, 92
Martin, Lisa L., 10
McClelland, C.A., 32, 33, 34, 49n1, 52n8
McCormick, J.M., 35
McNamara, Robert, 296
Mearsheimer, John J., 8, 124
Medvedev, Dmitry, 263, 268
Meir, Golda, 15, 102, 115
Mengistu Haile Mariam, 155, 156
Merchant, L.T., 195
Midlarsky, Manus, 8, 373
Miller, Linda B., 10
Milner, Helen, 10
Milošević, Slobodan, 95, 107, 121
Modelski, G., 17, 50n2
Mohammad Ali, Chaudhri, 186
Mohammed VI, King of Morocco, 161
Molotov, Vyacheslav, 216
Morgan, Roger, 355
Morgenthau, Hans, 11, 124, 328, 338
Morris-Jones, W.H., 351
Mountbatten, Louis, 15
Mudie, Francis, 347

Muhammad VI, King of Morocco, 170
Mujeeb, M., 352
Musharraf, Pervez, 199
Mussolini, Benito, 92, 95, 96, 97, 107, 116

N
Nagy, Imre, 99
Nasser, Gamal Abdel, 194, 239
Nazimuddin, Khwaja, 186
Nehru, Jawaharlal, 15, 92, 121, 179
Nguyen Chi Thanh, 300
Nicholson, Michael, 9
Niebuhr, R., 124
Nixon, Richard, 295, 296, 297, 298, 299
North, Robert C., 44, 366, 367
Nuri al-Sa'id, 241, 243
Nussbaum, Martha C., 355
Nye Jr, Joseph S., 9

O
Ortega, Daniel, 175
Osman Daar, Aden Abdullah, 153

P
Paasikivi, Juho Kusti, 213, 228
Pahlavi, Mohammed Reza (Shah of Iran), 195, 196, 200, 244, 246
Palme-Dutt, R., 349
Palmer, Norman D., 345, 352
Parel, Anthony J., 352
Park, Richard L., 351, 356
Park Chung Hee, 273, 274, 275, 280, 284, 290, 292
Perelmutter, Amos, 365
Peres, Shimon, 16

Pérez de Cuéllar, Javier, 168, 172
Peterson, V. Spike, 9, 34
Pettman, Jan Jindy, 9
Pfaff, R.H., 360
Pham Van Dong, 206, 300
Pilsudski, Josef, 229, 231
Pirzada, 92
Podgorny, Nikolai, 233
Popper, Karl, 334
Prittie, T., 359, 360
Pruitt, D.G., 34, 51n4
Putin, Vladimir, 263

Q
Quayle, Dan, 104
Qureshi, Shah Mahmud, 182

R
Rafsanjani, Akbar Hashemi, 259
Rahman, Musaid, 195
Ray, James Lee, 9
Retzlaff, Ralph H., 357
Reynolds, P.A., 343, 344
Richardson, J.L., 328, 367–8
Riker, W.H., 328
Roh Moo-Hyun, 275, 280, 282
Roosevelt, Theodore, 175, 232
Rosecrance, R.N., 29, 49n1, 51n4
Rosenau, James N., 9, 14, 29
Rosenblum, Herbert, 364
Rouhani, Hassan, 259
Rousseau, Jean-Jacques, 124
Rubenstein, Alvin Z., 352, 365
Rusk, Dean, 296
Russett, Bruce, 50n2, 328

S
Saakashvili, Mikheil, 262, 263, 268, 269
Sadat, Anwar al, 16, 195

Saddam Hussein, 95, 104, 105, 106,
    116, 121, 238, 239, 240,
    242, 244, 245, 246, 247,
    250
Schelling, Thomas, 328
Scolnick Jr, J.M., 374
Scowcroft, Brent, 104
Sharett, Moshe, 15
Shastri, Lal Bahadur, 15, 39
Shermarke, Abdi Rashid Ali, 153
Shermer, David, 362
Shevardnadze, Eduard, 262, 266
Shichor, Yitzhak, 366
Shlaim, Avi, 7, 121
Siad Barré, Muhammad, 153, 154,
    155, 156
Sidqi, Bakr, 237
Silverburg, S.R., 367
Simon, H.A., 337
Singer, J.D., 10, 29, 52n8, 333, 334
Singer, J.D. and Small, M., 49n1
Slawoj-Skladkowski, Felicjan, 229, 230
Smith, Steve, 9, 370
Somoza, Anastasio, 175, 177
Spear, Percival, 344, 353
Spykman, Nicholas, 11, 124
Stalin, Joseph, 95, 98, 116, 213, 214,
    215, 216, 229, 230, 231,
    232, 300
Starr, Harvey, 9
Stoll, R.J., 369
Stubb, Alexander, 268
Sykes, Christopher, 347
Sylvester, Christine, 9
Syngman Rhee, 272, 274, 275, 284,
    290

T
Tachau, Frank, 360
Tanter, R., 33, 34, 35, 44
Taraki, Nur Mohammad, 196
Tharoor, Shashi, 358
Thompson, W.R., 50n2

Thucydides, 124
Tickner, J. Ann, 9
Tikka Khan, 186
Tinoco, Federico, 173, 174, 175, 176
Tombalbaye, François, 148, 150, 151
Trotsky, Leon, 214, 215, 231
Trudeau, Pierre, 15
Truman, Harry S., 36, 92, 97, 116
Trumbore, P.F. and Boyer, M.A., 117
Truong Chinh, 206, 207

U
Urofsky, Melvin I., 365

V
Van Dong, 207
Vasquez, John, 8, 338, 373, 374, 375
Vertzberger, Yaacov, 10, 369, 370
Vo Nguyen Giap, 300

W
Waldheim, Kurt, 251
Wali Khan, 196
Walker, Stephen G., 10
Waltz, Kenneth, 34, 50n1, 50n4,
    51n4, 124, 329, 338
Wiener, A.J. and Kahn, H., 34
Wight, Martin, 124, 328
Wilkenfeld, J., 4, 10, 34, 81
Wilkenfeld, J. and Brecher, M., 7, 77,
    333
Wilson, Harold, 100
Wolfers, Arnold, 11, 124
Wright, Quincy, 328

X
Xi Ping, 308

Y

Yahil, Chaim, 362, 363
Yahya Khan, Muhammad, 92, 116, 186, 189
Yeltsin, Boris, 267
Young, Oran, 9, 28, 29, 34, 50n1, 50n4, 51n4

Z

Zafrullah Khan, Muhammad, 187
Zahir Shah, King of Afghanistan, 182, 184, 194
Zalewski, Marysia, 9
Zartman, I.W., 50n2
Zhou Enlai, 202, 305, 308, 312
Zia-ul-Haq, Muhammad, 186, 196, 199
Zimmerman, W., 50n2
Zinkin, Tara, 350, 353, 354, 355
Zinnes, Dina A., 9, 18, 27, 329, 358

INDEX

A
Abyssinia, 84, 91, 92, 95, 107, 116
Actor change, 41, 73
Actor (concept), 6, 7, 19, 31, 41, 60, 67, 73, 80, 93, 108, 279, 336, 340
Actor level, 7, 60, 67, 336
Afghanistan
  Soviet invasion, 99, 188
  Taliban, 182, 183, 185, 190, 196, 199, 201
Afghanistan/Pakistan conflict
  attempts at conflict resolution, 166, 191
  conflict behavior of adversaries, 147; decision, 147, 148, 180–186, 197, 200, 241; decision-makers, 92, 182, 185, 186, 188, 321; decision processes, 147
  conflict management by adversaries and mediators, 248
  conflict-sustaining acts by adversaries, 132, 133, 137, 143, 191
  historical roots, 179

Africa, 3, 17, 77, 78, 93, 96, 148, 151, 153, 156, 163, 319, 340
Aggregate data vs. case study methods of analysis, 335, 336
Alternative and Critical perspectives, 9
Angola, 321, 323, 325
Aouzou Strip, 148–152
Asia
  foreign policy crises, 1, 3, 4, 6, 7, 16, 54, 59, 66, 80, 83, 84, 91, 95, 96, 107, 118, 336
  international crises, 15, 24, 26, 38, 77, 78, 80–82, 88, 123, 198, 297, 332
  protracted conflicts, 15, 16, 22, 24, 82, 136, 139
Assessment of the Field of IR, 14
Attitudinal prism (concept), 5, 92, 108

B
Balance of capability (concept), 132, 135, 136, 138, 144, 146, 171, 199, 321, 326
Basic causes of conflict resolution

catalyst, 27, 32, 46, 55, 61, 62, 142, 144, 145, 177, 271, 299
changes in balance of capability, 132, 135, 136, 138, 144, 145, 171, 172, 201, 255, 317
collective exhaustion, 134, 135, 138, 198, 257, 290, 325
domestic pressures for conflict resolution, 143, 256, 290, 326
external pressures for conflict resolution, 226, 288
hypotheses on conflict resolution, 145
perceptual calculus, 132, 142–145, 228
reduction in conflict-sustaining acts, 142
reduction in discordant objectives, 132, 133, 137, 140, 143, 326
Berlin Blockade
background, 2, 77, 246
coping, 58–61, 65, 72, 96, 107, 110, 117, 123, 124, 177
decision-makers, 5, 16, 18, 45, 47, 56, 59, 64, 66, 92, 94, 95, 106
decisions, 45, 60, 64, 71, 79
de–escalation, 53, 55, 61–64, 68–70, 75, 108, 192, 250, 285
escalation, 53, 55, 61–64, 68–70, 75, 192, 250, 285
impact, 55, 72–74, 117, 120, 134, 137
intensity, 38, 61, 63, 142, 275, 311
onset, 4, 21, 48, 59, 61
perception, 34, 35, 44, 47, 57, 64
Berlin Deadline, 36
Bipolarity (concept), 5, 80, 97

Bipolarity, findings on
Bipolycentrism, findings on, 5, 22, 78–80, 83, 100, 125

C
Capability (concept)
as an interactor attribute, 54, 55
Chad, 136, 148–151
Chad/Libya conflict
attempts at conflict resolution, 148, 149
conflict behavior of adversaries
decision-makers, 150; decision processes, 150; decisions, 148, 150
conflict management by adversaries and mediators, 148, 149
conflict-sustaining acts by adversaries, 151
historical roots, 147
China, 23, 39, 69, 78, 82, 100, 102, 120, 140, 170, 202, 204, 205, 207, 208, 273, 279, 300, 303, 304, 306–309, 311, 313
China/Vietnam conflict
attempts at conflict resolution, 203, 207
conflict behavior of adversaries
decision-makers, 203, 206; decision processes, 150, 204; decisions, 204, 205, 207
conflict management by adversaries and mediators, 207, 208
conflict-sustaining acts by adversaries, 202
historical roots, 315
Closed-mind mentality in IR, 329, 330
Cold War, 5, 6, 75, 78, 193, 197, 222, 244, 301, 340

Conflict resolution model, 136, 138, 170, 172, 197, 201, 227, 268, 326
Conflict setting (concept), 26
Conflict sustains acts, 207
Constructivism, 9, 11, 12, 124, 329, 339
Consultation, findings on, 59, 60, 64, 66, 67, 71, 95, 97, 107, 116, 123, 126, 127, 183, 207, 222, 225, 231, 309
Correlates of War Project (COW), 23, 333
Costa Rica, 173–177, 320, 321
Costa Rica/Nicaragua conflict
  attempts at conflict resolution, 173
  conflict behavior of adversaries, 173; decision-makers, 174; decision processes, 175; decisions, 173
  conflict-sustaining acts by adversaries, 176
  conflict management by adversaries and mediators, 176
  historical roots, 173
Crisis definitions
  colleagues, coders and advisers, 2
  data sets and aggregate analysis, 7
  formative publications, 6
  objectives, 13, 18, 76, 77, 136, 140, 141, 173, 200, 226–228, 239, 242, 244, 255, 257, 281, 330
  origins, 1, 11, 22, 29, 49
  overview, 9, 53, 78
  overview of findings, 78
  qualitative analysis, 81, 85, 89
  rationale and methods, 3
Crisis domains/phases, 71
Crisis management techniques (CMTs), 64, 70
Crisis Onset Model, 55, 57

Crisis period, 5, 16, 60–66, 70, 71, 85, 91, 94, 95, 97–99, 101
Critical Theory, 9, 11, 12, 328, 329
Cuban Missile crisis, 5, 26
Cumulation of knowledge in IR theory vs. history as approaches to knowledge, 330

D
Decisional forum, findings on, 59, 60, 64, 66, 71, 92, 94, 95, 108, 109, 115, 116, 123, 126
Decisions (concept), 5, 18, 60
Decision-makers (concept), 3, 5, 45
Deductive vs. Inductive paths to theory, 330, 333
De-escalation phase, 16, 21, 53, 69, 70
Democratic People's Republic of Korea (DPRK), 4, 271–281, 283–286, 288–291, 293
Discordant objectives (concept), 140–142, 317–320, 322
Diversity in International Studies, 11
Dominant system (concept), 17, 36, 42, 49, 78
Duration (concept), 15, 47, 60, 62, 68, 69, 72, 91, 131, 134, 187, 189, 228, 277, 319

E
Economic discrimination
  as a conflict-sustaining act, 142, 147, 158, 217, 235, 278, 303, 313
End crisis period
  hypotheses on, 4, 55
Enduring international rivalry (EIR), 25
Escalation phase

hypotheses on, 62
Ethiopia, 4, 24, 90–93, 95, 96, 106, 107, 152, 153, 155–158, 316, 320, 321
Ethiopia/Somalia conflict
attempts at conflict resolution, 154
conflict behavior of adversaries, 152, 154, 156, 157; decision-makers, 153–154; decision processes, 154; decisions, 153–154
conflict management by adversaries and mediators, 157
conflict-sustaining acts by adversaries, 157, 158
historical roots, 158
Europe
foreign policy crises, 3, 84, 117
international crises, 42
protracted conflicts, 77

F

Feminist-gender perspectives, 9, 12
Findings for system structures, 122, 126
Findings on Attributes of foreign policy crises, 90
Findings on coping and crisis management, 5, 94
Findings on Coping and Crisis Management, 94
Finland, 211, 212, 214–228, 268
Finland/Russia-USSR conflict
attempts at conflict resolution, 222–228
conflict behavior of adversaries
decisions, 214; decision-makers, 212–215; decision processes, 213–216
conflict management by adversaries and mediators, 218–220, 223, 226

conflict-sustaining acts by adversaries, 216, 217
historical roots, 223
Foreign policy crisis (concept), 4, 21, 23, 44, 46, 47, 53, 55–58, 60, 63, 83, 90, 91, 115, 124, 128, 148
Foreign policy system (concept), 17, 18
Formal modeling (methodology), 12

G

Geographic distance, 60
Georgia/ Russia-USSR Conflict
Attempts at Conflict Resolution, 265
Conflict Behavior of Adversaries
decisions, 261; decision-makers, 261; Decision Processes, 262
Conflict Management by Adversaries and Mediators, 265
Conflict-Sustaining Acts by Adversaries, 263
Historical Roots, 261
Georgia/ Russia-USSR conflict
attempts at conflict resolution, 269
conflict behavior of adversaries
conflict management by adversaries and mediators, 266–269
conflict-sustaining acts by adversaries, 261, 263–265
Geostrategic salience, 21, 41–43
Germany, 26, 36, 46, 47, 77, 82, 90, 92, 97, 99, 101, 105, 137, 212, 216, 217, 219–223, 226, 229, 232–234, 256, 291, 294

H

Horizontal (breadth) vs. vertical (depth) focus of inquiry, 327, 330

Hypotheses and evidence on conflict onset, 316
Hypotheses and evidence on conflict persistence, 137, 199, 317–319
Hypotheses and findings on conflict resolution, 322
Hypotheses on Effects of Time and Impact of Stress
  Cognitive Dimension, 108
  commonality in coping with high stress, 88, 118
  Decisional Dimension, 109
  Test of Neo-Realism, 124
  shared response to stress, 117
  stress–behavior relationship, 128

I
Ideologies, competing, 29, 141, 280, 281, 287, 293, 316
India/Pakistan Crisis Over Kashmir 1965–1966, 37
Information processing, findings on, 59, 60, 66, 71, 94, 107, 122, 337
Institutionalism, 8, 11, 328
Intellectual odyssey
  concepts, 15, 17
  dynamics of the Arab/Israel conflict (Odyssey II), 16
  interstate crises and conflicts (Odyssey III), 15, 16, 76, 174, 190
  phases, 4, 15
  political leadership and charisma (Odyssey I), 15, 16, 135
  themes, 15, 16
Inter-Korea conflict
  attempts at conflict resolution, 278–280, 282–291, 293, 294
  conflict behavior of adversaries, 277–280, 282, 284–286, 288–291; decision-makers, 271, 272; decision processes, 272, 274; decisions, 270–274, 277, 278
  conflict management by adversaries and mediators, 278, 279, 281, 282, 284, 285
  conflict-sustaining acts by adversaries, 275, 276, 278
  historical roots, 292
International crisis (concept), 2, 4–6, 20, 21, 23, 24, 26, 37, 41, 46, 53, 55–57, 63, 81, 122, 166, 305
International Crisis Behavior (ICB) Project, 1–4, 6, 7, 19, 23, 24, 26, 27, 59, 75, 76, 81, 83, 91, 93, 121, 131, 152, 333, 336
International political economy, 1, 5, 7, 10, 12, 14, 20, 21, 23, 26, 32, 54, 78, 83, 85, 87, 89, 108, 124, 338
International system (concept), 18–21, 25–30, 37, 46, 79, 81, 124, 125, 128, 339, 340
Intolerance in IR, 328, 331
Intra-war crisis (IWC), 26, 86
Impact (concept), 4, 5, 21, 22, 27, 40–44, 54, 72–74, 141, 176, 207, 244, 245, 258, 277, 294, 303, 318–321, 324, 330
Impact Phase
  hypotheses on Impact, 74
Iran/Iraq conflict
  attempts at conflict resolution, 248–250, 255, 258
  conflict behavior of adversaries, 238, 240, 245, 248, 249,

251, 252, 255, 257, 259;
decision-makers, 240–242,
244; decision processes, 243,
244, 246–248; decisions,
240, 242, 244–246, 248,
249
conflict management by adversaries
and mediators, 248–250, 256
conflict-sustaining acts by adversaries, 257
historical roots, 236, 237, 248
Italy, 4, 90, 91, 95, 96, 98, 106, 116,
117, 121, 153, 155

K
Kashmir, 1, 22, 24, 37–39, 43, 47, 82,
102, 188, 320
Khomeini, Ayatollah, 238, 247, 250
Korea, North, 4, 82, 271–276, 278–
283, 285, 287, 289–292,
294, 340
Korea Nuclear Crisis, 281
Korea, South, 271, 273, 275–279,
281–283, 285–292, 294,
302
Korea War of 1950, 208

L
Large 'n' vs. small 'n' clusters of data,
328, 330
Latin America
protracted conflicts, 131, 172
Libya, 136, 148–152, 165

M
Militarized interstate disputes (MID),
23, 25
Military-security crises, 1, 58, 72, 157,
166, 172, 177, 305, 332

Millennial reflections project, 10, 11
Models
of de-escalation/end-crisis, 4, 21,
53–55, 61
of escalation-crisis, 4, 21, 53–55,
61
of foreign policy crisis behaviour, 6,
21, 53, 55
of international crisis, 3, 21, 53, 55,
56, 77, 336
Multipolarity, 5, 75, 78, 80, 83, 85,
125, 127
Multipolarity, findings on, 84

N
Neo-realism vs. neo-institutionalism or
constructivism, 328
Nicaragua, 173–177, 320
North America
international crises, 3, 25, 77
protracted conflicts, 24, 77
North Vietnam, 138, 202, 209,
294–302
North Vietnam/U.S. conflict
attempts at conflict resolution, 265
conflict behavior of adversaries,
296, 297, 299, 301, 303;
decisions, 298; decision-makers, 300; decision processes,
300
conflict management by adversaries
and mediators, 270
conflict-sustaining acts by adversaries, 302, 303
historical roots, 147

O
Onset phase
hypotheses on, 316, 317

P

Pakistan, 1, 17, 22, 24, 37–39, 41, 43, 77, 82, 92, 101, 102, 106, 107, 116, 120, 127, 128, 131, 136, 179–184, 186–201, 241, 256, 284, 323
Poland, 217, 228–235, 321
Poland/Russia
  attempts at conflict resolution, 167
  conflict behavior of adversaries, 233, 235; decisions, 228–234; decision-makers, 63; decision processes, 230, 233
  conflict-sustaining acts by adversaries, 233, 236
  conflict management by adversaries and mediators, 219
Polisario, 159–173, 319
Polycentrism (concept), 22
Post-crisis period, 4, 16, 53, 71, 75
Post-modernism, 9, 12, 328, 329, 339, 340
Precipitating causes (concept), 144, 145, 238
Pre-crisis period, 16, 53, 55–61, 64–66, 70, 95, 97, 101, 102, 104–107
Probability of war and escalation, 61–64, 71, 94, 119
Protracted conflict (concept), 4, 24, 25, 62, 77, 82, 86, 131, 133–135, 137, 139, 142, 144–146, 150, 155, 158, 160, 161, 167, 170, 172, 200, 201, 212, 215, 218, 220, 224, 225, 229, 233, 234, 236, 237, 244, 246, 248, 250, 254–256, 258, 262, 267, 268, 271, 278, 284, 286, 290, 293, 294, 298, 303, 307, 316, 317, 320, 321, 324, 341

Pushtunistan conflict, 189
Pushtunistan II, 190, 191
Pushtunistan III, 189

Q

Qualitative case-studies (methodology), 2, 4, 6, 12, 83, 84, 87, 89, 327
Quantitative methods (methodology), 4, 9, 89, 330

R

Radical Theory, 9
Rann of Kutch crisis, 38
Rational calculus vs. psychological constraints, 328, 330
Realism, 6, 8, 11, 117, 328, 338
Republic of Korea (ROK), 271, 274, 275, 284
Research fashions; retreat from science in IR, 327
Russia, 78, 105, 170, 197, 212, 214, 216, 218, 222, 228, 231, 234, 262, 264–267, 269, 288
Russia-USSR, 214, 215, 227, 228, 233, 261

S

Severity (concept), 21, 25, 27, 40–42, 54, 65, 73, 79
Shortcomings of IR, 33, 328, 330
Somalia, 152–155, 157, 158
Strategic rivalry, 25
Subordinate state system (concept), 17, 339
System change, 9, 27, 35, 44
Systemic crisis (concept), 32–35, 38, 45, 47, 48

System vs. actor, 328, 330

T
Taiwan, 82, 277, 303–306, 308–313
Taiwan Straits conflict
  attempts at conflict resolution, 309
  conflict behavior of adversaries
    decisions, 303–306, 332; decision-makers, 303, 307–309, 311; decision processes, 303
  conflict management by adversaries and mediators, 313
  conflict-sustaining acts by adversaries, 303–306
  historical roots, 315
Tangible variables, 24, 72, 244, 259, 283, 288, 291, 306
Territory
  as an actor attribute, 57, 61, 74, 92
Teschen crisis of 1919, 28
Time pressure, 34, 46, 47, 55, 60–62, 64, 70, 94, 111, 119, 124
Trigger, 5, 46, 47, 49, 56, 61, 63, 65, 79, 90, 108, 125, 332
Triggering entity (concept), 5, 81, 90, 108, 305
Trigger-value response nexus, 56

U
Unified model of crisis
  crisis onset model, 55, 57
  crisis period, 4, 16, 53, 55, 56, 60–62, 64, 66, 67, 75
  de-escalation phase
    hypotheses on de-escalation, 70
  end crisis period, 67
  escalation phase
    hypotheses on escalation, 62
  impact phase
    hypotheses on impact, 55, 74, 77
  onset phase
    hypotheses on onset, 315
  post-crisis period, 4, 16, 53, 55, 56, 60–62, 64, 66, 67, 75
  pre-crisis period, 4, 16, 53, 55, 56, 60–62, 64, 66, 67, 75
Union of Soviet Socialist Republics (USSR), 36, 41–43, 47, 80, 90, 95, 98, 107, 120, 156, 182, 191, 197, 198, 211–213, 215–217, 219–221, 229, 231, 232, 234, 235, 256, 301
Unipolycentrism, findings on, 5, 7, 14, 17
United Nations (UN), 20, 31, 39, 80, 90, 98, 101, 104, 105, 139, 153, 161, 164, 168, 170, 180, 190, 208, 254, 255, 257, 266, 275, 286, 306, 309
United States (U.S.), 8, 41, 46, 47, 78, 97–101, 103, 105, 138, 175, 183, 277, 284, 286, 288, 301
Unit–system linkages (concept), 44
Unresolved conflicts, 285, 320
USSR-Iran border conflict, 236–239

V
Values (concept), 21, 25, 45, 56, 62, 66, 93, 225, 259
Value threat, 26, 45, 54–56, 59–62, 64, 65, 70, 119, 131
Variables
  dependent, 88, 145, 237, 273, 333, 334
  independent, 15, 16, 82, 132, 135, 142, 144, 213, 222, 233, 280, 289, 292, 317, 334

INDEX 419

intervening, 132, 142, 145, 317, 334, 336
Vietnam, 24, 138, 203, 204, 206, 208, 209, 295, 298–300, 302, 303
Violence
  findings on, 3, 4, 145, 322, 324
  in international crises, 53, 78, 79

W
War
  as a crisis management technique, 25, 31, 63, 65, 164

conflict and crisis in, 1–4, 8, 20, 80, 81
Western Sahara conflict
  attempts at conflict resolution, 165
  conflict behavior of adversaries
    decisions, 160; decision-makers, 159–161; decision processes, 161, 162
  conflict management by adversaries and mediators, 163–167
  conflict-sustaining acts by adversaries, 158–160
  historical roots, 167

The manufacturer's authorised representative in the EU is Springer Nature Customer Service Centre GmbH, Europaplatz 3, 69115 Heidelberg, Germany. If you have any concerns regarding our products, please contact ProductSafety@springernature.com

Printed and bound by CPI Group (UK) Ltd, Croydon, CR0 4YY

23/03/2026

02076747-0011